D1432088

IE
STRANGER IN AMERICA

View of the City and Port, of Philadelphia, on the Delaware,
taken from Kensington.

The STRANGER, IN America

BY

Charles William Janson, Esqr

Front View of the Presidents House in the City of Washington.

Published by James Cundee, Albion Press London.

1807.

THE STRANGER IN AMERICA
1793-1806

BY
CHARLES WILLIAM JANSON

Reprinted from the London Edition of 1807

WITH AN INTRODUCTION AND NOTES BY
DR. CARL S. DRIVER
OF VANDERBILT UNIVERSITY

WITH REPRODUCTIONS OF THE ORIGINAL ENGRAVINGS

NEW YORK
THE PRESS OF THE PIONEERS, INC.
1 9 3 5

DESIGNED BY L. C. GANDY
PRINTED IN THE UNITED STATES OF AMERICA

INTRODUCTION

THE traveller from any European country to America in 1793 experienced many hardships not properly appreciated by individuals who now read the records of those who ventured across the Atlantic. The physical discomforts of the long voyage presented by no means the only obstacles to the travel-minded Englishman. The mental hazards were quite as difficult to surmount. The thought of a sojourn in the land of republican principles and supposedly boorish customs brought a chill to his enthusiasm for travel and a feeling of repugnance against the inquisitiveness of strangers. This attitude had been augmented constantly since the development among the colonists of a hostile spirit toward what they regarded as the unjust governmental policies of the mother country. The Revolution added to the resentment of the Americans and to what they conceived to be haughty arrogance on the part of the English, who never became reconciled to the loss of valuable natural resources.

The business man-of-the-world in England, however, did not allow his prejudices to interfere with his American trade. Yet the relationships which existed in matters of business did not dissipate the popular feeling that Americans in general were uncultured. During the years immediately following the war, the credit of the new republic steadily declined. Many Englishmen confidently expected the republican experiment to collapse, a belief fostered by desire as well as by a knowledge of conditions in the New World. Business relations became fewer, for foreigners evinced little desire to invest in any sort of speculation under the tottering power of the Confederation. But the firm hand of Washington and the protection assured to property under the Constitution brought their renewed interest in American resources. European men of affairs sought out the means of realizing quick returns from investments in bonds and lands. Alluring advertisements found their way into the hands of prospective speculators. Soon the man on the street talked again of the possibilities of his finding a place in the land of equality and privilege.

What manner of country was this land of promise? In the public prints of the time the occasional traveller recorded his experiences and sketched something of a contradiction of the colorful inducements portrayed by the realtor. During the last decade of the eighteenth century these travelogues increased in number and scope. By the first quarter of the new century they presented a phase of literature with which Americans should be more familiar.

Although the business man may have found a recompense for his general repugnance toward Americans, these observers failed to reconcile themselves to the distasteful customs which irritated most travellers. The English people desired information, and they read with avidity any book or article which purported to describe conditions in the United States. The writing of books about America became a profitable adventure. Not all were favorable; most of them, in fact, made a pretense of fairness. But their value does not lie entirely either in their pretended fairness or in their studied attempts at impartiality. The stranger saw peculiarities and characteristics that the native took for granted; he recorded that which might never have been mentioned in American prints.

Charles William Janson came to the United States for the purpose of investing in speculative enterprises. Little is known of his circumstances in England before he departed upon his venture or of his life after his return to his homeland. He must have been a member of a family of some means and social position — at least he assumed, by his own words, the prerogatives of such standing in his relations with Americans. His long residence in America and his financial adventures gave him an opportunity to observe with minute care the habits and culture of this republican country. In spite of his distaste for its people and their ways, his record bears the marks of authenticity and sincerity. His prejudices are readily apparent to even the casual reader. He was violently anti-French, an attitude engendered by the British reaction to the excesses of the French Revolution and by the international complications arising from that movement. Consequently, he detested the policies advocated by Jefferson and the party of Democratic Republicans who came into power in 1800 during his residence in the United States. The conservative Federalistic principles of Hamilton attracted his interest and support — especially since that party championed reimbursement of the Yazoo investors, into which speculation he had plunged eagerly. The reserve of the typical English gentleman led him to criticize bitingly certain characteristics which irritated him.

The literary style and organization of THE STRANGER IN AMERICA leave much to be desired. One English reviewer said that it was "... indeed one of the most unblushing examples of a *made-up* book that we have ever seen, even in this book-making age," and that the "... heterogeneous materials are thrown together with a wonderful disregard to all the principles of arrangement." But another commended the arrangement as being a welcome relief from the diary or journal style adopted by most travellers. Indeed, the English reviews, which called attention to this publication and devoted a large amount of space to discussions of its merits and contents, differed radically as to its worth and quality. One of the severest and most sarcastic comments outlined the motives for its publication in the following uncomplimentary terms: "The Europeans who visit America are generally drawn thither by some commercial speculation, or by some plan of acquiring lands. They are seldom men of liberal education or possessed of those enlarged views which might enable them fairly to appreciate what they see; or to estimate the merits and defects, the good and the evil of whatever is peculiar to the institutions and practices of the country which they visit. If they remain in that country we hear no more of them; but if they are disappointed in their views, and return, they make another speculation of their travels; and generally revenge themselves for their disappointments by abusing the people among whom they did not find that agreeable reception which they had too sanguinely expected. Such has undoubtedly been the origin of more than one volume of American travels, which has lately come under our review; and such, we apprehend, is the origin of the present work. . . . The work itself bears very evident marks of being put together in haste, and of being more adapted to advance the profit of the book-seller than the fame of the author."

And in the same vein, another critic commented that the work was ". . . a most hasty performance, by a person neither accustomed to laborious composition, nor qualified to write without labour; neither capable of selecting his materials, nor of arranging them; and not very eminent in that astuteness which enables a man well to observe or profitably to reflect on what he has witnessed. . . . In all this the hand is more employed than the head; and the reader's mental fatigue is perhaps nearly equal to the author's."

However, Janson did not lack supporters: "The volume before us contains much miscellaneous information. . . . It abounds with amusing and interesting anecdotes; the author has in many instances very characteristically exemplified the manners of the Americans; and, for the rectitude of his intentions in composing this work, we give him full credit." Another remarked somewhat facetiously: " 'I was a stranger, and they took me in,' says Mr. Janson of the Americans. By way of having his revenge, in his delineation of the country and people of the New World, he assiduously labours to prevent his readers, whether they remain at home or are disposed to emigrate, from being strangers to America, and subject to the same delusion by which he suffered." And then in a more serious vein, the reviewer continued: "We believe, however, that Mr. Janson means to be as accurate as he has certainly been indefatigable, and we perceive no reason for questioning the general fidelity of his narrative. He professes to notice whatever he deems worthy of observation; . . . and to speak truth without malice, as well as without extenuation . . . and when we are informed that he spent more than thirteen years in the United States, he cannot be regarded in the light of a cursory stranger, who picks up information as one of Astley's riders recovers his whip from the ground, at full speed, and who might have passed *through* America and yet remained in a great measure a stranger *to* America. . . . By transatlantic readers, however, Mr. J. will be reckoned a disappointed man and many parts of his book will be condemned as merely calculated for the meridian of England . . . it contains a mass of valuable information and presents such a view of the United States as the philosopher, who knows how to winnow the chaff from the wheat, will not be displeased to obtain."

Another less enthusiastic reviewer stated that "Making some allowances for disappointment, and for a little prejudice, much information is to be derived from THE STRANGER IN AMERICA." Some years later, in 1819, William Faux, then in Washington, made something of a final pronunciamento when he remarked that "Janson, author of THE STRANGER IN AMERICA, it is there said, came and returned a stranger."

Opinion of the merits of the book appears to have divided along the lines of the particular sympathies of the magazines which carried the reviews. The Anti-Jacobins gave it a great amount of space and lauded the author and his work. The less conservative journals scathingly ridiculed the production and the man who wrote it.

One journal took him to task in no lenient fashion for his "unlimited abuse of private characters," and ascribed this fault to Janson's contact with the American press and its ill manners. "He drags individuals into notice without scruple or ceremony. Sometimes he tells what he has picked up" about persons who were practically unknown. This critic showed his leaning toward the Republicans by saying: "As for his endless invectives against Mr. Jefferson and his party, they belong to another class of wrongs, and only obtain their share of the dignified contempt by which that eminently wise ruler has consigned to oblivion all the spoken and written scurrility of his enemies." It seems to be apparent, therefore, that the English readers received the work with either enthusiasm or disfavor, depending upon their political predilections.

The most serious faults of Janson's book were brought to light by his contemporaries. Its principal value to the modern reader may be found in its rather faithful and authentic characterizations of the average citizen of the United States. In spite of his deep-seated reserve and his irritation at republican manners, Janson acquired enough of them unconsciously to transmit to us an insight into the public mind of that era. Concerning some things, he possessed an extraordinary amount of information; in other matters he carelessly reflected only public gossip. If we forget the prejudices against Americans, which found expression partly because of the writer's frustrated aims, there remain a great residue of fact and, in some cases, a penetrating expose of the American scene. These, we may suppose, found a substantial response among English readers.

Years passed before the inaccuracies which the early travelers expanded regarding America had been corrected. The new country changed, too, as well as the notions concerning it. Janson described the land in which he resided as a stranger possibly with less literary skill than others who pretended to know a great deal about it, but with a more intimate knowledge of its people and their way of life.

Vanderbilt University CARL S. DRIVER.

CONTENTS

CHAPTER I

CHAPTER II

CHAPTER III

CHAPTER IV

CHAPTER V

CHAPTER VI

CHAPTER VII

CHAPTER VIII

CHAPTER IX

CHAPTER X

CHAPTER XI

CHAPTER XII

CHAPTER XIII

CHAPTER XIV

CHAPTER XV

CHAPTER XVI

CHAPTER XVII

CHAPTER XVIII

CHAPTER XIX

CHAPTER XX

CHAPTER XXI

CHAPTER XXII

CHAPTER XXIII

CHAPTER XXIV

CHAPTER XXV

CHAPTER XXVI

CHAPTER XXVII

CHAPTER XXVIII

CHAPTER XXIX

CHAPTER XXXIII

CHAPTER XXXIV

CHAPTER XXXV

APPENDIX

ILLUSTRATIONS

PREFACE

WHEN the Author of the following sheets, previous to his taking up the pen to commence his contemplated work, reflected on the many volumes which have already appeared on the subject, he must acknowledge that he felt no very strong inclination to add his own lucubrations to the list. Year after year has this impression contributed to restrain a rising desire to communicate to the public the result of his observations respecting our once trans-atlantic brethren, but now the only remaining republicans in the civilized world. The persuasions of friends, together with the favorable opportunities of obtaining a thorough acquaintance with the true character of the Americans, afforded by a long residence among them, and the avocations he pursued during that time, have at length induced him to give to the world his ideas on the subject. He disclaims the vanity of aspiring to a place in the class of authors; had this been his ambition, he might have gratified it several years ago with equal facility.

In perusing the contents of this volume, the reader should bear in mind this circumstance, that the author did not visit the United States for the purpose of making a regular tour through the territories comprized in them. He removed to that country with an intention of passing a considerable part of his life there; but the disappointments he met with often caused him to change his residence; occasioning a journey first in this direction, then in the other, and his return, several times, to the same point. To this cause must be ascribed the want of regularity and of plan which some may think fit, at first sight, to alledge against this work. On a nearer examination, however, it will be found that, in his remarks on each state, the author has preserved, as nearly as possible, the geographical arrangement, commencing at the north, and ending at the south. In what year, month, or day this observa-

tion was made, or that circumstance happened, must be matter of perfect indifference; in their accuracy alone can the reader feel interested, and on this subject the writer assures him, that he has introduced nothing into his work but what resulted from personal observation, or rested on the most indubitable authority.

To a portion of the readers into whose hands this book may chance to fall, some of the anecdotes contained in its pages may probably be familiar. For the younger and the most numerous class, he flatters himself that they will have the charm of novelty; the circumstances to which he alludes having occurred while they were yet unborn. If he has occasionally had recourse to the writings of others, it has only been for the purpose of illustrating the subject under review, or supporting his opinions by their testimony. In some instances, it is true, it will be found that he has endeavored, and, as he hopes, with success, to refute error, and to combat misrepresentation.

The great length of time to which the author's visit to the United States was prolonged, was far from being agreeable to his inclination, for an English traveller will find his curiosity thoroughly satiated in as many moons as fortune assigned years to him, in a country in every respect uncongenial to English habits, and to the tone of an Englishman's constitution. During the early part of his residence in America, and about the time he was planning his return to Europe, specious and tempting offers induced him to risk a considerable sum in a land-speculation, (a fatal snare laid for every emigrant) and the hopes of again realizing some portion of it, prevented his departure. He is obliged to confess the commission of a second act, equally injudicious — the embarkation of another sum in mercantile concerns, which eventually proved unfortunate, owing, in a great measure, to the unprincipled conduct of the commanders of the vessels in his employ. Thus were his hopes beguiled, from day to day, for more than thirteen years!

The rooted aversion in the hearts of the Americans against the inhabitants of Britain, was to the author a source of perpetual uneasiness. Among the lower order, in spite of his endeavors to adapt his behavior to their satisfaction, he was regarded as proud and haughty; while a distant kind of envious obsequiousness, tinctured with an affectation of superiority, was but too evident in the majority of his equals. Such being the case, it cannot be surprising that he was never so happy as to form a true friendship with an American. From Germans and Frenchmen, numbers of whom are found in different parts of the United States, he received many civilities, and these he doubts not would have been extended to acts of friendship, had he needed them.

His opinion of the American character is not the effect of premature prejudice, nor is it founded on precarious observation. Had the author, like an ordinary traveller, merely rolled through the country, in the stage waggons, his strictures might with some shew of justice have been challenged as the effusions of spleen, or unbecoming partiality. So far from being influenced by feelings of this nature, he trusts he shall be believed when he asserts, that he never would have embarked for America, had not his mind been powerfully biassed in favor of the United States and their inhabitants. Nor was it till long experience had uniformly exhibited them in a point of view very different from what he had fondly expected, that he adopted his present sentiments, which have been strengthened and confirmed by an attentive study of the genus, habits, and manners of these people, during a constant intercourse with individuals of every class and description.

The author is perfectly aware of the reception these remarks will experience in America, and that a host of scribblers will rise up in arms to attack his work. He will, however, anticipate an answer. Americans make a point of denying every truth that in any way tends to expose a defective habit, or a national error. They bow before the shrine of *adulation, fondly conceiving themselves the merited favorites of heaven; and the United States "a country where triumph the purest principles of legislation which ever adorned civil society; a country in which the human character is already elevated to a superior species of man, compared with the miserable wretches of Europe."**

All nations, it is true, have their follies, their caprices, and their imperfections; but the manner in which they are affected by the exposure of them, is widely different. For instance — John Bull † laughs at the recital of his own follies; while the slightest sarcasm rouses a spirit of resentment in the bosom of the sullen Yankee.

Though the Americans declaim so loudly in favor of liberty and equality, yet no where are those terms more unworthily prostituted. That equality, the establishment of which was a favorite object of the revolutionary republicans of France, is still the idol of the mob in the United States. The meanest plebeian would be quite ungovernable, did he barely suspect you of harboring the idea that he was inadmissible to equal rank with the best informed of his fellow-citizens. Hence you are accosted by people of the lowest description with familiarity, and answered with carelessness. This, it is obvious, cannot be a very enviable state of society for a person educated in European notions of the decorum necessary to be observed in civilized life.

With such chimerical ideas of liberty, the degradation of the slaves, and the large proportion of their numbers to that of the white population, in some parts of the American republic, must form a striking contrast in the mind of every reflecting reader. It will be seen, with horror, that the cruel-

* Austin's Letters from London, Boston, 1804.

† This humorous personification of the English character is most ably delineated in the comedy under the same title, written by the ingenious Mr. Colman, who does not hesitate to lash the vices and follies of his countrymen, with unrelenting severity; and the universal approbation this piece has experienced proves the good temper which John preserves under this kind of castigation.

ties practised on this unfortunate race in that land of freedom, *can scarcely be exceeded in the West India Islands. That this state of things cannot be of long duration, must be evident to the most superficial observer; and accordingly it appears, that very just apprehensions begin already to be entertained on this subject in the American States. The principle of the trade in human flesh, is too horrible, even for those most deeply interested in it, to defend: however they may value its profits, they cannot possibly withstand the conviction of its injustice. It is rather a singular circumstance, that the last discussion, at which the author was present, in the house of representatives, in the city of Washington, related to this abominable traffic, and that, on his first entering the house of commons, after his return to London, he there heard an interesting and animated debate on the same subject. The eyes of governments appear to be opened to a serious consideration of the mischiefs which the prosecution of the slave trade must, sooner or later, entail on the regions to which its influence extends; but whether the present be a seasonable moment for its suppression by the administration of Britain, he does not attempt to decide.*

America, however, labors under none of the embarrassments which an implacable enemy has found means to throw in the way of the commerce of England. The question under the consideration of congress last year, was the propriety of imposing a tax on imported slaves, till an entire stop is put to the nefarious traffic, which, by a provisionary act passed some years since, will take place in 1808. Though no one can be a more decided advocate for an amelioration of the condition of these wretched blacks, than the author, yet he is convinced that their emancipation would be attended with imminent danger, as he has endeavored to show in the subsequent pages treating of South Carolina. Some evil even attended the manumission of the slaves of the late General Washington. The author has frequently heard the measure reprobated in the neighborhood of Mount Vernon, where he died. With a great part of them, liberty was prostituted to the purposes of licentiousness, which was supported by plunder. Many robberies were committed at this time, and great mischief done to the negroes still in bondage; who, doubtless, were anxious to participate in the outrages and idleness committed and indulged in by their free brethren.

The author has been at some pains to unfold the prospects that await the European emigrant in America. On this subject he is qualified to speak, not only from his own experience, but from that of many other persons, whose delusive hopes have terminated in disappointment. He has endeavored to expose the knavery of American land-jobbers, and to shew the fallacy of all that native writers have advanced relative to the facility and small expence of forming an establishment in the western regions of the republic. The history of the author's friend, Mr. Gilpin, furnishes a striking and melancholy example to such as repair to the new world on agricultural speculations.

The United States may still be considered as a new country, in every acceptation of the term. As such, therefore, it is but natural to suppose that those arts which supply the prime necessities of man, would there experience the greatest encouragement, and be held in the highest estimation. Accordingly, the farmer and the mechanic must stand a better chance of success than any other classes of emigrants, and when we so often witness the failure, even of their hopes, can we be surprised at the yet more frequent disappointments of the professors of the liberal arts and sciences; or of such whose occupations are subservient only to the luxuries of life? These can prosper only in the countries where society has arrived at a high degree of civilization, and where flourishing manufactures and commerce have diffused ease and opulence. Society is still in a state of infancy in America. What encouragement is held out to the study of architecture, for instance, in a region where many of the inhabitants are satisfied with log-houses; or what progress can be expected in the arts of design, if, from want of education, or deficiency in taste, their beauties are neither felt nor relished? America has, comparatively speaking, no manufactures; and how intimately the prosperity of arts and sciences is connected with these, it is unnecessary for the author even to attempt to demonstrate.

All his observations on emigration flow from no other motive than regard for the welfare of his country, and the happiness of his deluded fellow-subjects. Impressed with this sentiment, he has developed the illicit practices of American traders on the northern coasts of Ireland, and the injury which not only the revenue, but likewise the empire at large must sustain from their continuance. He flatters himself that he may be the means of directing the attention of the British administration to a subject which appears to him of no trifling importance; and if his endeavors shall lead to the application of a remedy to this national mischief, or shall prevent only one discontented fellow-citizen from quitting the substantial blessings he enjoys at home, in order to seek imaginary comfort, happiness, and wealth amidst the unproductive wastes and unsociable inhabitants of another hemisphere, his time and trouble will not have been in vain.

During his residence in America, the author was no inattentive observer of passing objects and events in the extensive territories of the United States. Accordingly, the notes and observations which he made are both copious and varied. From them he has selected the subjects of the following sheets, and on the reception they may experience will depend the publication of a second volume, much valuable matter still remaining unemployed in his possession.

Aware that many imperfections may be found in the following sheets, yet conscious of the rectitude of his motives for publishing his observations, in which he has been guided by a sincere desire that they may prove beneficial to his countrymen, the author throws himself upon their candor, and solicits the exercise of their indulgence in the perusal of them.

THE STRANGER IN AMERICA

CHAPTER I

MOTIVES OF THE AUTHOR FOR GOING TO AMERICA — HE EMBARKS IN AN AMERICAN SHIP — CHASED BY A FRENCH PRIVATEER — CONDUCT OF HER CREW — SEIZURE AND RECOVERY OF THE AUTHOR'S PAPERS — SPECIMEN OF AMERICAN MANNERS — A SQUALL — SINGULAR MANNER OF CATCHING A SHARK — TREATMENT OF THE PASSENGERS — AMERICAN DUPLICITY — NOCTURNAL ADVENTURE — ARRIVAL AT PORTSMOUTH — CURIOSITY OF THE AMERICANS — BOSTON.

FIFTEEN years have elapsed since I first entertained the idea of undertaking a voyage to the United States of America. In early life, my mind was inflamed with a desire to visit foreign countries. Under this influence, I first proceeded to France; and there my ardor to cross the great Atlantic was encreased by the description of America, given to me by some French officers who had served in Count Rochambeau's army in the revolutionary war of that country. My fortune, with a little frugality, was adequate to carry my designs into execution. I accordingly hastened my departure from France, and returned to London to make preparations for this important undertaking. I was advised to place my property in the American funds. This step, I was told, would not only be the safest remittance, but I might calculate upon considerable gain, from the late great demand for that stock. I therefore lodged all my ready cash, having sold my English stock, in the hands of Messrs. Bird, Savage, and Bird, who procured for me American six per cents. and shares in the National Bank. So far, however, from being a gainer by this measure, when I had occasion for money I was obliged to sell at from five to fifteen per cent. loss. The breaking out of the French war had a fatal effect on the American funds, which having been artificially raised to a great height at the time of my purchase, fell considerably previous to my arrival.

An American vessel, called the Snow Industry, of Wiscasset, in the province of Maine, under the command of David Trask, wafted me to the happy land, as my imagination had pictured it. My fellow-passengers in the cabin were, a Mr. Minchin, his wife and child, Mr. John Plank, and Mr. Lemuel Cravath. The first of these gentlemen represented himself as a lieutenant in the British navy, and as having served under the Duke of Clarence. Mr. Plank had been a diamond merchant, and had suffered much from the depreciation in the value of the article in which he dealt, at the beginning of the French revolution. Mr. Cravath was a Boston merchant, on his return from a visit to different parts of Europe, on his commercial concerns.

I had flattered myself with the hopes of gaining much information respecting the new world from Mr. Cravath, the only American passenger on board. The captain was completely a salt-water boor; the mate somewhat communicative, with ideas which did not extend farther than the ship's way and his log book; and the seamen were an ignorant, motley crew, collected from the various American States. I was farther encouraged to prosecute my enquiries, from the circumstance, that our vessel was bound to Boston, the place of residence of a fellow-passenger; but I had the disappointment to find Mr. Cravath extremely reserved upon every subject relating to his country; and, though for some time I neglected no opportunity to lead him to my favorite topic, I generally received evasive answers. He, however, promised to introduce me to a good boarding-house on our arrival in Boston.

Our voyage was prosperous for a week; but on the eighth

day, when the passengers were at breakfast, the man at the helm called out "a sail astern." Not having yet beheld any thing but the immense Atlantic and the sky, we hurried upon deck; and by means of my telescope (the only one on board), discovered a vessel under a press of sail, evidently in chase of us. The war of 1793 had commenced, for it was now the latter end of the month of May, in that year. Finding the strange sail gaining fast upon us, and fearing an interruption, we determined to take an early dinner, before she spoke us. During this repast, the chasing vessel fired a gun, though at such a distance as to have been scarcely perceived by those on deck. We continued our course for half an hour, when another gun was fired from the same quarter, which left us no doubt of their intention. Our captain therefore ordered his crew to hoist the American flag, and to back the topsails, for we had no defensive weapon on board, unless my fowling-piece could be so denominated. In an hour the enemy was nearly along-side, with English colours flying at the main-top, and we were hailed in our own language. After the usual interrogatories and answers, we were ordered to hoist out our boat and the captain, with his papers, was directed to come on board. During the latter part of the chase our commander was decidedly of opinion that the enemy was English, but by constantly using my telescope, I perceived the greasy cap of liberty ornamenting the masthead of the sans-culottes, and therefore told him to prepare for a fraternal hug.

We represented, by means of our speaking-trumpet, that our boat was leaky, and therefore to comply with their demand would be dangerous; at the same time inviting them to board us. To this we were answered: "Out with your boat, or we will sink you." Our captain, who, like a great majority of his countrymen, was an inveterate enemy to England, could no longer contain his passion; he cursed the English, and swore that nothing but one of their "d——d privateers" would act in this manner. "Go, captain," I replied, "to your friends the Monsieurs, and receive the benediction of equality." While he went below for his papers, and his shore coat, the privateer fired another gun, lowered her English colors, and hoisted the tri-colored flag of France. I immediately hastened after the captain, and told him that his friends were impatient; for they now spoke the language of his heart, which was legible at their main-top mast-head. He understood me, and in sullen silence put his bill of sale, manifest, and clearance into his pocket; and then came upon deck, while the crew were launching our leaky boat. The mask being thrown off, *Monsieur le capitaine* loudly vociferated, "*Depêchez vous, depêchez vous!*" Both vessels, their sails a-back, had now edged within a stone's throw of each other, when Lieutenant Minchin, on their again threatening to fire into us, roared out, in the true style of a British seaman, "Fire and be d——d." This, fortunately, was not understood, except by an Englishman, in "durance vile," on board the privateer, and who, by threats, was compelled to fulfil the derogatory office of hailing our vessel. His miserable companions in captivity were confined below the deck.

Half an hour had Capt. Trask undergone the ordeal of Gallic scrutiny, when we perceived four armed *sans-culottes* descend into our shattered boat, which pushed off, rowed by two of our crew, who had conducted their captain on board the privateer. They were soon on the deck of the Industry, for the sea was not much agitated. It is not in my power to describe the appearance of this gang of raggamuffin marauders. The leader was a tawny, squat, savage-looking Frenchman, in height not more than four feet and a half. over his shoulders was a thread-bare blue coat,with red facing. His paunch, and posteriors, which were disproportionably enormous, were covered with a greasy and coarse red cloth. This, as well as his coat, glared with yellow buttons of extraordinary size, on which were embossed the wretched emblems of liberty and equality. Round his waist was girt a monstrous sabre, which a trooper would find it difficult to wield. At least a third of this instrument of death he dragged after him, while he strutted and gasconaded on our quarter-deck. A pair of large ship pistols were stuck in his belt. On his head, in which nature had sported until all proportion was lost in overgrown size, was an enormous cocked hat, surmounted with a monstrous plume of coarse feathers. Though at the mercy of this ludicrous figure, we could not restrain our risibility. His self-importance was evident to all, though no person on board understood one word of his menaces, save myself, nor could I immediately adjust the features of my face to accost him. I had, however, sufficient command over my feelings, not only to subdue the strong impulse I felt to throw the animal overboard, but even to offer a complimentary introduction. I told him, in French, that I thought the gallantry of a Frenchman would have restrained him from intimidating a lady. Mrs. Minchin was near me. Having in some degree appeased the affected wrath of the intruder, who charged us with altering our course to avoid him, he insisted on searching the trunks of the passengers, asserting, that he was sure we were English. This I stoutly denied; and believe me, reader, it was the only time I have been reduced to this choaking humility. Looking up at me, his saffron face nearly in contact with my breast, he sarcastically replied, *Je dis, encore, je suis sur au contraire.*

It was not till this moment that I recollected having the day before been employed amongst my papers, and that they lay in a deranged state and uppermost in my trunk. The fellow fortunately did not observe my confusion, yet nothing could have preserved my devoted papers. After ransacking various trunks of the other passengers, during which outrage he spared not even the linen of the lady, he came to my unfortunate property. Again looking up in my face, he roared out with the voice of arrogant authority, *Pourquoi, faquin, n'avez vous pas exposé cette malle la?* The other trunks had all been opened in rotation by their respective owners.

To what indignities had I reduced myself! The idea of revenge flashed with redoubled force across my brain — a moment might have overwhelmed me, and blasted all my golden prospects in the happy land for which I was embarked. An involuntary menacing motion with my hand was interpreted as an effort to find the key. He hastily demanded it, and I peevishly answered that I had lost it. He then gave orders to his savage followers to break open my trunk. At this instant one of the gang had taken up Mrs. Minchin's child, and the fears of the mother afforded me time to recover my calmness. The key was produced; seeing no alternative, I opened the trunk, and the result was such as I had apprehended. He scrambled up the papers, uttering an hundred *sacre Dieu's*, and grinned at me the most insulting sarcasms, while another of the crew ran upon deck to announce to his comrades *une bonne prise.*

With my papers crammed into a dirty handkerchief, taken from a still more dirty neck, the plunderers were regaining the deck. To me alone they were of the utmost consequence, yet I knew that, without explanation, we might all be involved in trouble. I followed them, and after intreating my fellow passengers, in vain, to accompany me, I jumped into the boat amidst the Frenchmen, and again offended the captor by my presumption. I now used a more haughty tone — insisted on going on board the privateer, observing to my misshapen tormentor, that there I would require justice of his superior. The Frenchmen nimbly got on board, and handed the bundle to the captain; then like true sons of equality, indiscriminately crowded round the companionway, where the examination began. I followed, but found little prospect of gaining the place of search. The privateer was full of men, of a description calculated to recal to the imagination Falstaff's picture of his company of soldiers. Without exertion, I saw that I might be condemned, and our vessel also, without a hearing; for the *Monsieurs* were confident the papers would make us a good prize.

Taking, therefore, one of the ragged rascals by the collar, and pushing another aside, at the same time calling out *avec permission,* I reached the companion-way. I found the French captain, dressed *à la mode Angloise,* in plain clothes. I addressed him in French, and he answered me with politeness. He had, by this time, given a parchment (the counterpart of a lease I had granted of a house in England) to an apostate American, one of the crew, and who was recognized by one of our people to be a native of Connecticut. This fellow, who scarcely knew his own name on paper, blundered out the first line of the deed, as far as "in the thirtieth year of the reign of our sovereign lord George the Third," when he threw it down, and swore it was a commission from old George. After the uproar of *diable's* and *mon Dieus'* had ceased, I perceived the captain looking at me, as if for an explanation. On this point I gave him entire satisfaction; and finding no instrument remaining which looked so formidable as the lease, he returned my papers, and, with Parisian complaisance, apologized for the trouble he had given me. He then invited me to drink a glass of claret with him, which the hurry of my spirits, and the exertions I had used, rendered most grateful. I therefore filled a large tumbler to the brim, thanked him, and drank it.

This privateer was called L'Esperance, and had taken some prizes. I was highly gratified in reading, a short time after my arrival in America, that she did not long remain a pest to the ocean; but that being taken by a vessel belonging to her enemy, she was conducted into an English port. I could not, on this occasion, restrain a wish that my little dingy hero had been consigned to the voracious inhabitants of the deep.

On taking leave of the privateer, I was accosted in English by a respectable looking man, who had been confined until it appeared that there was no danger from our resistance, and who informed me, that he had been taken by the Esperance a few days before, in an American vessel which he commanded. This man gave me his name, with that of his ship, and requested me to hand it to a printer on my arrival. I accordingly gave the particulars to Major Benjamin Russell, printer of the Columbian Centinel, who inserted it next day in his paper. These names I have forgotten; indeed, at this remote period they would be but of little use. This captain likewise informed me, that we had experienced a lucky escape, as the most trifling suspicious circumstances would have thrown us into "the bloody jaws of Marat."*

The privateer veered round while I was again getting on board the Industry: the crew manned the yards, and gave us three cheers. This manœuvre, however, the lady was prevented from witnessing, for many of the Frenchmen were literally *sans culottes*, and being in this situation elevated on the yards and shrouds, presented objects not exactly adapted to the eye of female modesty. We returned them three hearty curses — but not before we thought them out of hearing.

We had contracted for our passage with Capt. Trask for thirty guineas each, including our provisions. This was a large sum to a man who confessed that he never had carried a passenger across the Atlantic. He was to lay in an ample stock of provisions, a certain quantity of wine and porter, to which were added, at our own expense, some bottled cyder, and spirituous liquors. We had also requested him to procure a plentiful supply of other articles, so that we might not suffer by a voyage of longer duration than usual, and promised, in that case, an additional remuneration. We were greatly surprised to find on the first day a dinner of salt beef, but as he apologized by observing that things were not yet in order to cook fresh provisions, we made no comments. While at this our first meal on board, a specimen of American effrontery was given us by Bob, the cook-boy, a sprig of a

* See Burke's Speech on the French Revolution.

true-born Yankee,* who, reaching his dirty arm across the table, took a tumbler and deliberately filled it with equal parts of rum and water. Amazed at this behavior, we waited the result. He looked round, and familiarly nodding his head, "Good folks," said he, "here's to ye." Then with perfect *sang froid,* he swallowed the contents, and looked round for approbation. We stared at each other, but no one spoke, till Cravath, the American passenger, exclaimed, "Ah! pure nature!" We, however, perceived that Bob's countryman was not well pleased with this first exhibition of American equality. Bob was laughed at, and soon found that he had not hit upon the right plan to obtain a glass of grog. In return, he sometimes muttered among his companions, "the proud English!"

A few days after our adventure with the privateer, arrived the fourth of June.[1] It was not till after dinner that we were aware of the circumstance, on which we agreed to have a bottle of wine each, in honor of the day; but under a resolution of subsequent economy in the consumption of our store of that grateful beverage. The first glass was scarcely filled before the Englishmen, with one accord, toasted "The King," in which the American passenger joined. We then gave "The President of the United States," in compliment to Mr. Cravath, who seemed highly gratified. The great and good Washington, who then filled that office, merited the remembrance. Sentiments were then proposed, and Mr. Plank, in his turn, gave "Bloody noses to the French." This too was drunk by Mr. Cravath, without comment; but when he was called upon, he reversed the toast, and drank "Bloody noses to the English." This had nearly put an end to our conviviality. The impropriety of my countryman's

* This is so far from being considered a term of reproach by the inhabitants of New England, that it is employed by them in the same manner, and perhaps with greater complacency, than a native of Old England applies to his countrymen the appelation of "John Bull." It should likewise be observed, that the term is confined only to the people of the New England states, who are even called Yankees by those of the southern states.

behaviour, in our then situation, forcibly struck me the moment he pronounced the toast; but I had hoped it would have been passed over, and therefore took no notice of it. I mention this trifling circumstance, to shew the reader the sentiments entertained at that time by Americans towards England. Mr. Cravath was a mild man, of few words, and never introduced politics, yet rancour against his mother-country was not eradicated from his mind; and I fear its seeds still vegetate in those of three-fourths of his country-men. Mr. Plank was about to make a severe retort, when I interfered, by observing, that he had himself given occasion to the obnoxious sentiment, by inconsiderately wishing discomfiture to his enemies, in the presence of one whose country was at peace, and in treaties of amity with them. Here the matter rested; the Englishman was good-natured, and the American joined in wishing that nothing had been said, at such a time, by either of them, respecting the French. Thus, hilarity was restored, and the day concluded, as it always should with Englishmen — in good humour.

Fourteen days we had run before the wind; not a sheet or a tack had been altered: we were one evening congratulating each other on the fair hopes of a very short passage, when, on retiring to our respective cabins, Mr. Minchin observed that the vessel heeled a good deal. He immediately ran upon deck, and found a heavy squall coming on, while the mate at the helm was giving directions to take in the top-sails. American mariners do not always follow the example of the English in taking in their small sails before night approaches, and we severely felt the consequence of this omission. The braces and sheets having been long neglected in consequence of favorable gales, great confusion and delay took place in securing the vessel. The wind had suddenly shifted, and it now blew a heavy gale. The noise on deck alarmed us — the lady was shrieking, and fear seized all the inmates of the cabin. It would be ridiculous to deny that I was not in a state of great dread; for it was the first gale I had ever encountered upon the ocean. The captain was roused from his sleep, and ran upon deck with no other cloathing than his shirt; he seized the helm, while the mate, with Mr. Minchin, used every exertion to get in the sails. This was accomplished in about half an hour, when the latter relieved our fears in the cabin, by informing us "that the vessel was now snug." I then ventured upon the deck, where the foaming of the waves, and the whistling of the wind, by no means tended to dispel my apprehensions. I applied to the mate, who had resumed his post at the helm, for consolation. He laughed at my anxiety, and said it was only a sudden puff; adding, "d——n her, she did to be sure run off like a scalded hog."

Such, however, are the perils of the ocean, that the mind of a passenger can never be said to be truly at ease. When he lies down to rest, he dreads the dangers of the night; while his meals are often interrupted by the unpleasant call of "All hands upon deck." This gale continued four days, during which the vessel lay to, under a double-reefed fore-sail. On the morning after the squall overtook us, I went upon deck, and was greatly alarmed at finding no person there, and a heavy sea running. I fancied the crew had abandoned the ship, and, under this impression, I called out for the captain or the mate. "What do you want?" replied one of the seamen, stretching out his neck from behind the binnacle. I told him my apprehensions, at which he laughed immoderately. I fancied the fellow an insulting savage; but, when he had sufficiently indulged his risibility at my expense, he told me that the crew could do nothing while the wind continued in that point, and nothing more was required than "a hand to look out." I now proceeded upon the main deck, and looking down, saw the mate busily engaged with his reckoning, some of the crew asleep, and others employed as they thought fit.

We had now to contend against adverse winds, and a tremendous sea, till we reached the banks of Newfoundland, of which we were apprized by the thick fog that enveloped us. The sea became tranquil; and, as it were, yielded to the influence of the fog.

The following incident occurred not long before to a ship, in the latitude in which we now were: The cook had slung overboard a piece of salt beef, in order to wash and freshen it for dinner; and not as a bait for the rapacious tenants of the deep. The barrel being nearly empty, he was unable to reach the beef without the assistance of a harpoon, which happened to be at hand, and which he had struck so forcibly into it, that, finding some difficulty in drawing out the instrument, he threw the whole over the side of the ship, first fastening it to a rope. A shark of an enormous size, must, unperceived, have followed their track, for, in a very few minutes, one of the seamen observed the coil of rope, to which the cook had attached the meat, diminishing at a great rate. Ignorant of the use to which it had been put, he seized it, and finding a great resistance, called for aid, by which the course of the ravenous animal was checked, and they soon discovered it writhing in agony. It was drawn alongside, and with considerable difficulty hoisted upon the deck. On the cook's explanation, it became a matter of surprise how the shark could be held; but, upon examination, they found that a bone in the beef had been started by the introduction of the harpoon, in such a direction, that, on being swallowed, it completely operated as a hook, and thus rendered all the animal's attempts to disengage itself utterly unavailing.

This circumstance affords another confutation of the assertion of Linnæus, who says, that the shark devours her own young. On extracting the beef, three young sharks followed, in full vigour. Had the old one received them into the stomach as food, life would, undoubtedly, have been extinguished before the expiration of half the time that had elapsed from her being hooked, to the extracting of the bait. We find that Sir Richard Hawkins, in his account of his voyage to South America, upwards of two centuries ago, says, that he has observed the young sharks have free egress and regress into the mouth of the dam, and that he has found them in the stomach.[2] Of late years, Dr. Mosely on the subject, asserts, that the young sharks retreat into the stomachs of the old ones, in time of danger. In this instance, the young ones struggled upon the deck with great activity; and, small as they were, they excited so great a terror, that few chose to venture too near them. The cook, to whom they were consigned, dressed them for dinner, and it required but little effort in the crew to banish their prejudice, when placed on the table.

In the stomach of the old shark, which measured fourteen feet, two inches, in length, were found a variety of both finny and testaceous fish, a turtle half digested, several crayfish, two of which, having been lately swallowed, were eaten at supper; and several large bones. They were unable to determine the species of animal to which many of the latter had belonged.

I have already observed that Captain Trask was to receive thirty guineas per head for our passage, and that he was promised a further recompence in case of a long voyage and sufficient sea stores. He purchased about three dozen fowls, the great part of which died from improper treatment, the first week; two dozen ducks; two dozen bottles of port wine; two gallons of rum; two of brandy; not more than two or three dressings of fresh beef, and a single joint of veal; with some tea and sugar, potatoes and cabbages. We often calculated the cost of these articles, and found they could not amount to the price of one passage. The vessel, too, was not accommodated for passengers, being, in fact, a lumber-carrier, trading with timber of every description from Wiscassett, one of the most northerly ports of the United States, to Great Britain. Neither the want of accommodation, nor the rudeness of the captain, was regarded at the moment of embarkation. I know not to how much greater inconvenience we would have submitted, to be blessed with a sight of the far-famed land to which we were bound. How sweet are the delusive dreams of imagination! — But to return to our captain.

Our fresh provision of butchers' meat were consumed before the end of a single week, while the fowls were dying at the rate of three or four a day. We were therefore already upon what is called "Ship's allowance." This was beef, pork, and biscuit. Such is the constant fare of seamen; and, being used to no other, they look not for variety. We too, though now for the first time obliged to live like seamen, should have been content, had the provisions been good. To our vexation, we found them difficult to masticate, and disagreeable to the palate. The mate, whose name was Nye, told me, that the beef was American, and by no means the best — that it had crossed and re-crossed the Atlantic he knew not how often; the pork, he added, was not worth mentioning, because there was but very little left; the biscuit, to which we were also reduced, was of a similar description with the beef, being worm-eaten and rotten; while our water was nearly in a state of putridity. Our wine and spirits too were entirely gone. It appeared that Citizen Bob made free with our liquors, notwithstanding the rebuff he experienced upon his first attempt, changing only the mode, by taking his glass behind our backs. Now, Bob had almost as many different offices to fill on board, as Scrub enumerates to Archer: he was steward as well as cook, and in this capacity he had the care of our cabin-stores. He was also the only individual of the crew who had for some time entered the cabin; for our captain had long fled from our reproaches, and had made himself a berth in the steerage. This stewardship in a considerable degree contributed to the premature exhaustion of our liquors; for Bob (and I never met with an American who did not), loved his glass. This, however, could not have made such obvious ravages in his charge, had he confined his glass to himself. We discovered, when, alas! too late, that our Yankee "helpmate," — for, reader, we must not use the word servant, as you shall hereafter know, — had made frequent repetitions of "Here's to ye," with company more suited to his taste. In short, Bob had not only made pretty free himself, but had been most liberal to his shipmates, taking our liquor by wholesale in return for our laughing him out of his glass. — A cork was probably drawn as often under the fore-scuttle as in the cabin; and thus, our store of liquor was exhausted before we reached the banks of Newfoundland.

The discovery of these misfortunes greatly encreased our clamours against the authors of them. Our captain now seldom came even upon the deck, except when called by his indispensable duty, in the performance of which he took care to shield himself against our attacks. I have omitted to mention, that, very early on our voyage, our captain contrived to obtain from each of us the whole of our passage-money. This business was moved by the captain's countryman, our fellow-passenger, Cravath, who first paid up the balance of his thirty guineas before the whole commonwealth of the cabin. Americans are a people who seem to gather from the habits of every European nation, something which they turn to their own advantage; and to elucidate this, it is only necessary to observe "that they stick together like Scotchmen when abroad." The example of Cravath was followed without suspicion, and a week previous to the discovery of the rapid decay of our subsistence the whole of our passage-money was paid. Now, had I been taking my passage from a British port, and in a British bottom, for Lisbon — nay, even for Calais, I should not have paid a shilling till I was safely landed at my destined port. The case was here far different: and, with Doctor Pangloss I would mentally exclaim, "Am I not with the true sons of freedom? — am I not about to pay them a domestic visit?" The idea of that caution which I had ever found most useful, when a separation was to take place between my purse and my cash, I would not now for a moment endure. With what pleasure did I pay my balance to the captain! How eagerly did I then question him upon the distance still before us! My heart beat with a sensation not to be described, when this *child of nature* was flattering me with the fair prospects of a short passage, while he pocketed my money.

Our situation was a constant source of discontent, and the English passengers appeared impatient to land, that they might wreak their vengeance on the captain, the moment they should catch him out of his vessel. The esteem I entertained for him was converted into indignation; and being, perhaps, of too sanguine a constitution, it was with some difficulty I forbore taking some revenge on his person while on board. I however repressed the impulse, but on every opportunity loaded him with reproaches. In his society, for he now messed with his crew, by way of retaliation, he branded me with the appellation of "*The Grumbler;*" and I am ready to confess that I put myself foremost in our struggle for a redress of grievances. This new title was soon handed by Bob into the cabin: my companions at first made themselves merry upon it; while I could not cordially join with them, for it served rather to irritate than to soothe my mind. I replied, in order that Bob might carry my observation back by way of answer, that if ever we arrived at Boston, he should have an opportunity of calling me *The Flogger,* as well as the grumbler; for, unless he returned me a good part of the money of which he had completely swindled me, be the consequence what it might, I would exercise my horsewhip upon him. In a few minutes the captain was in full possession of my threat, with as many aggravating circumstances as Bob could invent; but on the next day a negociation was opened between him and the malcontents through the medium of Mr. Cravath. After some time spent in debate, a restitution of five guineas each was proposed, together with the contrition of our commander; and this was accepted. I had now not only the gratification of playing off my adopted name with great advantage, but observed to the crest-fallen captain, that I had worked his shame, and that he had paid me five guineas for my *grumbling*.

Peace was now restored; the captain, in order to insure his entire safety on landing, told us that we might most likely procure some spirits, or spruce-beer, from the fishing vessels, which began to appear in sight. This observation was made in consequence of two large halibuts, a rich, fine-flavored fish, being caught, from the Industry; yet, after regaling on them, we had nothing to drink but stinking water: for a breeze springing up, favorable to our course, the captain would not hail the fishermen. We would have compounded with the sacrifice of a whole week longer in our unpleasant situation, and even offered a guinea each for a single gallon of spirits and a barrel of fresh water; yet we could procure no farther supply till our arrival.

We now approached the land, which was evident, as well from the birds, as from an alteration in the color of the water. The reckoning, both of the captain and of the mate, was run out; but Mr. Minchin, who also kept one, declared that we were not so near as the others asserted. The long-wished for object was the next day descried from the mast-head by the mate, who called out "land under the starboard bow." Those alone can form a judgment of our sensations, who, for the first time have been plowing, during six weeks, the uncertain ocean, and who have been opposed by adverse winds, with intervening discord on board their little bark. The land descried was the mountain called Agnamenticus, in New Hampshire, a land-mark for mariners. We made the shore, with a fresh gale, and gained the river Piscataway, on which is situated the town of Portsmouth. We were boarded, on our entrance into this river, by a custom-house boat, with an officer, who exhibited a grotesque appearance. He was clad in the fashion prevalent among the lowest class of the country people of England in the earliest years of my youth, and his garments had suffered much in his service. Our captain, anticipating our well-grounded complaints, apologized to him for a lack of entertainment, by observing, that our long passage had entirely exhausted our stores of liquor. This unwelcome information, added to our only making the river for a harbour (being bound to Boston), soon caused him to take his leave. Before we could come to our moorings, the wind blew hard, and the rain drove the passengers into the cabin. Another night were we doomed to pass without relief in our prison, for so the vessel now appeared to us. About midnight, *honest* Bob roared out in the midst of his sleep, and his cries, predominating over the wind and the rain, roused us from our cabins. Hastening to that part of the vessel where he lay, I found that he had been bitten by a rat, and his upper lip was much swelled, and bleeding. He was soon thrown into convulsive fits, and it was with difficulty that we could confine him to his bed. The captain wished him to be bled, but, such is the wretched state in which many American vessels are fitted out, though the government have, by law, provided to the contrary, that no kind of article of relief, medicinal or surgical, was to be found on board. In my pocket-book was a lancet, and on making this known, the captain intreated me to produce it, and to bleed the patient. As I could not reconcile the idea of this operation to my present situation, I declined the proffered honor of drawing American blood. Mr. Nye, the mate, then took the lancet; after many unsuccessful attempts he opened a vein, and poor Bob revived. He had been more terrified than hurt by the disgusting animal.

The morning arrived, and the passengers prepared to go on shore. To Mr. Minchin this port was more agreeable than that of Boston, inasmuch as it was about sixty miles nearer the place of his destination. He informed us that he was bound to Halifax, of which place, his wife's uncle, Mr. Wentworth, was the British governor. Mr. Cravath's affairs in Boston requiring every possible dispatch, he determined to take the stage, by which conveyance he might arrive there in one day. A boat was procured, which received Mr. and Mrs. Minchin, the child, and their baggage, while the remainder of the passengers got into the ship's boat, which had been repaired, and after rowing two miles, landed us at Portsmouth, in New England.

This town is beautifully situated, about four miles from the mouth of the river Piscataway. It is nearly as large as Gravesend, but built chiefly of wood; and about twenty sail of vessels were lying at the wharfs.

On landing, we were surrounded by a motley group, from the well-dressed merchant, down to persons whose appearance bespoke the most squalid indigence. The first salute we received, was from at least a dozen voices, inquiring the news from England. We had been apprised that unbounded curiosity was a prominent trait in the character of the Americans. While I was attempting to satisfy one party, another had gathered round Mr. Plank. This gentleman had a little of the humorist in his composition. He answered his surrounding enquirers, with much gravity, that there was great news from England. "Fifty thousand men," continued he, "rose in the town where I embarked, the morning we sailed." Here again it was very evident what satisfaction a large majority received from a supposed misfortune to old England. "What then? what did they do then?" was the next question. "Why," replied Plank, "I do not know, but I judge" — "What? what?" — "That at night they went to bed again!"

It would have required the pencil of a Hogarth to depict the various countenances of the Yankees. Rage, it is true, appeared but momentary — the sense of rebuke drove some away — some laughed — and one, with a better turn of mind, observed, that he was glad to find Englishmen merry on their arrival in the country. Mr. Cravath, no doubt, dreading delay, hurried to the post-house, and we saw no more of him till our arrival at Boston. Good-humor being in some measure restored, the intelligence of the tranquillity of England, of the distraction of France, of our detention on our voyage, with a variety of other particulars, was received by our auditors with apparent gratification.

The impression made by this inquisitive disposition upon the mind of a stranger, is at first favorable. He concludes that these interrogatories will lead to acts of kindness; conscious that Englishmen would not take the trouble — nay, would not dare to question each other without making, at least, an offer of services. In England, every one appears to find full employment in his own concerns; — here, it would seem that the people are restless until they know every person's business. If the Americans have any national trait, which has been denied by some writers, it is this intrusive *curiosity*. Nor is it to acquire useful information that these people pester strangers; it is habit, for they act in the same manner towards each other; and on meeting, they propose, as it were, in one breath, a long string of questions to each other. If, however, a question is asked them by a person apparently a foreigner, they hesitate, and avoid giving a reply by demanding his business, leaving the stranger under that most unpleasant sensation which is produced by a doubtful and ambiguous reception. This habit, to those unacquainted with them, indicates suspicion that he comes among them to gain unfair information, or to outwit them in some favorite speculation. If he would avoid insult, he must bear with this and have in readiness an uniform set of answers, for which in travelling he will have abundant occasion, wherever he stops in his progress through New England.

No farther attention was paid us, but we were left to continue our way to the market to purchase fresh provisions. As every principal town in America has a daily market, we found no difficulty in supplying ourselves, having submitted to all impositions. We purchased tolerably good beef at fourpence per pound; lobsters at three-pence, according to weight; and bread was nearly the same price as in England at our departure. The dollar is here at six shillings; the reader may therefore rate the beef at three-pence, and the lobsters at two-pence farthing sterling per pound. We soon discovered that we had paid at least a halfpenny per pound more than the market price; but in other countries, the perversion of the scriptural expression "I was a stranger, and ye took me in," is perhaps still more strikingly exemplified.

On the next day we again continued our voyage, and anchored in the harbor of Boston, without meeting with any incident worth relating. All animosity being now at an end, Mr. Plank and myself, the only passengers remaining on board, invited the captain and mate to regale with us in the cabin.

Boston is a large commercial town; the port was full of shipping, and the bustle of business appeared in all the streets leading to the harbor. Mr. Cravath, agreeably to his promise, soon came on board, and conducted me to a lodging-house, kept by Mrs. Archbold, behind the old church, at the head of State Street, one of the best in the town. Mrs. Archbold was an elderly married lady, but her husband was a mere cypher in the house, while three or four daughters completely filled the circle. Her price was seven dollars per week, but the extra charges, which, in all such houses in America, are unconscionable, amounted, during the week I remained there, to four more, making two pounds and twelve shillings sterling money![3] For washing I was charged one dollar each dozen pieces, and the smallest handkerchief is charged equal to a shirt. It is not the price of provisions which causes these exorbitant charges, nor public taxes, nor house-rent; all these things are moderate. It is on the score of *trouble* that every thing is rendered dear in America. If you comment upon the price of an article, you are sure to have the answer end with, "*and then consider the trouble.*" If I had judged them at the time by my own feelings, I could not have demurred, for I confess it was great *trouble* to me to move — to eat — I had nearly said to drink; which would have been a gross falsehood, for I drank the whole day long, and at night still craved for drink. The heat to me, just landed from the cool sea-breezes, and ever used to temperate climates, was almost insupportable. So profusely did I perspire, that I changed my shirt several times in a day, until I was cautioned against a too frequent repetition of that comfortable practise, and told to remain with it thoroughly wet, rather than run the risk of checking perspiration by putting on cold linen. In Carolina, where the thermometer is much higher, I did not suffer in such a degree. The reason was evident; my constitution was in some measure inured to the climate before I visited that unhealthy country. Had I landed in Charleston, instead of Boston, I am of opinion that nature would have sunk under the effects of the excessive heat.

NOTES — CHAPTER I

1. Evidently they were celebrating the birthday of George III, then King of England.

2. Sir Richard Hawkins, *The Observations of Sir Richard Hawkins, knight in His Voyage into the South Sea.* London, 1593.

3. Henry Bradshaw Fearon in his *Sketches of America* reported that boarding at a moderately respectable house cost eight dollars a week for a "transient man" or five or six dollars for a three or six months' resident. Elsewhere he said the charges varied from eight to fourteen dollars a week. In Boston he paid 3£ 1s. 8d., and was served neither beer nor cider. Brandy and rum were served, and the charges were made upon the assumption that the guest availed himself of them.

CHAPTER II

EXCESSIVE HEAT — BED-BUGS AND MUSQUITOES — PROCESSIONS — ORATIONS — BUNKER'S HILL — DEATH OF MAJOR PITCAIRN — VAULTS CONTAINING THE REMAINS OF THE OFFICERS WHO FELL AT THE BATTLE OF BUNKER'S HILL.

WE landed in Boston on the third of July, and the fourth was the day of Jubilee — the anniversary of the declaration of American independence. The fatigue of getting my baggage on shore in the excessive heat of a meridian sun, had nearly exhausted me before I reached my lodgings. I, however, met with no detention or aggravating circumstance at the custom-house — no extortion — no demand of fees. An oath was administered to me, that the baggage was for my own private use; and this was the only ceremony I underwent.

By dinner time I had lost all appetite, and, suffering under a most profuse perspiration, had thrown myself upon my bed, from which I had no inclination to rise. Instead of dinner, I substituted large draughts of weak punch; and for supper, tea. I now endeavored to compose myself to sleep, but soon found the night to be more intolerable than the day. No cool breeze accompanied it — not even a breath of air; tormented with myriads of bugs and musquitos, which blistered me all over,* I contended against their united efforts

* The bite, as it is called, or rather the puncture of the musquito, though seldom felt at the moment it is inflicted, is attended with great irritation; and sometimes, if improperly treated, with dangerous consequences. It is the buzzing noise the insects make while on the wing, added to the sense of having felt the effects produced by their bite, which causes a most unpleasant sensation. A traveller who visited part of the United States some years ago, Mr. Weld, speaking of this insect, says: "General Washington told me, that he never was so much annoyed by musquitos in any part of America as in Skenesborough, for that they used to bite through the thickest boot." This is told with an air of gravity, and no doubt the author meant that it should be believed. I confess, though I have been in a part of the country through which this author never

until the morning's dawn drove them from their prey. Thus relieved, I had fallen into a refreshing sleep, from which I was soon roused by one of the Miss Archbolds, a pert virgin, though growing a little antique. She summoned me to rise and join in the festivity of the day — a most unwelcome message for a man in my situation. I craved a respite, and requested more tea; but I found that nothing could be obtained, without a promise of rising. On my entering the parlour, the ladies were seated at breakfast, dressed, and ready to join in jocund sports; than which, nothing could just then have been more irksome to me. I found their anxiety for my presence arose from the use they intended to make of me as their gallant to the Mall, the Parade, and the Orations; while they intimated how much I might think myself favored by their preference, adding a torrent of empty compliments and insipid jokes. I shrunk with disgust from the familiarity of persons to whom I had been known but a few hours, and whom I expected to have found attentive to the accommodation which a stranger on landing from a long voyage must naturally require. To add another wound to my feelings, my body still smarting from the attacks of my midnight tormentors, one of the young ladies began to question me in the usual manner of the country. I had passed

penetrated, where the climate and situation are more favorable to the musquito, I never saw or heard of such dangerous wounds as those must be which are inflicted by an insect capable of biting through the thickest boot. This is more than even a rattle-snake has the strength to do; for I have seen the marks of the teeth of one on the leather breeches of a man in North Carolina, which entirely resisted the bite. I have often heard this assertion of Mr. Weld's commented upon in America — not as to the possibility of the fact itself, but as an instance of the misrepresentations of Europeans with respect to their country. It has even been treated in a contemptuous manner in their provincial newspapers; and in some places I have heard it quoted, when an improbable anecdote was related, "that's like the musquitos that bit General Washington through his boot!" Some observed that it must have been a joke; while other replied, that the General was no jester. In making this comment, I would not be understood to decry Mr. Weld's publication; it arises from a duty I owe to some friends in America, and to fulfil a promise I made them of explaining mistakes. There is truth in most of Mr. Weld's observations.

the *ordeal* on my first interview, while bargaining for my apartments, but unluckily one of the family was not present, and I found that I must satisfy the absent fair one on this all important subject. Contemplating, therefore, the advantage I should derive from getting through the business expeditiously, I immediately repeated my tale. This had a good effect; and in order to evade the *favors* intended to have been heaped upon me, I pleaded a promise made to my fellow-passenger, who lodged in another part of the town, to call upon him immediately after breakfast.

My friend, before I could give him an idea of my situation, began *his* lamentable story of his sufferings during the night, and I had only to reply that my case was exactly similar. He approved of my declining to attend the ladies, declaring that he should feel some repugnance at parading about with boarding-houses misses. Little did we then know the etiquette of equality. We, however, concluded that it was good policy to appear in public; and that on no account should we give cause of offence to the people whom we were now among. The thirteen stripes were flying before the window — guns were firing, and the drums beating, giving notice to attend. In no very pleasant mood, we sallied out, once more to encounter the rays of the sun, first providing ourselves with umbrellas, an indispensable article in America, in the heat of summer. We now joined a crowd which led us to the Mall, from which we had a view of the military parade. Here were assembled a great number of citizens of both sexes, and of all descriptions. The ladies appeared in the fashions of England about two years antecedent, but more gaudy; the gentlemen had their hair dressed, and full powdered, and their clothes of the best materials. During the hot weather it is a custom here to wear light dressing or morning gowns, but very few were to be seen on this day of jubilee.

Of the military, about five hundred infantry made a fine appearance; and as many more, without regimentals, formed a perfect contrast. The manœuvres consisted of salutes, marching in columns, and firing *feu de joyes.*

A part of the duties of the day was to move in procession to some church, to hear an oration pronounced from the pulpit, by a layman. That to which we repaired was greatly crowded, and not being early apprized of the circumstance, we could barely get within the doors, and consequently heard the orator but indistinctly. From what we could collect, however, his address was abundantly interlarded with invective against England for her oppression before, and cruelties during the revolutionary war. I could not see the policy of this method of proceeding. The two countries were at peace, and their faith was plighted to each other to continue on terms of amity. The very Indian, on making peace with his enemy, *buries the hatchet* — which denotes an oblivion of all animosities; yet the descendants of Britain to this day continue to impress on the minds of the rising generation the most rancorous hatred against the country from which they sprung.

Next day I presented my letter of credit to "the honourable Thomas Russell, Esq." Titles of honour are given to legislators; and that of bishop to the dignified clergy, in America. I found in Mr. Russell, a sensible and attentive gentleman, and I greatly regret, that my short stay in Boston, and his death, which happened before I again visited that town, deprived me of his farther acquaintance. He offered me his services in the most friendly manner, and gave me some information which proved of much utility in my progress through the country.

Having somewhat recruited myself, I became anxious to ascend Bunker's Hill, where so many gallant men lost their lives. Mr. Archbold, whom I must call my landlord, offered to be my guide. Accompanied by Mr. Plank, we set out, crossed the bridge which divides Boston from Charlestown, and followed the track of the British troops till we reached the summit of the hill. The old gentleman, our conductor, perfectly remembered the event; indeed, he was a spectator of some part of the transactions of the desperate and unfortunate engagement which there took place. "Here," said he, pointing to the spot, "Major Pitcairn fell, — and here General Warren died. There are the remains of the redoubt, — and (pointing to the river) from thence the English men of war covered the landing of their troops." The scene excited melancholy sensations — it could not otherwise have affected an American — for brave men on both sides fell on the ground we trod.

By a man whom we met on the road, we were informed, that when the British forces rallied, and again ascended the hill, led on by Major Pitcairn, they had advanced near to the redoubt, when the major called to his soldiers to hasten their speed, as the enemy had abandoned the fort. A boy, who, he observed, was then a shoemaker in Boston, replied from behind the trench: "We are not all gone," and instantly fired his musket, which proved the death of Major Pitcairn. No officer fell more regretted, for he was beloved — even by his enemy. Previous to the war, he had been the military commandant at Boston; and, in that situation, had endeared himself to the people.[1]

On our return, we visited the vaults of the church in Boston, which contained the bones of some of the British officers who lost their lives in that memorable battle. The tomb in which were deposited the remains of the gallant Pitcairn, was empty.[2] The sexton informed us, that his brother, Dr. Pitcairn,* of London, had obtained permission to remove them; but we saw many skeletons, which, we were told, were

* This gentleman, who was highly esteemed for his professional skill and ability, was, at the time of his death, in October, 1791, treasurer of Bartholomew's, and physician of Christ's Hospital. Early in life he had been tutor to the Duke of Hamilton, with whom he made the tour of the continent. On the opening of the Ratcliffe library in 1749, he was presented with the degree of doctor of physics, and a year or two afterwards was elected physician of St. Bartholomew's Hospital, in opposition to Dr. Barrowby. He was several years president of the College of Physicians, and fellow of the Royal Society.

the relics of some who held commands under the Major. On one of them hung the remains of regimentals, and a pair of leather breeches, in high preservation. The pipe-clay, with which the latter had evidently been cleaned, probably for the fatal occasion, appeared fresh and white; but the flesh of the body was entirely decayed. Another presented a fractured bone; and the whole formed a painful picture of mortality. The effect it produces on the spectator is so much the more powerful, as these bodies are not deposited in coffins, but lie exposed one upon another in the vault, without any farther covering. — Gallant, but unfortunate men! No weeping relative, no beloved wife, no fond sister, no dutiful child, was at hand, to close your eyes in death! Separated by the wide Atlantic from all the objects of earthly affection, ye had no friends to superintend your obsequies, or to drop the tributary tear on your untimely graves! —

The remainder of my week's stay in Boston was principally passed in my room, where I employed myself in reading such publications as treated of the country of which I had become an inhabitant. I was informed of a singular custom appertaining to the charter of this town, but it was not practised upon me. It consists in a warning given to strangers to leave the place; and, after this ceremony, they are debarred from ever receiving parochial relief.[3]

Boston is the capital of New England, one of the oldest towns in North America, and the third in size and rank in the United States. It is built upon a peninsula at the bottom of Massachusetts Bay, of an irregular figure, connected with the continent only by a narrow isthmus, on the south, which leads to the town of Roxbury. When the town was threatened to be stormed by the Americans under Washington, the British commander, General Gage, cut off all communication with the inhabitants by placing a chain of sentinels across the isthmus; but he soon found it expedient to give it up, on consideration of its not being pillaged, and a quiet evacuation by his army.

Boston bears considerable resemblance to an old city in England. It is two miles in length, but of unequal breadth, being seven hundred and twenty-six yards at the broadest part. It contains about 3500 dwelling-houses, many of which are built of wood, besides a great number of store-houses, and nearly 28,000 inhabitants. This town is famed for a wharf, leading from State Street into the harbor, 1743 feet in a direct line, and in breadth 104 feet. On approaching it from the sea, it appears to the greatest advantage. At the back part is Beacon Hill, which greatly adds to the prospects. On the top of this hill is a column, on which are inscribed the achievements of those who fell by the swords of the British during the revolutionary war. At Boston they distil large quantities of that detestable spirit, there called New England, but in the Southern States, Yankee rum, and in this employment there are near forty large distilleries. It is made of the worst and the damaged molasses, and its baleful effects are severely felt in every part of the union. In Virginia, the Carolinas, and Georgia, it foments quarrels, which produce combats like those of bears and wolves — gouging, biting, kicking, and tearing each others' flesh; of which I shall make more particular mention when I speak of those states. It is sold for about an English half-crown per gallon, is strong, and has the most execrable smell with which any kind of spirit ever assailed my nasal organs.

The first dramatic exhibitions at Boston were performed in a temporary wooden theatre, a short time previous to my arrival; under the management of Mr. Harper. He met with great opposition from the puritanical sects, who even proceeded to pull down his building.[4] He was summoned to answer for his conduct before the select men* of the town, and found it necessary to employ counsel in his behalf. The affair became the principal topic of the day; — those of a liberal education, and generally the younger part of the inhabitants, taking a decided and active part in favor of the children of Thespis;

* Magistrates whose duties are equivalent to those of aldermen of London.

while the Quakers, Presbyterians, Baptists, and Methodists, strenuously opposed them, declaring them vagrants, and their pursuits an abomination. The matter at length came before the court, and, chiefly through the influence of the gentlemen of the bar, the muse triumphed; and a subscription was opened for the erection of a large brick theatre in Federal Street.[5] This was soon filled; and when the building was finished, a company from England, under the management of Mr. Powell,[6] celebrated for his performance of *Bagatelle*, at the Theatre Royal, Covent-Garden, opened the season with Brooke's patriotic tragedy of Gustavus Vasa. The novelty of these rational amusements, rendered the season so productive, and so great was the rage for theatricals, that another place of performance, larger than the first, but of wood, was built in the Haymarket;[7] where the New York company, under Mr. Hodgkinson, performed. The town of Boston has frequently, of late years, suffered by fire, which makes dreadful havoc amongst the old wooden buildings. In a calamity of this nature, the old theatre, as it was then called, was destroyed;[8] but the proprietors immediately erected upon its ruins, one still more commodious. It has been discovered that, in many instances, towns in different parts of the United States, have wilfully been set on fire; and, from Boston to Savannah, suspicions to that effect have, at different times, been entertained; but I never heard of a discovery being made of the perpetrators of such dreadful and atrocious offences.

The bridge connecting Boston with Charlestown, over which we passed to view Bunker's Hill, is a surprising work. It is of wood, with a draw for the admission of vessels, and is 3483 feet in length, and 40 feet wide. On the same river, and not above two miles farther up the country, is another bridge of this nature, 1503 feet long, and 42 in width. The principal manufactures of Boston are, sail-cloth, cordage, hats, wool and cotton cards, pot and pearl-ashes, paper-hangings, plate and common glass, loaf sugar, tobacco, chocolate,

Drawn under the Direction of the Author, and Engraved by M. Marigot.

View of Boston, from the Bay.

and an immense quantity of playing cards, on which they counterfeit the English figures with great exactness. The reader may judge of the propensity of Americans to the abominable spirit above-mentioned, in preference to that agreeable and nutritious beverage, malt liquor, when he finds that only two breweries can barely be supported by this large town and its populous vicinity; — in fact, by all New England, for I never heard of another brewery in the four states and one province which form it: namely, New Hampshire, Massachusetts, Rhode Island, Connecticut, and the Province of Maine.

NOTES — CHAPTER II

1. Major John Pitcairn, son of David Pitcairn, a minister of Dysart, and his wife, Catherine Hamilton, was born at Fifeshire, Scotland, c. 1740. He entered the marine service and became a captain in 1765. In 1771 he was promoted to the rank of major. During the seven years he was stationed in Boston, he won the respect of the citizens by his just treatment of complaining colonists. General Gage sent him with the force to destroy military stores at Concord on April 19, 1775. Major Pitcairn maintained until his death that the minute men had fired first. He died at Boston on June 17, 1775, of wounds inflicted by a negro soldier as he led the fourth charge in the battle of Bunker Hill. His body was returned to England by his brother, Dr. William Pitcairn.

2. Major Pitcairn was buried in Old Christ Church. Like many of the old churches in Boston, it has its vaults underneath for the reception of the dead, and with them, of course, its legendary lore. The officers of the British army were interred in the churches and their cemeteries. Many of the bodies were later sent home. The soldiers in the ranks who died of disease or of wounds received at Bunker Hill were buried in the Common Ground.

3. The commissioners of the city appointed a citizen to have charge of warning such undesirables as came from other towns to leave Boston during the time prescribed by law — fourteen days.

4. No one was permitted to build a theater in Boston until 1792. In 1750 two English actors attempted to give a performance of Otway's *The Orphan*, an audacious enterprise followed by a small riot. The Commonwealth then not only forbade play acting but rendered liable to a heavy fine any one who by his presence gave countenance to anything of the kind. In 1790 Hallam and Henry made a formal appeal to the Massachusetts Legislature to be allowed to open a theater, but they were refused. As time went on, a group of theater lovers formed an association which subscribed funds for the erection of a building which was to be a theater in everything except name.

They purchased ground on Broad Alley, near Hawley Street, and erected the

"New Exhibition Room," which accommodated about 500 persons. On August 10, 1792, it was formally opened under the management of Joseph Harper. The first program consisted of an address by the manager, a song by Mr. Woolls, and dances by M. and Mme. Placide. On September 26 all disguise was thrown off, and Home's *Douglas* and O'Keefe's *Poor Soldier* were put boldly on the bill. The first regular dramatic season in Boston had begun.

All went well until the night of December 5, when during a performance of *School for Scandal,* the sheriff entered the theater and arrested Mr. Harper. Many of the spectators, furious at the interruption, leaped to the stage and tore down the coat of arms of the State. The following day Harper was arraigned in court but released on a technicality. This episode, which brought the absurdity of the law against the theater to the attention of the more intelligent people, really aided the drama. In 1793 another determined attack on the law resulted in its repeal.

5. Following the repeal of the law against theatricals, subscriptions were taken for building a theater in Boston. A commodious brick building with card and tea rooms for those bored by the play was erected at the corner of Federal and Franklin Streets. Charles Stuart Powell was appointed manager. In June, 1793, he sailed for England to engage a company. On February 3, 1794, the first performance was given in the building, called the New Federal Street Theater. The season lasted until the following July, and the repertoire included the best of classic and contemporary drama.

6. Charles Stuart Powell, born in England in 1749, was the son of the manager of a strolling company. After acting at Covent Garden, he came to Boston in 1792. From 1794 until 1796 he was manager of the Federal Street Theater, and later of the Haymarket Theater. On April 26, 1811, he died at Halifax, N. S., where for some years he had acted as manager of the Halifax Theater.

The Haymarket Theater opened on December 26, 1796, under the direction of Charles Stuart Powell.

8. Federal Street Theater burned during the afternoon of February 2, 1798. Opponents pretended to see the hand of God at work in its destruction. However, it was rebuilt during the summer and reopened on October 29.

CHAPTER III

EXTENT OF THE UNITED STATES. — PRESENT NUMBER OF INHABITANTS. — ACQUISITION OF LOUISIANA AND THE FLORIDAS. — CONJECTURES ON THE DURATION OF THE FEDERAL GOVERNMENT. — STATISTICAL SURVEY OF THE UNITED STATES.

THE United States, according to an American geographer, are estimated to comprise upwards of a million square miles, or six hundred and forty million acres of land, exclusive of the lakes, and other large waters of that country. This estimate was made previous to the purchase of Louisiana,* the extent of which has never been accurately defined. Already a region too extensive to be subject to one general government, the people of the northern and southern states differing as much in manners as in climate, they have, by this acquisition, added an extent of territory nearly equal in magnitude to the federal states. Since the peace of 1782, this country has been extending its limits on the frontiers by purchase, and treaties with the different tribes of Indians. The

* The cession of Louisiana by Spain to the ruler of France, formed one of the articles of the treaty of Saint Ildefonso — a treaty which has never yet been carried into full effect on the part of the latter. The purchase of that extensive country by the United States, is an event too recent and too well known to require any farther notice from me. Though the acquisition of the Floridas has not been officially announced by the American government, yet no doubt exists, that the sum of two millions of dollars, shipped for France about a year ago, on the demand of Buonaparte's diplomatic agent Turreau, was the price of those provinces. The conduct of Napoleon in this transaction, is well worth an observation. By means of a treaty which he never intended to execute, he obtained the sovereignty over those vast regions; but knowing that, from the naval superiority of England, he could derive no advantage from these distant possessions, he transferred them on the point of the sword to the Americans, whom he bullied into a purchase, in order to recruit his exhausted treasury. From the readiness with which they have complied with all his requisitions, I should not be surprised to hear that he had disposed of his imperial island of Hayti, as another *good bargain,* to those complaisant republicans.[1]

thirteen states are already swelled into sixteen, and the territories of Mississippi and Indiana, each sending a delegate to congress, will, doubtless, very soon be added to the number. The province of Maine, in the north, has also long looked forward to become an independent state; and when Louisiana is incorporated with the union, it is not improbable that we may find twenty-six united states of America for some short time recorded in history.

The present population of this extensive country, justifies the assertion, that many centuries must elapse before the whole is under cultivation. In the year 1791, a census was taken by order of government; when the inhabitants were found to be in number 3,929,326

In 1801, by another census then taken, there were 5,305,638

Making an increase in ten years of . . . . 1,376,312[2]

According to this average, exclusive of the great increase of population by emigrations from Europe since the year 1801, there must be, exclusive of Louisiana, 6,337,072 souls, under the federal government. If the whole of this country were under improvement, it would require, allowing forty acres of land to each, sixteen millions of families; and, estimating such families at five persons, it would support eighty millions of souls. In this way it has been calculated in America, that to people the whole territories belonging to the United States, including Louisiana and the Floridas, it would require three hundred and twenty millions. It likewise appears, that were the population of this immensely extended republic proportioned only to that of Great Britain, instead of five or six millions, it ought to contain two hundred and thirty-nine millions of inhabitants.

Notwithstanding this vast disproportion between the population and the territory of the United States, the Americans are still farther extending their limits. Considering the opposite interests of the northern and southern states, it is surprising that the federal constitution has so long maintained itself, and triumphed over contending parties. Some of the best informed men are, however, of opinion, that the compact will not hold much longer, and that the next election of a president will sever the states, and leave New York or Pennsylvania the boundary between them. The northern states are firm federalists; that is, of Washington's system: in the south, they are violent democrats, bawlers for liberty in the very midst of slavery. The latter have twice elected Mr. Jefferson as president; and it is conjectured that, should the federals fail in their majority at the next election, it will be the *tocsin* of disunion.

For the information of the statistical inquirer, I have subjoined a table which affords a perspicuous and comprehensive view of the relative extent, population, &c., of the various states, and their newly-purchased possessions. Though, in some of the amounts, it may slightly differ from the preceding statement, yet I believe it to be as correct upon the whole, as it is possible to make such a survey of so extensive an empire. Every reader must be aware that, on subjects of calculation, scarcely any two writers are agreed; and this cannot be surprizing when the difficulty of procuring accurate data is considered. I shall further premise, that, from my personal knowledge, in this table the number of slaves is under-rated.

NOTES — CHAPTER III

1. The "Two Million Dollar Act" passed the Congress of the United States in January, 1806. The appropriation was intended for use in negotiating the purchase of Florida. The "agent," Turreau de Garambouville (1756-1816), served as French ambassador to the United States from 1804 to 1810.

2. Louisiana was admitted in 1812, and Maine in 1820. The population as given by Janson evidently included the inhabitants of the territories. A slight discrepancy exists here. The inhabitants in the United States proper according to one report numbered 3,893,635. Another gave the population as 3,929,625. In 1800 the number in the same area was reported as 5,247,355.

A STATISTICAL VIEW OF THE UNITED STATES.

Names of States.	*Length in Miles.*	*Breadth.*	*Latitude of North and South Extremes.*	*Longitude of E. and W. extremes from Philadelphia.*	*Area in Square Miles.*	*Area in Acres.*	*Population in 1790.*	*Slaves.*	*Population in 1801.*	*Slaves.*	*Increase in Ten Years.*	*Increase of Slaves.*	*One Slave in Persons (1800.)*	*Persons to One Square Mile (1801.)*	*Chief Towns.*	*Chief Rivers.*	*Population of Chief Towns 1801.*
Vermont	156	96	45. 42. 44.	3. 17. E. 1. 44. E.	10,000	6,400,000	86,000	20	160,000	10	74,000			16	Windsor Rutland	Connecticut Otter	2,500 2,200
N. Hampsh.	168	90	45. 15. 42. 41.	4. 33. E. 2. 45. E.	9000	5,760,000	142,000	160	185,000		43,000			20½	Portsmouth Concord	Connecticut Merrimack	5,500 2,200
Maine	240	377	48. 43.	7. 36. E. 4. E.	30,000	19,200,000	100,000		155,000		55,000			19 2-3	Portland Hallowell	Kennebeck Penobscot	4,000 1,400
Massach.	155	90	42. 52. 41. 32.	5. 2. E. 1. 42. E.			380,000		425,000		45,000				Boston Salem	Connecticut Merrimack	25,000 10,000
R. Island	47	37	42. 41. 22.	4. E. 3. 11. E.	2000	1,280,000	70,000	1000	70,000	400			18	35	Newport Providence	Wood Pawtucket	7,000 7,700
Connecticut	100	72	42. 2. 41.	3. 20. E. 1. 50. E.	5000	3,200,000	240,000	3000	250,000	1000	10,000		250	50	New Haven Hartford	Connecticut Thames	4,200 5,500
New York	335	316	45. 40. 32.	3. 6. E. 5. W.	50,000	32,000,000	340,000	22,000	485,000	16,000	140,000		27	9¾	New York Albany	Hudson Mohawk	61,000 5,200
N. Jersey	160	52	41. 20. 39.	1. 24. E. 0. 25. W.	7500	4,800,000	185,000	12,000	215,000	15,000	30,000	3000	14	18 2-3	Trenton Brunswick	Delaware Rariton	
Pennsylvania	261	161	42. 39. 43.	0. 20. E. 5. 20. W.	50,000	32,000,000	440,000	4000	600,000	2000	160,000		300	12	Philadelphia Lancaster	Susquehan. Ohio	75,000 4,500
Delaware	92	33	39. 38. 29.	0. 0. 40. W.	2000	1,280,000	60,000	9000	65,000	6500	5000		10	32½	Wilmington Dover	Christiana Nanticoke	
Maryland	198	130	39. 43. 37. 56.	4. 21. W. 0. 2. W.	10,000	6,400,000	320,000	105,000	350,000	100,000	30,000		3	35	Annapolis Baltimore	Potowmack Patapsco	 26,800
Virginia	373	291	40. 39. 36. 30.	0. 7. W. 8. W.	75,000	48,000,000	750,000	300,000	880,000	350,000	130,000	50,000	2½	11 2-3	Richmond Norfolk	Ohio James	7,000 3,000
N. Carolina	450	180	36. 30. 33. 50.	9. 30. W. 1. W.	45,000	28,800,000	400,000	100,000	480,000	140,000	80,000	40,000	3½	10 2-3	Newberne Edenton	Yadken Nuse	2,500 1,400
S. Carolina	270	250	35. 32.	3. 34. W. 9. 20. W.	30,000	19,200,000	250,000	110,000	350,000	150,000	100,000	40,000	2 2-3	11 2-3	Charleston Columbia	Santee Pedee	21,000
Georgia	660	260	34. 53. 31.	4. 42. W. 16. 17. W.	120,000	76,800,000	85,000	30,000	165,000	60,000	80,000	30,000	2 2-3	1½	Savannah Augusta	Savannah Altamaha	5,200 2,200
Kentucky	370	200	39. 10. 36. 30.	7. 22. W. 15. 15. W.	45,000	28,800,000	75,000	12,500	220,000	40,000	45,000	27,500	5½	5	Lexington Frankfort	Kentucky Green	1,800 650
Tenessee	412	104	36. 30. 35.	7. 45. W. 16. 56. W.	50,000	32,000,000	36,000	4,000	110,000	15,000	74,000	11,000	6 2-3	2 1-5	Knoxville Nashville	Tenessee Cumberland	400 350
Missip. Ter.	384	97	32. 23. 31.	9. 52. W. 16. 20. W.	40,000	25,600,000			10,000	4000			2½	¼	Natchez	Mississippi Mobile	1,700
N. W. Ter.	1,170	800	50. 37.	6. W. 23. W.	350,000	224,000,000			50,000	150			1-7	1-7	Marietta Greenville	Mississippi Ohio	
Totals and averages.	U. S. 1250	1,040	48. 31.	7. 36. E. 23. W.	930,000	595,000,000	3,894,000	712,680	5,235,000	818,660	1,341,000	172,980	4	5 2-3	Philadelphia New York Washington	Mississippi Ohio Hudson	
Louisiana	1,400	1,000	50. 29.	29. 12. 30.	750,000	480,000,000			50,000	12,500			4	1-15	N. Orleans N. Madrid	Mississippi Missouri	10,000 1,000
Totals and averages					1,680,000	1,075,000,000			5,285,000	898,160			4				

CHAPTER IV

GENERAL OBSERVATIONS ON THE HISTORY OF AMERICA — PROVINCE OF MAINE FIRST EXPLORED BY THE ENGLISH IN SEARCH OF GOLD — ARTIFICE OF THE NATIVES — ANECDOTES OF SIR WILLIAM PHIPPS — FREEBOOTERS — PRODUCTIONS OF THE PROVINCE — PORTLAND — FALMOUTH.

THE outlines of the general history of America have been so often traced and described, that it is needless to enlarge on that subject. Every reader knows, that Columbus claimed the merit of discovering the New World — that the Spaniards, led on by Pizarro and Cortes, accompanied by priests bearing the cross of Christ, for gold, destroyed a race of their fellow-creatures, far exceeding the population of Old Spain. It is equally well known, that Canada was wrested from the French in battle, and that the conquest was sealed with the blood of the brave General Wolfe, at Quebec. Various religious sects first took possession of New England. The revolt of the thirteen colonies — their declaration of independence — the seven years' war in which they struggled against the mighty arm of their mother country — the treachery of the King of France in aiding the colonies against her, by which the acknowledgment of their independence was obtained, but which eventually brought down ruin upon his devoted head, and all those distractions that long rent the bosom of France; while they involved nearly the whole of Europe in the flames of war — are well-known to be events connected with the history of America.

It appears, from more ancient records, that several years had elapsed from the time of the discovery of Columbus, before human nature was disgraced by the rapine and murder committed upon the unoffending natives of Mexico and Peru, by the Spaniards. The Spanish commanders having discovered the mines of precious metals, the exercises of chivalry were neglected — the knights preferring adventures in the New World; while tilts and tournaments gave place to the more interesting game of plunder.

A party of adventurers inflamed by the success of the Spaniards in the south, determined to explore the regions of the north, not doubting that the earth produced gold in every other part of the continent. Tradition reports, that a number of Englishmen landed in the neighbourhood of Casco bay, in that division of New England, now called the Province of Maine, subject, however, to the State of Massachusetts. It is, at this time, a flourishing country, abounding with the best timber, of which large quantities are exported to the British dominions. The climate, however, like almost every other part of the United States, is unfavorable to the English constitution. To strangers, the heat in the summer is almost insupportable, while the severity of winter is scarcely to be endured. The spring and autumn are, certainly, delightful; the month of November, which is proverbially fatal to Englishmen, is, in America, one of the most delightful in the year. The sun has then declined to such a point, that his rays diffuse a most comfortable temperature, the frosts of winter being no farther advanced than to act as a bracer to the relaxed constitution. In this month, I could, without the least inconvenience, pass the whole day, from morning until sun-set, either in the active sports of the field, or seated upon the rocks, angling for the various species of fish, with which the coast of New England abounds.

The European adventurers who first explored this province, it has already been observed, were in pursuit of gold. At what period their enterprize was undertaken, I could not learn. Circumstances appear, however, to concur in fixing it during the religious persecutions in England, in the reign of Queen Mary. They landed on different parts of this coast, and some appearances of their search are said to remain until the present time. It is, however, very certain that success did not reward their labors; for no gold or silver has ever been discovered upon the "iron-bound coast" of New England.

An American writer, after describing the hardships which the first settlers here met with, and particularly the disappointments of the gold searchers, relates, that the natives were drawn near to the spot where the English were perforating the earth, in a hunting excursion, and thus they first beheld the white man.

The savages, it seems, were at first inclined to smoke the pipe of peace with the strangers. They soon discovered the leading passion of their visitors, and encouraged their fruitless attempts by informing them of mountains of ore which never existed, and of riches in the interior of the country which have never been found. The White Mountains, northwest of Casco bay, have a singular appearance; their tops are white like snow. There was an early expectation of finding a gem of immense magnitude and value in this mountain. It was rumoured that a carbuncle was suspended from a rock over a pool of water, at the foot of the mountain. While this belief was current, every one was afraid lest his neighbor should become the fortunate discoverer and proprietor of the prize.[1] To keep them as long as possible in suspense, a tale was invented by the natives, that the place was guarded by an evil spirit, who troubled the waters, and raised a dark mist on the approach of human footsteps. Thus the savages, by their cunning, obtained presents from the credulous adventurers, more valuable to them than the gold sought for would have proved, if found, to Englishmen.

Another tradition reported, that three hills of rocks, situated up Saco river, about forty miles from the sea, were as full of silver as the mountains of Peru. Impressed with this belief, William Phipps, of Saco, purchased these mountains in 1660, but neither he nor his posterity have ever discovered the expected wealth.

Under an influence so very unfavorable to the interests of society, as well as subversive of the quiet of individuals, an accident produced in the minds of the people of New England a still more powerful impression. A Spanish galleon had been lost near the Bahama Islands. The vessel had a great quantity of bullion on board, and the expectations of vast numbers were fixed upon obtaining a treasure by finding the wreck. William Phipps was supposed to have been the fortunate adventurer. In those days, the puerile delusions of visions, dreams, witchcraft, and spirits, were current in New England. They who had dreams, which the distempered mind interpreted into the miraculous, or that the wandering imagination supposed to have been verified, were considered as prophets, and believed to be in the secrets of the Lord. Many innocent persons fell victims to this strange delusion; under an accusation of their having entered into a league with the Devil, and of deriving miraculous power from the foul fiend. Mr. Phipps had removed to Boston, where he followed the business of ship-building. It was reported that he had been informed in a dream of the situation of the galleon. Whether animated by an extraordinary spirit of enterprise, and taking advantage of the temper of the times, he pretended to the favor of a vision which he never had, in order to procure assistance in an undertaking which a rational calculation might not consider worthy of the hazard attending it; or whether, having fixed his imagination upon the scheme, his mind embraced the object in an agreeable manner when he was asleep, is not decided. It is, however, certain, that he attempted it, and that his success raised him to honor and wealth. He was afterwards governor of Massachusetts, and had the dignity of knighthood conferred upon him.[2]

The spirit of the people about this time in America, would not bear a debate on the greatest absurdity, or a contradiction of the most palpable error, without the danger of contentions or commotions. It was doubtless, owing to this superstitious folly, that Sir William Phipps never disclaimed the idea of a divine interposition in his favor.

In the early period of civilization in America, her maritime power was unable to protect her seas from pirates; and the infant government was too feeble to prevent depredations on the sea-coast. Rovers of this description were numerous, and long enjoyed an unmolested plunder with impunity; but necessity will bring every thing within the power of human exertion. They were at length subdued, and numbers were executed — no less than thirty suffered death together at Newport, in Rhode Island.[3] Some of them, between the time of condemnation and execution, flattered the persons to whom they had access with stories of great wealth being concealed by them in different places. These confessions were made only with a view of obtaining pardon, for no money was ever found where they pretended that it was deposited.

After the death of Charles the First, the district of Maine underwent many changes, both in proprietors and forms of government; and was finally purchased by the colony of Massachusetts. The trifling sum of £1,200 was paid to the grandson of Sir Ferdinando Gorges for his patent.[4] The wars with the Indians rendered this country a scene of blood, from the year 1691 to 1702; even so late as the year 1748, the English were molested by them, and some lives lost. The growing importance of Maine will soon produce a political separation from Massachusetts, when it will, in all probability, raise itself to the rank of an independent state. It is three hundred miles long, and two hundred and four miles in breadth, lying between 43 and 46 degrees, north latitude, and extending to the British dominions. The climate is healthy to the natives, but subject to extremes of heat and cold. The inhabitants often live to a great age. The land produces Indian corn, rye, barley, oats, peas, beans, potatoes in astonishing quantities, and of fruit, apples, pears, plums, peaches, cherries, etc. The butter made here is said to excel that of every other part of New England, owing to the sweetness of the grass. This is a wonderful country for timber, abounding in stately and extensive forests, and the lumber trade is consequently very lucrative. The numerous rivers afford abundance of salmon, and the sea coast furnishes such quantities of cod, that their fisheries are very extensive and profitable. The country produces deer of various kinds, beavers, otters, sables, bears, wolves, rabbits, mountain-cats, porcupines, and other animals. The sportsman may find sufficient amusement among the partridges,* squirrels, and an infinite variety of water-fowl. There are no venomous serpents to the eastward of Kennebeck river. The people, as in every other part of New England are very inquisitive to

The principal town in the province of Maine, is Portland. It has grown into consequence within a few years; being till 1786, a part of Falmouth. The town of Portland is beautifully situated on a neck of land, at high water nearly insulated by the sea, which renders it healthy and pleasant. I have not met with a more agreeable place in America, and have ever thought that this town claimed a preference, in many respects, to all others which I have visited on this vast continent. The harbor is always open, very commodious, and the trade and inhabitants rapidly encreasing. A spirit of enterprise and industry prevails in Portland, which cannot fail, with its natural advantages, to render it a populous and wealthy place.

The town of Falmouth adjoins Portland, and before the incorporation of the latter, was the capital of the province. The contention of politics between England and America did not extend to Falmouth till the year 1770. At that time it had a custom-house, and various officers under the crown. The appearance of a change will too frequently alter a man's political opinions. The crown-officers had no doubt that the parliament possessed a right to legislate for the colonies in all cases, and the committee of the town was as clear in the reverse of the proposition. Added to this, the Episcopalian minister conceived the hierarchy to be in danger, unless the supremacy of the king was supported in church and state. To have an ecclesiastical head, without civil authority, would

* The partridge, throughout all the states, is similar to what is called in England the quail. It is, in fact, a partridge in miniature.

be a fundamental error, according to the dogmas of the church; the minister, therefore, took a decided part in favor of the parliamentary claims. Civil disputes can generally be managed with calmness and humanity, unless there is a mixture of religious tenets with political opinions. The animosity between the parties denominated Whig and Tory, daily encreased, and finally became so extremely bitter, that the Episcopalian minister, the custom-house officers, with numbers of the Tory party, fled for protection to the British army at Boston.[5] This was a prelude to the hostilities which caused the declaration of independence.

NOTES — CHAPTER IV

1. Nathaniel Hawthorne's use of this legend in his *The Great Carbuncle,* is, of course, known by every school child. James Sullivan in his *The History of the District of Maine,* published in 1795, tells the story of the carbuncle and says that even then the legend was not entirely discredited.

2. The story of Sir William Phipps is comparatively well known. He was born February 2, 1650, one of twenty-one sons in a family of twenty-six children. In 1687 he discovered a Spanish plate ship among the rocks near the Banks of Bahama on the north side of Hispanola. Although it had been submerged for more than forty years, gold and silver to the value of £300,000 sterling were taken from it. For leading an expedition for this purpose, William Phipps was knighted by James II. He served as governor of Massachusetts, but he was unpopular and not particularly outstanding. He died February 18, 1694-5 and was buried in London. Additional facts about him may be found in Cotton Mather's *Magnalia.*

3. In 1723 two pirate sloops unwittingly attacked a British sloop of war, the *Greyhound,* off Long Island. One pirate vessel escaped. The other was captured and taken to Newport, where an admiralty court tried thirty-six of the pirates and condemned twenty-six to be hanged. They were executed July 19, 1723.

4. Lois K. Matthews, author of *The Expansion of New England,* gives the purchase price of a large portion of the district of Maine in 1677 as £1250.

5. William Goold, *Portland in the Past with Historical Notes of Old Falmouth,* gives a full account of the part Falmouth played in the Revolutionary troubles, especially concerning the difficulties with Captain Coulson and Captain Mowatt, the burning and bombarding of the town by Mowatt, and the aid given by the town to Boston when that post was closed. No mention, however, is made of the flight to Boston of the minister and the customs officials. This would have been a logical consequence of the difficulties there as described by the author, who claimed he had access to letters and other documentary sources.

CHAPTER V

CONNECTICUT — NEW LONDON — RIGBY'S MOUNTAIN.

THE reader will, doubtless, think it high time to return to my narrative.

Wearied with my situation in Boston, particularly on account of the excessive heat, I determined to seek a place visited by cooler breezes; and for this purpose took my passage in a sloop bound for New London, in Connecticut. The place of my immediate destination was immaterial, and, pleased with the manners of the captain, I agreed with him for eight dollars, and to find my own provisions. Our course lay over the dangerous shoals of Nantucket, which we passed in safety. On our voyage we caught a quantity of haddocks, of an excellent quality.

At New London, I went to Minor's Tavern, but wishing for more quiet than an inn afforded, I took two rooms in the house of Mrs. Wilson, who was stigmatized by the appellation of an old Tory. The unconscionable charges of boarding-houses were now apparent, for I lived as well by catering for myself, and infinitely more to my satisfaction, at one-fourth of the rate charged me in Boston.

New London, a high-sounding name, is not larger than a middle-sized English village. It is situated four miles up a river, called the Thames, which empties itself into Long Island Sound. It is pleasant, healthy, and gratefully refreshed by the sea breeze. The inhabitants evinced a disposition to sociability, and I was frequently invited to join in shooting and fishing parties. Here I shot the woodcock in the month of July, similiar to that in England; but, some years afterwards, I found that the bird so named in the Southern States, resembles the jay, both in its size and chatter, though of a more beautiful plumage. The fish we caught by angling from the rocks, were various and excellent. One kind resembles the tench, but is of a superior flavor. The Indian name of this fish is *totog*, but it is commonly called the *black fish.* The bottom of the waters here must be nearly covered with lobsters; a great number of vessels being employed in carrying them to New York, and other places. The price of them is about twopence sterling per pound, and they are equal, in all respects, to those caught upon the English coast. In the Bay of Fundy they are taken of an immense size. In order to give me some idea of their magnitude, a person informed me that ten hungry men sat down and supped on one lobster, and that the fragments would have served another!!*

Near Middletown, in this state, is some mountainous land, called Rigby's mountain, which I was induced to ascend. The road lay through a forest, winding and rocky. On the opposite side is a frightful cliff, in many places nearly perpendicular. The vale beneath affords a pleasing variety of landscape, but the view was frequently interrupted by shrub-oaks and cedar, until we reached the summit. Our horses had been left at a considerable distance, and our ascent was attended with much labor.

At the top we enjoyed a prospect of a beautiful country as far as the eye could view, terminating with Long Island, a distance of near thirty miles. When on the brink of this precipice, Shakespear's description of the view from the Dover Cliffs forcibly recurred to my mind. Ours, however, was a land prospect — the cattle grazing in the plain appeared no larger than sheep — horses at plough, at a farther distance, were diminished to the size of a child's toy — the driver to an atom scarcely visible. One of our company durst not approach within many yards of the verge — he said he felt a dreadful propelling sensation, as though he could with difficulty restrain himself from rushing forward, and plunging into the tremendous abyss. I soon felt giddy,

* The public prints of America have likewise recently given an account of a lobster, on which seven persons dined, and yet left sufficient to satisfy another hungry man.

and retired; but others amused themselves with throwing stones, and observing their progress, with the loose rocky fragments, which tumbled, on being touched, to the bottom. The sound occasioned by their fall was awful, and the whole formed a scene that was truly sublime.

Among the curiosities of Connecticut, where we must now consider ourselves, are the caverns and other hiding-places where three English parliamentary officers, who served under Cromwell, secreted themselves for a great number of years. These were the Generals Whalley and Goffe, and Colonel Dixwell, three of the judges on the mock tribunal which condemned King Charles the First. The account of the hardships they underwent, collected and transcribed on the spot, is here presented to the reader.

CHAPTER VI

ADVENTURES OF GENERALS WHALLEY AND GOFFE, TWO OF THE JUDGES WHO CONDEMNED KING CHARLES I. — THEIR LONG CONCEALMENT IN VARIOUS PARTS OF NEW ENGLAND — WHALLEY'S SECOND CHILDHOOD DESCRIBED BY GOFFE — ACCOUNT OF COLONEL DIXWELL — STRICTURES ON DR. STILES'S PUBLICATION RELATIVE TO THESE REGICIDES.

THE restoration of Charles II. in 1660, it is well known, proved fatal to all those who had taken an active part under the parliament. The most obnoxious could only appease the young king by their death; and sixteen of those who sat in judgment on his father saved themselves by flight. Three of the fugitives, Major-general Edward Whalley, Major-general William Goffe, and Colonel William Dixwell, took refuge in America. They all had commanded in the army of Cromwell, and were among the most enthusiastic enemies of the crown.*

Whalley and Goffe landed at Boston on the 27th of July, 1660, having escaped only a few days before King Charles the Second was restored to the throne, the intelligence of which event they received in the English Channel. Goffe kept a journal of every remarkable incident which happened to them for seven years from the day they left Westminster. After his death, this journal came into the possession of Governor Hutchinson; who kept it till the populace demolished his house, in the tumults occasioned in Boston by the stamp-act, when this curious manuscript was destroyed.[1] It was written in characters, but which were readily decyphered. The governor, however, had fortunately taken from it some extracts; these, together with the particulars related to me

* Cromwell himself once contemplated a flight to America. The circumstances which prevented his embarkation are well known.

on the subject in Connecticut, enable me to give an accurate account of the sufferings of these unfortunate men.

When they first arrived at Boston, they did not attempt to conceal their persons or characters, but immediately went to Mr. Endicot, the governor; who received them courteously. They were visited by the principal inhabitants; even Colonel Crown, a staunch royalist, introduced himself to them. They resided at Cambridge, a village four miles from Boston. They attended public worship, and received the sacrament. They were grave and devout; and such was the respect paid them, that being once insulted, the offender was bound to keep the peace. It is not strange that they should thus have experienced so favorable a reception upon their landing; for, though they were known to have been two of King Charle's judges, yet no official news of the restoration had reached America. Reports soon afterwards arrived by way of Barbadoes, that all those who sat in judgment on their sovereign would be pardoned, except seven. When it appeared that the royal clemency was not extended to Whalley and Goffe, the officers of government at Boston were alarmed; while pity and compassion pervaded the bosoms of the inhabitants. By some they were assured that the general court would protect them; and others advised them to make a speedy retreat. On the 22d of November, 1660, the governor summoned a general court of assistants, to take into consideration the propriety of putting them under confinement, but it broke up without coming to any decision. Finding it unsafe to reside longer at Cambridge, they left the place, and arrived at Newhaven, (about one hundred and fifty miles distant) on the 7th of March. Information of their retreat having been given in England, a hue and cry, as Goffe terms it in his journal, was set on foot; and day after they left Cambridge, a warrant was issued against them; and they were pursued, but without effect.

At Newhaven they were at first received as at Boston; but on the arrival of the king's proclamation, they were obliged to abscond. On the 27th of March they removed to New Milford, where they made themselves known; but at night they privately returned to Newhaven, and were concealed by Mr. Davenport, the minister, until the 30th of April. About this time the intelligence reached Boston that ten of the judges had been executed; and the governor received a royal mandate to apprehend Whalley and Goffe. This alarmed the country, and the most diligent search was made, but the fugitives found friends, who gave them intimation of their danger. It was now too hazardous for Davenport to secrete them any longer: they therefore went into the woods, conducted by two of the inhabitants of Newhaven. They first took refuge in a mill — then in a place called Hatchet Harbor, where they concealed themselves till their friends had prepared a cave on the side of a hill in the woods, where they remained from the 15th of May to the 11th of June. To this place they gave the appropriate appellation Providence Hill; for while they resided there, a most diligent search was making after them; and many of the king's messengers passed near to the spot. There existed proof of their having been at Davenport's, and large rewards were offered for information by which they might be secured. Davenport was threatened, and the unfortunate but grateful wanderers, offered to deliver themselves up, rather than that any one should suffer for the hospitality afforded them. The hardships they had suffered, and to which they were still exposed, together with the little chance they saw of escaping, would not, perhaps, have proved sufficient to induce them to make such an offer. Honor has often been found to prevail even over the love of life. Influenced by this principle, they actually gave notice to the deputy governor of the place of their concealment: but he paid no attention to their magnanimous intimation, and the next day they were advised not to surrender.

In this solitary abode they met with several disasters, some of which had nearly proved fatal. One dark night, when they were both laid down to rest, they were suddenly terrified by an animal of the tiger genus. It had advanced to the cave, forced its head through the aperture, and presenting its horrid eyes, which appeared to flash fire upon them, gave a dreadful roar; but departed without attacking them. At another time they were in still greater danger, but from a different cause. Having ventured too far from their concealment, they were overtaken by Mr. Kimberly, the sheriff, with a warrant in his pocket for their apprehension, They defended themselves with their sticks, and repelled the officer, who, leaving them to obtain assistance, afforded them an opportunity of regaining the woods. On another occasion, being closely pursued, they hid themselves under a bridge; while their pursuers passed over their heads. At Newhaven they were several times concealed in houses, while they were searched by the officers of government.

As soon as they thought that their enemies had given up their search, they ventured to the house of one Tomkins, near Milford, where they remained two years, without even daring to walk into the orchard adjoining the house. Hearing that commissioners from the king had arrived at Boston, Whalley and Goffe, thought it necessary to retire again to their cave. Soon afterwards some Indians in their hunting excursions discovered the place of their concealment, which caused them to bid a final adieu to Providence Hill. They wandered about in the night, and retired to the woods in the day, till they arrived at Hadley, in Massachusetts, near one hundred miles from the cave. Here they were received by Mr. Russell, the minister of the place, by whom they were concealed between fifteen and sixteen years. They frequently received remittances from England, and some friends to their cause often relieved them. One donation, by Richard Saltonstall, Esq., who was in the secret of their concealment, amounted to fifty pounds. It is, therefore, to be presumed that Parson Russell found them profitable boarders.

These unfortunate men were said to have lived in constant

terror, even when all enquiry after them was at an end. A strange reverse of fortune from the times of Cromwell! Several years they had been principal actors in the affairs of a great nation. Whalley defeated Prince Rupert, and Goffe turned the members out of the house of parliament, and was intrusted by Cromwell with the custody of the king.

At Hadley they complained that they were banished from society, and that their lives were miserable and burthensome. Goffe married Whalley's daughter, with whom he corresponded by the name of Walter Goldsmith, addressing her as Frances Goldsmith: and the correspondence was carried on as between a mother and son. Their letters are replete with fanaticism, and crowded with quotations from the Bible. The following extract from a letter from Goffe, describing Whalley's second childhood, in which he continued the last few years of his life, is interesting:

Your old friend, Mr. R. (Whalley) is yet living, but continues in that weak condition of which I have formerly given you an account, and I have not much to add. He is scarce capable of any rational discourse; his understanding, memory, and speech doth so much fail him, that he seems not to take much notice of any thing that is either done or said, but patiently bears all things, and never complains of any thing, though I fear it is some trouble to him that he hath had no letter for a long time from his cousin Rich, but he speaks not one word concerning it, nor any thing you write in your last; only after I had read your letters to him, being asked whether it was not a great refreshment to him to hear such a gracious spirit breathing in your letters, he said it was none of his least comforts; and indeed, he scarce speaks of any thing but in answer to the questions that are put to him, which are not of many kinds, because he is not capable to answer them. The common and very frequent question is, to know how he doth, and his answer, for the most part, is, very well, I praise God, which he utters in a very low and weak voice. But sometimes he saith, not very well, or very ill; and then if it be further said, do you feel pain any where? to that he always answereth, no. When he wants any thing, he cannot speak well for it, because he forgets the name of it, and sometimes asks for one thing, when he means another, so that his eye or his finger is his tongue; but his ordinary wants are so well known to us, that most of them are supplied without asking or making signs for them. Some help he stands in need of in every thing to which any motion is required, having not been able for a long time to dress or undress himself, nor to feed, nor ease nature either way, orderly, without help, and it's a very great mercy to him that he hath a friend that takes pleasure in being helpful to him. I bless the Lord that gives me such a good measure of health and strength, and an opportunity and a heart to use it in so good and necessary a work; for though my help be poor and weak, yet that ancient servant of Christ could not well subsist without it; and I do believe, as you are pleased to say very well, that I do enjoy the more health for his sake. I have sometimes wondered much at this dispensation of the Lord towards him, and have some expectations of more than ordinary issue. The Lord help us to profit by all, and to wait with patience upon him, till we see what end he will make with us.

Thus far I write for myself. I will now ask him what he would have me say to his friends concerning him. The question being asked, he saith, I am better than I was. And being asked what I should say more to his cousin R. or any other friends; after a long pause, he again said, the Lord hath visited me in much mercy, and hath answered his visitation upon me. (I give you his own words.) Being desirous to draw more from him, I proposed several questions, and the sum of his answers was, that he earnestly desires the continuance of the fervent prayers of all friends for him.

During their residence at Hadley, these unfortunate men received a pretty regular consolation in letters from England; and this was the only remission of the highest degree of mental anxiety and distress they experienced since their proscription. Their fanaticism strengthened their hopes, as they expressed it, of the fulfilment of the prophecies; and this delusion kept alive the idea of their deliverance. They appeared to be greatly disappointed when the year 1666 passed without any remarkable political event, but flattered themselves that the Christian æra might be erroneous.

During their abode at Hadley,[2] the most famous and

memorable Indian war of New England took place. This was called King Philip's war. Philip was a powerful sachem, and resided at Mount Hope, in Rhode Island; where he was soon after this war put to death by Colonel Church.[3] All the new frontier towns of New England were attacked, and Hadley was then exposed as a place of that description. The time the savages fixed upon to make the assault was while the inhabitants were assembled in the meeting-house to observe a fast-day; but fortunately it had been some time a custom for the men to attend public worship, armed. Had the town been taken, the discovery of Whalley and Goffe would have been inevitable. The men took up their arms, and attempted a defence, but were soon thrown into confusion, when (as it is related to this day) a stranger suddenly appeared among them, of venerable aspect, and different in his apparel from the inhabitants; who rallied, and disposing them in the best military manner, led them to the charge, routed the Indians, and saved the town. In the moment of victory their deliverer vanished. The inhabitants, unable to account for the phenomenon, believed that they had been commanded by an angel, sent from heaven for their protection.

This supposed angel was Goffe, who never before ventured from his concealment. Whalley was then in a state of second childhood. Such was their caution to prevent a discovery of their retreat, that the inhabitants never knew them, or who it was that so ably led them against the savages, until they both had paid the debt of nature. In a country where the leading feature of the mind is the most familiar, and, indeed, impertinent curiosity; it is a matter of wonder how they could for so long a time conceal themselves from the prying eyes of the inhabitants. What rigid confinement they must have endured! What solitary hours they must have passed! But their fanaticism animated them with the hope of better days.

Another story of Goffe is still current among the old

inhabitants of Boston, which proves him to have been very expert at the exercise of the sword. It is thus related in a print which fell into my hands there.

While the judges were at Boston, there appeared a gallant person there, some say a fencing-master, who, on a stage erected for that purpose, walked several days, challenging and defying any person to play with him at swords. At length one of the judges, disguised in a rustic dress, holding in one hand a cheese wrapped up in a napkin, and in the other a broomstick, the end of which he had besmeared in a dirty puddle of water; and thus equipped, he mounted the stage. The fencing-master railed at him for his impudence, asked what business he had there, and bid him begone. A rencounter ensued; Goffe received the sword of his antagonist in the cheese, while he drew the dirty end of his stick across his mouth. Another pass was made, and again received in the cheese; and in return, he gave another mark across the fencer's eyes. At a third lunge, the sword was again received as before, and the stick rubbed over the other parts of his face. The enraged master of arms then threw aside his weapon, and took up a broad sword, with which he advanced. Upon this, Goffe told him to stop, and added, that he had hitherto only played with him, without attempting to hurt him: but as he came on in rage, with the broad-sword, his life would pay the forfeit. The fencer, struck with the manner this was said, and fearing the event, asked Goffe who he was; adding, that he must be either Whalley, Goffe, or the Devil, as no other could beat him. The disguised conqueror retired, leaving the boasting champion to the diversion of the spectators. Hence it became proverbial in New England, in speaking of a champion, to say, that no one can beat him but Whalley, Goffe, or the Devil.

Whalley died at Hadley in the year 1688. After about a year from the time of his decease, all tradition of Goffe is lost. The only conjecture that can be formed is, that he did not long survive his friend, and was privately buried near him at Hadley.

Colonel John Dixwell, another of the members of the court which condemned King Charles the First, also fled to America. He visited Whalley and Goffe in their retirement on the 10th of February, 1664, after which he went to Newhaven, where he lived until his death, under the assumed name of James Davids, Esq. Cautiously concealing his character, he was not molested. He married in America, and left several children; but upon his death-bed he discovered his real name and former situation in England; and executed a will, signed "John Dixwell, alias James Davids." He acquired some property by marriage, on which, with occasional remittances from England, he lived comfortably, and left some property among his children.

A learned American divine, Ezra Stiles, S. T. D. L. D. President of Yale College, published, in 1795, a large volume, which he calls "The History of the Three Judges." A work more eccentric I never saw. A variety of subjects, from the rebellion in the time of Charles, to the recent revolution in France, are there jumbled together, interspersed with old women's tales, in the most trite and barren language; and spun out, by an insufferable tautology, to three hundred and fifty-seven pages. But the doctor published by subscription, and something voluminous was liberally paid for before it went to press. Had not this work been eagerly read, and by some greatly admired, I should not have noticed it. Of my American readers, some may be gratified, while others will be displeased at my comments; but upon subjects collected in my travels, I hold it my duty to notice whatever I may think worthy of observation. After reading Governor Hutchinson's account of Whalley and Goffe, I found nothing in the performance of Dr. Stiles but what provoked my risibility, or created my contempt; for, indeed, nothing more could be added on the subject. Lest my friends on the other side of the Atlantic, however, may think I treat their collegian with too much asperity, and to give my countrymen a specimen of this production of a literary character of the new world, I shall quote some paragraphs.

The learned divine is solicitous to ascertain where the remains of his heroes were interred; and in about twenty places he impresses his reader with the importance of this discovery, as though it were of any consequence where a man's bones are consigned to their parent earth. Cromwell's carcase rested as quietly under the gallows as it did in Westminster Abbey; and where I may moulder, or to what unworthy uses Alexander's dust may have been converted, is matter of the utmost indifference. On this subject, the Doctor thus *narrates*: —

What I have before *narrated** is delivered upon sure documents. I shall now *narrate* what is only conjectural, and leave it to every one's judgment, only observing, that if it ever did take place, no one will doubt but that Dixwell was concerned in it. There is somehow preserved, not in universal or general, but in particular and strong lineal tradition, at Newhaven, which is to be considered more largely hereafter, that another of the regicides, besides Dixwell, lies buried in our burying-place, and that this other was Whalley. This is particularly preserved among the sextons or grave-diggers, who, it seems, for many years, and perhaps ever from the time especially of Dixwell's death, have shewn the stone marked E. W. for Whalley, as they have that marked J. D. for Dixwell. I have not found the least tradition of Goffe, till I myself conjectured it, January 1793, inferring in my own mind, without a doubt, that if Whalley, who certainly died at Hadley, was afterwards removed here, Goffe must be here also. But of this, I mean as to Goffe's being here also, I can find no tradition, yet I find it tenaciously adhered to, especially in the line of the grave-diggers, that Whalley is here. I have often examined the E. W. stone, but consider the matter without proof, yet possible, but by no means certain. Nor do I wish, and least of all attempt, to gain any one's credulity to it, leaving every mind perfectly free and unprejudiced. But as I know that whoever takes the pains that I have done, to trace out, and collect, and digest the traditions in Newhaven, will find this among others, however it originated among us; so, after this precaution and notification, I shall proceed, &c.!!

It is then supposed by some, that Whalley lies buried in Newhaven. If so, his corpse must have been taken up and secretly con-

* This *narration* consisted of extracts from Hutchinson, copies of old records, letters, &c., &c.

veyed here, for, without repeating the proofs, it is certain he died at Hadley. Who will doubt this removal was at the procurement of his friend Dixwell; None. If done before 1685, none but Dixwell, Jones, and Bishop, in Newhaven, and Russell, Tilton, and perhaps Smith, were privy to it; and yet probably it was after Randolph's* rage burned and became dangerous, which was after 1680, when Goffe was either dead or abdicated. At all events, the five or six I have mentioned must have been the persons concerned in this removal. If so, Dixwell, must have been deeply concerned in the affair; and this event and transaction, however secretly performed, must become an important anecdote in his life, as being the last care and office of surviving friendship to the memory and to the security of the ashes of a venerable fellow-exile and brother judge. In this Governor Jones was unquestionably the efficacious agent. He and Mr. Tilton must have been the men who procured the corpse to be conveyed, &c.†

If Goffe died at Hadley in 1680, as is probable, the same reasons which would induce the removal of one, would induce the removal of the other, and perhaps from a preconcerted plan, that all the three exiles should be deposited and sleep in the dust together, until they should rise together at the resurrection of the just.

The Doctor concludes with some incoherent ravings, truly indicative of a mind labouring under religious phrenzy. He is a most violent enthusiast in the cause of his heroes; and would, if possible, immortalize the arch-traitor Cromwell. He calls Monk the Dumouriez of Britain; and places Bradshaw, Ireton, and the rest of the *judges*, as he calls them, among the martyred patriots. Of Cromwell's character, after lavishing encomiums too gross to offer at the shrine even of a *saint*, he concludes in these words: — "O Oliver! how I love thine open, thine unabashed, thy undissembled, and undisguised religion!"

The frontispiece of this learned and pious work is ornamented with the portrait of its author, in sacerdotal robes.

* One of the officers of King Charles the Second.

† The Doctor must have forgotten that, a few lines above, he fixes this *procurement* upon Dixwell.

As I turned over the pages I hoped to meet with similiar representations of his heroes, or, at all events, of his friend Oliver, but in this I was disappointed.

NOTES — CHAPTER VI

1. It would seem that Janson had access either to Hutchinson's *History of Massachusetts,* as he intimates, or to Ezra Stiles' *A History of Three of the Judges of King Charles I.* (Hartford, 1794.) A note on page 32 of the *Diary and Letters of His Excellency, Thomas Hutchinson, Esq.* (London, 1883), compiled by Peter O. Hutchinson, gives the following fact concerning the journal of Governor Hutchinson: "It is enough to say that it has not been seen since the night of August 26, 1765, when the mob sacked his house, and destroyed or stole everything in it."

2. Samuel Drake, *History and Antiquities of Boston,* gives the date of the arrival of Whalley and Goffe as July 27, 1660: "The most memorable event which occurred this year in Boston, perhaps, was the arrival of General Edward Whalley and Colonel William Goffe, two of the individuals who had sat as judges at the trial of King Charles the First." A paper read before the Pocumtuck Valley Memorial Association examines the story of the Indian attack upon the town of Hadley and Goffe's part in its defense. It is a very careful and discriminating study, which concludes that no attack occurred during this time and that the legend of Goffe's appearance "either as man or angel — is pure romance." See George Sheldon, "The Traditionary Story of the Attack upon Hadley and the Appearance of General Goffe, September 1, 1675. Has It any Foundation in Fact?" *History and Proceedings of the Pocumtuck Valley Memorial Association, 1870-1879,* I, 202-19.

3. Evidently Colonel Benjamin Church.

CHAPTER VII

EXTREMES OF HEAT AND COLD IN NEW ENGLAND — STATE OF VEGETATION AND THE PRODUCE OF THE FIELD — DIRECTION OF THE WINDS — METEOROLOGICAL OBSERVATIONS ON THE RAIN — UNCERTAINTY AND STATE OF THE WEATHER.

CONSIDERING the latitude of the New England states, the extremes of heat and cold can neither be conceived by an European, nor fairly accounted for by an American. Some of the latter writers on the subject ascribe the intense cold to their back lakes, and high lands. That this may contribute in a small degree towards that extreme is not impossible, though I am not inclined to adopt the opinion; but I have not met with even a probable conjecture as to the other.

New England is situated in latitude 41° to 46°, yet in the months of July and August the heat is often as intense as in the West Indies. An American geographer, in describing the climate of this region, says, "The heat in summer is intense, and the cold in winter equally severe. All fresh-water lakes, ponds, and rivers, are usually passable on ice, from Christmas till the middle of March. The longest day is fifteen hours and sixteen minutes; and the shortest eight hours and forty minutes."

For several days together in the hottest weather there is not a breath of air; and the nights, with the additional annoyance of swarms of that aggravating and poisonous insect the musquitoe, upon which some observations have already been made, are nearly insupportable to an European. He will undergo a complete perforation of the skin, and every wound will poison to the diameter of half an inch, till his blood is reduced to the state of that of the natives, or the temper of the climate when he may find respite from their nocturnal attacks. They make a buzzing noise nearly equal to that of the honey-bee, and yet, with this notice, you cannot guard against their assaults. The croaking of the toad, of which there are infinite varieties — the creeking of the locust — and the no less offensive chirping of the grasshopper, together with the noises of many other restless reptiles, join in dismal discord to deprive the way-worn traveller of his rest. With these his disturbed fancy may associate the birds and beasts of prey under his window. Custom will, however, reconcile man to all things. He will soon find that these inharmonious sounds will as effectually lull him to rest, as the most soft and soothing strains. In addition to all these inconveniences, he will be sure to find his bed overstocked with bugs* and fleas, which will attack him in one quarter, while the musquitoes seize him in another. Curtains of thin gause are some defence against the latter, but, from the harbour the former find in the coarse woollen bed-chamber furniture, they rove at large and uncontrouled.

To many days intense heat, a violent storm of wind and rain will perhaps succeed, attended with tremendous thunder and lightning; which often sweeps away whole fields of corn, and deluges the earth; then again will the heat break out with redoubled violence, causing fevers, dysenteries, and agues, which of late years have proved a dreadful scourge in America.

The following observations on the atmosphere in New England will shew the heat of the summer of 1795.

On the first of August, the thermometer, being placed in the north shade, was,

At 8 o'clock, A. M.	74.	At 3, P. M.	79.
2nd of August	78.		88.
3rd	72.		74.
4th	73.		76.
5th	72.		88.
6th	85.		92½.

* The inhabitants call bed-bugs, *chintzes*.

On the last-mentioned day, when moved where the sun shone upon it, in a few moments the mercury rose to 124 — and when moved back again, into the north shade, it fell to 92.

When we consider that 98 is blood-heat, and 112 fever-heat; we may conceive what effect such a climate would have upon an English constitution. The diurnal prints of New England about this time were full of accounts of people being suddenly killed by the *coup de soleil*, or stroke of the sun. Strangers would do well to provide themselves, during the hot weather, with white hats, the advantages of which are obvious.

The houses in America are, for the most part, built of wood, slightly put together, and covered with the same materials, made into shingles.[1] This is but an indifferent protection from the cold. Added to this, though the continent in many parts abounds with coal, yet they use but little of that comfortable article. Wood is almost their only fuel, and though the country is abundantly furnished with that also, yet the consumption renders it daily more difficult to be procured. This article, before you get it to your fire-place, in the state of Rhode Island, will cost seven dollars, or one guinea and a half, a cord;* and a cord a month is the calculation for one fire. Several masters of families have told me, that their wood alone cost them three or four hundred dollars per year; a sum upon which many families comfortably subsist in England.

Water will freeze within a few yards of a large fire in ten minutes and out of doors in two minutes. In the year 1790, the thermometer, on the 18th of December, was 16 below 0.

* On the vast influx of French people from St. Domingo, this article rose considerably, with every other necessary of life, at the sea-port towns. The strangers never questioning the demands of the dealers, they, of course, made the most of the circumstance; and have since tenaciously kept up the greatest proportion of the advance then demanded.

26th of January, 1792, ... 15¾ ditto.
28th ditto .... 11 ditto.

In the succeeding winter to that in which I have above given the observations on the summer's heat, the thermometer was,

January 31 .... 10 below 0.
February 1 .... 7 ditto.

Another view of the climate may be taken from the common operations of nature, the vegetable and animal productions. The times when the trees and plants put forth their buds, leaves, flowers, and fruit; or when the different seeds are planted, spring up, are in blossom, produce their fruit, and are gathered; also when the birds of passage, or other migratory animals, make their approach or departure. Observations upon such phenomena are, perhaps, the truest that can be made to ascertain the relative temperature of different climates.

The following tables of the state of vegetation, taken from an American writer, will shew the seasons of harvest in New England.

TREES AND SHRUBS.

	Buds.	Leaves.	Flowers.	Maturity.
Elder.............	April 5	April 14	June 15	
Gooseberry........	---- 6	---- 16	May 9	July 20
Currant...........	---- 6	---- 16	---- 1	---- 1
Raspberry.........	---- 6	---- 17	---- 27	---- 5
Strawberry........	---- 20	---- 20	---- 4	June 28
Wild Cherry.......	---- 20	---- 28	---- 4	---- 28
Wild Plumb........	---- 20	May 4	---- 1	Aug. 12
Apple Tree........	---- 22	---- 1	---- 12	---- 18

PRODUCE OF THE FIELD.

	Sown.	Flowers.	Gathered.
Flax	April 16	June 25	Aug. 1
Spring Wheat	---- 15	May 30	---- 15
Winter Wheat	Sept. 1	---- 26	---- 1
Oats	April 20	June 7	---- 20
Pease	---- 16	May 26	July 1
Barley	---- 20	June 10	---- 28
Rye	Mar. 20	May 27	---- 28
Indian Corn	May 15	July 12	Oct. 1
Hay			July 10

The frost commences about the beginning of October, and continues in a slight degree till the middle of May; but it is seldom severe till December, and generally ceases at the end of March. The first effects are not sufficient to freeze the leaves of the trees, or other vegetables; it only produces the congelation of the dews and vapors, and as these are only to be found in low and moist land, such places first feel the effects of the frost. Where the ground is not covered with snow, the frost penetrates three or four feet, and waters have been frozen thirty inches.

"God tempers the wind to the shorn lamb," is a saying not more trite than true. Accordingly, we find that the severest weather never kills the young trees, and rarely freezes the young cattle, although they are seldom housed during the winter. The human constitution too, seems inured to the cold, the winter season being the most healthy.

The winds in North America receive their general direction from the situation of the sea-coast, mountains, and large rivers. Hence south-west, and north-east winds prevail. The former are warm, moist, and relaxing — the latter dry, cooling, and bracing. They sometimes rage with great fury for two or three days, and whirlwinds are too frequent.

The following Table of the directions of the winds, at different places on the continent, will give the best view of their comparative courses — deduced from a number of observations.

	N.	N. E.	E.	S. E.	S.	S. W.	W.	N. W.	No. of Observats.
Maryland - - - - -	9	59	71	72	53	45	8	207	524
Virginia - - - - - -	122	110	104	45	22	185	70	82	740
Pennsylvania - - -	31	56	25	32	45	97	69	111	466
Massachusets - - -	61	127	111	36	86	271	177	226	1095
Vermont - - - - -	153	13	16	76	272	182	125	258	1095
Quebec - - - - - -	1	194	0	1	14	261	2	35	508
Hudson's Bay - - -	169	78	86	51	83	70	159	359	1055
Rhode Island - - -	59	127	109	50	93	280	166	220	1095

The quantity of rain which falls in America, where meteorological observations have been made, is found to be more than double that which generally falls in the same latitude in Europe; and yet the lands often suffer by drought in some places. These observations are best explained by a general Table.

RAIN IN	MEAN ALTITUDE IN INCHES.			
	S. Carolina.	Virginia.	Massa-chusets.	Vermont.
January	2,624	3,195	3,503	3,497
February	3,735	2,049	2,618	2,784
March	3,329	3,950	2,516	3,102
April	2,074	3,680	2,725	3,112
May	3,975	2,871	5,861	4,716
June	6,009	3,571	2,083	3,914
July	5,840	4,497	2,221	2,313
August	6,964	9,153	2,278	2,313
September	4,944	4,761	3,791	2,481
October	2,450	3,633	2,466	5,662
November	1,195	2,617	1,851	4,101
December	1,523	2,877	3,483	3,491
	47,666	47,038	35,396	41,179

On the 22nd of October, 1785, was the greatest fall of rain ever remembered in one day in this part of the globe, being 5,217 inches.

The climate has altered considerably within a few years, and the same observation is made in Europe. Cæsar says, that during the winters of his wars, he passed with his army the frozen rivers of Germany and Gaul, in his line of march, with his baggage, &c. A similar circumstance favored the French in the year 1795, but that winter was uncommonly severe in Europe, and mild in America. Instead of remaining fixed and settled as formerly, the climate is perpetually changing and altering, in all its circumstances and affections; and this change of late has been so rapid and constant, as to become the subject of common observation. This has been remarked in every part of the United States, but it is most sensible and apparent in a new country, suddenly changing from a state of vast uncultivated wildness, to that of numerous settlements and extensive improvements. When the settlers move into a new township, their first business is to cut down trees, clear the land, and sow grain. The earth is no sooner laid open to the influence of the sun and winds, than the effects of cultivation begin to appear. The surface of the earth becomes warm and dry; and as settlements increase, these effects are more general and extensive. The cold decreases, the earth and air become warm, and the whole temperature of the climate becomes more equal and moderate. The stagnant pools disappear, and redundant waters are every where carried off. The snows decrease; the winds receive new directions; and the seasons become much altered. These changes every where attend the cultivation of the country, and have produced a remarkable change of the climate in those states which have been long settled.

The effect of cultivation with regard to the heat of the earth, so far as it can be collected from experiment, is great. The exposure of the land to the full force of the solar rays in this latitude, will produce heat at the depth of ten inches below the surface, ten or eleven degrees greater than that which prevails in the uncultivated parts of the country; and this effect continues, so that such rays are sufficient to increase the heat of the earth. This additional heat in the earth will suffice to effect the same alteration in the temperature of the air; for, whatever degree of heat prevails in the earth, nearly the same will be communicated to the lower parts of the atmosphere. Thus, the earth and air, in the cultivated parts of the country, are heated in consequence of their cultivation, ten or eleven degrees more than they were in their natural state.

In new settlements, this change is effected in two or three years. Fields of corn and wheat are attended with the most rapid vegetation, and the greatest increase on land, which, a few years before, had been inundated with standing waters. One of the best effects of cultivation is the dispersion of these waters, by which a swamp is changed into a fertile meadow.

Though the seasons have become more variable and uncertain, yet the heat and cold in the different seasons are as intense as at the first attempt to plant New England; but not perhaps of such long duration. The winter season is of late years subject to great and sudden thaws. The spring is very uncertain: — after two, and sometimes three weeks of inviting weather, which tempts the gardener to commit his seed to the earth, a sudden and severe storm of snow, attended with frost, will, in a night, blast his hopes of an early crop. In the year 1795 I experienced the vexation produced by such a flattering spring. I had cultivated my little garden, and was anticipating the pleasure I hoped to derive in beholding the progressive advances to maturity of some botanical and culinary plants not common in England, when, on the twenty-seventh of March, there fell the deepest snow for the time I had ever seen. This was preceded by a sharp frost, which destroyed my work, and almost discouraged me from a second attempt. This variation between heat and cold is not only unfavourable to vegetation, but attended with danger to the health of the inhabitants. Tempted by a succession of warm spring weather for a few weeks, they throw off their winter garments, and are too often unexpectedly caught by a cold north wind, bringing along with it a heavy fall of snow.

The spring, from the month of April to the end of June, and the autumnal season, are delightful. The harvest is not finished till the end of November; indeed, this month is one of the most agreeable of the year. The distressing fogs usual in England about this time, are rarely to be seen; they are, however, frequent in the summer.

Annual courses of meteorological observations properly reduced, will afford the most complete information of the weather and meteors in different parts of North America. The following statement is taken from a philosophical work lately published in New England.

The state of the Weather at sundry places in North America, deduced from annual observations.

Places.	Time.	Fair.	Cloudy.	Rain.	Snow.	Hail.	Fog.	Thunder.	Aur. Bor.	Hazy.	No. of Observat.
Maryland - - -	1753 & 1754	314	179	145	21	7	10	39	—	—	493
Philadelphia - -	1748 to 1749	235	141	83	21	2	11	13	7	—	376
Massachusets -	1784 to 1788	564	531	71	25	4	16	22	22	—	1095
Vermont - - - -	1789	452	643	89	41	7	37	15	21	—	1095
Quebec - - - - -	1743 & 1744	277	128	88	32	4	14	7	—	—	405
Hudson's Bay -	1768 & 1769	360	432	36	76	25	31	4	5	155	792

I have observed, that the winters become less severe in America as the country increases in population. In some degree, this effect contributed to the alteration of climate in many parts of Europe. The vast forests, into which Cæsar with difficulty penetrated, are now cut down, and the dreary wastes over which he marched are now luxuriant fields of corn. It is, however, certain, that in the populous cities of New York and Philadelphia, the cold is much more intense than under the same latitudes in the regions of Europe.

NOTE — CHAPTER VII

1. The author must be speaking in very general terms and without exactness. His statement was true of only a part of the houses at that time. See Alice M. Earle, *Home Life in Colonial Days,* for a full discussion of the buildings in the various colonies.

CHAPTER VIII

MULTIPLICATION OF WILD PIGEONS IN NEW ENGLAND — THEIR ABUNDANCE IN CAROLINA — FECUNDITY OF FISH IN NEW ENGLAND.

MR. RICHARD HAZEN, a land surveyor, who, in 1741, drew the line which divides Massachusets from Vermont, gives an interesting account of the multiplying power of nature in the wild pigeon: —

For three miles together, says he, the pigeons' nests were so thick, that five hundred might be reckoned on beech trees at one time; and could they have been counted on the hemlocks as well, he did not doubt but that five thousand might be seen at one turn round.

Twenty-five nests were frequently found on one beech tree in New England. The earth was covered with these trees and with hemlocks, thus loaded with the nests of pigeons. For an hundred acres together, the ground was covered with their dung, to the depth of two inches. Their noise in the evening was extremely troublesome, and so great, that the traveller could not get any sleep where their nests were thick. About an hour before sun-rise they rose in such numbers as to darken the air. When the young pigeons were grown to a proper size, it was common for the first settlers to cut down the trees, and gather a horse load in a few minutes. The markets at this season, even at Philadelphia, are often overstocked with them; a score having lately been purchased for sixpence. But as the land becomes settled, they retire into the black forests, where they are at this day in equal numbers.

In North Carolina, wild pigeons or doves pass over the country, in such numbers as to darken the air, devouring all kinds of grain in their progress. A large musket, loaded with small shot, fired among them, has killed scores; and boys knock them down with sticks and stones. I did not see this destructive phenomenon, but was credibly informed at Edenton, that it occurs about once in seven, and sometimes in ten years. During my residence in that state, I cut holes in the top of my barn, and by placing food on the roof, soon noticed about half a dozen from the adjacent woods. In a short time they became domesticated, and fed with the fowls; affording a constant and an agreeable food. When I left my residence, they had, notwithstanding the use I made of the young ones, increased to many score. They grew so familiar, that they would watch my appearance in the morning, and perch upon me, in hopes of obtaining food, with which it was my practice to supply them. They distinguished me from my domestics, whom they would not suffer to approach them. They would permit me to go into their dovecote, without retreating, and the dam would often oppose my taking her young ones.

In the production of fish, nature seems to have been equally prolific in every part of America. Almost all the different species that inhabit the European seas, are found there in great numbers; but I have not observed the turbot or the sole. This deficiency is amply supplied in New England by a firm and delicious fish called the sheepshead; also the black fish, or totog, which we have not in England; the sea bass, abundance of halibut and sturgeon. The rivers of New England abound with salmon, shad, trout of different sorts, and nearly every other species of fish found in those of Europe. Testaceous fish are also in the greatest plenty. There are oyster beds on the shores of New York, Boston, and almost every other sea-port, of an unknown thickness producing oysters five times the size of those esteemed in London; and which, with the same management, would prove equally good.

The natural quality of the uncultivated soil in this part of the globe is such as wonderfully to promote the increase of fish. A dam was formerly built across a brook in New England, between twenty and thirty feet wide, and two or three deep, in which were the trout and the sucker. This dam was built for the purpose of supplying water for a saw-mill, and covered, by estimation, about a thousand acres, where the trees were thick, and the soil had never been cultivated. In two or three years, the fish were multiplied to an incredible number. They had become so numerous, that at the upper end of the pond, where the brook fell into it, in the spring, the fish were seen running one over another, embarrassed with their own numbers, and unable to escape from any attempt that was made to take them. They were caught by the hand at pleasure; and the swine could catch them without difficulty. With a net, the fishermen often take a bushel at a draught, and repeat their labor with the same success. Carts are loaded with them in as short a time as the people could gather them up, when thrown upon the banks; and it is customary to sell them in the fishing season for a shilling per bushel. While they have thus augmented their numbers, they have become more than double their former size. This extraordinary increase seems to be derived from no other cause than that of collecting the waters in such a quantity as to form the pond, and thus augment the means of subsistence by carrying the water over a large tract of rich, uncultivated land. Circumstances of a similar nature generally take place when an artificial pond is made in any part of the country, not before cultivated, and probably from the same cause.

CHAPTER IX

MOUNTAINS OF THE UNITED STATES — THE BLUE RIDGE — THE WHITE MOUNTAINS — THE ALLEGANY MOUNTAINS — LAKES — SURVEY OF THOSE WITHIN THE TERRITORY OF THE AMERICAN REPUBLIC — LAKE SUPERIOR — HURON — ERIE — ONTARIO — LAST ENGAGEMENT BETWEEN THE AMERICAN TROOPS AND THE SAVAGES.

NATURE is exhibited upon a large scale in America. The lakes, rivers, and mountains are of a greater extent and magnitude than in any other known parts of the earth, and the quadrupeds are larger and stronger than those of Europe.

The loftiest part of the Andes or Cordilleras mountains in South America, has been found by some geographers to be 20,663 feet; and by others 20,590 feet in height,* which is 4,917 feet higher than Mount Blanc, in Savoy. This is the highest known mountain in the world, and though in the torrid zone, is constantly covered with snow. In Virginia, according to Mr. Jefferson, the mountains of the Blue Ridge, and those of the Peaks of Otter, are thought to be of the greatest elevation, measured from their base. "From data," saith he, "which may be found a tolerable conjecture, we suppose the highest peak to be about 4000 feet perpendicular."

In New England, the White Mountains of New Hampshire are the highest. The history of that state by Belknap does not give their height by geometrical observation, but says, that their summit is below the point of perpetual congelation. On the 19th day of June, 1774, on the south side,

* The American Geography, by J. Morse, describes the Andes in South America, to stretch along the Pacific Ocean, from the Isthmus of Darien to the Streights of Magellan, 4300 miles: and the height of *Chimborazo*, the most elevated point of this vast chain of mountains, to be 20,280 feet, which is above 5,000 higher than any other mountain of the known world.

in one of the gullies, the snow was five feet deep. On the first of September, 1783, the tops of the mountains were covered with ice and snow. In July, 1784, snow was seen on the south side of the highest mountain; as it also was in August, 1790. These are the hottest months of the year in America. In general, the mountains begin to be covered with snow in September; but it goes off again, and seldom becomes fixed until the end of October, or the beginning of November. These mountains are in latitude 44 deg. 15 min. north.

The Allegany Mountains are also of surprising extent. They reach, with but few broken ridges, from Hudson's River to Georgia, from about 45 to 32 deg. north latitude. In these mountains are large veins of coal; and though that article is procured with far greater facility than at Newcastle and Sunderland, it is more than three times the price, and of a much inferior quality. Iron and other metals are supposed to lie buried in these mountains, but the variety of objects which are daily presenting themselves to the citizens of the United States, in trade and speculation, have hitherto prevented their being explored.

An American bard,[1] who styles himself M'Fingal, but whose doggrel proves him to be no relative of the ancient Caledonian bard of that name, in a poem written during the late war, and greatly admired by his countrymen, comparing the extent of Great Britain with the size of their lakes, says,

> Its *small* extension, long supply'd
> By *vast* immensity of pride:
> So small, that had it found a station
> In this new world at first creation;
> And for its crimes transported over,
> We'd find full room for't in Lake *Erie*, or
> That larger water pond, *Superior*,
> Where *North*,* on margin taking stand,
> Would not see shore from either strand.

* Lord North — Imputing to him the long continuance of the war, the Americans by no means venerate his character.

The late geographer to the United States, Mr. Hutchins,[2] has given the following survey of those parts of these lakes, or inland seas, within the territories of the American republic:

	ACRES.	
Lake Superior, ...	21,952,780	
Lake Michigan, ...	10,368,000	Wholly in the United States.
Lake Huron, ...	5,009,920	
Lake Erie, ...	2,662,800	
Lake Ontario, ...	2,390,000	
Lake of the Woods, . .	1,333,800	
Bay Puan, ...	1,216,000	
Red Lake, ...	551,000	
Lake Rain, ...	165,000	
Lake St. Clair, ...	89,500	

Lake Champlain, which was crossed by General Burgoyne's army, is not noticed in this report. Its length is two hundred miles, reckoning from Fairhaven to Saint John's. It is from one to eighteen miles broad, and the mean width about five miles. It therefore will be found to cover one thousand square miles, or 640,000 acres. It is of sufficient depth for large ships; and contains several islands, one of which called Grand Isle, is twenty-four miles long, and from two to four miles wide.

The survey of Mr. Hutchins extends only to that part of these waters comprised within the territory of the United States. As the division line, or boundary, strikes nearly through the middle of these lakes, except Lake Michigan, we may infer that they are nearly twice as large as the idea conveyed by this computation; but this may be made more clear by pursuing the American geography.

Lake Superior is confessedly the largest body of fresh water upon the earth. According to the French charts, it is fifteen hundred miles in circumference; but Mr. Carver,[3] one of the most accurate writers on America, supposes, that if the utmost extent of every bay was taken, it would exceed sixteen hundred. A great part of the coast is bounded by rocks and uneven ground. The water is pure and transparent, and appears generally throughout the lake, to lie upon a vast bed of rocks. Dr. Halley[4] has given it as his opinion, that *all* perennial lakes are saline, either in a greater or less degree, and that this saline quality increases with time; and on this foundation he proposes a method for determining the age of the world.

There are lakes in many parts that, from their vicinity to the sea, are impregnated with salts. But this wonderful body of water, called Lake Superior, has been found by chemical process to be as free from salt as an inland brook; and although the surface, during the heat of summer, is affected by the sun, yet on letting down a bottle to the depth of a fathom, the water drawn up is so excessively cold, that when taken into the mouth it has the same effect as ice.

This lake lies between 46 and 57 degrees north latitude, and between 9 and 18 degrees west longitude from the meridian of Philadelphia. It contains many islands; one of them called Isle Royal, is about an hundred miles long, and forty miles broad.

The Nipegon and Michipicooton, two large rivers, empty themselves into Lake Superior. Not far from the former is a small river, remarkable for a perpendicular fall, of upwards of six hundred feet, from the top of a mountain. Surveyed at a distance, it appears like a white ribband suspended in the air. Upwards of thirty other rivers discharge themselves into this lake. On the banks of one, there is abundance of virgin copper, and copper ore in immense beds. It is ascertained that this valuable metal might be conveyed through the different lakes and rivers nearly to Philadelphia; yet it lies neglected. Lake Superior abounds with fish, particularly trout, which have been caught of the surprising weight of fifty pounds. It is agitated by storms, like the Atlantic Ocean; and like that sea, is in many places unfathomable, or out of soundings.

There is but one outlet to this great body of water. It is called the Streights of Saint Mary, through which, it is conjectured that not one tenth part can pass. How the superabundance is disposed of, is yet unknown. Nearly forty rivers are constantly running into it, and some of them almost as large as the outlet of St. Mary.

From Lake Superior, through the Streights of St. Mary, we come to Lake Huron. The American Geography says that this lake "is next in magnitude to Lake Superior."[5] The boundary line through Lake Huron reserves the greatest part of it to Great Britain; in this, part is an island called Manataulin, or the place of spirits, which is held sacred by the Indians. This lake communicates with Lake Michigan by the Streights of Michillimackinac. It is remarkable that although there is no diurnal flood or ebb to be perceived in the waters of these streights, yet, from an exact attention to their state, a periodical alteration has been discovered. It has been observed that they rise by gradual, but imperceptible degrees, till, in seven years and a half, they have reached the height of about three feet; and in the same space of time they gradually fall away to their former state, so that in fifteen years they complete this inexplicable revolution.

From Lake Huron, through the small Lake of St. Clair, (though this *small* lake is ninety miles in circumference) we come to Lake Erie. "It is *nearly* three hundred miles long, and *about* forty in its broadest part." The American bard would therefore have been puzzled to place Great Britain, or even that part of it called England, in these dimensions.

Poets, however, must in all parts of the world have unlimited licence: and, doubtless, England might have floated on Lake Erie in this bard's brain. Were we not to allow the poets their flights of fancy, we might have lost the Trojan wars, Milton's heroic devils, and many other sublime productions of the human mind.

Lake Erie is the most dangerous, both for navigation and the numerous species of serpents with which it abounds. It was, perhaps, on this account that the American, M'Fingal, wished to assign this situation to England. "The margin of this lake in many places is covered with the large pond lily, the leaves of which float on the surface of the water so thick as to cover it entirely for many acres together. On these leaves, in the summer season, lie myriads of water snakes, basking in the sun." Mr. Carver's account of the *hissing snake* is supposed to be fabulous.

This lake at the north-east communicates with Lake Ontario, by the river Niagara. On the eastern shore of this river the British established a fort, and kept possession of it until the commercial treaty with America, though decidedly within the boundary line of the United States. Another fort was in like manner maintained by Great Britain on the banks of the Miamis river, near Detroit, between the Lakes Erie and Ontario. In the vicinity of the latter fort, the last battle took place between the troops of the United States and the savages. This engagement was an interesting event to America, and having nearly involved a question that might ultimately have been attended with serious consequences to England and the United States, a short sketch of the event may not be unacceptable to the reader.

The cause of this war is well known; and it is scarcely necessary to observe that the Americans charge the Indians with being the aggressors.

In the summer of 1794, Major-General Wayne, at the head of an American army, amounting to about three thousand effective men, marched against the warlike tribes of Indians, on the north-west of the Ohio, consisting of the Delawares, the Shawanese, the Miamis, the Wyandotts, and some others, then at war with the United States. They were assisted, according to the general's report, by the Canadian militia, and some volunteers.

On the 13th of August he arrived in the vicinity of the enemy, when he issued a proclamation, inviting them to terms of peace; which was disregarded. On the 20th his army marched in columns. After his advanced party, which consisted of cavalry, had proceeded five miles, they received so severe and sudden a fire from the Indians, who were concealed in the woods and high grass, as compelled them to retreat. The general immediately formed his army in two lines, principally in a thick wood, which extended several miles on his left, and for a considerable distance in front. The ground was covered with fallen timber, probably occasioned by a tornado, which rendered it impracticable for his cavalry to act with effect; he therefore attempted to turn the flank of the savages with them, by a circuitous route. He had discovered his enemy drawn up in three lines, within supporting distance of each other. At the same time he ordered his front line to advance, and charge with trailed arms, to rouse the Indians from their coverts, at the point of the bayonet, and when up, to fire and charge, so as not to give them time to load again. Another legion of cavalry was directed to attempt to turn their left flank. By these manœuvres the Indians were soon dislodged; but they killed many of the general's troops in their retreat. The vanquished fled through the wood, and the Americans pursued them under the guns of the British garrison on the banks of the Miamis. The American army destroyed all the houses and corn-fields for a considerable distance, both above and below Fort Miamis. They lost in this action, one captain, one lieutenant, three sergeants, and twenty-eight privates, killed; also four captains, two lieutenants, one ensign, four sergeants, four corporals, two musicians, and eighty-four privates, wounded. The loss on the part of the savages was not ascertained. The bodies of more than thirty of them were found after the engagement; and from their sudden retreat, it is probable that this was nearly the whole loss they sustained.[6]

The Indians alleged that they were taken by surprize; for, having waited in ambush two days without food, and conceiving that General Wayne had pursued a different route, they were taking some refreshment at the very moment he suddenly came upon them, and began the action. This is highly probable, for, had the Americans fallen into their ambush, they might have shared the fate of Braddock and St. Clair. Be it as it might, the savages received the Americans with a resolution which induced their commander to believe that they were assisted by the British from Fort Miamis, in sight of the field of battle. Under this impression, a detachment advanced in a menacing manner to within pistol-shot of the fort. Upon this, the commanding officer, Major, since General Campbell, of the 24th regiment of foot, wrote to General Wayne to know in what light he was to view such conduct, observing, that he knew of no war between the king whom he served and the United States. The general, in his answer, alluded to the battle of the preceding day with the hordes of savages, in the vicinity of the fort and asserted that, in case the Indians had been driven under the influence of the British cannon, they would not much have impeded the progress of his victorious army. After this, Wayne, *in person, descended* to approach the fort, and insult the British flag, as it were to provoke the garrison to fire, and thus involve the two countries in the calamities of a new war. Major Campbell then wrote, that if he should, after that notice, "approach his post in the threatening manner he was at that moment doing, his indispensable duty to his king and country would oblige him to have recourse to those measures which thousands of both nations might have cause to regret, and which he solemnly appealed to God he had used his utmost endeavours to avert." This spirited remonstrance appears to have irritated the American commander, as, in reply, he demanded, in the name of the president of the United States, that he should immediately desist from acts of hostility or aggression, by forbearing to fortify the place, and withdrawing the troops, artillery, and stores, under his command. The major, whose force did not exceed two hundred effective men, answered in these words, "permit me to inform you, that I certainly will not abandon this post at the summons of any power whatever, until I receive orders from those I have the honour to serve, or the fortune of war should oblige me. I must still add here, Sir, to the purport of my letter this morning, to desire that your army, or individuals belonging to it, will not approach within reach of my cannon, without expecting the consequences attending it."

The Americans charged the British with assisting the Indians, and General Wayne, in his account of the battle, makes use of this expression, "the Indians and *Canadian Militia,* and *Volunteers,* were driven from all their coverts."[7] There might probably have been some young Canadians, who are scarcely a degree removed from the savage, in the Indian army, but the charge of militia or volunteers, organized under the British government, assisting them, was without foundation. It has since appeared, that when the Indians found the English did not fire upon General Wayne's army, which they were taught by the Canadians to expect, should he shew himself before the fort, and that no assistance whatever was given to their cause by the British, they sued for peace, and commissioners soon settled the terms with the savage chiefs.

The Americans having buried their dead, marched off the ground, without replying to Major Campbell's last notice, or making any attempt upon the fort. Thus happily ended this very critical affair, which might have been attended with the most dreadful consequences to both countries.

In naming this subject, Mr. Weld says: "Before they began to eat, the Indians had divided themselves, I must observe, into three divisions, in order to march into another quarter, where they hoped to surprise the army of the United States. In this situation, however, they were themselves surprised by General Wayne. He had received intelligence from his scouts, now equally cunning with those of the Indians, of their proceedings, and having made some motions as if he intended to move to another part of the country, in order to put them off their guard, he suddenly turned, and sent his light horse pouring down on them when they least expected it. The Indians were thrown into confusion, a circumstance which with them never fails to occasion a defeat; they made but a faint resistance, and then fled with precipitancy."— And again,

"How absurd this whole plan was, however, was plainly to be deduced from the following circumstance, allowed both by the general and his aides-de-camp, namely, that during the whole action the American army did not see fifty Indians; and indeed, every person who has read an account of the Indians, must know that they never come into the field in such regular array, but always fight under covert, behind trees or bushes, in the most irregular manner."

NOTES — CHAPTER IX

1. John Trumbull, born at Westbury, Connecticut, on April 24, 1750, His *McFingal,* begun in 1775 and completed in 1784, gives in poetical form a general account of the American revolution, with descriptions of particular characters and manners of the time.

2. Thomas Hutchins, a military engineer, received the designation of "Geographer of the United States" by Congress on July 11, 1781.

3. Jonathan Carver, *Travels through the Interior Parts of North America in the Years 1766, 1767 and 1768.* London, 1778, p. 132.

4. Dr. Edmond Halley, the English scientist and geologist.

5. See Jedidiah Morse, *American Geography.* London, 1792, pp. 38-9.

6. This statement checks with the official report of the encounter. See *American State Papers, Indian Affairs,* I, 490-92.

7. See General Wayne's report to the Secretary of War, August 28, 1794. *American State Papers, Indian Affairs,* I, 491.

CHAPTER X

EXCURSION IN CONNECTICUT — SUBSTANTIAL BREAKFAST — DINNER — HORSE — CORN — GENERAL ASPECT OF THE COUNTRY — FROGS — MANNERS OF THE INHABITANTS — EFFECT OF REPUBLICAN PRINCIPLES — DANGEROUS PASSAGE OF HELL GATE — NEW YORK — DESCRIPTION OF THE CITY — MACHINATIONS OF GENET, THE FRENCH AMBASSADOR — DALLAS, THE AMERICAN SECRETARY OF STATE.

AN excursion through Connecticut, and part of Massachusets, afforded me an opportunity of observing the mode of travelling, and the accommodations on the road. In order to view the country at my leisure, I purchased a horse, which with a tolerable bridle and saddle, cost me sixty dollars. Upon my new purchase I set out, before the break of day, from New London, in order to arrive at Norwich before the sun acquired his full power. After riding three hours, I stopped at a decent looking house, with a vile daub of General Washington for a sign, in order to feed my nag, which had ingratiated himself in my favor by this morning's performance, and to take breakfast. I was greatly surprized to see a hot beef-steak, swimming in grease and onions, brought upon the table; and still more so find this substantial dish followed by another of fried eggs and bacon. My ride had sharpened my appetite, so that the fume of these smoaking dishes was by no means unpleasant. They remained upon the table till nearly cold, before a single person came into the room. My patience was exhausted — hunger drove away ceremony; I could no longer restrain its calls, and therefore commenced an attack, for the first time in my life, upon a clumsy beef-steak, at eight in the morning. I saw no appearance of tea or coffee, and concluded that I must make a dinner instead of a breakfast, but in a little time the room began to fill with country-looking people of both sexes, to my confusion — for I was stared at with looks not very prepossessing, till I observed, that being a stranger, in haste to pursue my journey, not knowing company were expected, and above all, the steak cooling, I had begun to eat. Very little notice was taken of my apology, but each followed my example, with stomachs not a whit less keen than my own. If, methought, looking round the table, and fixing my eyes upon a pretty girl, who was too deeply engaged with a plateful of eggs and bacon to notice me, — if you make a practice of breaking your fast thus, pretty damsel, you must surely be a maiden of the days of Queen Bess, preferring "to such slip-slops as tea the leg of an Ox." A few days convinced me that this is the daily custom in the morning with this class of people, who must have something hot and substantial. Beside this fare, let me not forget to mention, we were served with some most detestable coffee. I wished for ale or porter after my steak, but was offered "*Yankee rum*," the most execrable spirit ever distilled; and at length I allayed my thirst with a glass of sour cyder.

Again mounted, I proceeded on my excursion till I came to a place where the road branched out in different directions; one of them was to be pursued, and confident that I could not miss the stage-road, I had made no minute enquiries, and not a soul appeared to direct me. After several minutes consideration, I chose the wrong branch, and thus did not get under shelter till between two and three, greatly fatigued by the heat, and the length I had contrived to make the stage. On asking for dinner, I was roughly answered by the landlord that they *had all dined long ago;* and was about to make him understand that I had not, but before I could so, he espied some swine in his garden, which the window overlooked, and, upon this, ran roaring out the disaster, and left me to entertain myself as I pleased. In vain I might have waited his return, for I saw him very deliberately take a spade and begin to repair the disorder made among his cabbages. I now began to explore the house, but met not a single individual till I reached the kitchen, where a girl was clearing away the fragments of the family dinner. The inmates had dispersed, as usual in America, immediately after a meal has been hastily dispatched, in several directions, and to their different avocations. To this Maid of the Kitchen I made known my wants, and though greatly out of humour, I was aware if I betrayed myself, my situation would not be mended. Assuming, therefore, a pleasant air, through the medium of a little flattery, I succeeded so far as to hear her express concern that there was nothing for me to eat in the house. I pointed to some fowls scratching on the dunghill, and observed, that one of those, accompanied by a piece of bacon, might soon be converted into an excellent repast. The good creature took the hint, and in an instant twisted off the head of a fine chicken. To pass the time until the business of cooking was concluded, I returned to the stable to view the condition of my horse, who was still gaining favor with his new master, and I was determined to be grateful by attending to his accommodations. The food they give horses here is the leaves of the Indian-corn stalk, which is a substitute for hay, and what Englishmen call a feed of oats and a few beans, is here half a galloon of the corn which grows upon that stalk. Thus, the whole food of a horse is produced from one single plant! but it is not so good as hay and oats. The corn is of so heating a nature, that an over-feed often founders the cattle, so as to render them unable to proceed on a journey. They are so fond of this grain, that they would eat to an excess, which would prove fatal; while the leaves are given them to use at pleasure. Thanks to the pigs, I saw nothing more of my landlord, and I afterwards found that in this respect, I was very fortunate, these fellows in Connecticut being more troublesome to their guests, by prying into their business, than persons of any other description.

Having made a good dinner, and being refreshed by two hours' sleep, a practice here in the afternoon with travellers, when they can spare time for such refreshment, I determined to proceed to Middletown, distant only a few miles. As the sun declined, this part of my day's journey was delightful, through a fine cultivated country on the banks of the beautiful river Connecticut. Could the English quick-thorn hedges have been added to the scene before me, I could have fancied myself travelling along the bye-roads of Kent. Crossing the ferry, I arrived in Middletown as the family of the inn were sitting down to supper. This meal in America is also very different from the usage of England. It is prepared and on the table between seven and eight o'clock, and consists of broiled salt fish, slices of ham, the relics of the dinner, bread and butter, with coffee; and this is their last meal for the day, after which, the female part of the family generally take a walk, or pay visits. To this recreation I was invited by two pretty daughters of the landlord, having, during supper, gratified them with the history of my movements, as usual; and by these means I avoided a *tête a tête* with mine host — of all things the most irksome. On my return, having visited the stable, I retired to bed, and had my choice of half a dozen, in a room the full length of the house, being fortunately the only guest for the night. It was scarcely dark, when, on lying down, my ears were suddenly assailed by a noise perfectly new, and for which I was at a loss to account, till, by enquiry in the morning, I learned that it had proceeded from the frogs in an adjacent pond, and the creeking song of the locust. Among the discord, like the bass in a band of music, was a kind of roaring, which particularly surprized me. It resembled the distant bellowing of the enraged bull; and this I found proceeded from what they aptly call the bull-frog. These animals are four times the size of the English frog, and raise their heads above the water for the space of two minutes, at intervals, (for I have since particularly noticed them,) when they continue this most discordant noise. I could seldom find them out of water, and when I came upon them by surprize, on the margin of a pond, they fled to it by prodigious jumps. I had made many efforts to catch one of them in vain, but returning one evening from a shooting-party, being about to draw my charge, and observing one in a marsh near me, rising to make his roar, I discharged the contents of my piece, and immediately saw it floating on the water. A dog which had accompanied us brought it to me. It measured six inches in length, and its hind legs were nearly as long as the body. In colour, and somewhat in shape, it more resembled the toad than our green-speckled frog. I severed its body, and brought home the hind quarters, more delicate in appearance than those of a chicken. In France I had conquered my repugnance to the flesh of a frog; and having heard that some people in America extolled such food, I resolved to have a little fricassee made of this part of the bull-frog. In accomplishing my purpose I had many difficulties to combat. Not a domestic of the house would touch it, and determined to carry my point, I seized the stew-pan, procured the necessary ingredients, and cooked a dish greatly to my satisfaction — and I can assure my reader, that if he could conquer that enemy to the mind, prejudice, he would find the legs of a frog nearly as excellent as those of a woodcock.

I have been thus prolix in order to draw a picture of my first day's peregrination in the interior of America; but shall hereafter avoid repetitions of this subject, there being little variation in the treatment you meet with in New England. I must, however, observe, that I was greatly indebted to fortune throughout the twenty-four hours; therefore, to give a general view of travelling in this part of the world, in the private manner I had adopted, I shall now shew the reader, without the most distant idea of giving offence, what must sometimes be endured from the manners and customs of the people.

Arrived at your inn, let me suppose, like myself, you had fallen in with a landlord, who at the moment would condescend to *take the trouble* to procure you refreshment after the family hour, and that no *pig*, or other trifling circumstance called off his attention, he will sit by your side, and enter in the most familiar manner into conversation; which is prefaced, of course, with a demand of your business, and so forth. He will then start a political question (for here every individual is a politician), force your answer, contradict, deny, and, finally, be ripe for a quarrel, should you not acquiesce in all his opinions. When the homely meal is served up, he will often place himself opposite to you at the table, at the same time declaring, that "though he thought he had eaten a hearty dinner, yet he will pick a bit with you." Thus will he sit, drinking out of your glass, and of the liquor you are to pay for, belching in your face, and committing other excesses still more indelicate and disgusting. Perfectly inattentive to your accommodation and regardless of your appetite, he will dart his fork into the best of the dish and leave you to take the next cut. If you arrive at the dinner-hour, you are seated with "mine hostess" and her dirty children, with whom you have often to scramble for a plate, and even the servants of the inn; for liberty and equality level all ranks upon the road, from the host to the hostler. The children, imitative of their free and polite papa, will also seize your drink, slobber in it, and often snatch a dainty bit from your plate. This is esteemed wit, and consequently provokes a laugh, at the expence of those who are paying for the board. No check must be given to these demonstrations of unsophisticated nature; for the smallest rebuke will bring down a severe animadversion from the parent. Many are the instances that could be pointed out, where the writer has undergone these mortifications, and if Mr. Winterbottom[1] has ever travelled in the country parts of the United States, he can, if he pleases, attest the truth of these observations.

The American farmer, (says this gentleman) has more simplicity and honesty — we more art and chicanery; they have more of nature, and we more of the world. Nature, indeed, formed our features and intellects very much alike; but while we have metamorphosed the one, and contaminated the other, they have retained and preserved the natural symbols of both.

If we credit these assertions, we must admit that the inhabitants of the new world, far excel us, also, in mental acquirements; but I take the very contrary to be the fact. A republican spirit makes them forward and impertinent — a spirit of trade renders them full of chicanery — and under a shew of liberty, they are commonly tyrants to each other. This is observable at their public meetings, when the fumes of whisky or apple-brandy begin to operate — the more opulent will lord it over his poor neighbor; while the robust will attack the weak, till the whole exhibits a scene of riot, blasphemy, and intoxication.

An English farmer, in the north especially, when asked the price of his grain, will answer with modest diffidence: nay, will often be abashed at the attempt to undervalue the article. In America, the meanest planter must go through his routine of interrogatories, and perhaps mount his political hobby-horse, before you receive an answer to your question. Should you happen to observe that you can purchase for less than he demands, he will give you the lie, accompanied with a grin and an oath, and tell you to go where you can obtain it cheaper.

With the other sex, whose curiosity is generally admitted in other countries to be by no means inferior to that of the men, you may naturally expect to fare no better. This I likewise found by manifold experience. One instance, which occurred during the excursion described in this chapter, shall here suffice. Seeing a pleasant little cottage on the river Connecticut, and understanding that it was to be let, I knocked at the door, which was opened by a woman, of whom I enquired the rent of the house — "And where are you from?" — was the reply. — "Pray madam," I again asked, "is this house to be let?" — "Be you from New York or Boston?" said the inquisitive dame. The place was situated about half-way between those two towns. Impatient at this mode of reply — "I'll thank you, madam," I repeated, "to acquaint me with the price demanded for this little place?" — "Pray what may you be?" rejoined she, as if fully determined not to satisfy my enquiry till I had gratified her curiosity. I was not less resolute than herself, and turned my back in disgust.

Among the females, a stranger may soon discover the pertness of republican principles. Divested, from that cause, of the blushing modesty of the country girls of Europe, they will answer a familiar question from the other sex with the confidence of a French Madamoiselle. I would not, however, be understood to question their chastity, of which they have as large a portion as Europeans; my object is merely to shew the force of habit, and the result of education.

The arrogance of domestics in this land of republican liberty and equality, is particularly calculated to excite the astonishment of strangers. To call persons of this description *servants*, or to speak of their *master* or *mistress*, is a grievous affront. Having called one day at the house of a gentleman of my acquaintance, on knocking at the door, it was opened by a servant-maid, whom I had never before seen, as she had not been long in his family. The following is the dialogue, word for word, which took place on this occasion: — "Is your master at home?" — "I have no master." "Don't you live here?" — "I stay here." — "And who are you then?" — "Why, I am Mr.——'s *help* I'd have you to know, *man*, that I am no *sarvant;* none but *negers* are *sarvants.*"

I have frequently heard of an *amusement* in New England, and particularly in the state of Connecticut, called *bundling.*[2] It is described as being resorted to by lovers. The young couple retire to bed, with their clothes on, and there the lover tells his soft tale. One author says, that "*bundling* has not its origin in New England, as supposed. It has been practised time immemorial in Wales, and is also a general practice in the Isle of Portland. I was informed that servant-girls in Connecticut demand liberty to do so on hiring — they receive their gallants in the night in bed, with their petticoats tied to their ancles. In Holland, too, this is practised amongst the peasants, who call it *queesting*."

Another author mentions *tarrying* in New England. If parents approve their daughter's choice, the lover is permitted to *tarry* with his love a night in *bed*, but not undrest; and there they either agree to marry or part for ever. Sometimes, however, a child has been the fruit of this *tarrying*, in which case, the lover must marry, or be excommunicated!

I confess I never knew a single instance of this bundling or tarrying; indeed, during my residence in New England I was not happy enough to become a *lover*.

From New London I took my passage to New York, in Captain Harris's packet, wishing to view Long Island sound, and to pass through the narrows, called Hell Gate. We were becalmed soon after we had cleared the river Thames, and at noon had proceeded on our voyage no farther than the Long Island shore, nearly opposite to New London. Several of the passengers and I among the rest, went ashore to make an excursion in this beautiful spot, till the tide should favor our proceeding for New York. We were hospitably received by a Dutch farmer, who gave us milk and cyder; but before we could avail ourselves of such information as he might communicate respecting the country, a breeze sprung up, which was the concerted signal for us to return to the boat. This we accordingly did with all expedition, the sails were immediately hoisted, and the gale proved propitious. We passed the town of Newhaven at a great rate, and before dark were at the head of Hell Gate. Our captain was not inclined to pass these streights that evening, as there is great danger unless the tide suits, or the wind enables you to stem the current. We pressed him to make the attempt, and giving way to our solicitations, though with reluctance, he continued his course. This passage may well be called Hell Gate, for it has a most terrific appearance. In one place the water boils up with a great foam, and this they call the pot, a place extremely dangerous when approached too near; on one side are sunken rocks, called the Hog's Back, and on the other, (a place of equal danger,) denominated the Frying-pan. I fancied myself between Scylla and Charybdis; and grew very uneasy on observing the countenance of our captain, who at length evinced evident signs of apprehension for the safety of his vessel, and reflected on himself for being persuaded against his own judgment to pass through at such a time of tide. In fact, we were in greater danger than we conceived; for the wind, which was brisk on our entrance, at once lulled and we were irresistibly drawing towards the Gridiron, a place equally fatal with those already described, where, in our crowded state, many lives might have been lost, though within a few yards of Hancock's rock. On this place, perhaps one hundred yards in circumference, we observed fragments of the rock that had been piled up by the crew of a vessel which had the misfortune to strike upon the Gridiron, to shelter themselves from the inclement wind until the tide permitted a boat to come and take them off.*

In this situation, such was the apprehension of our crew, that, with one accord, they got out their sweeps, or long oars, and the passengers assisted in tugging. With great labor we checked the sloop's way, by which her head swung round towards the city, and thus we fortunately avoided this imminent danger. Our captain now swore and protested

* The following anecdote is related of a black man, the pilot of the Experiment of 50 guns, who took her through Hell Gate, a passage before deemed impracticable for ships of war, to the great astonishment of Lord Howe, then commander-in-chief of the British naval force in those parts. At the moment of the greatest danger, Sir James Wallace, the Captain, gave some orders on the quarter-deck which, in Mungo's opinion, interfered with the duties of his office. Advancing, therefore, to Sir James, and gently tapping him on the shoulder — "Massa," said he, "you no peak here." The captain felt the full force of the poor fellow's remonstrance; and, to the extreme surprize of all those acquainted with the difficulty of navigating a ship through Hell Gate, the negro carried the Experiment safe to Sandy Hook. The addition of this ship was a most

that he would never again be "over-persuaded," as he termed it, by any set of passengers. The wind had fallen, and we had to wait the return of the tide, being now at anchor, and safe, at any rate, from being swung on this watery gate of hell; yet the idea of remaining on board all night was far from one of the most pleasing, as there was not a third part of the births, or places to lie down to rest, required by the passengers. At midnight we were abreast of the city, and at that late hour, when the sober inhabitants are in bed, the boat was soon filled by such of the passengers as chose this alternative to remaining on board till morning. I stepped into the boat, and landed, but soon lost sight of all my companions, who had, for the most part, some friend or relative to whose house they could repair. Behold me then at this unseasonable hour, in the extensive city of New York; the night was dark, a few straggling lamps reflected a dim light, and the watchmen, in monotonous discord, announced the hour. I had gone through two or three streets without seeing a single house open, when two well-dressed men before me, knocked at a door. I determined to avail myself of this opportunity; for by a lamp I discovered that the house at which they were demanding admission, was a tavern. I stopped, and hearing them converse in French, addressed them in that language, and acquainted them with my situation. They behaved with a degree of complaisance peculiar to Frenchmen, and requested me to

seasonable reinforcement to the little fleet under Lord Howe, and so highly did his lordship appreciate the skill and adventurous spirit of the negro pilot, that he settled on him an annuity of fifty pounds for life. Had the Experiment taken any other than this unusual route, she would have infallibly have fallen into the hands of the enemy, as she afterwards did in the course of the war. — A British frigate which attempted this passage during the same contest, less fortunate than the Experiment, was totally lost.

Two French frigates blocked up last year (1806), in New York, by the Leander and another English ship of war, gave their antagonists the slip, by pushing through this dangerous channel. The perils of the land, air, or ocean, dwindle into nothing in the estimation of the French, when compared to those of a meeting with the *unmannerly* tars of Old England.

follow them. I soon found that I was in a French house; several of these lively people being in conversation, while others were amusing themselves with the game of domino. I was invited to join, but urging want of rest, I was shewn to a good bed in a very filthy room, with which I was nevertheless, well pleased.

The city of New York is built upon an island, fourteen miles long, and about a mile in breadth, formed by the north and east rivers; a situation which, to a stranger, would appear to insure the health of its inhabitants. The southern part opens to the sea, and the tide flows with great rapidity. From the battery, which is now used as a public walk, there is a charming view of the Jersey shore, and Long and Staten Islands. New York is a place of great trade, several hundred sail of vessels being generally at the wharfs and at anchor. It is the depôt of European goods, for the supply of retailers in every state in the union; and of late years it has far exceeded Philadelphia in a commercial point of view.

The duties paid at the port of New York during four years, commencing April 1, 1801, and ending March 31, 1805, amounted to	12,862,020.14
For the like time, Philadelphia produced	7,777,965.14
Boston, ditto	6,408,400.28
Baltimore, ditto	3,861,963.08
Charleston, ditto	3,061,693.54

This at one view shews the comparative trade of the five largest commercial towns in America.

New York was built by the Dutch, who called it New Amsterdam; and, following their usual mode of building in Europe, the houses presented their gable-end or back to the streets, which were laid out according to the fancy of the owners of the ground. Thus they became narrow, crooked, and inconvenient in many parts, and some of the old Dutch tenements still continue to disgrace the city. This circumstance, however, cannot give rise to those pestilential fevers which have raged there every summer, in some degree, since the year 1794. Volumes have been written on this subject. Medical men have opposed each other's opinions with much asperity, so that the patient is bewildered in their contradictions. On its first appearance, it was generally believed to have been imported; but its regular return, particularly in New York and Philadelphia, clearly shews it to be engendered there by the operation of excessive heat upon uncleanliness. Great attention has of late been paid to the cleansing of those cities so subject to the fever; yet we find it at an alarming height in both, so late as in the year 1805. It is a singular circumstance, that this scourge never appeared in the country until 1793, the very year of the revolt of the negroes, and the massacre of the white people in St. Domingo, when thousands of French fled to the United States from that devoted island; and very few indeed suffered by it, though raging in Philadelphia, where numbers of them landed.[3]

New York has greatly increased, both in size and population, notwithstanding the havoc made by the yellow fever. The distracted state of Europe has caused an influx of inhabitants scarcely credible; and as the summer destroys, the winter brings in a fresh supply. The Broad-way, leading from the south battery through the park, and the whole length of the city, is a wide, handsome street. I was informed, that a piece of ground in the park, which, seven years ago, was not worth fifty dollars, had been recently disposed of, for the purpose of building upon, for five hundred, pounds, currency of the state, which is eight shillings to the dollar.

The time of my arrival in New York was during the reign of terror in France; the baleful consequences of which were severely felt in America. Robespierre's faction sent an ambassador to the United States, who would have brought immeasurable evils on the country, had not the wisdom and firmness of President Washington counter-acted his plans. This minister was Genet, whose embassy was intended to sow the seeds of a second revolution, to cause a rupture with England, and by availing himself of the consequent anarchy and confusion, to secure to France an ally, by means of a treaty offensive and defensive. The encouragement he met with from the Jacobin interest, then espoused by the most numerous, though least respectable part of the community greatly encouraged him in prosecuting the object of his mission. From Charleston to New York he was flattered by success equal to his most sanguine wishes. A thread may lead a multitude; a bauble, be it a crown or a greasy red cap, is sufficient to procure the adulation of a mob, when held up to view by such a political juggler as Genet. He well knew the temper of the people he was among — unstable and violent in political discussions, yet tenacious and jealous of that liberty, of which it was his aim to deprive them. This required great art, consummate hypocrisy, and undaunted resolution, joined, in case of emergency, to the most desperate measures. That he was competent to the task, and that he would too well have succeeded, had not Washington counteracted his machinations, the event fully proved. This great and good man, an Achilles in war, and a Mentor in peace, again saved his country from the rapacious grasp of insatiable France.

Clubs upon Jacobin principles were formed in the large commercial cities; the flag of France and America supported the cap of liberty in the club-rooms, and the tri-colored cockade was assumed by the whole party of Genet.

General Washington was invested, in many instances, with power equal to the king of Great Britain. He saw with pain the rapid strides of faction, and was determined to crush the monster. He was aware that foreign influence was subtle and fatal poison to the states of America; and the deplorable condition of the countries conquered by France has since fully justified his opinion.

Drawn under the direction of the Author and Engraved by M. Merigot.

View of Hell Gate; the Entrance from Long Island Sound to New York.

An army was raising in the western country, and privateers were fitting out in the ports of the United States, commissioned by the French ambassador; and when *Dallas*,[4] one of the officers of state, attempted to remonstrate with him, and to express the disapprobation of government upon this infringement of the law of nations, he flew into a rage, and declared that he would "appeal to the people from the decisions of the president." This was the language of the French generals in Europe, where they imagined that art would avail. Washington, however, was neither to be duped nor intimidated. He first dismissed Duplaine,*[5] the vice-consul of the French republic at Boston, by revoking and annuling his diplomatic functions. Against this proceeding Genet protested, in a furious remonstrance to Mr. Jefferson, then secretary of state. He declared, "that he did not acknowledge† its validity, because the constitution of the United States has not given the president the right which he now appears desirous to exercise."

This proclamation drew forth the pen of the whole faction. The underlings adopted the language of their chief: they, too, questioned the right of the president to dismiss a foreign vice-consul: they reviled, insulted, and abused the virtuous magistrate. Who then can expect to avoid the shafts of calumny? Where is the man that may hope to escape censure?

These vipers to their country asserted, that the English had agents there, whose business it was to seduce them from the friendship of their great and good allies — to break the

* Duplaine was the principal engine of Genet in New England. The district attorney for Massachusetts had already presented three bills of indictment against him to the grand jury of the circuit court, but the French faction had found means to throw them out. It was therefore high time for the executive to begin with Duplaine.

† The proclamation of the president of the 10th October, 1793, declared, that Duplaine had, under colour of his office, committed sundry encroachments and infractions on the laws of the land; and in consequence he did no longer recognize the said Duplaine, &c., &c.

bonds of rational compact by rousing an unjust indignation against the majesty of their sister republic. Every deceitful art was used, every sophistical argument advanced, to incense the people against the president. The ghost of Franklin was brought forward uttering the following extract of his letter from Paris, to Dr. Mather, in the year 1784, which was with great industry circulated through the public prints of the union:

> This powerful nation (speaking of France) continues its friendship for the United States. It is a friendship of the utmost importance to our security, and should be carefully cultivated. Britain has not yet well digested the loss of its dominion over us; and has still at times some flattering hopes of recovering it. Accidents may increase these hopes, and encourage dangerous attempts. A breach between us and France would infallibly bring the English again upon our backs; and yet we have some wild beasts among our countrymen, who are endeavoring to weaken that connection. Let us preserve our reputation, by performing our engagements and our contracts; and our friends by gratitude and kindness, for we know not how soon we may again have occasion for all of them.

Could the ghost, thus conjured up, have been again animated, and vital warmth once more have been restored, old Franklin would have recanted this political prognostication; and have called those fools and rebels who thus unseasonably brought forward his prediction.

The curious remonstrance and daring threat of Genet, was followed by a demand from him to the attorney-general of the United States, to prosecute John Jay, the chief justice, and Rufus King, one of the members of congress.[6] His charge against these gentlemen was, laughable to relate, that they had falsely asserted that he, "Citizen Genet, as minister plenipotentiary of the French Republic, one and indivisible, &c. declared his resolution of appealing from the president to the people." These gentlemen, friends to their country, came forward, and not only publicly attested the truth of Genet's threats, but gave the names of Hamilton and Knox, men at that time high in office, who confirmed the fact. A confutation like this, would have brought the blush of shame and guilt into any other cheek than that of a revolutionary Frenchman. In the mind of Genet it added fuel to the flames of discord: he even had the temerity to repeat his application to the attorney-general in dictatorial terms, charging Messrs. Jay and King with the additional crime of a coalition with the secretary at war and the secretary of the treasury, Messrs. Knox and Hamilton, whom he called authors and abettors of vile machinations against him, and threatening to apply to the head of the executive power to oblige him to carry on the prosecution. The answer to this demand, till then new in the United States, with Genet's reply, I shall give at length.

PHILADELPHIA, *December 18th*, 1793.

Sir,

I had the honor of receiving yesterday the second communication which you purposed to make to me. When we conversed together on Friday the 13th instant, I doubted for a moment, whether you did not mean, that I should wait for the instructions intended to be asked for me, from the president of the United States; but as I want no special order to discharge my real duty, and the opinion which you request must be the result of my own conviction, I do not think it proper to delay my answer.

You apply, Sir, to me as the attorney-general of the United States to prosecute Mr. Jay and Mr. King for their publication on the 12th of August and 26th of November, 1793. The act constituting my office declares my duty to be "to prosecute and conduct all suits in the supreme court in which the United States shall be concerned," and I have been sworn to its faithful execution. But while I admit it to be incumbent on me to prosecute without distinction of persons, when the law will support me, I do not hold myself bound, nor do I conceive that I ought to proceed against any man in opposition to my decided judgment. With these impressions, I must beg leave to decline the measures which you desire, persuaded, as I am, that this case will not sustain the prosecution which you meditate.

But, Sir, if it would not seem modifying with an apology this determination of mine, founded upon principles which need none, I would take the liberty of adding, that any other gentleman of the profession, who may approve and advise the attempt, will be at no loss to point out a mode which does not require my intervention.

I have the honor, Sir, to be, with sincere respect and attachment for the nation whom you represent,

Your most obedient servant,

EDM. RANDOLPH.

M. Genet, Minister Plenipotentiary of the French Republic.

P. S. December 20*th*, 1793.

Since I wrote the above, I have received, Sir, a letter from the secretary of state on the subject of your request. As no change is rendered necessary in the foregoing sentiments, I do myself the honor of sending my letter as it originally stood.

PHILADELPHIA, 21*st December*, 1793,
2*d year of the French Republic.*

Citizen Genet, &c. to Mr. Randolph, Attorney-General of the United States.

Sir,

SINCE you refuse cause to be rendered to my nation, the ally of yours, the justice claimed by its representative, I will apply immediately to the judges, and should they refuse to admit my complaint, I will cover myself with the mantle of mourning, and will say America is no longer free.

Accept, Sir, my profound respect for and my attachment to the United States, of which you are attorney-general.

GENET.

The penetrating eye of the president had some time been fixed on the motions of the French party: he was now convinced of the danger of Genet's mission; and he therefore deemed it his duty to extend that power which he had already exercised upon Duplaine. It was also the best answer that could be given to the threatening remonstrance to the secretary of state, and it was the seal of approbation of the conduct of the attorney-general. The functions of the dread minister plenipotentiary himself were suspended, and a complaint against him forwarded to France. In due time he was superseded by Fauchet, and recalled to Paris to answer for his conduct; but the wily republican, regarding the bloody scenes there, which he had but lately assisted in, declined obeying the latter part of the mandate. He chose rather to sink in soft repose in the arms of beauty, than to meet the pikes of enraged republicans. Adopting the country he had attempted to divide, he married into a respectable American family,[7] retired to a snug private seat, "far from the court and the tumultuous city," where he can shed with impunity, no other blood than that of his own mutton.

The conduct of this man, in his official capacity, will not appear extraordinary, when we recur to his instructions. As a justification of his proceedings, he published them in America. Consummate art and deep intrigue, are the leading features of the whole. A few lines may give the reader an idea of modern republicanism:

> In this situation of affairs, we ought to excite, by all possible means, the zeal of the Americans, who are as much interested as ourselves in discouraging the destructive projects of George III in which they are probably an object. Their own safety still depends on ours; and if we fail, they will sooner or later fall under the iron rod of Great Britain.

Such were the inflammatory orders of President Monge to Genet, and such was his encouragement to carry them into full effect by the American faction; at the head of which appeared Dallas, then a secretary of state. This man is described by Cobbett,[8] who published the best diurnal print in America, under the name of *The Porcupine Gazette*, to have been a strolling player, of such inferior abilities as to have been hissed off the stage in the island of Jamaica. "Wonderful turn of the wheel of fortune," continues Mr. Cobbett. "A man rejected as a diverting stroller in a British colony, is found very fit for a secretary of state in the republic of America!"

NOTES — CHAPTER X

1. William Winterbotham, author of *An Historical, Geographical, Commercial, and Philosophical View of the American United States.* London, 1795. 4 vols.

2. Bundling appears to have been practiced in the United States until the last decade of the eighteenth century. Numerous travellers in this country comment upon the custom. For a comprehensive account of it, not only in the United States but in various other countries, see Henry Reed Stiles, *Bundling, Its Origin, Progress and Decline in America.* This interesting study was reprinted from the scarce edition of 1871 in 1928 at Harrisburg, Pennsylvania.

3. Yellow fever had made its appearance, even as an epidemic, as early as 1699 in Philadelphia. It came to be known as the Barbadoes distemper, because it was supposed to have been brought in by ships from the West Indies. Samuel Faulke mentioned it again in 1762. The disease broke out as a raging epidemic in the summer of 1793, making its first appearance in July. Due to unsanitary conditions, it spread rapidly. All sorts of stories arose as to its origin. Some thought that French fugitives from Santo Domingo, who fled from the slave uprising on the island, carried it to Philadelphia. Others believed it to have been brought on a coffee ship. One correspondent said that "a great deal of Invention was us'd to satisfy the People which way the Disorder came." About 5,000 died in three months.

4. Alexander James Dallas, at this time Secretary of the Commonwealth of Pennsylvania.

5. See the *Writings of Thomas Jefferson,* edited by Paul Leicester Ford, VI, 401, and 404; *American State Papers, Foreign Relations,* I, 178-82; *Annual Reports of the American Historical Association* (1903), II, 281, Correspondence of Genet, edited by F. J. Turner.

6. See Correspondence of the French Ministers to the United States, 1791-1797, edited by F. J. Turner, in the *Annual Report of the American Historical Association* (1903), II, 278-79.

7. Genet married Cornelia Tappen Clinton, daughter of Governor George Clinton, on November 6, 1794. For some years he lived on a small farm on Long Island. About 1800 he moved to a farm in Rensselaer County. After the death of his first wife, he married, on July 31, 1814, Martha Brandon Osgood, daughter of Samuel Osgood, a former Postmaster General of the United States.

8. Cobbett's gossip here, as in many other instances, seems slightly exaggerated. Dallas was induced to come to the United States from Jamaica, where he was Master in Chancery, by Lewis Hallam's descriptions of this country. Arriving in Philadelphia in 1783, he signed citizenship papers within ten days. On account of a prohibitory statute, he could not practice law in Pennsylvania for two years. Following the return of Hallam from Jamaica in the spring of 1784, he and Dallas attempted to introduce regular drama into Philadelphia. Dallas prepared a memorial to the Legislature, and even turned his pen to dramatic plots. That he had been a strolling player in Jamaica seems unlikely.

CHAPTER XI

STATE OF RELIGION IN THE UNITED STATES — SUNDAYS — GENEROSITY OF THE ROMAN CATHOLIC BISHOP OF MARYLAND — SHAKERS — BAPTISTS, ANECDOTES OF THEM — CAMP MEETINGS OF THE METHODISTS.

SOON after Mr. Jefferson's advancement to the presidency, the tythes of the episcopal clergy were entirely abolished, and the church lands sold for the use of government.[1] All religious sects are therefore on the same footing, without supremacy, or limited salaries. In the New England States, Presbyterians and Baptists are the most numerous. New York has a large proportion of adherents to the church of England, which many of the Dutch also attend. New Jersey contains a mixture of Quakers, Baptists, and Presbyterians. In Pennsylvania, founded by William Penn, a rigid quaker, a great part of the inhabitants are consequently of that persuasion. Being subject to no restraint, this non-resisting sect are, by many Americans of other denominations, charged with overbearance in all matters where they are concerned, and with a busy intermeddling meanness in the affairs of other sects. Maryland, like Pennsylvania, follows the religion of the ancient proprietor, Lord Baltimore. About one half of the people are therefore Roman Catholics, In Virginia, the Methodists bawl out their tenets with the greatest success amongst the lower orders of people. They are said to do great mischief among the slaves, whom they receive into their congregation, and place among the most select part of their white brethren. They certainly terrify the uninformed negroes; and, in many instances, serve to aggravate the hardships of their situations, by disordering their minds. In the Carolinas, (to use Dr. Morse's observation) "Religion is at a very low ebb."[2] The inhabitants of these states he calls Northingarians. Sundays are there passed in riot and drunkenness; and the negroes indulge uncontrolled in tumultuous sports and licentiousness. At night they prowl about stealing wherever they find opportunity, at the risk of a severe flogging in the morning. At Charleston, they make some shew of religion on the sabbath, but, perhaps, with as little devotion as in the other parts of the state. Of Georgia, I cannot, from my own observation, say much; but there is every reason to believe that, with respect to religion, it is nearly on a par with the Carolinas; *gouging* being in equal vogue in the four southern states.

In Connecticut, the sabbath is kept in the most rigid manner; a great majority of the people being Baptists and Presbyterians. There the traveller is *compelled* to take his rest at the miserable tavern where he may have arrived on the Saturday, until Monday morning; for the running of stages is prohibited on the Lord's day. I actually sustained a considerable loss by being detained at Newhaven on a Sunday in the spring of the year 1794, on my road to New York, which, in consequence of this delay, I reached too late to transact my contemplated business. Many instances have occurred of travellers on horseback, who have attempted to pass a meeting-house during service being forcibly dismounted, and compelled to hear a doctrine, perhaps repugnant to their tenets.*

In all the other states, Maryland excepted, the principal merchants and men of property are chiefly of the church of England. The Roman Catholics are the most moderate and orderly of the other sects. They have handsome churches

* This kind of religious persecution has been noticed by different English authors, and denied by Americans. I can, however, affirm, that as late as the year 1793, such cases as that described above frequently occurred. Mr. Harper, manager of a company of comedians, informed me that an attempt was made to stop him on passing a small building, which he supposed to be a meeting-house, on a Sunday forenoon, in Connecticut, and that he preserved his freedom by hastening his speed. The player was witty in commenting on his situation, observing, that he was taken by surprise, for had he only told them his errand (he was going post to Boston to open a theatre), the Puritans would have avoided him as a pestilence.

in New York and Philadelphia. At Baltimore, a Metropolitan cathedral is building, on an extensive scale, under the patronage and protection of Bishop Cleggett, a man of good sense and erudition, who governs the Catholic church throughout the United States with much propriety. To provide funds, he prevailed upon the government to grant a lottery, in which the Bishop drew the highest prize, and magnanimously appropriated it to the use of the church, affording a brilliant example to the other dignified clergy to "go and do likewise."

Amongst the numerous religious sects in the United States, there is one, which for extravagance of action, during their orisons, is certainly pre-eminent. These people are called *Shakers*. The first society was formed at Harvard, in the State of Massachuesetts, by Ann Leese,[3] who denominated herself their *mother;* and she associated herself with William Leese, her *natural* brother, as her second; John Parkinson, who had formerly been a baptist preacher in England, the chief speaker; and James Whitaker, second speaker.

These people had converts in numbers, and from distant parts, who laid up stores of provisions for such as tarried at Harvard. Their meetings, which continued day and night for a considerable time, consisted of preaching, singing and dancing; the men in one apartment, the women in another. These meetings were attended by converts from a great distance, who staid from two to twenty days. They had missionaries in the country making proselytes, and confirming others in this fancied millenium state. Those were taught to be very industrious at home, that they might be able to contribute to the general fund, and many devoted their whole substance to the society. They vary their exercises of devotion. Sometimes they dance, or rather jump up, and down in a heavy manner till they are exhausted by the violence of the exercise. The chief speaker will sometimes begin to pray, they then desist to listen to him, and when he has finished, immediately renew their dancing with increased vigor. Then generally follows the shaking, as if shuddering under an ague, from which they have received the name of shakers. They sing praises to David during the dancing; but I could not learn what holy man or saint they invoke in their shaking fits. The women are equally employed in the fatigues of these exercises under the eye of the mother in another apartment, where they jump and scream in dreadful concert. Sometimes there will be short intermissions, but in a minute or two, one of the chiefs will spring up, crying, "as David danced, so will we before God;" the others follow this signal; and thus, alternately dancing, praying, and singing, they pass night after night, and often until morning. Mother Leese's followers have formed societies at New Lebanon and Hancock, in the state of New York, and in other parts the shakers, who call themselves believers, are spreading with enthusiastic rapidity.

At Edenton, in North Carolina, the people are so far lost to the sense of religion, that they have suffered a handsome brick episcopalian church, the only place of public worship in the town, to fall into decay. In many parts of the southern states, there is a total neglect, not only of religious, but often of moral duties. The church-yard at Edenton is open to the carnivorous beasts which prowl about that country; and when cattle have grazed, and hogs rooted in it, they retire to rest in the neglected church. Having driven their minister away, the ceremony of marriage is performed by a justice of the peace, who having first freely indulged at the festive board of the happy couple, and generally late in the evening, hiccups over a few lines, and this serves as a bond for life. The baptism and the burial service are dispensed with. This church was built and flourished under the British government, when benevolent and spirited merchants gave a rank and consequence to the town, when hospitality and unanimity spread their benign influence, and somewhat ameliorated an unfriendly clime, by the exercise of the social and moral virtues.

These religious liberties, like the civil code of republicanism, is often grossly abused. The episcopalians in many of the states have their *bishops*, and even the ranting methodists have their Lord's anointed; notwithstanding Doctor Currie boldly advances that there are no ecclesiastical orders in the country. The baptists are also a formidable sect in some parts; and, like the other seceders, are bitter enemies to the old established code of religion.

I was present at a baptism according, as they say, to the doctrine of Saint John, in Rhode Island. The day was one of the severest in the month of January, and in that part of the world it is many degrees colder than in England. The thermometer was, at the time, 10 below 0.

A concourse of people near the water-side attracted my attention. I joined the crowd, and found that it was assembled to witness a baptism by immersion. The ice, which was about a foot thick, had been cut through to the distance of twenty or thirty yards, but so intense was the frost, that some of the *elect* were obliged, with poles and staves, to keep the hallowed water from freezing. A few minutes would have cemented the whole again. In order to turn the hearts of unbelievers, and to reclaim such as have gone astray, the baptists on these occasions are particularly prolix. They assert that the spirit enures them to this rigid penance, making to them the day mild, and the water of the summer's temperature. I had waited for the end of the minister's exhortation, after which he was to lead his flock to the water, until my limbs ached with cold. At length the penitents appeared. They consisted of the members of the meeting, two and two; then followed the devotees, about twelve in number, of both sexes, in long gowns, resembling a *robe de chambre*. At the head of the noviciates was the priest, alternately praying and singing, in honor of Saint John the baptist: and thus without slackening his pace, or altering his dress, he plunged into the freezing stream, till he was nearly breast-high in the water. His disciples, with wonderful resolution, hand in hand, followed; while the members who had already been purified by immersion, ranged themselves along the margin of the deep. The pastor then turned round and began a solemn exhortation on baptism, which continues a few minutes; a dreadful interval in his situation! He then seized the nearest devotee, and with great dexterity immersed him entirely in the water. Another short prayer succeeded, then another immersion; and this was repeated till the whole had thus received the holy sacrament. They returned, giving thanks to God, after suffering the severity of the freezing water, at such a season, about ten minutes.

During this unnatural ceremony, I was no less entertained with the remarks of the spectators. One of them observed that, severe as the discipline was, they seldom took cold, or suffered subsequent bodily pains; adding, that their enthusiasm was so great, and their minds were wrought up to such a degree of religious phrenzy, that no room was left for reflection, or sense of danger. Another related a story of a public baptism of this nature in Connecticut, which was attended with a fatal circumstance. "It was about the same time of year," continued the narrator, (for the severer the weather the greater their faith) "when I was present at one of these *duckings*, (as he termed it.) It was performed in a small but rapid river, then covered with ice, except a place cut for the purpose. The minister with his followers, advanced to the proper distance into the water: after the usual introductory prayer, being in the act of immersing the first, he accidentally lost his hold of the unfortunate person, who was in an instant carried down the stream, still running under the ice, and irrecoverably lost. The good man finding his subject gone, with a happy serenity of mind exclaimed, "The Lord hath given, the Lord hath taken away, blessed be the name of the Lord: — come another of you, my children." The remainder, astonished and confounded, lost their faith, and fled.

A third spectator declared, that one of his relations, an

elderly man, had suddenly become a frequenter of the baptist meetings, and offered himself a candidate for a place among the elect. The penance necessary to endure is severe and the probation arduous, before the repentant sinner can pass the ordeal of the ministers and elders. The old man had, it seems, obtained the blessed sanction, and a distant day was appointed for his regeneration by baptism. Upon reflection, finding that it would happen in the greatest severity of winter, at the next meeting he petitioned that the ceremony might take place in warmer weather; alledging that it would certainly prove his death to be put under water in time of frost and snow. The congregation murmured, while the priest, without a reply, read his sentence of excommunication, with the most severe anathemas on his head as an unbeliever, possessing neither faith nor the holy spirit; and never could he recover the effects of his indiscretion, or be again admitted into the number of the elect.

The methodists assemble in the summer season in surprising numbers, in different parts of the United States. These are called camp-meetings,[4] and converts will travel to attend them several hundred miles. A place is fixed upon at a convocation of the preachers, at which their bishop sometimes presides, and a distant time appointed for these meeting, which also draw together the neighboring inhabitants for a considerable distance from motives of curiosity. They sometimes continue during a fortnight, and this time is passed in the field, in prayer. They bring with them provisions, tents, or blankets, and support the numerous body of preachers, who continue bawling to the people in turns, day and night. When signs of conversion begin to be manifest, several preachers crowd round the object, exhorting a continuance of the efforts of the spirit, and displaying, in the most frightful images the horrors which attend such as do not come unto them. The signs of regeneration are displayed in the most extravagant symptoms. I have seen women jumping, striking, and kicking, like raving maniacs; while the surrounding believers could not keep them in postures of decency. This continues till the convert is entirely exhausted; but they consider the greater the resistance the more the faith; and thus they are admitted in what they term the *society*. The men under the agony of conversion, find it sufficient to express their contrition by loud groans, with hands clasped and eyes closed.* The following is an exact copy of an advertisement of a camp-meeting, taken from a newspaper printed, at Trenton, in New Jersey:

CAMP-MEETING

THE public is hereby informed, that a Camp-Meeting will be held near Mr. Minard Farley's, in a grove, about a quarter of a mile from New Germantown, in Hunterdon County. To commence on Saturday, the 29th of September, and to continue three days, under the superintendence of the ministers of the methodist church.

As camp-meetings are generally attended by several thousands from far and near, and commonly continue day and night, it will be best for those who may come a distance to bring provision for themselves and horses if possible, and to tarry on the ground till the meeting ends.

All friendly ministers and praying people are invited to attend said meeting.

THOMAS WARE,
JOSEPH TOTTEN.

Trenton, Sept. 10, 1804.

* That such things should take place even in America, excited in me a considerable degree of astonishment. But who would expect to find extravagancies equally ludicrous practised in this enlightened age in South Britain! In the Gentleman's Magazine for Dec. 1806, I find the following passage:[5]

"In a town called Bala, in North Wales, there is a sect of enthusiasts called *Jumpers,* who assemble together once every year to the amount of four or five thousand persons; when, after being inflamed almost to madness by venting their fanatical doctrines, they begin to groan, and howl, and foam at the mouth, and then jump violently about, and struggle with each other till they are quite spent and exhausted, and obliged to be carried home to their lodgings to recover their strength for the next day, when the same frantic scene, and savage cries, and extravagant gesticulations, and jumpings are repeated."

NOTES — CHAPTER XI

1. An act which directed the selling of the glebe lands of the church was passed on January 12, 1802. See *Statutes at Large of Virginia from October, Session 1792 to December 1806*, edited by Samuel Shepherd. **II.**

2. In his *History of North Carolina*, Samuel A. Ashe states that the condition of religion in the sparcely inhabited settlements was deplorable. Paine's writings were widely read, and the French Revolution influenced the people to a considerable degree. Dr. Caldwell, President of the University, wrote in 1797: "In North Carolina, particularly in that part that lies east of us, every one believes that the first step he ought to take to rise into respectability is to disavow, as often and as publicly as he can, all regard for the leading doctrines of the scriptures." This statement is surely somewhat overdrawn, but it gives expression to the prevailing tone of that society. The camp meetings in 1801 and after that time modified the attitude toward religion.

3. Shakers is the name often applied to the United Society of True Believers in Christ's Second Appearing. The designation originated in the somewhat violent and irregular motions once a part of their worship. Ann Lee (or Lees), founder of the Shakers in America, was born in Manchester, England, on February 29, 1736. The daughter of a blacksmith, she was sent to work when young, and she never learned to read nor write. In 1758 she joined the society called Shaking Quakers or Shakers, founded in Manchester eleven years before as a result of a revival conducted by exiled Camisards. In 1762 she married Abraham Standerin, known in Shaker history as Stanley or Standley. After losing four children in infancy, she became morose and obsessed with repugnance against marriage. In 1770, imprisoned for profanation of the Sabbath, she received such an extraordinary illumination of the "mystery of iniquity, of the root and foundation of human depravity" she became the acknowledged leader of the Society, and was called Ann the Word or Mother Ann. A vision in 1774 directed her to America. She, her husband, her brother, William Lee, and a few others went to New York, where she remained until 1776. Then she joined her brother at Watervliet, near Albany, where they founded the first Shaker settlement in America. Before Ann's death in 1784 two new communities were founded, one at Hancock, and another at Mount Lebanon. There also were scattered groups in New England.

4. The great period for the Camp Meeting in the west began about 1800. These meetings were not confined to the Methodists; Presbyterians and Baptists also participated as well as other smaller sects. They were accompanied by many emotional exercises, and resulted in an increase in church membership as well as in schisms in some denominations. Many sources describe these gatherings. William Speer, *The Great Revival of 1800;* Catherine C. Cleveland, *The Great Revival in the West, 1797-1805;* J. R. Rogers, *The Cane Ridge Meeting House;* William W. Sweet, *Circuit Rider Days in Indiana;* and Richard McNemar, *The Kentucky Revival* are among the most interesting and authentic sources.

5. *Gentleman's Magazine*, LXXVI, pt. 2 (1806), 1091. From an article in reply to criticism of the Bishop of London for not suppressing the Methodists.

CHAPTER XII

AMERICAN PUBLIC CHARACTERS, LIVING OR RECENTLY DECEASED

GENERAL GATES — GENERAL HAMILTON — COLONEL BURR — GENERAL PINCKNEY — GENERAL PUTNAM — MR. ALBERT GALLATIN — MR. JOHN RANDOLPH — MR. LEVI LINCOLN — LORD FAIRFAX — SIR JOHN OLDMIXON — THOMAS LAW, ESQ. — PAUL JONES — CAPTAIN HACKER CAPTAIN PETER LANDOIS — GENERAL ARNOLD.

THE avidity with which the particulars of the lives of conspicuous characters are, in general, perused by the public, has induced me to devote a portion of my work to the subject of American biography. Presuming that it will not prove uninteresting to the majority of my readers, I shall not apologize for the length of this chapter. To many, perhaps, it may appear too short. Some may be inclined to find fault with the omission of such names as Washington, Adams, and Jefferson; and to these I would say, that I was more solicitous to collect facts which are not universally known in this country, than to repeat what every individual must already be acquainted with. This being premised, I shall now proceed.

GENERAL GATES

This venerable officer paid the debt of nature on the 10th of March, 1806, full of honors, and greatly lamented in America. He had attained the seventy-eighth year of his age, and, like his great commander, Washington, passed the winter of his life in retirement on his estate.

General Horatio Gates[1] was by birth an Englishman, and when very young, entered into the British army, where he acquired his first knowledge of military tactics under the late Duke of Brunswick, at that time Prince Ferdinand. He went to America as captain of infantry under General Braddock, and continued in that service till the peace of 1763, when he returned to his native country. It appears that during this time he had imbibed so great a partiality for the new world, that he sold his commission, and purchased an estate in the colony of Virginia, where he resided till the breaking out of the unfortunate war, and upon that event he joined the standard of his adopted country. The qualifications he possessed gained him so rapid a promotion, that he was appointed commander in chief of the Northern American army; and in this situation he obtained distinguished celebrity by the capture of General Burgoyne, and the English army under his command.

His humanity to his captives was equal to his success; and the attention he shewed to Lady Harriet Acland[2] will ever render his name respected in England. The complicated distresses, the extraordinary fatigues, and the heroic resolution of that amiable lady, were subjects of astonishment to the contending armies. The particulars of her adventures were given in the publications of that day. Thirty years having, however, elapsed since the fatal turn of this conflict, and her history being in some measure connected with that of her generous enemy, a brief sketch of it will give the reader, then unborn, some idea of the miseries attending that unnatural war.

In the year 1775, the regiment of which John Dyke Acland, esq. of Devonshire, was major, was ordered on the American station and his wife, Lady Harriet Acland, determined to accompany him. This resolution was not to be shaken by any intreaties to relinquish so dangerous a project; and in the beginning of the ensuing year she was in Canada, where, during the first campaign, she traversed a vast extent of country, in different extremes of the season; encountering difficulties that an European traveller will not easily conceive, for the purpose of attending the major, who was confined by sickness in a wretched hut in Chamblee.

On the opening of the campaign of 1777, she was restrained from offering to share the fatigue and hazard expected before Ticonderoga, by the positive injunctions of her husband. The day after the conquest of that place, he was badly wounded, and she crossed the lake Champlain to join him.

As soon as he recovered, Lady Harriet insisted on following his fortunes through the campaign. The artificers of the artillery, for this purpose made her a two-wheeled tumbril. Major Acland commanded the grenadiers, who were always the advanced post of the army. From their situation, these troops were obliged to be so often on the alert, that none of them slept out of their clothes. In one of these positions, a tent, in which the major and Lady Harriet were asleep, suddenly took fire. An orderly serjeant of grenadiers, with great hazard of suffocation, dragged out the first person he laid hold of. It proved to be the major. At the same instant his wife, unconscious of what she did, and perhaps not perfectly awake, providentially made her escape by creeping under the walls of the back part of the tent. The first object she beheld on the recovery of her senses, was the major on the other side, and in the same instant again in the fire in search of her. The serjeant once more saved him, but not before the major was very severely burned in the face and different parts of the body. Everything they had with them in the tent was consumed.

This misfortune befel them shortly before the army passed Hudson's River. It neither altered the resolution nor the cheerfulness of Lady Harriet; and she continued her progress, sharing on every occasion the fatigues of the advanced corps. The next trial of her fortitude was of a different, nature, and more distressing, as it was of longer duration. On the march of the 19th of September, the grenadiers became liable to the hazards of an action at every step. She had been directed by the major to follow the route of the artillery and baggage, which was not exposed. At the commencement of the action she found herself near a small, uninhabitated hut, where she alighted. When the engagement was becoming general and bloody, the surgeons of the hospital took possession of the same place, as the most convenient for the care of the wounded. Thus was this lady in hearing of one continual fire of cannon and musquetry for four hours together, with the presumption, from the post of her husband at the head of the grenadiers, that he was in the most exposed part of the action. She had here three female companions, the Baroness of Riedesel, and the wives of Major Harnage and Lieutenant Reynell. Major Harnage was soon brought to the surgeons, very badly wounded; and a little afterwards came intelligence that Lieutenant Reynell was shot dead. Imagination can scarcely conceive the state of the whole group.

From the date of that action to the 7th of October, Lady Harriet stood prepared for new trials, and it was her lot that their severity should increase with their number. She was again exposed to the hearing of the whole action, and at last received the shock of her individual misfortune, mixed with the intelligence of the general calamity, that the troops were defeated, and that Major Acland, desperately wounded, was a prisoner. The 8th was passed by Lady Harriet and her companions in inexpressible anxiety — not a shed, not a tent was standing, except what belonged to the hospital; their refuge was among the wounded and dying. The army retreated that night, and at break of day on the 9th, reached very advantageous ground. A halt was necessary, to refresh the troops, and to give time to the batteaux, laden with provisions, to come abreast.

When the army was on the point of moving, Lady Harriet sent a message to General Burgoyne, proposing to pass to the camp of the enemy, and request General Gates's permission to attend her wounded husband. General Burgoyne was astonished at the proposal. That a woman, after so long an agitation of the spirits, exhausted, not only for want of rest, but absolutely for want of food, drenched in rains for twelve hours together, should be capable of delivering herself up to the enemy, probably in the night, and uncertain into what hands she might fall, appeared to him an effort too great for human nature. The assistance which he could render her was small indeed; he had not even a cup of wine to offer her. All that he could furnish was an open boat, and a few lines, written upon dirty and wet paper, to General Gates, recommending her to his protection.

Mr. Brudenell, the chaplain to the artillery, readily undertook to accompany her, and with one female servant, and the major's valet-de-chambre, who then had in his shoulder a ball received in the late action, she was rowed down the river to meet the enemy. But her distresses were not at an end. The night was advanced before the boat reached their out-posts, and the centinel refused to let it pass, or even to come on shore. In vain Mr. Brudenell offered the flag of truce, and represented the state of the extraordinary passenger. The guard, apprehensive of treachery, and punctilious to his orders, threatened to fire into the boat if it stirred before day-light.

Here then behold a delicate female, who had all her life been a stranger to bodily hardship of every kind, who had never known the want of any of those indulgences that are usually enjoyed by the daughters of affluence — behold her, destitute of every earthly comfort and convenience, exposed, for seven or eight dismal hours, in an open boat, beneath an inclement American sky, to the accumulated horrors of the most cruel anxiety, of darkness, hunger, rain, cold, and fatigue! Say then, ye beauties whose presence gladdens the crowded assemblies of this brilliant metropolis, ye gay votaries of dissipation, who know no fatigue but what ye experience in devising new pleasures; whose keenest disappointments proceed from the negligence of your milliner, jeweller, or coach-maker; who are strangers to vexation, save that which ye feel when eclipsed by some more ingenious fair one in the vanities and elegancies of fashion; — which of you could renounce the allurements of the great world; which of you could resolve to encounter all the distresses incident to a military life, purely from motives of affection to the man of your choice? Few, very few, I fear, would be found among you to imitate the example of the virtuous and heroic Lady Harriet Acland!

The reflections of that lady during so long an interval of painful suspense, could not inspire her with very encouraging ideas of the treatment she was afterwards to expect.

Morning arrived, and General Gates being apprised of her situation, sent instant orders to conduct the fair sufferer to his quarters, where he set before her every refreshment which he could procure, lamented that he had not been informed of the conduct of the sentinel, and treated her with all the humanity and respect that her rank and her merits deserved. She was then conducted to her husband, who, through her tender care, recovered from his wounds.

It was not many days after this, that General Burgoyne's whole army, worn out with fatigue, destitute of provisions, and greatly reduced by losses, were compelled to capitulate. The British officers bore testimony to General Gates's moderation and humanity on this occasion. He endeavored to sooth the distress of mind in which the circumstance involved his adverse commander, and sought, by every possible means, to render his situation and that of his officers less irksome.

Having conquered in the north, General Gates was invested by congress with the command of their southern army; but there fortune did not second his exertions. He was defeated in his turn by Lord Cornwallis, who thus, for a time, subdued the Carolinas. Being superseded by General Greene, he retired to his estate in Virginia, quitting "the trade of arms," perhaps not altogether without disgust at the manner in which congress deprived him of his command. I have conversed on the subject of this his last engagement with American officers, who agreed that no blame could attach to their commander, whose orders were to check the rapid progress of the British force, superior to his own, both in number and appointment.

The private virtues of General Gates were many and eminent. He was charitable — humane — just in all his dealings — inflexible in his friendship — and ever acted under the impulse of a good heart. He was the scholar, the soldier, and the gentleman.

GENERAL HAMILTON

The talents and integrity of the much-lamented Alexander Hamilton[3] raised him to an estimation which no man, Washington excepted, has obtained in America since the revolution. He was descended from a respectable Scotch family, but was born in the West Indies, and came into the British colony of New York at the age of sixteen.* Early in life he displayed a taste for literature, and, on his arrival, entered upon a course of studies with such assiduity, that, at the age of nineteen, he was qualified to take the degree of Bachelor of Arts, in the college of New York, and to lay a foundation, by preparatory reading, for the future profession of the law. About this time, the American revolution caused him to exchange his pen for the sword, and his principles induced him to join the American army, which he entered as a captain of artillery. His abilities soon attracted the notice of General Washington, who appointed him his aid-de-camp. In this situation Mr. Hamilton served until the peace. Though his appointment impeded his promotion, yet the

* His grandfather was Alexander Hamilton, of Grange in Ayrshire, who married Elizabeth Pollock, daughter of Robert Pollock of Renfrewshire, by whom he had a numerous family. James Hamilton, father of the subject of this sketch, was the fourth son of Alexander, and went to the West Indies, where he was born, in the Island of St. Vincent. His mother was an American lady, and to her friends the youth was sent, as related above.

gratification of possessing the confidence of the commander-in-chief was greater than the acquirement of rank.

Mr. Cobbett, speaking of General Hamilton, says, "that he entered into the American army at a very early period of the contest, and was soon distinguished for his discretion and his valor. His high reputation for both procured him the post of aid-de-camp to General Washington, whose fame is perhaps more indebted to Mr. Hamilton than any other intrinsic merit of his own.

"In the history of the war, we find Mr. Hamilton rising from rank to rank, till, at the siege of York Town, we see him a colonel, commanding the attack of one of the redoubts, the capture of which decided the fate of Lord Cornwallis and his army. Mr. Hamilton's conduct on this occasion was such as marks the true hero. Previously to the attack being made, La Fayette, who was high in command in the American army, proposed to Washington to put to death all the British officers and soldiers that should be taken in the redoubts. Washington replied, 'that as the marquis had the chief command of the assault, he might do as he pleased.'* This answer encouraged the base and vindictive Frenchman to give a positive order to Colonel Hamilton to execute his bloody intention. After the redoubts were subdued, La Fayette asked why his order had not been obeyed, to which the gallant and humane Hamilton replied, 'that the Americans knew how to *fight*, but not to *murder;*' in which sentiment he was joined by the American soldiers, who heard the remonstrance of La Fayette with indignation and abhorrence."

Mr. Cobbett refers the reader, for a detail of these facts, to the American account of the revolutionary war, published by Dobson of Philadelphia, and inserted in the American edition of the Encyclopædia Britannica.

On the peace, the legislature of the state of New York

* If this statement be correct, such compliance must be a great drawback in the public opinion from the fame of General Washington.

appointed this officer one of their representatives in congress. He now settled in the city of New York, and commenced the practice of the law with great ability and reputation, when he was again reluctantly drawn into public life. He became a member of the convention which framed the present constitution of the United States, and having taken part in that measure he considered himself under an obligation to lend his utmost aid to set the machine in motion.

General Washington was unanimously called upon by his country to exert his talents in the cabinet, and accepted the troublesome office of President. Here, as in the field of battle, he summoned the aid of Hamilton, whom he appointed Secretary of the Treasury. Though qualified for this situation by the most eminent abilities, yet neither he nor the President could escape the shafts of calumny. He met with many intrinsic difficulties, and many artificial obstacles, engendered by passions not very commendable, and which act with the greatest force in republics. He raised his country to a commercial rank among distant nations, by establishing public credit, and introducing order into the finances. Public offices need not to be eagerly sought in the United States. The income of Mr. Hamilton at this time was scarcely a thousand pounds sterling per annum, a sum inadequate to defray the expenses attending an office of such importance. The love of his country superseded all other considerations: from this motive he relinquished his practice at the bar, which would infallibly have led to affluence. Having established a regular system of finance, the consideration of an increasing family determined him, as soon as his plans were matured, to withdraw from office.

Accordingly, in the year 1795, Mr. Hamilton resigned his office of Secretary of the Treasury, with a reputation high in the estimation of every friend to his country; yet under the opprobrious slander of the French faction, which at that time was at the zenith of its influence.

During his services in the army, he became acquainted

with the amiable family of General Schuyler, and married his second daughter, by whom he had several children. To his abilities alone he was indebted for his rank and eminence, and early in life were they displayed. On the breaking out of the war, when he was not eighteen years of age, his juvenile pen asserted the claims of the colonies, against the political writers in favor of the British government. The unknown author was sought after, and for some time his performances were imputed to Mr. Jay, since chief justice, and ambassador to the court of London. The truth could not long be concealed, and it was discovered that in her rank of sage advocates and patriots, was a youth whose pen gained more partizans than their ablest leader. In General Washington's family, he had opportunities of studying one from whom no other man was too great to learn — of analyzing those qualities which were combined in his character, and of improving his own exalted mind, by an unrestrained intercourse with the magnanimous chief.

When he retired from office, in the duties of which he had expended a considerable portion of his private fortune, the idols of faction actually accused him of purloining the public money. This will no longer remain a matter of surprise, when it is known that Duane, an Irishman, and printer of a daily Philadelphia newspaper, styled the virtuous Washington *the man who is the source of all misfortunes to the country*, (the United States); and that Callender, who fled from justice from his native country, Scotland, in his book entitled "The Prospect before us," denominated President Adams *a hoary-headed incendiary — the scourge, the scorn, the outcast of society*. This is what republicans call the liberty of the press!

The cause which led to the catastrophe that terminated in the death of General Hamilton, was of a political nature. It appears that some officious partisan had asserted that Hamilton had, in a conversation, said of Colonel Burr, then Vice-President of the United States, a man of a violent character, and opposite to him in opinion, "that he was a dangerous person, and not to be trusted." In answer to the colonel's application by letter to be informed of the truth of this report, Hamilton wrote, that he had no recollection of the conversation alluded to, but if the colonel would specify any particular conversation, or state any particular words, he would immediately avow or deny them. The colonel replied, that it was not in his power to specify the particulars of the conversation, but insisted that General Hamilton should declare whether he ever had in any conversation made use of words derogatory to his character. To this demand the general replied, that he did not think himself bound to answer, but again expressed his willingness at once frankly to acknowledge or deny any particular conversation which might be specified. Burr sent a challenge: Hamilton answered, that as the court was then sitting, and his services were retained in several important causes, he could not feel himself at liberty to fight till after the court should rise; and then, first devoting a few days to the arrangement of his private affairs, he would inform him of the time and place of meeting. The general went through the business of the court, and spoke often with his usual animation in long and intricate suits. He then made his will, and the next day attended to finish some business in his office, where he gave one or more elaborate opinions in writing, and appeared in his usual good spirits. The day after, he made the fatal appointment; and on the road to the place, he declared to his second, Mr. Nathaniel Pendleton, that he should not fire at Colonel Burr, as he had not the most distant wish to kill him. His antagonist soon appeared — Burr was attended by Mr. W. P. Van Ness as his second. The place of meeting was in the state of New Jersey, which adjoins to New York.*

* Affairs of honor are generally decided in the adjoining state to that where the parties reside. This is done to evade the law, as each state being independent of the rest, the offenders, in case of the commission of the crime of murder, can only be apprehended where it was committed; and by this means, Burr escaped with impunity.

Hamilton fell without firing, lamented by every good man within the United States.

The wounded hero was carried to a boat, and landed at Greenwich, near New York, where he had ordered his carriage to wait for him, and was thence removed by his own request, to the house of his friend Mr. Bayard, where he lingered nearly two days; and having forgiven his murderer, and received the sacrament from the hands of Bishop Moore, he expired without a groan, in the forty-eighth year of his age. His remains received all the honors which his country could bestow on the man second only to the good and great Washington.

It is usual in the United States to pronounce orations on the death of eminent men. On this melancholy occasion almost every town produced an orator. At New York, Governor Morris undertook this affecting task. He appeared upon a temporary stage in the church where lay the body, and in front of the pulpit, attended by four sons of the deceased.* The scene was most affecting. Grief choaked the voice of the orator when he began, while an immense crowd were bathed in tears of unfeigned sorrow.

The British frigate Boston, lying at anchor within Sandy Hook, fired minute guns all day; the French frigates off the battery had their colours half-mast high, and also fired minute guns on the occasion. The shops in the city were shut, no business was done, and all the inhabitants mourned his loss.

The coroner's jury brought in their verdict "Wilful murder against Aaron Burr, Vice-President of the United States,"

* A fatality appears to have attended this family from the abhorred practice of duelling. A short time previous to the untimely fall of the father, he had to mourn the loss of his eldest son Philip Hamilton. This youth was engaged in a political dispute, and had fought once without receiving injury; but such was the height of party animosity, that he was called out a second time, and notwithstanding the father's interference in order to bring about an accommodation, he went out and was killed. The situation of her, who, by the same cause, untimely lost a husband and a son, is truly pitiable!

and a warrant was issued for his apprehension. He, however, chose to insure his safety by flight.

I cannot take leave of the lamented subject of the preceding pages without introducing the following eulogy on his character, which formed part of the funeral oration pronounced by Mr. Otis of Boston. At the same time that it does justice to the memory of General Hamilton, it will afford the English reader a very favorable specimen of American eloquence:

The principles, says Mr. Otis, professed by the first leaders of the French revolution, were so congenial to those of the American people; their pretences of aiming merely at the reformation of abuses were so plausible; the spectacle of a great people struggling to recover their "long-lost liberties," were so imposing and august; while that of a combination of tyrants to conquer and subjugate, was so revolting; the services received from one of the belligerent powers, and the injuries inflicted by the other, were so recent in our minds, that the sensibility of the nation was excited to the most exquisite pitch. To this disposition, so favorable to the wishes of France, every appeal was made which intrigue, corruption, flattery, and threats, could dictate. At this dangerous and dazzling crisis, there were but few men entirely exempt from the general delirium. Among the few was Hamilton. His penetrating eye discerned, and his prophetic voice foretold, the tendency and consequence of the first revolutionary movements. He was assured that every people which should espouse the cause of France would pass under her yoke, and that the people of France, like every nation which surrenders its reason to the mercy of demagogues, would be driven by the storms of anarchy upon the shores of despotism. All this he knew was conformable to the invariable law of nature, and experience of mankind. From the reach of this desolation he was anxious to save his country, and, in the pursuit of his purpose, he breasted the assaults of calumny and prejudice. "The torrent roared, and he did buffet it." Appreciating the advantages of a neutral position, he cooperated with Washington, Adams, and the other patriots of that day, in the means best adapted to maintain it. The rights and duties of neutrality proclaimed by the President, were explained and enforced by Hamilton in the character of Pacificus. The attempts to corrupt and intimidate were resisted. The British treaty was justified and defended as an honourable compact with our natural friends, and pregnant with advantages, which have since been realized and acknowledged by its opponents.

By this pacific and vigorous policy, in the whole course of which the genius and activity of Hamilton were conspicuous, time and information were afforded to the American nation, and correct views were acquired of our situation and interests. We beheld the republics of Europe march in procession to the funeral of their own liberties, by the lurid light of the revolutionary torch. The tumult of the passions subsided, the wisdom of the administration was perceived, and America now remains a solitary monument in the desolated plains of liberty.

Having remained at the head of the treasury several years, and filled its coffers; having developed the sources of an ample revenue, and tested the advantages of his own system by his own experience; and having expended his private fortune; he found it necessary to retire from public employment, and devote his attention to the claims of a large and dear family. What brighter instance of disinterested honor has ever been exhibited to an admiring world! That a man upon whom devolved the task of originating a system of revenue for a nation; of devising the checks in his own department; of providing for the collection of sums, the amount of which was conjectural; that a man who anticipated the effects of a funding system, yet a secret in his own bosom, and who was thus enabled to have secured a princely fortune consistently with principles esteemed fair by the world; that such a man by no means addicted to an expensive or extravagant style of living, should have retired from office destitute of means adequate to the wants of mediocrity, and have resorted to professional labor for the means of decent support, are facts which must instruct and astonish those who, in countries habituated to corruption and venality, are more attentive to the gains than to the duties of official station. — Yet Hamilton was that man. It was a fact always known to his friends, and it is now evident from his testament, made under a deep presentiment of his approaching fate. Blush then, ministers and warriors of imperial France, who have deluded your nation by pretensions to a disinterested regard for its liberties and rights! Disgorge the riches extorted from your fellow-citizens and the spoils amassed from confiscation and blood! Restore to impoverished nations the price paid by them for the privilege of slavery, and now appropriated to the refinements of luxury and corruption! Approach the tomb of Hamilton, and compare the insignificence of your gorgeous palaces with the awful majesty of this tenement of clay!

We again accompany our friend in the walks of private life, and in the assiduous pursuit of his profession, until the aggressions of France compelled the nation to assume the attitude of defence. He was now invited by the great and enlightened statesman who had succeeded to the presidency, and at the express request of the commander-in-chief, to accept of the second rank in the army. Though no man had manifested a greater desire to avoid war, yet it is freely confessed that when war appeared to be inevitable, his heart exulted in "the tented field," and he loved the life and occupation of a soldier. His early habits were formed amid the fascinations of the camp. And though the pacific policy of Adams once more rescued us from war, and shortened the existence of the army establishment, yet it is sufficient to secure to him the love and confidence of officers and men, to enable him to display the talents and qualities of a great general, and to justify the most favorable prognostics of his prowess in the field.

Once more this excellent man unloosed the helmet from his brow, and returned to the duties of the forum. From this time he persisted in a firm resolution to decline all civil honors and promotion, and to live a private citizen, unless again summoned to the defence of his country. He became more than ever assiduous in his practice at the bar, and intent upon his plans of domestic happiness, until a nice and mistaken estimate of the claims of honor, impelled him to the fatal act which terminated his life.

COLONEL AARON BURR,

LATE VICE-PRESIDENT OF THE UNITED STATES.

This man has rendered himself more conspicuous by the fatal duel in which General Hamilton fell by his hand, than by a long reign as a leader of the democracy which still rules the United States of America.

On the election of a president and a vice-president, Colonel Burr[4] had an equal number of votes with Jefferson, for the office of chief magistrate. The house of representatives, by the law as it then stood, were, in such case, to decide by ballot which of the candidates should be president, and the other was of course to be vice-president. This business took up more than a week, and the house sometimes continued ballotting during the night. It was carried on with the greatest obstinacy by the contending parties; members were brought to vote, from the bed of sickness, and it was even feared that there would be no election, which, leaving the country without a president, at such a period of political animosity, could not fail of being attended with fatal consequences. The democratic party proceeded to threats, but the Federals were not to be intimidated. Mr. Adams, the late president, and Mr. Pinckney, the candidates proposed by them, having lost the election, the Federal party were left to choose one of the Democratic candidates who had been successful. They preferred Burr to Jefferson, which gained the former the greatest number of individual votes in the house of representatives. A majority of the states was, however, required, to determine the matter: of these Jefferson had eight, namely, New York, New Jersey, Pennsylvania, Virginia, North Carolina, Georgia, Kentucky, and Tennessee. The states that voted for Burr were, New Hampshire, Massachusetts, Connecticut, Rhode Island, Delaware, and South Carolina. During this singular contest, the votes of the members of the house of representatives were, for Burr 54, and for Jefferson 51. Two states, Vermont and Maryland, were divided and it therefore became necessary that a member for one of these states should recede, in order to put a stop to the approaching scene of anarchy and confusion. This expedient was actually resorted to; Jefferson thus acquired a majority, and the impending political tempest was averted.

The division on this important occasion tends to confirm

the opinion I have already expressed relative to a future separation of the American states. We here find those of New England unanimously voting the same way, except Vermont, which was divided, and in direct opposition to all the southern states, save South Carolina, which, with Delaware, were with the Federal interest.

In order to prevent a similar election, but more, as the Federals say, to secure Mr. Jefferson's re-election at the expiration of four years, a law was passed, by which the electors are to designate by name, in their tickets, the person for whom they vote, as president, and in like manner for vice-president. By the former mode the man who had the greatest number of votes was president, and the next vice-president — the Federals supporting one party, and the Democrats another.

The two presidential chairs were taken without farther resistance, and Colonel Burr attended in his seat as president of the senate, generally about one half of the sessions. The inutility of this office has long been a subject of private discussion and complaint, and many consider it little more than a sinecure, except that in case of the death or removal of the chief magistrate the vice-president officiates till the time arrives for another election. In his absence the senators elect one of their own body president *pro tempore*, and they went more smoothly through their business when Colonel Burr was away.

Vanity is a predominant passion in this gentleman. I was informed by Mrs. Slacum, of Alexandria, who attended the balls given at Washington during the sitting of congress, that she saw the vice-president at one of them, though he seldom appeared at these assemblies. Being asked by a lady of his acquaintance why he did not oftener favor them with his company, he replied, "that he saw his presence awed the company, and he did not wish to be a restraint upon them." This was long the tea-table chat; when the ladies turned up their noses at the idea of being struck with awe at the sight of so insignificant a being as Burr. The colonel is certainly rather diminutive in person, but his ambition is great indeed.

On the subject of these balls, I was informed by the same lady, that our fair coutrywoman, Mrs. Merry, wife of the British ambassador, offended the American dames. They charged her with great reserve, which they termed English *hauteur*, and asserted that on entering the room, she walked round it, chatted a little with the diplomatic characters, or the ministers of state, and then retired. Such was the ground on which they founded their dislike. They were offended because she did not join in their dances, and skip through their reels with them. The lady's dress was called in question, on which, craving a truce, I took the hint of the subject of their comments, and walked off.

Mr. Burr, more terrified at the popular clamor against him, than alarmed at the verdict of the coroner's jury after his affair with General Hamilton, privately left the city of New York, and passing into the state of New Jersey, where the duel was fought, he was conducted by a friend to Cranberry. Hence he was conveyed in a light waggon to Lamberton Ferry, where he crossed the Delaware, and arrived at Bristol, about twenty miles from Philadelphia. A newspaper printed in one of the towns through which he passed, observes, "the same route through Jersey was some time ago pursued by Thomas Paine, and doubtless with the same view, to escape the scrutinizing eye and dreaded observation of the public."

It was said that at a tavern a few miles beyond the Delaware, he was recognized by the landlord, who, unapprised of his wish to be concealed, addressed him as usual; and that the *vice-president* requested him not to use his name while he remained at his house.

"How degrading," continues the editor of the same paper, "to the majesty of our government, that its second officer should thus be under the real or fancied necessity of travelling with studied privacy, through bye-roads, and in unusual vehicles. It becomes the man, however, who has extinguished the bright constellation of genius and worth, himself to walk in darkness and obscurity. It manifests some deference to public opinion and the energy of the laws."

Mr. Burr proceeded to Philadelphia, and excited much private indignation by a public appearance; but though not pursued by the arm of justice, his situation could not be agreeable, for we soon find him in the state of Tennessee.[5] There he was a land-holder, and he took this memorable occasion to visit his possessions, which also afforded him a safe retreat; the victim of his resentment being little known in that part of the Union.

In this retirement he was still vice-president, and it is no less surprising than true, that pending his recent violation of the law, and though the warrant of one of the federate states was in force to apprehend him, he still exercised the functions of that office. I saw him repeatedly sit in the vice-presidential chair, without any other notice than the whispers of resentment among the auditors in the galleries of the senate-chamber. He presided during the whole trial of the learned and persecuted Judge Chace. "The guilty sits in judgment on the innocent." — "The fugitive from his country, arraigns at the bar of justice the judge himself." Such were the comments I frequently heard among the auditors during the proceedings of that impeachment. The venerable federal magistrate, called to the superior bench of justice by Washington, was by a democratic senate honorably — most honorably acquitted.

For upwards of two years after the unfortunate recontre with General Hamilton, did Mr. Burr execute the office of vice-president of the United States; and not until the expiration of the time for which he was elected did he retire into obscurity. He returned to Tennessee; but as these sheets went to press, accounts have been received of his being there apprehended on a charge of attempting a revolution, in order to separate the western territory from the federal union.

It appears that Mr. Davies, attorney-general for the district of Kentucky, on his own affidavit, moved the district court of the United States, "that Aaron Burr should be arrested and compelled to find security for his appearance; and that a writ should be issued for compelling the attendance of witnesses, and a stop be put to all further proceedings of the said Aaron Burr." The affidavit of the attorney-general filed in court stated: —

That he was in possession of the most satisfactory evidence, that Aaron Burr, Esquire, had formed an association for making war against Spain, invading Mexico, and forming a distant empire in the western country; and that he was raising forces, and purchasing the necessary provisions and stores for that purpose.

The latest accounts received from America respecting this character, say, that when General Eaton was at Washington last winter, he was introduced to Colonel Burr, who was then at the seat of government. Having heard the bold, adventurous, and enterprising character of this hero: believing him to be a mere soldier of fortune, and that, like himself, he was ready to engage in any cause, either good or bad, which promised a harvest of military glory, Burr proposed to him that he should join his desperate fortunes — go with him to the Mississipi — take the rank of a general-officer under him as commander-in-chief — erect the standard of rebellion against the government of the United States — sever the union — and establish a distinct and independent government, to be composed of all the states west of the Alleghany Mountains.

Such was the general project, the minute details of which were particularly stated. General Eaton was struck with horror, and stood aghast at the proposal. He soon afterwards, in the true spirit of patriotism, communicated the conversation to the president of the United States, who treated it with perfect indifference. Recent occurrences in the western territory, such as the building of boats on the Ohio, and a variety of movements, indicating a spirit of revolt, have drawn the attention of the government to that quarter of the union.

Other accounts state that Colonel Burr has come forward and surrendered himself, but that the attorney-general of the district of Kentucky has declined to prosecute. In addition to this, a Pennsylvanian newspaper of the 5th of December, 1806, informs us, that about three hundred young gentlemen from Pittsburgh and the neighbouring counties, some of whom are of the first respectability, had the week before descended the Ohio, to join, it was supposed, the expedition under Colonel Burr. The measure is represented as very popular in that country; and it was imagined that the general rendezvous for persons residing in the western countries, would be at Natchez.

Though this is the precise statement of the American prints yet the truth of it appears extremely doubtful.

GENERAL CHARLES COTESWORTH PINCKNEY

This gentleman, a character eminently distinguished in America, who took an active part in the revolutionary war, and has since been employed in a diplomatic capacity in France and Spain, was supported by the Federalists at the last election for president, in opposition to Mr. Jefferson.

South Carolina is the native country, and still the residence of General Pinckney.[6] He was born in the year 1740. When that state was a British colony, his father was the chief justice until the commencement of the war. At this momentous period, when the best men knew not which part to take, or by what means to avoid engaging in the dangerous and destructive contest, the family of the Pinckneys at length determined to join those who were opposed to the measures of their mother-country. Mr. Pinckney was then a member of the general assembly of South Carolina, which situation he resigned in order to join the American standard. He first entered the ranks as one of the Charleston volunteers, from which he was appointed major of the first regiment of the line raised by the state of South Carolina, under the command of Colonel Gadsden; on whose promotion he succeeded to the command. The first engagement in which this regiment took part, was in the defence of Fort Moultrie, which was attacked by Sir Peter Parker and General Clinton. The gallant conduct of Colonel Pinckney was so much approved by the commander-in-chief, General Washington, that he appointed him one of his aids-de-camp, in which situation he served at the battles of Brandy-wine and German-town.

The southern states being again attacked by the British forces, Colonel Pinckney obtained leave to return to his native country, and he accordingly resumed the command of his regiment, at the head of which he made an assault on Savannah; and shortly after he was appointed by General Lincoln, commander of Fort Moultrie.

Charleston being now besieged by land, and bombarded by a part of the British fleet, the colonel's regiment was ordered to its defence, when, after a gallant resistance, he was, with the remainder of the garrison, taken prisoner, under honorable terms of capitulation — such, in fact, as were granted to Lord Cornwallis, on his surrender to the combined armies of France and America, at York-town, in Virginia. This event appears to have terminated his military career, as he could not procure himself to be exchanged till towards the conclusion of the war.

It is with infinite regret I am obliged to state, that while Colonel Pinckney was a prisoner of his parole on honor, his enemy burnt his mansion near Charleston. With respect to such shameful and flagrant acts of cruelty to individuals, we have, however, the consolation of knowing that they were, with very few exceptions, committed by native Americans who had joined the king's forces, and were by them called Royalists, but by their enemy stigmatized with the appellation of tories.

On the conclusion of the peace, by which the independence of America was acknowledged, Mr. Pinckney was appointed a delegate to the federal convention, and signed the present constitution of the United States in the year 1788. On the score of gratitude to the French, though an impulse very different from *friendship* caused them to take the part of America, he, with many leading characters in the United States, was the avowed advocate of that nation, and so continued till their enormities changed those sentiments to the contempt and hatred of all good men. Mr. Pinckney has additional cause to despise them; for the then insolent republic refused to acknowledge him as the minister plenipotentiary at Paris.

We next find him commander in chief of the militia of South Carolina; about the same time he was offered by President Washington the office of secretary of state, on the resignation of Mr. Jefferson, and after his refusal, a seat on the bench of the supreme court, which he also declined. The aggressions of France increased to an intolerable degree. The American trade to the British West India Islands was almost ruined, and the French privateers committed depredations on their very coast. Government, still pursuing the most pacific measures, determined to send a remonstrance by a diplomatic mission, consisting of Mr. Pinckney, General Marshall, and Mr. Gerry, who to a certain degree, succeeded in the object of their voyage.

An insurrection, called the *Whisky Rebellion*,[7] having broken out in the back part of Pennsylvania, had arrived to such an alarming height, that President Adams applied to General Washington to take the command of an army raised to quell the insurgents. That great and good man had retired to the peaceful shades of Mount Vernon, having resigned his military commissions, and again become a private citizen. The venerable soldier and patriot replied, that though he had anticipated repose from worldly labors, yet, when his country called for the renewal of his services, he would cheerfully attend the summons. He accordingly again repaired to the scene of danger, appointed General Hamilton the second, and Pinckney, then a major-general, third in command. The insurrection was happily quelled without bloodshed, and the newly raised army again disembodied.

In politics, General Pinckney is unfriendly to the present system of government, acting upon the principles of his great master, Washington; and it cannot be denied that the minority contain the greatest portion of men of abilities. Among them are numbered Marshall, Morris, Dayton, Adams, Ames, Griswold, Otis, Bayard, Rutledge, Tracy, Dana, Pickering, Lee, J. C. Smith, Broom, Thatcher, Goddard, Tallmage, Hastings, Quincy, Tenney, and many others who have not lately stood forward as members of the legislative body.[8]

GENERAL PUTNAM

This officer[9] was in the British service several years previous to the conquest of Canada by General Wolfe; and in the revolutionary war, having espoused the American cause, he was promoted to the rank of major-general in their army. He was a man of undaunted courage, and of an enterprising disposition.

When the French army lay encamped at Ovens near Ticonderoga, the British commander pitched upon Putnam, who then held the rank of captain of a company, to reconnoitre the position of the enemy; Lieutenant Robert Durkee was named for his companion. The outset of this expedition had nearly proved fatal, for Captain Putnam narrowly escaped being taken prisoner; and in his flight was on the point of killing his friend.

In the Canadian wars it was customary for the British to place fires round their camp, which frequently exposed them to the enemy's scouts and patroles. The French and Indians adopted a different, and a more rational practice. They kept their fire in the centre, lodged their men circularly at a distance, and posted their centinels in the surrounding darkness. In the present instance, the reconnoitring party, on approaching, concluded that the centinels were within the circle of fires, and were creeping upon their hands and knees till, to their utter astonishment, they found themselves in the thickest of the enemy. They were discovered and fired upon; Lieutenant Durkee was slightly wounded in the thigh. They fled, and Putnam, who was first, from the utter darkness of the night, soon found himself plunging into a deep pit; and Durkee immediately tumbled in after him. Conceiving himself to be pursued by the enemy, he had already uplifted his weapon to deal a dreadful blow, when Durkee spoke, and he recognized his voice. They now scrambled out, and effected their escape amid a shower of random shot. They passed the remainder of the night in the woods, out of the reach of the enemy. Putnam had provided a little rum, which he carried in a canteen slung over his shoulder, and on lying down, recollected the supposed treasure, but to his great mortification, found the vessel empty, having been repeatedly pierced with musket balls.

Soon after this, the subject of these anecdotes was promoted to the rank of major. A strong party of observation was now ordered upon the dangerous service of watching the motions of the enemy, who lay off Ticonderoga, under the command of Majors Rogers and Putnam. This force was divided, and the commanders took different positions, but being discovered by the enemy, they again joined, and began their march in files through woods — the right led on by Rogers — the left by Putnam, and the centre by Captain D'Ell.[10] The first day they reached Clear river, on the banks of which they encamped, near Old Fort Ann, which had been formerly built by General Nicholson. Next morning, previous to quitting the ground, it is said, that Major Rogers imprudently laid a wager with one of the officers, to be decided by firing at a mark, and which was immediately determined. Major Putnam remonstrated in a very pointed manner against this unsoldier-like conduct, in the very neighbourhood of the enemy, but as Rogers commanded, he could not put a stop to their proceedings. After this, they continued their march in columns, Putnam in the front, D'Ell in the centre, and Rogers in the rear; circumstances and the nature of the ground, rendering this disposition of the force most favorable.

The French had received information of this expedition, and had sent Colonel Molong, a most active and enterprising officer, with five hundred chosen men to intercept it. He was so near, that he heard the firing at the mark; and immediately placed himself in ambush. Putnam, at the head of his column, had just cleared his way through some thick brush-wood into the more open part of the forest, where the enemy sprung upon him, with the most horrid yells and war-hoops from the Indians, who formed a part of Molong's detachment. Putnam in an instant recovered from his surprise, calmly drew up his men, and returned the fire; sending off at the same time to the other divisions to come up with all possible speed. D'Ell soon came up, and the action, though widely scattered and fought between man and man, was soon general and desperate. The contending parties adopted the Indian mode of warfare, which is irregular and ferocious; indeed their situation precluded the possibility of practising tactics. During this dreadful contest Major Rogers did not come up, assigning afterwards as a reason that he formed his men in a circular file between the other columns and Wood Creek, to prevent their being taken in the rear, or enfiladed.

Major Putnam was not disheartened. He found he could not cross the creek, and therefore determined to keep his ground; and his officers inspired by his bravery and his personal exertions, encouraged their soldiers, who defended themselves against superior numbers with the most determined resolution. Sometimes they fought in small bodies; then each man against his antagonist; and often three or four upon one, while others fired from behind trees and under cover. The commander had been from the first in the heat of the battle; and had used his fuzee so often, that it missed fire while presented to the breast of an athletic savage chief, who, taking instant advantage of the circumstance, leaped upon him, and with a war-hoop and uplifted tomahawk compelled the gallant major to surrender. The savage disarmed his prisoner, bound him to a tree, and then returned to the battle.

The command now devolved upon D'Ell, who was bravely seconded by Captain Harman; but they were soon compelled to give way, which the savages considering as a total defeat, rushed on with impetuosity, and with horrid hoopings and dreadful cries. The British troops rallied at the orders of their officers, and gave their pursuers such a reception as caused them in their turn to retreat beyond the spot on which the battle began, where they made a stand. This movement placed the tree to which Putnam was tied, between the fires of the contending parties; the balls from either side struck the tree and passed through his clothes. In this state of jeopardy, unable to move his body or stir his limbs, he remained above an hour — so equal and desperate was the fight. At one instant, when the battle inclined in favor of the enemy, a young savage chose an odd way of indulging his humor. He discovered Putnam bound, and might consequently have killed him in an instant; but he chose another way of gratifying his passion of torture. He threw his tomahawk at the prisoner's head, with a view of shewing how near he could throw it without touching it; and he struck the tree several times within the smallest distance possible of his mark. When the Indian had finished his amusement, a French serjeant, a much greater savage in his nature, came up, and levelled his musket within a foot of the major's breast, but it happily missed fire. In vain did he claim the treatment due to a prisoner of war. The degenerate Frenchman did not understand the language of honor, or the laws of nature; but deaf to their calls, he repeatedly pushed the muzzle of his gun against the ribs of the bounden man, and completed these acts of barbarity by a dreadful blow with its butt end on his jaw-bone.

The intrepidity of D'Ell and Harman,* seconded by the valor of their followers, at length prevailed. They drove the enemy from the scene of action, leaving behind their dead, who were ninety in number. As the conquered fled, the Indian who had first made Major Putnam prisoner came up, untied, and took him away. Having been conducted to some distance, he was stripped of his regimentals, stockings, and shoes, loaded with the effects of the wounded, and strongly pinioned, his wrists being drawn tight together with a cord. After being driven many miles over the roughest roads, the party, greatly fatigued, halted to breathe. The miserable prisoner was now in a dreadful state of torture. His hands, from the tightness of the ligature, were immoderately swelled; and the pain had become intolerable. His feet were scratched, bruised, and cut, and streaming with blood. The burthen imposed upon him was too heavy for his strength; and, frantic with torments, exquisite beyond endurance, he entreated them to kill him and take his scalp, or to loose his hands. A French officer instantly interposed, ordering his hands to be unbound, and some of the load taken from his back. The Indian who claimed the prisoner had been absent with the wounded, but now coming up, gave him a pair of *macasons*, and shewed great resentment at his unworthy treatment.

The duty of this chief being with the wounded, he returned, leaving the advanced party, consisting of about two hundred Indians, to go on before the French troops, and to encamp for the night. They took with them Major Putnam, on whom, besides many other outrages, they had the barbarity to inflict a large wound on his left cheek with a tomahawk. His sufferings in this place were to

* A late American publication, from which these facts are principally taken, says, that this brave officer was living at Marlborough, in the state of Massachusetts, in the year 1804.

have been consummated, and a scene of far greater horror was preparing. — The savages had determined to roast him alive; and, in pursuance of this horrid doom, they led him into a dark part of the forest, stripped him entirely naked, bound him to a tree and piled around him dry brush-wood and other fuel. They accompanied their labours by dances and the yells of death, and then set the pile on fire; but a sudden shower of rain damped the rising flame. They laboured to rekindle it, and at length it began to blaze round the circle. The victim soon felt the heat, and being able to move his body, he instinctively shifted sides as the fire advanced. This sight, at which all but savages would shudder, afforded the highest diversion to his inhuman tormentors, who demonstrated the delirium of their joy by every extravagant gesticulation.

Major Putnam, convinced that his final hour had arrived, summoned all his resolution, and composed his mind, as far as the shocking circumstances would admit, to bid an eternal adieu to all he held most dear. The bitterness of death, painful and lingering as it would be, was in a manner past — nature, with a feeble struggle, was quitting its hold of sublunary things — when a French officer rushed through the crowd, opened a way by scattering the burning brands, and unbound the victim. It was the gallant Molong, whom one of the savages, unwilling to see another human creature immolated, had made acquainted with the dreadful proceedings. The commander spurned and severely reprimanded the barbarians; and fearing to trust the major with them again, kept him in safety till he delivered him into the hands of his master, the savage chief who made him prisoner.

This providential escape will by some appear to savor of the fabulous as it did to me when I first heard it related. I took some pains to make enquiries on the subject, in passing through those places where General Putnam was personally known, and found the tale was not doubted. I also met with an old officer, Colonel Martin, of New Brunswick, who was acquainted with him, and who gave full credit to all the accounts of his sufferings and miraculous escape. He added, that the general, though arrived at that advanced period of life when men often become garrulous, generally declined a conversation on the subject.

To return to the narrative. — It appears that the savage approached his prisoner with kindness, and seemed to treat him with affection. He offered him some hard biscuits, but finding that he could not chew them, on account of the blow given him by the Frenchman, this more humane savage soaked some of them in water, and made him suck the pulp-like part.* Determined, however, not to lose his captive, the like refreshment being taken, he took the macasons from his feet, and tied them to one of his wrists; then directing him to lie down on his back, upon the bare ground, he stretched one arm to its full length, and bound it fast to young tree — the other arm was extended and bound in the same manner, and his legs were stretched apart and fastened to two saplings. Some slender branches were then laid across his body; on each side of him lay a number of Indians, to prevent the possibility of an escape; and in this disagreeable state he remained till morning. In the account given of these sufferings by the major himself, he said, that during this night, the most dreary and painful, apparently also the longest of his life, he felt a ray of cheerfulness sometimes dart across his mind, while he entertained the hope that he should yet be restored to his family. He even indulged his fancy in reflecting upon the ludicrous group around him, in which he sustained the most ridiculous part; and how fine a subject it would make for a painter.

* Though instances have occurred of some traits of humanity faintly beaming from the breasts of certain savages, yet, I cannot suppose that the chief in question was entirely moved to this act of goodness by pure philanthropy. He knew from his arms, cloathing, and accoutrements, that his prisoner was a man of rank among his enemy, and consequently expected a considerable gratuity by way of ransom; and the anxiety he shewed to prevent an escape, serves to confirm this opinion.

The next day he was allowed a blanket and a pair of macasons, and was suffered to proceed with the party without carrying a load, or receiving insult. To allay this extreme hunger a little bear's flesh was given him: this he moistened and sucked through his teeth. At night the party arrived at Ticonderoga, where the prisoner was placed under a French guard; and after having been examined by the commanding officer, the Marquis de Montcalm, he was ordered to be conducted to Montreal, whence he soon returned to the English army.

ALBERT GALLATIN

Let the declaimers against the corrupt influence sometimes employed in monarchical governments, turn their eyes to the history of Mr. Albert Gallatin — a foreigner — a traitor[11] to the country which had adopted him, now exalted to one of the highest and most important official stations in the American commonwealth!

Mr. Gallatin is a native of Geneva. He removed to America about the year 1779, and after surveying the United States in different directions, at length took up his permanent residence in the western part of Pennsylvania. Whatever doubts might have existed respecting this stranger, the time and manner of his coming into this country was certainly suspicious at least, yet no notice was taken of him by any of the leading men in America at that time; nor was it till many years afterwards that he began to attract public attention. Settled in a place where many of the inhabitants were foreigners, and most of them illiterate and lawless, Gallatin, with Findley, Breckenridge, and Bradford,[12] undertook, in 1792, to excite an opposition to the law of the general government relative to the excise. General Washington, who was then president, used every gentle means in his power to prevail on the insurgents to submit to the law, but to no purpose. Accounts were received of immense crowds of these people meeting, and resolving, in the language of rebellion, to oppose the law. Gallatin acted as clerk to these meetings, the result of which was, the destruction of some houses, and the loss of several lives. Thus then this stranger, instead of gratitude for the hospitality afforded him, reared the banners of insurrection to overturn all law and order.

The President, always anxious to spare the sufferings of deluded citizens, issued a proclamation to forgive all those who would return to their duty, and obey the law. Not one accepted his proffered mercy at this time, and it was absolutely necessary to march an army against them. Another proclamation was issued, to give them further time to repent their misconduct. And here it must be observed, that these deluded wretches were made to believe that an army would not be raised to conquer them, but that the whole United States would make *their* opposition to the laws a common cause. They were, however, soon undeceived; and it was at the period when this was ascertained that the great Mr. Gallatin (as he is called by foolish partizans) let fall all his bristled feathers, and sneaked into town to receive the benefit of the amnesty. It was not until the *last hour* of the *last day*, and of the *last proclamation*, that this man availed himself of the condition of the president's forbearance. Thus, Albert Gallatin was first a conspicuous insurgent. The resolutions published at the time with his name, and never denied, are undeniable evidences of the fact.* Another proof,

* These were to the following effect:

"At a meeting of sundry inhabitants of the Western Counties of Pennsylvania, at Pittsburg, on the 21st day of August, 1792,

Col. *John Cannon* was placed in the chair.

ALBERT GALLATIN appointed *Clerk*.

The Excise Law of Congress being taken into consideration, a committee was appointed to prepare a draught of resolutions, expressing the sense of the meeting on the subject of said law.

Adjourned to 10 o'clock to-morrow.

The committee appointed yesterday, made report, which being *twice* read, was unanimously adopted:

"And whereas some men *be* found amongst us so far lost to every sense of virtue and feeling for the distresses of this country as to accept offices for the collection of the duty:

"*Resolved therefore,* That in future we will consider such persons as unif more were wanting, is, that he came into open court, and confessed his guilt of treason by subscribing the amnesty. From that time, to the accession of Mr. Jefferson, the conduct of Gallatin was of the same complexion. He steadily opposed the measures of government, right or wrong, and had very justly become hateful to good men of all parties, who were not deceived.

Such then is the man to whom Mr. Jefferson has thought fit to delegate the important trust of Secretary of the Treasury! The office is unquestionably of more importance in the government than any below the presidency; since the whole wealth of the country is in his hands. "Through all ages of society," says an American writer on this subject, "in every civilized country, the crime of treason stands prominently infamous in the eyes of mankind. The hateful criminal is shunned. Even a *philanthropic philosopher* would hazard his reputation by shewing him any kind of respect. But alas! in this age of revolution — in these days of fatal delusion, the experience of the world for many centuries is to be forgotten and despised in the rage for change; and the fury of party! — Posterity will blush, that the same President Jefferson who delivered the liberal *and honied inaugural speech*, should, in the face of his countrymen, and contrary to every maxim of government for the peace and happiness of mankind, bestow the best offices in his gift upon foreigners, — the revilers of Washington, the calumniators of our best citizens, and the authors of insurrection!"

Previous to the election of his friend Jefferson, Gallatin found means to obtain a seat in the house of representatives,

worthy of our friendship: *Have no intercourse or dealings with them,* WITHDRAW FROM THEM EVERY ASSISTANCE, *and* WITHHOLD ALL THE COMFORTS OF LIFE, which depend upon those duties, that as men and fellow-citizens, we owe to each other, and upon all occasions treat them with the contempt they deserve, and that it be, and it is humbly, and most earnestly recommended to the people at large, to follow the same kind of conduct towards them."

(Signed) "JOHN CANNON, Chairman.
"ALBERT GALLATIN, Clerk.

and there he had an opportunity of displaying abilities, which he possesses in an eminent degree. He was for some time the leader of opposition, and though his foreign accent would often in debate render him almost unintelligible, yet his speeches were in the highest degree beneficial to his party. French politics were then in vogue, and the virtues of the sister republic were echoed through the nation. At length his party prevailed, and he obtained the summit of his wishes.

Mr. Gallatin has been charged with injustice towards General Miller,*[13] who commanded a body of troops which were ordered to quell the insurrection above alluded to. It is true that, soon after his appointment, he discharged the general from the office of Supervisor, without assigning any reason; but, in other respects, Mr. Gallatin has conducted himself with ability.

JOHN RANDOLPH

This gentleman, the ex-chancellor of Mr. Jefferson's administration,[14] has been many years a member of congress, and, until the last session, was uniformly attached to the democratic party, of which he was one of the chief supporters.

From various passages in this volume, the reader will perceive that Mr. Randolph is a man of considerable talents. Nature has, however, been niggardly to him in some respects. Though forty years of age, so juvenile is his appearance, that, the first time I saw him in his place in the house of representatives, I took him for the youthful son of one of the members, who had, for some reason, obtained permission to sit among them. He is tall, but of a slender make, of a weak habit, and, as I should judge, in a wasting consumption. He is ever complaining of indisposition, and frequently adverts to his weak state of body in his speeches, by way of asking the indulgence of the house. His voice,

* The reader will hereafter find that General Washington rewarded the services of his officers when they were disbanded after a successful war, by civil appointments.

like his person, is very effeminate, and his action ungraceful.

During the presidency of Mr. Adams, the appointment of a respectable navy was among the measures of his administration. This was opposed by the democrats, and, in a speech to the house on the question, Mr. Randolph animadverted with some asperity on the naval service. On the recent debate on the bill prohibiting the importation of English manufactures, after an interval of nearly ten years, he perseveres in this opinion. On that occasion he says, "I am averse to a naval war with any nation whatever. I was opposed to the naval war of the last administration,* and I am ready to oppose a naval war of the present administration, should they meditate such a measure. What! shall this great Mammoth of the American forest leave his native element, and plunge into the water in a mad contest with the shark? Let him beware that his proboscis is not bitten off in the engagement! † Let him stay on shore, and not be excited by the muscles and periwinkles on the strand, or political bears in a boat, to venture on the perils of the deep! Gentlemen say, — Will you not protect your violated rights? and I say, why take to water, where you can neither fight nor swim? Look at France; see her vessels stealing from port to port, on her own coast, and remember she is the first military power on earth, and as a naval power, second only to England. Take away the British navy, and France to-morrow is the tyrant of the ocean."[15]

* Mr. Adams would not suffer the French to commit depredations upon his country with impunity. He raised a respectable navy, and sent frigates to make reprisals, and to protect the commerce of the West Indies. Commodore Truxton attacked a French frigate of equal force, and took her after a well-fought engagement. The enemy was brought into a port in the United States, repaired, and put in commission by the government of the captors. She was manned, and sent upon a cruise in the same latitude where she was taken, but is supposed to have foundered, with every soul on board, no accounts having been heard of her since sailing from the United States.

† Several members proposed making war upon Great Britain; while Crowninshield, a violent democrat, from Massachusetts, was for confiscating the national debt!!!

Mr. Randolph's former speech gave great umbrage to the naval officers. He was attacked by Captain M'Knight and Lieutenant Michael Reynolds, one evening at the theatre, on the subject.[16] They did not, it is true, strike him, for a blow would, perhaps, annihilate the legislator; but they reflected upon his conduct in terms of severity. He appealed for redress by letter to the president, to whom he complained that he had been grossly and publicly insulted by several officers of the army and navy, for words of a general nature, uttered in debate; conceiving it to be an attack on his independence and rights as a legislator. The president sent a message to the house of representatives, with the letter of Mr. Randolph. The officers upon receiving notices, attended the house, and denied the allegations laid to their charge. A committee was appointed to enquire into the matter, and Mr. E. Goodrich, the chairman, reported: "that in executing the task assigned to them, it is with great pleasure they noticed the respect shewn by the president to the rights and privileges of this house, in the message he had transmitted to them. On the style of Mr. Randolph's letter to the president, they forbear to make any remark, than to express a regret that he conceived himself justified in deviating from the forms of decorum customary in official communications to the president, which they conceive so justly due to his office and character, and so essential to that harmony which should be circumspectly cherished between the different branches of the government, by its respective members — that they consider the appeal in this instance to the executive authority, however otherwise intended, as derogatory from the rights of the house, it being exclusively cognizable by them, as it respects the privileges which are inherent in its own bosom, and derogatory to both its honor and independence, and the inviolability of its members — that having heard the parties, give it as their opinion although some circumstances took place at the theatre, which appeared to Mr. Randolph and others present to manifest hostility towards him, yet, as some of those circumstances had been sufficiently explained, and others were of a nature too equivocal to justify reprehension and punishment, there does not appear sufficient reason for the interference of the house on the ground of a breach of privilege."

This was a severe mortification to Mr. Randolph. He was not then so eminently qualified for a statesman as he has since appeared, or he would not have adopted a wrong course in endeavouring to obtain redress.

The intemperate warmth shewn by the ruling party towards Great Britain, and their tame acquiescence in the measures of Buonaparte, at length disgusted their leader. He began by rebuking Mr. Madison, the secretary of state, for acceding to the demand of Turreau,[17] the French ambassador, who followed it by an observation — "that France was in want of money, and that she *must* have some from the United States." The pretext, as we have already mentioned was payment for the Floridas.* Mr. Randolph next withdrew himself from the confidence of the president, and then repeatedly told the house of representatives that there no longer existed a cabinet council. His strenuous opposition

* On this subject an American print has the following observations:— "We have already informed the public of the issue of the secret sittings, a secret bill authorizing the purchase of the FLORIDAS. What will the public say to such conduct? After purchasing and PAYING for Louisiana, including as we thought a country of almost unbounded extent, and a considerable portion of the Floridas, we discover, to use an old adage, that we have been buying a pig in a poke. It now appears that a secret article between France and Spain, of which our minister and government were kept in ignorant, deprives the United States of all Florida and a portion of Louisiana. Thus have the government and people been most egregiously deceived in the value of the purchase. And we are now about to sanction the deception by appropriating millions more for another purchase in the extent of which we possibly may be again deceived! It was in developing this business, that the conduct of John Randolph was above all praise. The *amor patriæ* of this gentleman will ever command our highest admiration. The magnanimity of his spirit, and the independence of his mind, shone conspicuously in the midst of the assembled sages of his country; and his eloquence, splendid, luminous, and manly, as it was, failed to rouse those whose souls had heretofore been moulded to his will."

to the government making restitution for the sums of which innocent purchasers were *swindled* by the state of Georgia, the particulars of which infamous transaction I shall hereafter mention, is an undeniable proof of private rancour.[18] His hatred to Gideon Granger, the post-master general, who is greatly interested in that business is well known. The acrimonious manner in which he conducted the impeachment of Judge Chase is another proof of an irascible temper; and his attempt to abolish the senate because they acquitted the injured man, displays passion bordering on phrenzy.[19] Great as his abilities are, no man in the United States has acquired more enemies than John Randolph.

Mr. Randolph has lately rendered himself exceedingly conspicuous by his opposition to the non-importation act of congress, and deprecated their conduct towards Great Britain. To such a height did the debate on this subject proceed after he had delivered his celebrated speech on that question, that his name-sake,* in attempting to answer him, lost the government of his passions, and vehemently called upon his new antagonist in terms tantamount to a challenge. A duel was expected to follow; but next day the president's son-in-law apologizing in his place in the house, the matter ended.

The following extract from the speech of Mr. John Randolph, alluded to, must be interesting to every reader, both in Britain and America: —

> But a great deal is said about the laws of nations. What is national law but the national power, guided by national interest? You yourselves acknowledge and practise this principle where you can, or where you dare — with the Indian tribes for instance. I might give another and more forcible illustration. Will the learned lumber of your libraries add a ship to your fleet, or a shilling to your revenue? Will it pay or maintain a single soldier? And will you preach and prate of violations of your neutral right, when you tamely and meanly submit to the violation of your territory? Will you collar

* Thomas Man Randolph, son-in-law to President Jefferson, and little related to John Randolph.

the stealer of your sheep, and let him escape that has invaded the repose of your fire-side; has insulted your wife and children under your own roof? This is the heroism of truck and traffic — the public spirit of sordid avarice. Great Britain violates your flag on the high seas. What is her situation? Contending, not for the dismantling of Dunkirk, for Quebec, or Pondicherry, but for London and Westminster — for life. Her enemy violating, at will, the territories of other nations — acquiring thereby a colossal power, that threatens the very existence of her rival. But she has one vulnerable point to the arms of her adversary, which she covers with the ensigns of neutrality. She draws the neutral flag over the heel of Achilles. And can you ask your adversary to respect it at the expence of her existence? — and in favor of whom? — an enemy that respects no neutral territory of Europe, and not even your own. I repeat that the insults of Spain towards this nation, have been at the instigation of France? That there is no longer any Spain. Well, Sir, because the French government do not put this into the Moniteur,[20] you choose to shut your eyes to it. None so blind as those who will not see. You shut your own eyes, and to blind those of other people, you go into conclave, and slink out again, and say —"a great affair of state!" It seems that your sensibility is entirely confined to the extremities. You may be pulled by the nose and ears, and never feel it; but let your strong-box be attacked, and you are all nerve —"Let us go to war;" Sir, if they called upon me only for my little *peculium*, to carry it on, perhaps I might give it: but my rights and liberties are involved in the grant, and I will never surrender them whilst I have life. The gentleman from Massachusetts (Mr. Crowninshield) is for sponging the debt.[21] I can never consent to it. I will never bring the ways and means of fraudulent bankruptcy into your committee of supply. Confiscation and swindling shall never be found amongst my estimates, to meet the current expenditure of peace and war. No, Sir. I have said with the doors closed, and I say so when they are open, "Pay the public debt." Get rid of that dead weight upon your government, that cramp upon all your measures, and then you may set the world at defiance. So long as it hangs upon you, you must have revenue, and to have revenue, you must have commerce — commerce, peace. And shall these nefarious schemes be advised for lightening the public burthens? will you resort to these low and pitiful shifts? will you dare even to mention these dishonest artifices, to eke out your expences, when the public treasure is lavished on Turks and infidels; on singing boys and dancing girls; to furnish the means of bestiality to an African barbarian?[22]

The concluding words relate to the late Tunisian embassy, the account of which will be found in the subsequent pages.

Another observation delivered on the same occasion tends farther to prove that Mr. Randolph is by no means blinded by any partiality to the French interest: — "The Marquis Yrujo," says he, "has bearded your president to his face, insulted your government within its own peculiar jurisdiction, and outraged all decency. Do you mistake this diplomatic puppet for an automaton? He has orders for all he does. Take his instructions from his pocket to-morrow, they are signed, *Charles Maurice Talleyrand*."[23]

After having taken such a decisive part in the opposition to this measure, we cannot wonder to find Mr. Randolph one of the most strenuous advocates for its repeal.

LEVI LINCOLN

This gentleman was bred to the bar. He is of obscure origin,[24] being descended from a plain private family in the State of Massachusetts. He is indebted to the misplaced officiousness of a partisan, for creeping into public notice. From a mere bawler of democracy, he found means to ingratiate himself with Mr. Jefferson, who, among many other promotions which have sullied his name, appointed Lincoln to the office of attorney-general. His fitness for this important situation will appear from strictures on his conduct, occasioned by an observation in Mr. Jefferson's paper, entitled "The National Intelligencer," printed at the City of Washington. In one of these was the following absurd panegyric:

"The short period during which he (Mr. Lincoln) held his seat in Congress, had not admitted of a development of his talents, but he entered the body with the reputation of eminent talents." — We should be glad (says the writer who takes up the subject) to know with what reputation he left it? The truth is, that he entered the body with the reputation of being one of the writers in a Worcester (Massachusetts) paper, called the AEgis, and was supposed to be one of the authors of a series of essays, (if a mass of slander, personal, vindictive and unjust, deserves the name) called the "Farmer's Letters";[25] this was the only evidence which the public had received of his talents, and with this reputation he entered the house, and with this reputation only he left it. It is true, that a farther "development of his talents" did not take place during his stay in Congress; but it is not true that it was owing to "the short period" to which it was confined. He remained sufficiently long to have developed his talents on the many important and interesting topics which were each day the subjects of discussion. Awed by the splendor which surrounded him, he dared not expose his prate to the keen animadversion of his contemporary opponents. Having just sense enough to practise the maxim of "*vir sapit qui pauca loquitur*," he shielded himself in a stupid silence, and sat scowling at the eminence which he had not the power to resist. He therefore went out of Congress as he came in, with the reputation of being a very weak spoke in the wheel of government.

Mr. Lincoln was now appointed attorney-general of the United States, and during the long period in which he has held, we will not say discharged that office, he has permitted a farther development of his talents, by making one speech and an half in the Supreme Court.

The first speech was a sufficient development of his talents, to induce administration to believe that in any future development, it might be necessary for the interests of the country, that he should be assisted by other counsel, and therefore, in the celebrated case of the Sugar Refiners, Mr. Dallas was employed, at the expence of several hundred dollars, to render this assistance. The cause was tried at the capitol, in Washington, during the sitting of Congress, before Chief Justice Marshall, and Judges Chase and Washington. The hall of the court was crowded with spectators, among whom were observed many foreigners of distinction, and members of Congress. The honourable Levi Lincoln arose — one hand was rested on a large pile of law books, which it would seem he intended to use, the other contained a roll of manuscript notes of the case, to which it would seem he intended to refer. He neither used the one nor referred to the other. He was on the floor about ten minutes, when, having concluded his prefatory remarks, he said, "I will now inform this honourable Court, of the first point which I have taken in this case." — He paused, "I say, may it please your honours," (continued he, after a little hesitation) and paused again. — The court listened with the utmost attention; the spectators who were at a little distance from the bar, anxious to witness the event which this illustrious instance of the "*montes parturiunt*," seemed to promise, closed up in a semicircle around the balustrade of the forum. "As I was saying, (said Mr. Lincoln) I have made a point." — He had so. He had reached one which he could not surmount. He told the court that he begged their kind indulgence; that he felt exceedingly embarrassed, and wished a few minutes for recollection. The court bowed assent, and Mr. Lincoln sat down.

After a pause of fifteen minutes, during which there was the most solemn stillness, Mr. Lincoln rose again. He continued to speak about ten minutes more. His manner was wild, incoherent, and unargumentative, and seemed to be an unconnected, promiscuous, and irregular assemblage of words, without the smallest attention to the *ordo verborum*. "I have now come, (said he) may it please your honours, to the second point proposed — I say — the second point which I have taken is this — I have got (said he) to the second point." He, however, was never able to get any farther, and the Court remain yet to be informed what that second point was. Mr. Lincoln was obliged once more to apologize to the Court for being unable to proceed. He said, he felt an embarrassment which he could not conquer, and that Mr. Dallas would go on with the cause. A confused murmur was heard throughout the hall; it was the hum of vexation, disappointment, and keen remark. Some of the auditory felt chagrined at this debasement of our national dignity; some felt disappointed and astonished, that this exertion of forensic eloquence should have terminated in such a mortifying development of the talents of their attorney-general; and others laughed at the impotency which they had predicted — whilst the poor Mr. Lincoln sat down at the bar, and covered his face with his hands.

He was, soon after this probation, removed from the atttorney-generalship, and returned to his original obscurity.

BRYAN VISCOUNT FAIRFAX

Lord Fairfax,[26] who becomes an object of American biography, from his very long residence in the United States, was a viscount of the kingdom of Ireland, his ancestor being elevated to that dignity by king Charles the First, in the year 1628. The name of Fairfax is one of the most distinguished of those that occur in the history of the civil war which brought that monarch to the block, in the middle of the seventeenth century. We find the very nobleman who was thus indebted to the king for his title, among the most active of his opponents. His son also was a most useful instrument in the hands of the designing Cromwell.

It would appear that the spirit of republicanism had been transmitted through the intermediate generations of this family. Bryan Viscount Fairfax, settled in America previous to the revolutionary war; and I am told officiated therein as a chaplain, having been educated for the church. After the peace he settled on his estate in the neighbourhood of Alexandria, and lived a very retired life. He privately relinquished his titles, which had become unfashionable, when the country assumed a republican form of government. He occasionally exercised the sacred functions of his office, and died greatly lamented, about the year 1801, leaving several children; and as the heir at law has become in every sense an American, and also renounced the title, I presume it may be considered as extinct.

SIR JOHN OLDMIXON

This gentleman[27] is a baronet of Great Britain: with the occurrences of the early part of his life, I am not acquainted. He became enamoured of Miss George, then a performer at Drury-Lane and the Haymarket theatres; and having obtained her hand, soon afterwards embarked with her for America. She was engaged, at a handsome salary, by Mr. Wignall, one of the managers of the Philadelphia theatre, where she became a great favorite, ranking as a singer next to the late Mrs. Wrighten.

Sir John took a small farm near Philadelphia; and being of a domestic turn, and partial to agricultural pursuits, he for some years lived with his lady there in retirement. Their union was productive of several children; and when her engagements required her attendance at the theatre, Sir John accompanied her in his market cart, in which he at the same time conveyed the produce of his farm. This he disposed of, while she was engaged at rehearsal; and when the entertainments of the evening were finished, the market cart was ever ready to take her home. In the bills of the day she dropped her title, calling herself Mrs. Oldmixon.

I could wish to draw the veil over the latter part of this gentleman's life. His misfortunes were not, however, of his own creating; they have befallen all conditions of men, from the peer to the peasant. Lady Oldmixon long retained her situation with no other imputation than that of being unhappily possessed of a violence of temper, which rendered her disliked by her contemporaries of the sock, and of course by no means agreeable to her husband. At length she fell into those temptations to which females on the stage are so eminently and constantly exposed; and that too, at a time of life when the duties of a parent had long required her attention. She yielded, as common fame reported, to the tender assiduities of one of the theatrical corps, who moved in a sphere no higher than that of a scene-painter, and with him, it is said, she quitted Philadelphia, and joined the company at Charleston. Sir John merited better treatment; he was esteemed a man of honour and a gentleman. The lady has more recently removed the scene of her theatrical labors to New York.

THOMAS LAW, ESQ.

This gentleman is son of the late bishop of Carlisle, and brother to Lord Ellenborough, lord chief justice of the court of King's Bench.

Early in life Mr. Law[28] went to the East-Indies under the patronage of Mr. Hastings, obtained through the interest of the bishop, and there acquired a splendid fortune. During his residence in the British possessions in the east, Hyder Ali had been successful in some partial engagements with the company's troops. He had taken prisoners General Baird and Colonel Bailey, and for some time kept the latter gallant officer bound in chains, weighing thirty-two pounds, which were afterwards put upon Captain James Wilson, late commander of the British ship Duff, laden with warlike stores for the squadron under Sir Edward Hughes, whose ammunition had been nearly exhausted in his different engagements with the French admiral Suffrein. Wilson endeavoured to escape from Cuddalore; and after encountering the most imminent dangers, and swimming across rivers deemed impassable without a vessel, as well on account of their width and rapidity, as from the alligators lurking in them, he was seized by a party of the tyrant's troops, sent back to the prison whence he had escaped, and driven back naked to Seringapatam. Here he was confined with a considerable part of Colonel M'Leod's regiment of Highland ers, and underwent sufferings and torments shocking to relate. The gallant and athletic highlanders first fell under their horrid treatment, and several of them died while chained to Captain Wilson.*

* The extraordinary adventures and the sufferings of this gentleman, which almost exceed belief, will be a sufficient apology for introducing here a few farther particulars of his active and useful life:—

Captain Wilson was bred to the sea from his earliest years, and served, during the American war, at the battles of Bunker's Hill and Long Island. He afterwards went as mate to one of the company's ships to the East Indies, where he determined to settle. During the war with Hydler Ali, he was employed, as related above, to carry stores for the British army, and while on this service was taken by the French, and carried to Cuddalore. Having received information that Suffrein, their admiral, had been bribed by Hyder Ali to deliver up to him all his prisoners, Captain Wilson resolved that very night to attempt his escape. This design he executed with his servant, a Bengalese boy. They ascended the rampart, forty feet in height; the captain leaped down, and pitched on his feet, but the shock of so great a descent caused his chin to strike against his knees, and tumbled him headlong into the river. Recovering himself, he returned to the foot of the wall, where there was a dry bank, and bidding the boy drop down, caught him safely in his arms.

He had passed in his flight three arms of the river, encumbered with the weight of the boy, who was unable to swim, but in attempting to cross a fourth in the same manner, they had both nearly perished. He returned to the shore, and recommending his attendant to the care of a friend, pursued his route alone.

On being retaken after he had swum over the main river, he was carried to the head-quarters, and interrogated by an officer, to whom he gave an ingenuous account of his escape. The Indian looked angrily at him, protesting he was a liar, for no man, he observed, was ever known to pass the Coleroon by swimming, as the alligators would infallibly have seized him, had he only dipped the tip of his finger in it. The captain, however, produced such evidence of the fact, that he could no longer doubt the relation; on which the Mahometan raised his hands and exclaimed: "This is God's man!"

For twenty-two long months was Captain Wilson confined, as described above, at Seringapatam. The prison was a square, round the walls of which was a kind of barrack for the guard; in the middle was a place covered over head, but open on all sides, and exposed to wind and rain. Here, with no bed but the earth, no covering but the rags wrapped round him, he was chained to another prisoner; and they were often so cold, that they dug a hole in the earth as a defence against the chilling blasts of night. So scanty was the allowance of the wretched captives, that a state of raging hunger was never appeased, and he was often afraid to trust his fingers in his mouth lest he should be tempted to bite them. Though he entered this abode of misery exhausted by fatigue and disease, yet for a year he enjoyed a better state of health than any of his fellows. At length, the complicated wretchedness he endured produced in him the symptoms that had carried off so many others. His body became enormously distended, his thighs swelled to the thickness of an ordinary man's waist, and death seemed to have marked him for his prey.

Reduced to the extremity of weakness, and his irons being so straight as to threaten mortification, he was released from them to lie down and die. The soldier to whom he was last chained, had served him with great affection, and thinking it might alleviate his pain, entreated permission to spend his daily pittance of about three farthings (allowed to buy firing and salt to cook his allowance of rice) for oil to anoint his legs. To this the captain objected, representing that he would have nothing to dress the next day's provision. The soldier shook his head. "Master," said he, "I fear you will be dead, and never want it." Providence, however, snatched him from the brink of the grave. The captain had that day exchanged his allowance of rice for a small species of grain called *ratche pier*, which he eagerly devoured, and slaked his thirst with the liquor in which they were boiled. The consequence was such an amazing evacuation, that he was in a few hours reduced to a skeleton, and though excessively enfeebled, he was completely relieved, and recommended the trial with success to many of his fellow-prisoners.

After his deliverance, Captain Wilson again engaged in the sea service, and having realized a fortune, settled at Horndean, in Hampshire. This retirement he voluntarily quitted, and gratuitously took the command of the ship Duff, equipped by the Missionary Society for a voyage to the South Sea Islands, with the particulars of which the public is already acquainted.

The victories of Sir Eyre Coote happily mitigated their sufferings. The tyrant was compelled to give up his prisoners. Mr. Law was sent to Seringapatam, and to him the prisoners were delivered. He found his countrymen weak, and emaciated with hunger and disease — many of them covered with ulcers, and unable to support their feeble frames. Of one hundred and fifty of M'Leod's regiment, only thirty-two remained, with Captain Wilson and a few more. It was some time before Mr. Law, with the assistance of the surgeon, who was in his retinue, could prepare the wretched captives for a removal from the scene of misery.

Mr. Law returned to England with, or soon after his patron. On the celebrated impeachment, it is well known that his brother was retained by Mr. Hastings as his leading counsel; and on that occasion Edward now Lord Ellenborough, fully displayed those abilities, which paved the road to the high honours he now possesses.

It appears, however, that during the trial it was thought adviseable that the subject of these anecdotes should retire to America, where he invested large sums of money in the speculative plan of building in the American capital, on the banks of the river Potomack, which divides Virginia from Maryland, and where a great part of his fortune is sunk in its failure. The city of Washington will never be made a great or a commercial place. Baltimore on the one side, and Alexandria on the other, having a free navigation, are barriers to its commerce; and the products of the extensive back countries, will ever be carried to the mart from which they can be most conveniently shipped.

About two years ago Mr. Law visited his native country, and left his wife at Washington. On his return he found that the lady had given cause to disturb his future peace of mind.

Rumour, with "her hundred tongues" had represented to him, that his frail partner had become particularly attached to the military, at the marine barracks in Washington; nay, that she had been seen dressed *à la militaire* in company with the officers. Be this as it may, a separation certainly soon afterwards took place. The lady was allowed a handsome provision, while Mr. Law, at the time when this was written, (1806) boarded, as a single man, in one of the edifices built by himself in the New Jersey Avenue, which is a boarding house for the members of Congress, and kept by one Mitchel, a Frenchman.

A few years ago, Mr. Law procured a bill to be passed in Congress, enabling him to raise a lottery to open the Tiber Creek, which runs up to the city of Washington, so as to render it navigable for ships of burthen. The lottery was drawn; Mr. Atkinson, a respectable merchant of Alexandria, having informed me, that he had disposed of a number of tickets for Mr. Law, and paid the prizes to the fortunate holders — but the creek is not yet opened.

The large sums of money which Mr. Law has expended in the city of Washington, and perhaps the hopes of again realizing a part of them, are, I should presume, the reasons that detain him in America. Poetry occupies many of his leisure hours; and many of his compositions are of a religious nature.

PAUL JONES

During the American war, this renegado[29] struck terror into the minds of the unoffending inhabitants of many of the northern parts of the British dominions. After all the invective which has been bestowed upon him, he certainly possessed a desperate courage, enterprize and activity in the cause in which he had embarked. Some of his exploits, however, have not yet come to public knowledge; and several of his aggressions were not mentioned in the London Gazette.

At Providence, in the State of Rhode Island, a privateer of about eighty tons burthen, and carrying the like number of desperate adventurers, was equipped under the command of Paul Jones. This vessel was named after the town where she was built, "The Providence," and mounted 16 guns. On her first cruize she fell in with the British transport ship Mellish, laden with military stores for the army in Canada, which had been recently augmented in consequence of the siege of Quebec by the Americans and Montgomery. The Mellish defended herself with great bravery for nearly three hours, when Jones succeeded in boarding her. The prize was brought into New Bedford, in Massachusetts, and amongst other valuable warlike stores, were 12,000 suits of regimental clothing. The American army at this time was half naked, and the clothes being sent to General Washington, the adverse parties were soon in the same uniform. This proved of great disadvantage to the British, who, in several instances, being convinced that the enemy were detachments from their own army, fell unprepared for resistance into their hands.

CAPTAIN HACKER

The privateer above-mentioned took many more prizes, and greatly annoyed trading vessels on the American coast. Paul Jones had now been promoted, and having sailed for France, the command of the Providence was given to another desperado, named Hacker.[30] This adventurer swore, that he would surpass the achievements of Jones, and, for this purpose formed a design of attacking the island of New Providence, in the West-Indies. This was considered as a mad and chimerical scheme, the inhabitants possessing many privateers then cruizing against the Americans, and being defended by a garrison. Hacker, however, persisted, and provided himself with every thing necessary for the expedition. He arrived at a favorable time off the island, and ran into the harbour in the night unperceived, though a sloop of war then lay at anchor. Without a moment's loss of time he landed a strong party, many of whom were well acquainted with the situation of the island, under the command of one John Trivett. In silence they reached the fort, and completely surprised the garrison, whom they made prisoners. This was done with such secrecy and caution, that the capture was not known to the inhabitants till the morning, when they were struck with astonishment and terror on beholding the rebel stripes flying above the British ensign, and the guns of the garrison turned upon them. The sloop of war slipped her cable and put out to sea, not knowing the force of the enemy, while Hacker's party exercised the right of conquest by an indiscriminate plunder. Having laden their privateer with the spoils, they spiked the guns of the fort, left their colours flying, and sailed for the port appointed for the place of rendezvous. This anecdote was penned by the author from the lips of Trivett himself, who was, at the time, a cabinet-maker at Newport, in Rhode Island.

CAPTAIN PETER LANDOIS

During the last sitting of Congress, where my private business required my attendance, being interested in a matter under consideration of that assembly, I daily observed a veteran French officer take the same seat in the gallery of representatives. On enquiry, I found that his name was Peter Landois,[31] and that he commanded the Alliance French frigate, one of the squadron of Paul Jones, when he attacked the Serapis frigate, and the Countess of Scarborough armed ship off Flamborough Head. He was a petitioner to the house. It appeared by his petition, that the squadron had taken three valuable British merchant ships, and had sent them into Norway. On the remonstrance of the British ambassador at the court of Copenhagen, they were seized by order from the king of Denmark, under the plea that America had not been acknowledged as a nation by that country.

The ships were restored to their owners, and Landois prayed a compensation from Congress for this loss of prize-money. For several sessions he had his case before them, and perhaps, to stop farther clamour, they granted him two thousand dollars. This paltry sum the veteran refused, alledging, that it would not remove his pecuniary difficulties, great part of which had been incurred by his attendance several sessions on Congress. The affair will therefore most probably be revised.

GENERAL BENEDICT ARNOLD

The war, in its most frightful and destructive form, was carried into New London by this officer, who, after betraying the cause of his country, was, by stipulation, appointed a brigadier general in the armies of Britain. Arnold[32] was born at Norwich, a very few miles from the town which he destroyed by fire and sword. It was believed that his object was to satiate his vengeance by proceeding to Norwich and burning the very roof under which he first saw the light of heaven; but that the resistance he met with at Groton, opposite to New London, obliged him to relinquish the horrible design.

It has been asserted, that "the injury done by war to the morals of a country, is inferior to none of the evils which it suffers. A century is insufficient to repair the moral waste of a short war." The hatred cherished by the inhabitants of this part of Connecticut against Britain, can be traced no farther back than the conduct of Arnold, when he gave orders to burn New London and Groton.

On the high land near Groton, were a few rude trenches, which the inhabitants had hastily thrown up, in order to check the movements of the British troops, and which they called a fort. To this place a few score of undisciplined countrymen repaired, with such arms as they could collect on the emergency, and placed themselves under the command of Major Ledyard, an officer in the employ of Congress. While Arnold entered New London with his main body, he detached a party to dislodge the enemy on the height, which, had they been provided with artillery, would have commanded the town. The Americans were at this time but ill supplied with that formidable engine of war. Sixty dwelling houses, eighty stores, a church, and many smaller buildings, were burned in New London; and the fort, after a spirited defence, was stormed. Major Ledyard fell; and his countrymen affirm, that he was killed with his own sword, by the British officer to whom he had presented it, on surrendering.

From the information collected upon the spot where he was born, it appears that early in life Arnold's restless disposition was evinced, by his entering on board a vessel in the West-India trade, contrary to the wish of his relations. From Connecticut a considerable intercourse is carried on with different West-India islands. Horses, neat cattle, hogs and poultry, are exported in great quantities, and thus Connecticut is supplied with luxuries in return. The vessels employed in this trade are called "Horse jockies," and in this occupation Benedict Arnold began his career. He soon became captain of a "Horse jockey" — and, such is sometimes the turn of the wheel of fortune, that from this command he was called to be a general officer in the army of the United States. He was second in command to Washington, when he attempted to betray the army; and he died a brigadier-general in the army of Britain with a yearly pension of five thousand pounds!!!

At the commencement of the war, Arnold resided at Newhaven, a sea-port town in Connecticut; and from the active part he took, he was chosen captain of a company of volunteers, who associated in defence of the American cause. He immediately mustered his company, and found it to consist of one hundred and fifty rank and file. Before their ardour had time to cool, the captain proposed an immediate march to the neighbourhood of Boston, where offensive operations were already begun. They consented, the drum beat, and they marched; nor did they halt, until by forced marches of 150 miles, they joined their countrymen now flying to arms under Washington.

This conduct could not fail to gain the approbation of the general, and Arnold was rewarded with the rank of lieutenant-colonel, and appointed to the command of a detachment ordered to join General Montgomery33 in an attack on Quebec.

This expedition was planned as a retaliation for the defeat on Bunker's-hill; but neither the force employed, nor the season of the year, promised success. In the middle of winter, which is of a severity unkown in Europe, Arnold determined to set out on a march of nearly one thousand miles, through deserts, and across mountains of snow. Thirty-one days, it is said, he was in the wilderness without seeing a house, in which time his detachment suffered severely from cold and hunger. On the banks of Chandiore he obtained a temporary supply, which enabled him to reach Port Louis, nearly opposite to Quebec.

On the 5th of December he was joined by General Montgomery, with the main body, destined to make an attack upon that city. In the attempt, Montgomery was killed, and Arnold, who led on his division with great bravery, was shot in the leg. Americans have been heard to declare, "that this wounded leg deserved military honours, but that the rest of his body would have disgraced a gibbet."

Montgomery hoped for Wolfe's success — vain hope! The American officer was nevertheless brave, and greatly beloved by his men.* He died in the breach like a soldier; and his remains were interred with honour by his conquerors.

The command of the Americans now devolved upon Arnold, who, in contempt of his wound, drew off the remnant of the repulsed army, and retreated to Crown Point.

* General Montgomery was by birth an Irishman.

We next find him in the character of a naval commander, on Lake Champlain. His force consisted of three schooners, eight gondolas, and three gallies. With these he engaged the forces of the British on the lake; and though he checked their progress, yet, upon a second attack, he fled, and ran his fleet on shore, in order to prevent his men from being made prisoners.

Arnold received credit for both these operations, though unsuccessful; and, in order to give a greater scope to his abilities, he was appointed a major-general. He was sent to oppose General Tryon in Connecticut, of whom, say the Americans, "Arnold learned the art of burning the country of the enemy." They also charge Tryon with setting fire to several towns in that state, particularly the flourishing places called Fairfield and Norwalk.

In a poetical performance, entitled "Greenfield Hill," published in 1794, by the Rev. Dr. Dwight, since president of Yale college, the author breaks forth into the following apostrophe on this subject:

> Say muse indignant! whose the hand
> That hurl'd the conflagrative brand
> A foe to human feelings born,
> And of each future age the scorn;
> TRYON, achieved the deed malign,
> TRYON the name of every sin.
> Hell's basest fiends the flame survey'd,
> And smiled to see destruction spread;
> While Satan, blushing deep, looked on,
> And Infamy disown'd her son.

An explanatory note to this poem says: "From Fairfield the British troops proceeded to Norwalk, which they burned the next day. It deserves to be remembered, that during the conflagration, Governor Tyron had his chair carried to the top of an eminence in that town, called Grammon's Hill; and there at his ease enjoyed the prospect, and the pleasure of the scene."

Arnold signalized himself in many of the engagements which took place between the contending parties. In one of them which happened near Redsfield, he was unhorsed, and escaped the point of a bayonet by shooting with his pistol the soldier who was about to run him through. His horse died of its wounds, and Congress presented him another, a singular mark, in those times, of the high sense that body entertained of his services. He relieved fort Schuyler, then besieged by Sir William Johnson, and Colonel St. Leger; and made a desperate attempt to storm the entrenchments of General Burgoyne, where he was wounded in the thigh, which occasioned a lameness during the remainder of his life, by contracting the limb.

In the year 1778, Arnold was appointed to the command of that part of the American army, which took possession of Philadelphia on its being evacuated by Sir William Howe. Here he appeared determined to outdo the British commander in his manner of living. To support the expences, he is said to have engaged both in trade and privateering. Being unsuccessful in these adventures, and having no funds to support his extravagance, he set up claims against congress, which were disallowed. This was the first cause of his disaffection, and his subsequent conduct subjected him to a trial by a court-martial, from which he received a reprimand. This circumstance served to encrease his hatred to his countrymen, and from that time he meditated destruction to their cause. He formed the plan which involved the fate of the gallant Major André; having engaged to deliver up the American army at West Point for 5000*l.*, the rank of brigadier-general, with the pay of a colonel in the British army. The failure of this enterprise is well known.

Arnold, on his plot being detected, escaped, and joined the British; and in the year 1781, was appointed to the command of a considerable force, with which he attacked Richmond, in Virginia, destroyed the tobacco warehouses, and did considerable damage. From that town he proceeded to Portsmouth, opposite to Norfolk, but was soon superseded by General Phillips. He was again saved by his good fortune in not being with Lord Cornwallis at the capture of York Town. After the peace he came to London, where, in 1801, contrary to the predictions of his countrymen, he died a natural death.

NOTES — CHAPTER XII

1. General Horatio Gates was born in England in 1728/9. He served in the British army as lieutenant under General Edward Cornwallis in Nova Scotia, then under Braddock, and finally joined the expedition of General Monckton to Martinique in 1761. He came to America in 1772 and entered the Revolutionary War on the side of the patriots. After the war he resided in Virginia until 1790, when he emancipated his slaves and removed to New York. He served in the New York Legislature in 1800-1801. His death occurred in 1806.

2. Lady Christian Henrietta Caroline Acland, generally called Lady Harriet, was born January 3, 1750, the third surviving daughter of Stephen, first earl of Ilchester. In 1770 she married John Dyke Acland, soldier and politician, who took his seat in Parliament in 1774, and soon became prominent among the supporters of Lord North's minority in his advocacy of strong measures of war. When her husband was ordered to America with Burgoyne's ill-fated expedition, Lady Harriet accompanied him. They returned to England, where he died in 1778 from exposure during a duel. She lived until July 21, 1815.

3. The sketch of Alexander Hamilton is substantially correct as to fact. The sympathies of the author with his subject are readily apparent.

4. The facts of Burr's life as given by the author are correct for the most part, but his antipathy for his subject reflects the general feeling of Hamilton's Federalist sympathizers.

5. Burr went south to St. Simon's Island on the Georgia coast for a time and then to Florida. He returned to Savannah and on to Washington by way of North Carolina and Virginia.

6. C. C. Pinckney was born at Charleston, February 25, 1746. He served in the Revolution, was captured at Charleston in 1780 by the British, and held prisoner until 1782, when he was exchanged. He received a commission as Major-General in July, 1798, and was honorably discharged in 1800. Washington tendered him high offices, but he did not accept them. He was a member of the constitutional convention in 1788. He lived until August 16, 1825.

7. The author evidently allowed his memory to lead him into error here. The Whiskey Rebellion occurred in 1794, and Washington placed himself at the head of the armed forces employed in suppressing the movement. Washington said he had settled the question of rank as follows: "The Rank of the Principal officers of the Army being first settled by me as follows — First — Govr. Lee of Virginia to be commander in chief if I do not go out myself. Second — Govr. Mifflin. Third — Govr. Howell. Fourth — Majr. General

Danl. Morgan or Majr. Genl. Irvine, according to the dates of their militia commissions."

The author appears to have confused the Whiskey Rebellion with the French war scare in 1798.

8. In all except a few instances, the identity of these members of Congress can be established definitely. The following comprises a complete list with the few doubtful cases indicated: John Marshall or Humphrey Marshall; Governeur Morris; Jonathan Dayton; J. Q. Adams; Fisher Ames; Roger or Gaylord Griswold; Harrison Gray Otis; James Asheton Bayard; John Rutledge, Jr.; Uriah Tracy; Samuel W. Dana; Timothy Pickering; Henry Lee; John Cotton Smith; James Madison Brown; George Thacker; Calvin Goddard; Benjamin Tallmadge; Seth Hastings; Josiah Quincy; Samuel Tenney.

9. The author appears to have had access to some of the same sources used by Oliver W. B. Peabody in his *Life of Israel Putnam* in Jared Sparks, *Library of American Biography,* (Boston, 1837), VII. There is a striking similarity in the language employed. It is possible that Janson used a source referred to by Peabody entitled "An Essay on the Life of General Israel Putnam addressed to the State Society of the Cincinnati in Connecticut. By David Humphreys."

10. D'Ell, a misspelling of Dalzell.

11. A judicious and compact account of Gallatin's part in the Whiskey Rebellion may be found in the *Dictionary of American Biography,* VII, 103-10, by D. S. Muzzey. He sums up this matter: "In this crisis Gallatin played a dominant role. With superb courage and persuasive oratory he faced the excited and armed crowd, enheartened the moderates, won over the wavering, and at last secured a vote of 34 to 23 in the revolutionary committee of sixty for peaceable submission to the law of the country. It is hardly too much to say that Gallatin saved western Pennsylvania from civil war." Hamilton tried hard to show Gallatin's connection with disloyal propaganda, but no proof could be found. What Gallatin called his only political sin consisted in his acting as clerk of a meeting of protesting farmers in Pittsburg two years before the crisis in 1794. Gallatin served in Congress from 1795 to 1801 and, as a leader of the minority party from 1797, directed the fight for election of Jefferson.

12. William Findley, H. H. Breckenridge, and David Bradford.

13. Evidently a reference to Brigadier-General Henry Miller of Pennsylvania, Quartermaster General of the troops sent into western Pennsylvania in 1794.

14. The "ex-Chancellor of Mr. Jefferson's administration" evidently refers to Edmund Randolph, whom Janson confuses with John Randolph.

15. From a speech delivered in the House of Representatives on March 5, 1806. *Annals of Congress,* 1805-7, I, 559.

16. Randolph hotly took up with the President the question of the conduct of McKnight and Reynolds. The alleged attack took place January 10, 1800, and President Adams presented the matter to the House of Representatives on January 14. It was referred to a select committee, which reported on the next day. The report contained the testimony of witnesses and affidavits of the parties concerned. It precipitated a debate which continued from January 24 to the 29, the results of which were not favorable to Mr. Randolph.

17. Baron Louis Marie Turreau de Garambouville, French minister to the United States.

18. The Yazoo Land Speculation.

19. This must refer to a resolution offered by Nicholson, on March 1, 1805, which proposed to amend the Constitution so as to give the State legislatures the power to recall United States Senators whenever they thought proper. Earlier on the same day Randolph had proposed a resolution to amend the Constitution and give the President the power to remove Federal judges upon a joint resolution of Congress requesting their removal.

20. A French journal founded on May 5, 1789. In 1800 it began to publish officially accounts of the activities of the French government.

21. Given as "sponging" in the *Annals of Congress.*

22. From a speech delivered by Randolph on March 5, 1806, in the House of Representatives during the debate on Gregg's resolution, which provided for non-importation of goods from Great Britain. *Annals of Congress, 1805-1807,* I, 568-69.

23. *Annals of Congress, 1805-1807,* I, 574.

24. Janson's account of Mr. Lincoln affords another striking example of his anti-Jeffersonian prejudices. The facts of Lincoln's career do not support the statements that he was unfitted for the office to which Jefferson appointed him, or that he returned to his "original obscurity" after quitting it.

Levi Lincoln graduated from Harvard in 1772, and practiced law in Worcester after studying at Newburyport and Northampton. He served as a member of the convention which drew up the first State constitution of Massachusetts, and in 1781 he shared in the famous cases which involved the question of the right to hold the negro in slavery. After the Republican-Federalist alignment in Massachusetts, he became a leader of the former and served both in the State House of Representatives and in the Senate. In 1800 he was chosen to fill an unexpired term in the Sixth Congress. He was elected to the Seventh Congress, but was appointed by Jefferson as Attorney-General and acting Secretary of State until Madison's arrival. After resigning from the Cabinet he resumed his political activity in Massachusetts, where he was elected to the Governor's Council and as Lieutenant-Governor. He also served as Governor after the death of James Sullivan. In 1812 Madison offered him a place on the bench of the United States Supreme Court, but he declined because of his rapidly failing eyesight.

25. "Letters to the People by a Farmer" (Salem, 1802), which assailed the political activity of the clergy.

26. "His very long residence" and his relationship with a titled English family seem to constitute the only reasons for Viscount Fairfax's recognition in Janson's book. He descended from an Anglo-Scottish family which dated back to the fifteenth century, when Sir Guy Fairfax became Lord Chief Justice of England during the War of Roses. His great-grandson, Thomas, was raised to the peerage by Charles I as Baron Fairfax of Cameron. The fifth bearer of this title married Catherine, daughter of Lord Culpepper, and thus acquired vast estates in Virginia. Their son, Thomas, sixth Lord Fairfax, settled there

permanently. Brian Fairfax, the eighth in succession to the title, born in 1737, never asserted his claim to the peerage, although it was recognized as valid by the House of Lords in 1800. He entered holy orders and in 1790 became rector at Christ Church in Alexandria. A lifelong friend of Washington in spite of their political differences, he tried to dissuade this patriot from taking part in the war against England. He died at Mount Eagle, Fairfax County, Virginia, in August, 1802.

27. Little authentic information concerning Sir John Oldmixon is available. He was the grandson of the John Oldmixon whom Pope included in his *Dunciad.* Sir John, a noted beau of his day, probably met Miss George, the daughter of a clergyman at Oxford, in 1787. She had made her debut at Haymarket Theatre in June, 1783, and before the end of the season had secured an engagement at Drury Lane. Sometime before May, 1794, when she first appeared in America, she had become Mrs. Oldmixon. Sir John died before January 17, 1809, when in an advertisement for a concert, Mrs. Oldmixon was described as "a widow with seven children dependent on a mother's talents for support, and those talents paralised by the closing of the Theatre."

28. Thomas Law was one of the outstanding citizens of Washington and that vicinity. Janson departed from the truth in some particulars concerning the life of Law and his activities in America. He was not the private secretary of Lord Hastings. His brother was not a bishop at the time he went to India. In India, Law distinguished himself as a judge over the district of Bahar. He left that country in 1791. In 1794 he came to America and two years later married Elizabeth Parke Custis, granddaughter of Martha Custis Washington. In 1804 he and his wife reached an agreement to live separately, and in 1811 he secured a divorce. In 1824 he published a denial of the insinuations regarding the causes for the separation, which were sketched in Janson's book, in Faux's *Memorable Days in America,* and in a review of the latter work in the *Quarterly Review.* His absentmindedness was proverbial. Mrs. Samuel Harrison Smith (Margaret Bayard) in *The First Forty Years of Washington Society* says that he went to the postoffice for his letters one day and could not remember his name until an acquaintance spoke to him. In another connection she wrote: "Of Mr. Law, I say nothing, it is impossible to describe this man; he is one of the strangest I ever met with; all good nature and benevolence; his ruling passion is to serve every one, which keeps him perpetually busy about others." The following story was current in the vicinity of Alexandria: One morning as Mr. Law sat at his solitary breakfast, his man servant said hesitatingly, "Master Law, Missis Law, she died las' night." "The h—l she did," replied Mr. Law, "hand the potatoes." In 1817 he retired to a farm near Washington, where he lived until July 31, 1834. The construction of many of the residences and business houses in the new Federal city was financed by Thomas Law.

29 The history of Jones's exploits is well known. The account by Janson represents the popular estimate of him. The account of the capture of the *Mellish* was regarded in New England as one of his greatest adventures.

30. Little material concerning Hoysted Hacker is available. He received appointment as a first lieutenant in the Navy on December 22, 1775, by Con-

tinental Congress. In 1779 he commanded the 12-gun brig *Providence* and defeated the English brig *Diligent* after an hour's sanguinary fighting. The ship was taken into port and later into the United States service. The author establishes an authenticity for the story of the attack upon New Providence by giving his source.

31. Peter Landais, a French naval officer, was given command of the 32-gun frigate *Alliance* in 1779. After difficulty in obtaining a crew to serve under a foreign officer, he was placed under the command of Captain Paul Jones. He captured three British vessels and sent them as prizes to Bergen, Norway, consigned to the French consul. However, the Danish government, which then ruled Norway, seized them and returned them to the British on the ground that the seizures were illegal. In 1806 he presented a claim to Congress for upwards of $12,000. Congress agreed to pay him $6,000, which should be deducted from the prize money to be obtained from Denmark through negotiation. This evidently was unsatisfactory, for the next year he presented another claim, but later withdrew it. Landais must have suffered a loss of popularity in the United States because of the part which he played in the battle between the *Bon Homme Richard* and the *Serapis*. He was discharged from both the French and the American navies because he fired into Jones's ship during the engagement. The belief that he was insane prevented a more severe penalty.

32. Arnold received £6,315 in money for himself, £500 a year for his wife, and £100 yearly for each of her children, and 13,400 acres of land in Upper Canada.

33. Brigadier-General Richard Montgomery was born near Raphoe, Ireland, on December 2, 1736. When he was killed on December 31, 1775, the regret in Quebec was almost as keen as among the men whom he led. Many of the garrison had been with him during the siege directed by General Wolfe. These Englishmen buried him with the honors of war.

CHAPTER XIII

RETREAT OF GENERAL WASHINGTON FROM LONG-ISLAND — EXECUTION OF CAPTAIN HALE, AN AMERICAN SPY — THE ARMY — OPPOSITION TO CAPITAL PUNISHMENTS — PAY OF THE ARMY ESTABLISHMENT.

DURING the unhappy American war, when the field of battle was three or four thousand miles from the mother country, it is easy to conceive that, in some instances, many Europeans might adopt the grossest errors, and be led astray by misrepresentations. It is not to be supposed that the English prints of those days could be possessed of every interesting circumstance attending that surprising revolution, even favorable to their cause; much less that they would insert incidents which might militate against the measures of the government.

The fate of Major André will ever be lamented — even in America. The commander of the American army on that occasion was reprobated in England on the account first being received, and the execution of this military sentence was considered as the effect of daring rebellion. Time and circumstances have, however, set that unhappy circumstance in its true point of view; and while we mourn the fate of our countryman, we must admit that the right of judgment was vested in the enemy.

It remains yet to be told to a considerable portion of British subjects that a precedent for the execution of Major André was recent in the case of Captain Hale, an enterprising young officer, who had joined the American standard like many others, unsolicited, and for the same plain alledged reason — "that they thought it *right* so to do."

It appears that in the year 1776, the American army was posted on Long Island, opposite to New York. General Howe, the British Commander, determined to drive them from a position of such importance to the first commercial city in America; and for this purpose landed a large detachment, which had already skirmished with the enemy. The following day was expected to produce the capture of their army, which lay entrenched next to New York. Washington saw his danger; and, while he displayed a preparation for battle, he was actually taking every secret step to cover a retreat. The armies were within sight of each other at the close of the day; and during the night the Americans shewed fires along their lines from which their soldiers were seen preparing their arms. At day-light the English trumpets sounded, and their drums beat to arms; their lines were instantly formed, and each captain had his respective command allotted him. In the American camp reigned the most profound silence. The advanced guard reconnoitered with caution; but no enemy appeared. Their wary chief had, by this manœuvre, covered the retreat of his whole army; except the few who remained to keep up the false fires.

This was the most critical moment for the American cause. General Washington, with very inferior numbers, was flying from the British; but want of correct information of their movements appeared to be his greatest difficulty. To procure this, he consulted his most enterprising officers, when Captain Nathan Hale, a native of Connecticut, and belonging to Colonel Knowlton's regiment, offered to assume the character of a spy. He reached Long Island in disguise, examined every part of the British lines, and possessed himself of every possible information of their situation and projected operations. He passed unsuspected until the very moment of his attempting to obtain a seat in a boat which would have landed him in safety.

André owed his fate to a too liberal offer to the American militia who stopped him. Hale, on the contrary, was detected in consequence of an ill-judged remonstrance on the exorbitant fare demanded for his passage.[1] Suspicions arose, and he was carried before Sir William Howe; where, unfavorable circumstances appearing against him, he confessed his situation, and was hanged.

An American writer* says, that Sir William Howe at once gave an order to the provost-marshal to execute him the next morning — that the order was accordingly executed in a most unfeeling manner; that the attendance of a clergyman in his last moments was refused, and, that the farewell letters he had written, were destroyed.

Americans are averse to a standing army, relying for defence on the militia. Four regiments of the line compose their regular troops, with artillery, and these are chiefly stationed on the frontiers. At the seat of government there are seldom more than one hundred and fifty soldiers. The articles of war by which they are governed, are founded upon those of Britain, though in few cases the sentence of death is delegated to a court-martial. Inferior crimes are punished with flogging, imprisonment, and the like. On the passing of this law on the 31st of December, 1805, the sanguinary punishments met with great opposition from some of the members of the house of representatives.

Mr. George Washington Campbell, a member for the state of Tennessee, moved to strike out in the sections — of the bill for punishing mutiny and desertion — for striking a superior officer — and, in fine, every where the word "death." He said, that every section of the bill was stained with blood; and compared a soldier to a *machine*, moving as his officer directs. "I am astonished," continued Mr Campbell, "and it ought to strike the world with awe to find a fellow-creature put to death!" Mr. Southard, of New Jersey, in seconding the motion, declared that several sections were unnecessarily marked with blood, and that when a man saw so many puishments hanging over his head, he would be deterred from serving his country. In reply, General Talmage, of Connecticut, was the advocate of severe meas-

* History of New England, from the settlement of the Federal constitution, comprehending a general sketch of the American war.

ures, without which, he declared it impossible to maintain an army in any country. In the revolutionary war, he observed, the spirit of mutiny had gone to a length which had nearly proved fatal to their cause. A soldier struck adjutant-general Read in the execution of his duty. General Washington instantly ordered the offender to be tried by a court-martial, by which he was sentenced to die. The commander-in-chief approved the sentence, and preparations were made to carry it into execution; but, finding what an effect was already produced in the army, and the horror with which all ranks were struck, the culprit was pardoned upon the spot, where he expected to expiate the crime with his life. It is well known that the Americans troops drawn up on the execution of Major André, their enemy, were bathed in tears during the dreadful ceremony.

Mr. Campbell's motion had but twenty supporters, and was of course lost. The following are the rates of pay to the army establishment:[2]

	Dollars per Month.		Dollars per Month.
A Major-General (the present highest rank)	166	Major	50
Brigadier-General	104	Captain	40
Quarter-master General	100	Lieutenant	20
Adjutant-general and Inspector	75	Ensign	20
Lieutenant-Colonel	75	Sergeant	6
(They have no rank of Colonel)		Corporal	5
		Private Soldier (besides rations)	3

The General and Field-staff of the Militia includes the following ranks and numbers of officers: — 70 major-generals; 183 brigadier-generals; 8 quarter-master generals; 15 adjutant-generals; 114 aids-de-camp; 1 state-engineer; 1 commissary-general purchase; 1 commissary-general of issues; 160 brigade-majors; 1 pay-master general; 1 physician-general; 1 apothecary-general; 1 deputy quarter-master general; 1 wagon-master general; 1 forage-master general; 22 brigade quarter-masters. The second list, viz. of Field-officers and Regimental-staff, comprehends the following ranks and numbers of officers: — 760 lieutenants-colonels commandants; 1509 majors; 432 paymasters; 587 surgeons; 362 surgeons' mates; 618 quarter-masters; 732 adjutants.

The return of the Artillery includes 14 lieutenant-colonels; 45 majors; 195 captains; 251 first-lieutenants; 159 second-lieutenants; 17 adjutants: 16 quarter-masters; 733 sergeants; 91 corporals; 359 musicians; 148 gunners; 62 alarm-men; 6853 matrosses.

The list of Cavalry embraces 37 lieutenant-colonels; 70 majors; 431 captains; 778 lieutenants; 399 cornets; 28 adjutants; 8 pay-masters; 25 quarter-masters; 1366 sergeants; 433 musicians; 27 farriers; 30 saddlers; 17,675 dragoons.

	Artillery	Cavalry	Foot
New Hampshire . .	452	1629	19160
Massachusetts	2109	2126	53316
Rhode Island .	36	57	4414
Connecticut . .	487	1290	13965
Vermont	324	1002	13708
NewYork	1143	1784	63744
New Jersey . .	186	993	21742
Pennsylvania	310	2382	83413
Delaware			
Ohio	43	50	8079
District of Columbia	81	43	1895
Mississippi Territory			1623
Indiana Territory		16	1710
Michigan Territory			
Orleans Territory			
Louisiana Territory			
In the United States . .	7083	17675	476095
			17675
			7083

Drawn under the Direction of the Author, and Engraved by M. Marigot.

High Street, Philadelphia, with an American Stage waggon.

Maryland				Number liable to militia duty, on the 30th of January last..........	2220
Virginia	1050	3096	61962		
North Carolina		238	37871		
South Carolina	778	1743	29185	Number of Militia, exclusive of officers, in those states and territories from which returns were received at different years	503073
Georgia	71	590	16650		
Kentucky			29886		
Tennessee		636	14285		

NOTES — CHAPTER XIII

1. That Nathan Hale was betrayed by his Tory cousin, Samuel, was the belief of his times and of his family.

2. The bill establishing rules and articles for the government of the armies of the United States was approved on April 10, 1806.

CHAPTER XIV

JOURNEY TO PHILADELPHIA — STAGE-WAGGON — MISERABLE ROADS — COMMUNICATIVE PASSENGER — PHILADELPHIA — POPULATION OF THE CITY — THE MARKET — METHOD OF REARING HOGS — EXTREMES OF THE SEASONS — PUNISHMENTS INFLICTED ON CRIMINAL OFFENDERS — ADVANTAGES OF THE CRIMINAL CODE OF AMERICA — THE JAIL — THE BETTERING HOUSE — THE HOSPITAL — THE BANK OF THE UNITED STATES — BEGGARS — WATER-WORKS — BRIDGES — THE LIBRARY — PEALE'S MUSEUM — AMERICAN MANUFACTURERS.

JOURNEYING towards the south, the traveller may proceed to Philadelphia by the stage-waggon, or by Amboy, which is chiefly performed by water-carriage, at much less expense. I took a place in the waggon, wishing to see the Jerseys. I was directed to the coach-office in the Broadway, in New York, where I paid the full fare, five dollars, and was desired to attend at nine the next morning, with my luggage. I did so, and found other passengers waiting; when, to my infinite astonishment, we were directed to cross the water at the confluence of the East and Hudson, or North Rivers, which appears nearly a league broad, and were informed that we should find the stage on the other side, at Paulu's Hook, in the state of New Jersey; and to add to this imposition, we each paid our own ferryage. Thus, though the stranger pays for his place from New York to Philadelphia, he, in fact, is carried only from Paulu's Hook to the latter city.

I had noted many particulars respecting the city from which I was now taking my departure, but on comparing them with those made in Philadelphia, the preference of the latter in beauty, regularity, architecture, and improvement, is so decided, that I have suppressed much respecting New York. Another reason operated in my mind in favor of this determination. The latter is an ancient city, and consequently much better known by the accounts of various authors. It is more resorted to by the English, and, upon the whole, greatly resembles an ancient English city, irregularly built; and such of the public edifices as merited notice, have been more frequently described than those of any other place in America. However, as during my long residence in this country, I have been repeatedly called upon business to this great commercial place, I may possibly hereafter find it applicable to enter into further particulars on the subject.

Having been safely ferried over to Paulu's Hook, a miserable place supported by travellers, all the New York stages and horses for proceeding towards the southern states being kept there, we saw a number of waggons with horses yoked, ready to depart; and groups of passengers assembled, forming a truly curious scene. I now mounted, for the first time, an American stage, literally a kind of light waggon. While I attempt to describe this clumsy and uncomfortable machine, I cannot suppress the wish of being possessed of one of them, with the horses, harness, and driver, just as we set off, in order to convert them into an exhibition in London. I should not doubt of their proving as attractive and as lucrative as Lunardi at the Pantheon, with his balloon and his quadruped companions in his first aërial voyage over that city. In order to aid my pen in this arduous task, I have given a correct representation of one of them in the view of the Main Street, in Philadelphia, to which I refer the reader.

This vehicle, which is of the same construction throughout the country, is calculated to hold twelve persons, who all sit on benches placed across, with their faces towards the horses.[1] The front seat also holds three, one of whom is the driver, and as there are no doors at the sides, the passengers get in over the front wheels, and take their seats as they enter; the first, of course, get seats behind the rest.

This is the most esteemed seat, because you can rest your shaken frame against the back part of the waggon. Women are therefore generally indulged with it, and it is often laughable to see them crawling to their seats; and if they happen to be late, they have to straddle over the men, who are seated farther in front. It is covered with leather, and instead of windows, there are flaps of that article, which in bad weather are let down, and secured by buckles and straps. In summer these flaps are folded up, and this is some alleviation from the repeated shocks you receive in going over the roads, many of which are never repaired, and stumps of trees left unrooted for time to consume, which yet impede your progress even in the much-frequented road between the two largest cities in the United States. Several miles immediately before you enter Trenton, the road is so very bad in some places, that the driver, with whom I chose to sit, the better to view the country, told me, that the last time he passed, his horses *stalled*, that is, they were for some time unable to drag the waggon through the worst places. He also said, that the road there had not been repaired in his memory, and he did not cease cursing and swearing till we entered the city of Trenton, which was late in the evening, a distance of sixty-six miles. This day's journey was rendered more disagreeable by a heavy rain falling in the very worst part of the road, and being myself, as I have already observed, in front, I was wet to the skin, which threw me into a fever on my arrival in Philadelphia. Those seated farther back were in a situation not much better; the leather sides being an indifferent shelter.*

* Since the journey now under observation, I have travelled many hundred, perhaps a few thousand miles, in similar carriages, and in almost every state in the Union; and though I find much truth in Mr. Weld's Travels, yet I confess I never witnessed such a circumstance as is described by him in the following passage:

"The great roads are so little attended to, that the driver frequently has to call to the passengers in the stage to lean out of the carriage, first at one side, then at the other, to prevent it from overturning in the deep ruts with

One of my travelling companions was Colonel Ephraim Martin, a loquacious old gentleman, who had served in the revolutionary war, and was then proceeding from his residence in New Brunswick, to attend the sitting of the state assembly at Trenton, of which he had been long a member. After supper, having dried my clothes, still on my back, I wished to retire to rest, as the waggon was to proceed no farther that night; but the old soldier detained me till a late hour, and long after all the other passengers had retired. On a more suitable occasion I should have enjoyed his garrulity. He told me of "the battles, sieges, fortunes he had pass'd," and sometimes from lapse of memory he recapitulated twice over the details of the same action. We had just passed over a part of the theatre of war, and he frequently pointed out, as we proceeded, the situation of the contending armies. Drenched with rain, and fearful of being *stalled*, I could not retain in memory much of his information. I, however, recollect his saying that a considerable body of British troops lay at Trenton at the time Washington, by crossing the Delaware at Christmas, took the Hessians by surprise at Princeton, only twelve miles distant; and made them prisoners. An American officer was a prisoner at Trenton, when the report of the artillery in the skirmish, before Washington completed his capture, was distinctly heard at the out-posts. This man, after his liberation, reported, on joining his countrymen, that a Scotch officer, whose name I cannot recollect, high in rank in the British army, had advised the adoption of vigorous measures, as the enemy were in the neighborhood; but, from the confidence of secur-

which the road abounds. "*Now, gentlemen, to the right;*" upon which all the passengers stretch their bodies half out of the carriage to balance it on that side. "*Now, gentlemen, to the left,*" and so on. This frequently happens a dozen times in half the number of miles." [2]

I have been frequently questioned on this subject in America by persons who have read Mr. Weld's book. Though the roads are in general very bad, yet the clumsy waggon is proportionably strong to encounter the shocks; and accidents but rarely happen.

ity, his suggestions were not attended to. The North Briton now upbraided his superior, observing, that "while they had rested in apparent safety, the d——d Indian was killing their people at Princeton." "By the Indian," continued Colonel Martin, "he meant Washington." I have related the anecdote just as the veteran told it, who greatly enjoyed his own story; not, however, from a knowledge that I was an Englishman, but from that innate satisfaction with which my Uncle Toby narrated the battles in which he had been engaged. Like him too, the colonel possessed a good heart. He observed, that the commencement of hostilities was a fatal blow to his circumstances. He found himself obliged to take some decided part, and this cost him much thought. He brought every circumstance to view — the attachment he had professed to the British crown — the cause of complaint — and the gloomy prospects which then overshadowed the American cause. He at length adopted the latter, but with a heavy heart. He had two sons advancing to manhood; one of them fell in battle against the British, and the other, having been bred to the study of physic, was appointed surgeon of a regiment, and survived. He added, that the English, individually, were dear to him as his own countrymen, and, in fact, he never had an enemy out of the field of battle. "I forgive the man that wounded me — I saw him strike me down, and I think," continued this worthy man, "I should still know him. I would, now the contest is over, take him to my arms, and give him the best my house afforded!" Would to heaven I could say that I had often heard such sentiments as these during my stay among Americans. They would have filled me, and indeed every man who heard them, with admiration and esteem; but alas! on the contrary, how often have I been branded with opprobium, because I was born — an Englishman. In vain may they deny the principle; in vain contradict what I advance whenever I speak of localities; but still I shall continue to aver that I sit down to write these sheets, not with a view to pecuniary profit, but, in the plain language of truth, to inform my countrymen of the result of some *experience* in the new world.*

On the next day I sensibly felt the ill effects of my journey. We set off at six in the morning, and were conveyed to the Franklin's Head, in North Second Street, Philadelphia, at two; having come thirty miles, making together ninety-six miles from New York. I found accommodations at a private boarding-house, where I remained an invalid for a fortnight.

The rapid growth of this beautiful city, in size, wealth, and splendor, and its increase of trade, has seldom been equalled in commercial history. The plan was laid by the purchaser of the soil, the celebrated William Penn. This enterprising man was one of the earliest members of the religious sect who denominated themselves Friends; and at this day a large proportion of the inhabitants of Philadelphia are of that persuasion. He obtained a grant from King Charles the Second, in the year 1681, and the next year, accompanied by about one hundred settlers, he arrived in the river Delaware, on the banks of which stands the city, at the distance of 120 miles from the sea.[3] The spot was then covered with timber; its foundation was a stratum of potters' clay; the harbour furnished a bed of sand; the nearest hills contained quarries of stone; the vicinity yielded lime-stone and marble; and iron and coal were discovered upon the navigable branches of the Delaware, long before the new settlement afforded hands to work them.

* Travelling charges are half a dollar for each meal. These only differ in there being vegetables at the dinner table, and spirits and water, as an execrable beverage. At breakfast and supper there are also hot dishes, and generally very indifferent coffee. The Englishman is said to live too grossly; but the American gorges on meat three times a day. One alleviation to the fatigue of travelling in this country is, that you are not *dunned* for money by the driver, but he will often smoke a segar on the road, the fume of which, by the progression of the carriage, is left among the passengers. The average price of conveyance is not quite four-pence British per mile.

The natives, Mr. Penn justly considered, had the claim of nature to the soil, and were in possession of the country. He accordingly entered into a negotiation with them for the extinguishment of such title; and under a tree, which is still standing, they transferred to him their right of possession. He also there entered into a treaty of amity with the tribe of Indians who hunted on the ground where the city is now built.

It is situated 40 degrees north of the equator, and 75 west of London, being in the same parallel of latitude with Spain, Italy, and Greece; climates whose happy temperature had indicated milder seasons than were found on the banks of the Delaware, which, during the winter, is frozen to such a degree, that loaded waggons pass over it on the ice.

Philadelphia is built on an extensive plain, five miles above the confluence of two navigable rivers, the Delaware and the Schuylkill; the former is a mile in breadth, and of sufficient depth to admit ships of 1200 tons to the wharfs, after being in part unloaded at a bar near Wilmington, the only obstruction to its extensive navigation. The Schuylkill is about half as wide as the Thames at Lambeth, and is also navigable for smaller vessels as high as the city.

The streets running from river to river are named after the produce of the woods formerly growing upon the spot, viz. Walnut-street, Chestnut-street, Pine-street, Vine-street, Mulberry-street, &c. Those running from north to south, according to the original plan, were named Front-street, second, third, fourth, fifth, and up to twelfth-street, and are now built upon. The centre of the city is Market-street, which also extends from the Delaware to the Schuylkill, and is much wider than the others running in the same direction. Where the streets intersect Market-street they are distinguished by north and south, as North Second-street, South Second-street. North Third-street, South Third-street.

The ground-plot is laid out with great regularity. Nine streets, two miles in length, (though not yet built upon to

Drawn under the Direction of the Author and Engraved by M. Marigot

View of Second Street, north from Market Street, with Christ Church.

the extremities) run east and west, from river to river, and twenty-three of a mile in length, intersect them at right angles from north to south. These streets are fifty feet wide, and they distribute the plan into squares, the interior of which was designed for yards and gardens. Two main streets, of an hundred feet wide, cross each other in the centre, and form a public square, of which four more were laid out in different parts of the city.* A range of houses, for the principal merchants, was intended to open upon the water, in the same manner as the celebrated Bomb Quay at Rotterdam; for which purpose, the warehouses, &c., along the river, were intended to have been kept back from the rising ground above the bank; but cupidity, perhaps convenience, has crowded the platform between the streets with narrow alleys; the public squares, except the centre, have been otherwise appropriated; and the bank of the river has been built up with a row of houses which are a disgrace to the city, and which entirely intercept the view of the port. This street has proved a scourge to the inhabitants for their encroachment on the noble plan of the proprietor. It is called Water-street, and is so very contracted and dirty, compared to the cleanliness of other parts of the city, that it is alone sufficient to engender disease in the hot months; and there contagion first makes its appearance.[4]

The houses are well built, chiefly of red brick, and in general three stories high. In some of the new streets uniformity is observed, particularly in Sansom-street, which may vie with those of the fashionable parts of London. A great number of private houses have marble steps to the street door, and in other respects are finished in a style of elegance.

The streets are paved with large pebble-stones in the carriage-road, and the foot-pavements, which are raised ten or twelve inches higher, with brick. They are tolerably well lighted and guarded in the night; the watchmen calling the

* The city extends, including Southwark and the northern liberties, nearly three miles along the Delaware, and about a mile and a half east and west.

hours as in London.* Many of the new streets have of late been planted with rows of poplars, whose rapid growth, and spiral form, peculiarly adapt them to shade the avenues of the city in the sultry season of the year. During the last summer, these trees harboured a caterpillar of very large dimensions, the bite of which was said to be extremely venomous. Reports were propagated of its causing death in several instances, and the demolition of the poplars was in contemplation. I, however, witnessed the proof of their being perfectly harmless, having seen a gentleman in Walnut-street suffer one of them to crawl over his hands; nor do I conceive that the bite, which, by all reptiles, is never inflicted but under the impression of fear or anger, would produce at most more than a local inflammation.

On the declaration of the independence of the United States, Philadelphia, then the capital and seat of government, was estimated to contain 6,000 houses, and 40,000 inhabitants. An American author, from whom some of these observations are selected, states that, "since the operation of the federal constitution, four or five hundred houses have been annually erected, no small proportion of which (it is said not less than two hundred) have been built by a single citizen, W. Sansom, Esq."[5] This is greatly over-rating the increase, as the eighteen years of the compact of the union, taking this writer's medium at 450, would produce 8,100; which, added to the original 6,000, would make 14,100 houses in Philadelphia. This writer is rather unfortunate in his calculations, for in the very next page he observes, that the city is supposed to contain 13,000 houses, and eighty thousand people — but even this is a high calculation. From a plan taken by a British officer of engineers, when General Howe's army lay in Philadelphia, it appears that it is now double the size; and, notwithstanding the

* The police is generally active and well regulated in all the large cities in the United States. They have justices of the peace, constables, and watchmen, according to the English system.[6]

ravages of the yellow fever, its population has increased in proportion.

The market is the great boast of the Philadelphians. It is a covered building, 420 of my steps, in length, exclusive of the intersections of streets, and I calculated my step to be a yard; but only five feet in breadth, including the butchers' benches and blocks. It is well supplied; and its regularity and cleanliness indicate good living and wholesome regulations. No article can be offered for sale here without first being submitted to the inspection of one of the clerks of the market, who seizes unwholesome articles, and a fine is inflicted upon the owner. The fish-market from its distance to the sea, is but indifferently supplied, though much pains is taken to procure a regular supply. Light carts are constantly coming in from New York, and Burlington in New Jersey, with the most delicate fish of the ocean, and packed in ice during the summer. The beef is good, but the mutton and veal far inferior to that of England and Ireland. Butter and poultry are excellent; and there is a profusion of vegetables. Butchers' meat, on an average, is ten to twelve cents (5d. to 6d.) per pound; but poultry is not one-third of the London price, and of a superior quality. Fowls of all kinds are within the compass of the purchase of the labourer. A turkey of sixteen pounds weight may often be bought in Philadelphia for a dollar, but I have seen them sold of this size, both in New England and in Virginia, for three shillings, and even still less, British money. Wild turkies are sometimes brought to market of the enormous weight of twenty-five pounds and upwards; but these birds retire from the country as it becomes more settled. Geese, ducks, fowls, rabbits, (there are no hares in the United States) are of a proportionate price. Quails, which they call partridges, are brought alive in large quantities, and sold for about two and sixpence per dozen.* Negroes, and sometimes white

* Great quantities of this game are, in the winter, caught with snares and traps.

people, bring opossums, which could not readily be distinguished from roast pig, when dressed in the same manner; squirrels, which are by many preferred to the rabbit, and sometimes racoons. The latter I never could be prevailed upon to taste; indeed, it is not held in any estimation, partaking too much of the species of the fox, though, I believe it is not carnivorous. Excellent butter is supplied by the German settlers, at about an English shilling per pound, and eggs at sixpence per dozen. The pork throughout the United States is excellent, and, from the quantity of mast, it is raised in abundance. Large herds of swine, which ran off at my approach, have often suddenly surprised me when on a shooting party in the woods. They range at large, and stray sometimes many miles from their owner, who, however, is anxious to accustom them to resort to his plantation. To effect this, he blows the conch-shell, which may be heard at a great distance. At this signal the hogs that are well trained set off at full speed; and, from its being sounded at one particular spot, the animals soon appear, and are rewarded with Indian-corn, which they prefer to all other food.* About the end of November begins the pork season. Neighbouring planters and farmers unite, and form a large party in quest of the herds of swine, that are entirely wild, which they pursue and shoot with a single ball in the head. Each person knows his hogs by marks which are given them when young. This pork, by the quantity, is generally in price from five to six dollars per hundred weight. It is very fat, but the flesh is not firm, from the animal feeding chiefly upon the acorn; this they call mast-fed pork.

Spirituous liquors are, unhappily for the lowest orders of society, still easier of attainment. This pernicious article is generally the cause of those outrages, the narration of which so much offends the ear of all civilized nations, and which

* I do not agree with the vulgar saying, "as stupid as a pig." I have, from observation, found swine the most sagacious quadrupeds of the farm.

will be particularly noticed in treating of Virginia and the more southern states. Windward Island Rum, by the hogshead, is generally under a dollar per gallon, and the various distillations of the country about half that price. The duty on imported spirits is very small, and according to the proof, averaging an English shilling per gallon.

What I have hitherto said must be understood to relate only to the market in the winter season. It is by no means well supplied in summer. Fresh meat will then keep no longer than the dinner hour of the morning it is killed; and the morning's milk turns to curd in the evening. This they call "*bonny clabber*," and eat it with honey, sugar, or molasses. It is by some thought equal to custard, and the females are particularly fond of it. They have their seasons for the articles of life, which, in London, we scarcely perceive. For example — after the season for fowls come the fisheries of the spring, which continue for about six weeks, when the people in the country live solely on shad and herrings, of which they also export large quantities. In the beginning and middle of summer it is difficult to procure fresh provisions of any kind. They then live on salt pork or bacon, and greens. In a progress of many hundred miles in the southern states, at this time of the year, a traveller will find no other fare. This was once a favorite dish with me; but so long have I been confined to it at different times in America, that my relish for it is, I believe, for ever gone. In the spring, it is true, you every where meet with veal killed at a month or six weeks old, having first been almost starved to death by the robbery committed upon the natural sustenance of the calf.

The heat in summer is oppressive — more so I thought than in Carolina. This is accounted for, by the reflection of the sun upon the brick houses and the brick foot-pavements. The thermometer is often above 90 for several days together, sometimes for a few hours 93 and 95, which alone is sufficient to propagate disease in a crowded city. With the disadvantage of the fever, and the total stop put to navigation several weeks from the ice, in winter, Philadelphia has sent from twelve to fifteen hundred sail of vessels in one year to every quarter of the globe, some of which, following the British, double the promontory of Africa, and explore the antipodes for the most costly productions of the east. Add to this, the Americans, during the present war, have been the carriers of the world, across the ocean. It is said that a gentleman now living, and by no means very old, remembers but three coaches kept in the city; and now there are computed to be above three hundred. — This is not improbable, for, in coming from the Theatre, I have seen a bustle of carriages similar to that in London upon these occasions.

During the extreme heat, few would voluntarily encounter the rays of the sun; yet the pursuit of wealth stimulates the American to run every hazard. The female part of the family, however, stay within doors till the cool of the evening. They shut up the windows on which the sun shines, as well to exclude the heat, as to render the myriads of flies and musquitoes inactive, from the darkness. The streets of Philadelphia in the evening are crowded. The ladies emerge from their confinement, and pay visits by moon-light; while the girls sport and play without hats or cloaks, uninterrupted often till near midnight.

The punishments annexed to criminal convictions, throughout almost every state, are worthy of imitation. The many public executions which take place in England, after every general gaol-delivery, are a subject which strikes Americans with horror. Among the lower orders of the community, the spectacle of fellow-creatures executed by the arm of the law, generally tends to harden their hearts, and divests death of its terrors; and upon the commission of a crime, the offenders, inured to behold the extent of the punishment, console themselves under the idea of dying "as brave as the best."

Though both the penal and common laws of England are

generally adopted in the United States, the punishments differ materially; but it will be admitted that they are sufficiently proportioned to the crimes. In very few cases indeed, in any state, is the punishment of death inflicted. Legislative bodies consider, that the laws of man should seldom extend to the extermination of that life which was given by the Almighty! In Pennsylvania, of late years, capital punishments are remitted in all cases I believe except treason, or murder in the first degree; and, in the latter case, death is seldom inflicted; but the culprit is sentenced to solitary confinement in a dark cell for a number of years, or perhaps for life. In the second degree, light is admitted into the cell of the prisoner, and his confinement is limited to seven or fourteen years. For burglary, which rarely occurs, the punishment is also solitary confinement. Such as are under conviction of theft and petty larceny are made to work in their cells, at the trade to which they were bred. Prisoners for inferior misdemeanors, midnight disturbers, vagabonds, and such as are detected begging or fighting, are kept at labour together.[7]

The philanthropic reader will rejoice to find that there are regions where more humane laws seem to upbraid the severity of those of England, whose criminal code has justly been said to be written with blood. From a recent publication on the metropolis of the Austrian dominions, it appears that the continental sovereigns begin to perceive the inadequacy and injustice of this system of rigour. With the year 1804 a milder code of criminal law there commenced its operation. Treason, insurrection, if attended with aggravating circumstances, forgery of bank notes, and murder, are alone to be punished with death; the penalty for all other crimes being various degrees of imprisonment, either for life, or for a longer or shorter period.

It is curious and pleasing to see and reflect upon the various useful occupations these people, hitherto dangerous to society, are obliged to follow in the prisons of America.

Manufactures of most kind are there carried on. Taylors, shoe-makers, and persons of other trades, have separate rooms; and such of the prisoners who have not followed any useful branch in particular, are instructed to make nails, by machines, of which large quantities are constantly manufacturing. The produce not only maintains the labourers, but leaves a considerable profit to the state. Thus, prisoners who are a great expence to the English nation, living in idleness, and plotting and teaching each other mischief, and new methods and devices for plundering the public, are there rendered valuable members of society. The punishment, so far from hardening them in turpitude, reforms them, and they generally, on their liberation, return to those habits of industry which, from compulsion, have become second nature. The task assigned them is so moderate, that each individual can with ease earn a daily surplus; and in this case, an account is taken of it, and it is delivered in cash to the respective claimants on liberation. Thus, the most industrious often accumulate a sufficiency to enable them once more to begin an honest business.

The state of Virginia has adopted similar punishments and regulations.[8] A penitentiary is built, on an extensive plan, at Richmond; and the prisoners are employed in useful avocations. For particular offences, and such as do not amount to solitary confinement, the men have one half only of the head and beard shaved, they are obliged to wear a party-coloured dress, and are thus exposed at work to spectators. In every place of punishment the women, and they often constitute the majority of the prisoners, are kept in like manner at work with the needle, making garments for charitable institutions, or slop-work for sale to seamen; and the more refractory are compelled to beat hemp, or to pick oakum.

The Goal in Philadelphia is situated in Walnut-street, at the rear of the state-house. It is a large, strong, stone building, and in every respect adapted to the purposes for

The Bank of the United States of America.

which it is destined. The regulations of this place of punishment are worthy of the imitation of European nations. It is regularly inspected by a committee of the inhabitants, who chearfully in turn undertake the office without reward. They examine into the cleanliness of the rooms and the prisoners, who are regularly washed, and in summer bathed, and then supplied with a change of linen. Their diet is also regulated, and no spirituous liquor, doubtless in most cases, the primary cause which reduced the people to their unhappy situation, is suffered to be introduced to state prisoners.

In the winter, which is very severe in Philadelphia, the poor are relieved, and a house is opened for their reception. This is called the Bettering-house,[9] but the inhabitants are not prisoners. They are supplied with the necessaries of life, and dismissed in the spring. The institution is defrayed by a tax on the city.

The hospital is another noble institution.[10] It is provided with nurses and with all the necessary accommodations for patients of every description. The principal physicians of the city attend in rotation, and pay the strictest attention to the diseases of the sick.

There are very few beggars in the United Stats; there is indeed no pretext for begging in a country where every individual can find employment and the infirm are maintained. By this I do not mean to assert that there are no poor in the United States, nor families in distress, as Dr. Priestly[11] wrote to his few converts who remained in Birmingham, in order to induce them to follow him. The climate alone twice a year, occasions a number of poor people to seek parochial and other relief; but not in the form of street begging. The extreme cold in winter for two or three months, renders it impossible for many of the inferior class to follow their respective avocations — the intense heat of summer debilitates the constitution, and thus paves the way for bilious or yellow fevers; and where the latter do not rage, the miserable victim will most likely have to encounter, by way of substitute, those tormenting and wasting complaints, agues and fevers.

I have been asked for alms in many parts of the United States, though very seldom in the large cities. These republican beggars generally prefer their requests in the same manner as a person would ask a loan, but certainly with some moderation. This description of beggars will also stipulate with you as to the sum they expect to be given them — they will name a quarter of a dollar, a nine-penny or eleven-penny bit;* if you were to offer cents, which are equivalent to English half-pence, you might expect to incur their displeasure.

The Bank of the United States does infinite credit to the nation. It is a superb edifice of the Corinthian order, with a majestic portico of six fluted columns of stone, found in abundance in many parts of the Union, similar to Portland stone. This building indicates the flourishing state of those finances which were organized by the much-lamented general Hamilton.

Every thing which can contribute to the comfort of the inhabitants, has of late years been supplied in Philadelphia, and if it rests with man to avert the malignancy of the summer fever, which, however, he has hitherto attempted in vain, the regulations of the police must greatly contribute to the consummation of so important an end. The city is well supplied by water from the river Schuylkill, by means of a steam-engine,[12] in a handsome building at the intersection of the two principal streets; connecting ornament with public utility.

The excess of the water runs back in a small stream to the

* The eighth part of a dollar is of various denominations, according to the currency of the states. In Pennsylvania it is eleven-pence, the dollar there being seven shillings and sixpence; hence it is called an eleven-penny bit. In New England and Virginia, where the dollars are six shillings, it is nine-pence; in New York, one shilling; in one part of North Carolina, fifteen-pence, and in another part of that state, one shilling and six-pence. In South Carolina the currency is sterling.

river Schuylkill. The water is for a considerable distance so warm as to be of a proper temperature for washing linen, and I observed many women availing themselves of the advantage. Water is thus raised upwards of thirty feet above the highest ground in the city, and is conveyed by subterraneous pipes to what they call hydrants; which are placed in the streets at equal distances. The water is not suffered to flow constantly, but upon the slightest touch of the small handle of the hydrants, it rushes with impetuosity through a tube of a bore of about an inch in diameter, and continues as long as you press upon it. There are also pumps in the principal streets, and it was in contemplation to remove the hydrants entirely, and supply their places with them. There is certainly great convenience arising from the use of these hydrants; but on the other hand they are liable to abuse, and often stand in need of repairs. I have seen boys, who run all day uncontrolled about the streets, playing with them for hours together opposite to the window of my lodgings; passengers would sometimes attempt to *persuade* them to discontinue their abuse of the water, but not till some other plan of mischief was agreed upon, would they desist a moment.

A covered bridge has lately been erected over the river Schuylkill.[13] This beautiful wooden structure, was designed by William Weston, Esq. of Gainsborough, in Lincolnshire. It contains 800,000 feet of timber, board measure; was six years in building, and cost 40,000 dollars. The length of this bridge, including the abutments and wing-walls, is 1300 feet, the width 52 feet; the middle arch 194 feet, 10 inches, two others 150 each; and the inclosed height over the carriage-way, thirty-one feet. The amount of the toll for the year 1805, was 13,600 dollars.

The library is an institution which does credit to the country. It is open the greater part of the day for strangers, who are attended by a librarian, ready to hand them such books as they may select from the catalogue.* He is paid by the society, which is an incorporated body. A handsome building was erected by them in North Fifth Street; and the late Mr. Bingham, of Philadelphia, presented the society with a fine piece of statuary, in white marble, representing Doctor Franklin at full length, and which is placed above the entrance from the street. I applied to the librarian for some particulars respecting this liberal endowment. On informing him of my intention of publishing my observations, he was very assiduous in communicating whatever respected the origin and progress of the institution.

The foundation of this library was laid in the year 1731, a period when Philadelphia afforded little assistance to the enquiries of the studious.[14] A number of gentlemen having raised the sum of one hundred pounds by subscription, a small library was founded upon principles the best calculated to disseminate knowledge; the books were not, as in many public libraries of Europe, confined to the apartments, but the subscribers were allowed to carry them home for a reasonable space of time.

The plan soon became popular; additions to the number of members took place, and the stock of books was annually encreased by purchases at the company's expence, and liberal donations from persons both at home and abroad. The then proprietors of Pennsylvania appear to have taken a patriotic pleasure in the encouragement of the plan. Beside several valuable donations, they granted a charter of incorporation in the year 1724.

A spirit of literary improvement made its way among all classes of people, and the philanthropy of that great and amiable character, Doctor Franklin, who suggested the plan, was gratified by tracing the books as well into the hands of the opulent, with whom literature is sometimes no more than one of the ornaments of civil life, as of those to whom

* On my return to my native country, I was, at Liverpool, refused admittance to different coffee-rooms, to read the public papers, because I was not a subscriber; an illiberality unknown in America, where all places of this nature are gratuitously opened to the stranger.

it renders a more substantial benefit. Letters, while they employ the leisure of the artist, reconcile him to his labor; by removing grosser relaxations, they promote his health, while they enlarge his mind: and prolong his life, while they teach him to enjoy it.

The great utility and success of this measure occasioned the formation of other libraries upon similiar principles. But, as it appeared more conductive to the interests of literature to be possessed of one large, than of several smaller collections of books, coalitions gradually took place among them, till the whole were blended with the library company of Philadelphia.

Since this event, which took place in the year 1769, the members and the property of the company have continued to encrease; there being now 676 members. The number of volumes at present, including the Loganian library,*[15] amounts to 20,000, the selection of which has, in general, been calculated to promote the more important interests of society. The stock of books is continually encreasing by occasional donations, annual importations, and purchases of every publication of merit.

Some valuable machines and apparatus for the purposes of natural philosophy, and a variety of other curious, artificial, and natural productions, also belong to the company, and are deposited in other apartments of the building.

Besides the collection, the personal property consists of

* This valuable collection, consisting principally of ancient books, was begun by the late James Logan, whose enlarged mind induced him to provide for extending to others the means of those pursuits he had himself successfully cultivated. With this view he built a suitable house for the reception of the library; and, by deed, vested it in trustees for the use of the public for ever; this deed he afterwards cancelled, and prepared, but did not live to execute another, in which some alteration was made in the funds and regulations. After he died, his children and residuary legatees conveyed the whole estate, intended by him, to trustees, who caused the books, amounting to more than 2,000 volumes, to be arranged in the building prepared for their reception. To this collection was added, by the late William Logan, of Bristol, 1,300 volumes, and the whole, consisting of 3,443 volumes, and handsomely endowed by the donors, for the use of the public for ever, is now annexed to the Philadelphia library.

some monies at interest; the sales of shares, which since the year 1768, have been fixed at ten pounds, and the annual payment of ten shillings from each member. A house and lot of ground which belonged to the Union Company; two lots of ground, one the generous donation of the late Thomas Penn, Esq., and several ground rents, constitute the real estate.

The members hold their property as tenants in common, and dispose of their shares by will or deed; but the assent of the directors, as well in such circumstances as in case of an original purchase, is previously necesary, a restriction early adopted, in order, as much as possible, to prevent improper persons from having access to a collection of a nature so liable to injury. The directors and a treasurer are annually elected by the members; and the directors appoint a secretary and librarian.

In the year 1803, the reverend Samuel Preston, of Chevening, in Kent, bequeathed his valuable library to this company, and some money, in the American funds, to be applied to the purpose of keeping the books, engravings, &c., in good order. A portrait of this gentleman, by his friend West, was presented by Mrs. Elizabeth West, and is suspended in front of his bequest.

In this library is an antique clock, on which is the following inscription: — "This clock is said to have been made for, and belonged to, Oliver Cromwell, the protector. It was formerly owned by Mr. Samuel Hudson, of this city (Philadelphia). After his death, in the year 1793, his son, William Hudson, presented it to the library company of Philadelphia. It is believed to be the oldest chronometer in the city — and tradition informs us, that Samuel Hudson's great grandfather purchased it at an auction in England, when the auctioneer told his audience that it had once been in the possession of Oliver Cromwell." —
"It is no doubt at least one hundred and forty years old." (1804.) On the face are these words, "Johannes Fromanteel, Londini, fecit." It is used as the time-piece of the library, and is in good repair.

This ancient specimen of the arts is, however, of later date than the history affixed to it assigns. It appears from an old record, that clocks with pendulums were not invented till 1662, and of course some years after the death of Cromwell, by one Fromanteel, a Dutchman, and who undoubtedly made the clock in question.

The librarian shewed me, as a favor, an ancient manuscript Bible, dated in the year 1016; also a Romish prayer-book, of 1060, which are esteemed great curiosities.

The museum is a striking instance of the persevering industry of an individual, while the grant of the Old State-House for its exhibition does honor to the city. The proprietor is Mr. Charles W. Peale,[16] by profession a painter, which he relinquished, and became a virtuoso. He says "that in the year 1785, he began his collections with some bones of the mammoth, and the paddle-fish, hereafter described; and that in the year 1802, the legislature of Pennsylvania, influenced by the idea of its increasing utility, granted the upper part of the State-House for the use of the Museum."

Considering the short time since this collection was commenced, it is surprising to find such a number of natural curiosities in this Museum. The paddle-fish, which Mr. Peale observes was one of the first articles, and from which he probably conceived the idea of making the collection, is four feet and four inches in length. The snout resembles in shape the paddle used by Indians in crossing rivers, and is eighteen inches long. This fish is an object of curiosity from its being caught in the Allegany River, and State of Ohio, many hundred miles from the sea.

The fossils were chiefly collected in England, and make a handsome appearance, from the judicious manner in which they are disposed. Several were found near Christchurch, in Hampshire, seventy feet from the surface of the earth; and near them is placed a shark's tooth, dug up at the great depth of one hundred feet, where it was found in a bed of chalk at Salisbury. You are shewn what was called the *yolk stone*, also found in England. It is a thin, polished, small stone resembling the cornelian. Here are also exhibited petrefactions of small fish, found on the top of a high mountain near Naples. On a slip of white paper are affixed several small insects, thrown up from a woman's stomach in Maryland;* and a horn, between four and five inches in length, which grew out of another woman's head. To these curiosities are added, a small ivory crucifix of curious workmanship, with a human scalp, found at the root of a tree near the Miama village, soon after the defeat of General Harmer. In a large cage, feeding voraciously on raw beef, I saw the Scarlet Ibis, of South America; a bird of the crane species, but smaller, and of a most brilliant colour; and in another, a bird from Louisiana, exactly resembling the English magpie, but much larger.

The evaporation of 220 gallons of pump water, taken from South Second Street, the most populous part of Philadelphia, is preserved in four large glasses. They contain: —

	oz.
Of Carbonic Lime	12
— Magnesia	17
— Salt Petre	32
— Common Salt	24

In the collection of shells, are two of the Chama, from the Indian Ocean. Of all testaceous fish, this is one of the most curious. The shell has been known to weigh 582 pounds; and this weight accumulates from the size of a cockle-shell. It is said that food has been found within it

* The School of Medicine at Paris has lately published in its transactions some interesting observations of Doctor Desfontaines, on a living insect which was found in the liver of a man who died at the age of thirty-three, of a disorder in the stomach and bowels. It is a worm of a genus hitherto unknown, being of the size of a full grown silk-worm, and of a brownish-red. The body moves by means of rings, regularly articulated, each articulation being marked with a white point, surmounted by a hair of a firm texture, and extremely acute. The head of the insect is armed with a species of horn, and the lower extremity of the body is terminated in a manner similar to that of a lobster.

High Street from the Country Market Place, Philadelphia,
with the Commemoration of the Death of General Washington.

sufficient for more than one hundred men; and that the power of the monstrous inhabitant is such, that it can cut asunder a cable, or sever the limb which might unfortunately present itself while the massy shells are opening to supply the body with nourishment.

Among the quadrupeds are, the long-clawed grisly bear, from the source of the Missouri — the American buffalo, or bison — the great anteater — the orang outang — the crested, the American, and the New Holland porcupine — the Madagascar and the hooded bat — the lama, or camel of South America — American elks — the peccary, remarkable for a secretory organ on its back — the sloth — a variety of antelopes, &c. &c. The price of admission to this part of the Museum is one quarter of a dollar.

I then proceeded to the Mammoth room, and viewed the skeleton of this non-descript animal. Mr. Peale calls the mammoth an antediluvian animal, and says that this skeleton was discovered in Ulster county, in the state of New York, in the year 1801. It is eleven feet ten inches high, and nineteen feet long. It has carnivorous grinders; in many respects differs materially from the elephant, and is much larger, though formerly supposed to be of the same species. The tusks affixed to the skeleton are artificial, but a part of the real tusk is shewn, from which the size and shape are ascertained.

Mr. Rembrant Peale, a son of the proprietor, attended me during my examination of these curious productions of nature; and, by his civility, added greatly to the satisfaction I derived from the spectacle.*

In the Model Room is a case containing 1400 elegant casts from antique gems, which are part of the collection in

* This gentleman invited me to accompany him to view the works of his brother, a celebrated portrait painter in Philadelphia. I there saw several portraits of public characters in America, which I immediately recognised. The elder Mr. Peale, the proprietor of the Museum, has several sons; and all artists. He named them after eminent painters — Titian, Rembrant, &c. They are an amiable and loving family.

the Antique Room; a silver salt seller, which belonged to Oliver Cromwell, presented by Mrs. Washington; antique pots, household gods, and bas reliefs, from the cities of Herculaneum and Pompeii; curiously fabricated earthen pots found in South America — (in case 3 is a pot resembling these, found in Tennessee, 25 feet deep;) Chinese instruments and ornaments, and a considerable variety of such as are used by the aborigines of North and South America, such as wrought tubes of stone, crystal hatchets, &c. Around the room are displayed some paintings, and a number of Indian curiosities, models of canoes, spears, bows and arrows, clubs, paddles, baskets, the phoonka, or great Chinese fan, Chinese match gun, and ancient bow-gun, &c. The price of admission here, is half a dollar.

Manufactures, the great source of national wealth, are at a very low ebb in the United States. The amazing tracts of uncultivated land draw the attention, even of mechanics. At Boston, Newhaven, and other places, some Englishmen lost their capitals by endeavoring to establish cotton manufactories. The high price of labor absorbed every contemplated profit; and the fickleness of the people, and their partiality for European goods, would be great impediments to the sale of an article, known to be of home manufacture. Thus the country girls, who weave beautiful cottons of various colors and patterns, and extremely durable, exchange the produce of their labor for flimsy Scotch callicoes; giving, to use their own terms, "yard for yard." Though this home-made cotton will outwear three or four garments made of that which they eagerly take in exchange, yet the latter is British, consequently fashionable; and the American mountain girls, like the belles of St. James's study the fashions of the day. Cordage and sail-cloth are brought to great perfection; but the manufacture which thrives best is, that of nails, which they cut of all sizes, and to considerable profit. In this branch they will soon be able to supply every part of the Union. They also excel in a certain branch, of which

Americans are great consumers; I mean, playing cards, which they make in Boston in great quantities, counterfeiting the English devices and wrappers with great exactness. Some of these are sold for an English shilling per pack. In Boston there is another card manufactory, and for a very different use. Here are made wool-cards, the teeth of which are contructed with a new and ingenious piece of mechanism; but as gamblers are more numerous than manufacturers, the playing-card makers have the advantage.

In Philadelphia and the adjacent towns a considerable quantity of stockings are made, and other small manufactures carried on, but for want of a regular demand, the manufacturers are obliged to attend the market twice a week. Thus they lose one third of their time in endeavoring to sell what they make in the other two thirds. This is not the greatest hardship under which they labor. The contempt shewn to domestic manufacture, generally prevents the manufacturer from disposing of his commodities in the market, which obliges him to make great sacrifices. Thus this industrious part of the community too often comes to poverty and distress.

A few patriotic individuals have lately associated themselves for the purpose of assisting these unfortunate people. They propose an application to the legislature for a charter to incorporate a company for encouraging the sale of American manufactures, of woollen, cotton, and linen. The funds of the proposed company are to arise from a subscription of one hundred dollars each, one instalment of which is to be called for as soon as the charter is obtained, and the residue, if wanted, at such times, and to the amount which may be necessary. A warehouse is to be opened for the reception of finished and marketable goods of the above-mentioned fabricks, where the articles shall be deposited at the makers' prices. They are then to be inspected by competent judges of the commodities, who shall say how much, in their judgment, they ought to sell for. The company are then to advance one half in cash on the amount of the price fixed, and the other half when the goods are sold, subject to a very small deduction, to form a fund, from which, after subtracting the expenses of the establishment, the profits or interest on the capital will arise. In order to encourage and stimulate the industry of persons of small means, and who may spin any yarns by hand, such yarns are to be purchased by the company, and paid for immediately. The owners of goods left for sale at the Warehouse may at any time withdraw them, on repaying the money advanced and the expenses incurred; and all goods that may remain unsold, and which the owner will not redeem, shall be sold by auction at stated periods, and if more shall be received for them than the money advanced, and the charges, the surplus shall be paid to the owner of the goods.

The advantages, say the society in the advertisement, resulting to the public from the foregoing plan, are obvious and considerable; independent of those which arise to the manufacturers and the community at large, from the calling into activity so great a mass of useful labour. Let it be considered what satisfaction and advantage every housekeeper will experience from having a warehouse to go to, stored with a variety of goods of the first necessity; where the lowest price at which it can be sold is marked upon every article; and where there is no inducement to the seller to ask more from one customer than another; besides the additional gratification of knowing that every penny laid out here will contribute to encourage the industry of their fellow-citizens, and the wealth and independence of the nation.

Gunpowder, iron ordnance fire-arms, writing and printing paper, are manufactured in the United States.

Hats and shoes are made in every state in large quantities, but those imported from England are preferred. There are no other manufactures of any extent, or deserving notice.

Before I proceed, I shall take this opportunity of observing, that in my intercourse with the superior classes of the inhabitants of the large American cities south of New York, I was not often annoyed with that impertinent curiosity which has already been mentioned as a peculiar characteristic of these republicans. This is confined to the lower orders in some degree in every state, but in New England it is generally prevalent. Among well-bred people, a stranger is questioned only from a natural and moderate thirst of information. Such circles, it should however be observed, are to be found no where but in towns which have connections and commerce with Europe. As the traveller advances towards the south, he will find a gradual diminution of this species of impertinence.

NOTES — CHAPTER XIV

1. Thomas Twining in his *Notes and Reminiscences* described a "mail-wagon" or coach: "The vehicle was a long car with four benches. Three of these in the interior held nine passengers, and a tenth passenger was seated by the side of the driver on the front bench. A light roof was supported by eight slender pillars, four on each side. Three large leather curtains suspended to the roof, one at each side and the third behind, were rolled up or lowered at the pleasure of the passengers. There was no place nor space for luggage, each person being expected to stow his things as he could under his seat or legs. The entrance was in front, over the driver's bench. Of course the three passengers on the back seat were obliged to crawl across the other benches to get to their places. There were no *backs* to the benches to support and relieve us during a rough and fatiguing journey over a newly and ill made road."

2. This statement is taken from Isaac Weld, Jr., *Travels through the States of North America*, London, 1800, pages 41-42, but Janson does not quote it correctly: "The roads in this state (Maryland) are worse than in any one in the union; indeed so very bad are they, that on going from Elkton to the Susquehannah ferry the driver frequently had to call to the passengers in the stage, to lean out of the carriage first at one side then at the other, to prevent it from oversetting in the deep ruts with which the road abounds. 'Now, gentlemen, to the right'; upon which the passengers all stretched their bodies half way out of the carriage to balance it on that side: 'Now, gentlemen, to the left,' and so on. This was found absolutely necessary at least a dozen times in half the number of miles."

3. For a detailed account of Penn's coming to America, see E. P. Oberholtzer, *History of Philadelphia*, I, 20-29, and O. P. Chitwood, *A History of Colonial America*, p. 250 ff.

4. See Oberholtzer, *op. cit.*, for a detailed description of the plan of the streets. Water Street was condemned by many writers for its uncleanliness. In 1798 the alleys were still narrow and filthy.

5. William Sansom.

6. The Watch was established in 1700, and continued to function well into the nineteenth century.

7. Pennsylvania was a pioneer among the States in the matter of prison reform. In 1786 the Assembly made the first step in changing its attitude towards criminals, and from that time it attempted to improve prison conditions.

8. The cornerstone of the penitentiary was laid on August 12, 1797, but the building was not completed until 1800.

9. The first almshouse was opened in 1732. The second, called the Bettering House, began operation in October, 1767. In reality there were two buildings, one for those able to work and another for those not able.

10. The first hospital, Pennsylvania Hospital, was chartered in 1751. In 1792 and 1796 the Assembly enabled it to complete its buildings. In the latter year the west wing was added, and separate apartments were assigned to the insane, who up to this time had been confined under ground. The central building, in partial use by 1800, was completed in 1805.

11. Joseph Priestley, born in Leeds, England, on March 24, 1733, was a scientist and author. He was the discoverer of many chemical compounds. In 1794 he came to America and built a laboratory at Northumberland, Pennsylvania, where his sons lived. Here he continued his scientific experiments until his death on February 6, 1804.

12. Work on this project began in 1799, with Latrobe in charge. On January 21, 1801, water was first pumped into the pipes.

13. This is said to have been the first covered bridge erected in America. It was opened to traffic on January 1, 1805. The cost of building it amounted to upwards of $300,000.

14. This library was an outgrowth of Benjamin Franklin's Junto, established in 1728. In 1731 he secured subscriptions at forty shillings each. The resulting Philadelphia Library became "the mother of all the North American subscription libraries." In 1740 the Assembly invited the collection to the State House; later it was housed in Carpenter's Hall. Finally, in 1790 it was moved into a building of its own on the east side of Fifth Street below Chestnut. The library was open daily from two o'clock until sunset.

15. James Logan suggested the names of the volumes purchased by the original library company. He became interested in the public library idea. Before his death he erected a building at Sixth and Walnut Streets, where he placed many of his own books for public use. This seems to have been the first library in the colonies to have a separate building. At his death, his heirs gave it to the city, and it remained the Loganian Library until 1792, when it merged with the Philadelphia Library.

16. Charles Wilson Peale seems to have been something of a universal genius, who interested himself in art, natural history, mechanics, and politics. For years he accumulated pictures, wax and stuffed figures, and various curiosities. In 1794 the American Philosophical Society invited him to move his collection into its new building, where it remained until 1802.

CHAPTER XV

WASHINGTON, THE FEDERAL CITY AND SEAT OF GOVERNMENT — SLANDER OF ITS FOUNDER — EXTRACT FROM THE AMERICAN HUDIBRAS — WRETCHED STATE OF THE ROADS ABOUT WASHINGTON — DISAPPOINTMENT OF SPECULATORS — THE CAPITOL — THE PRESIDENT'S HOUSE — CAUSES OF THE DEPLORABLE STATE OF THE CITY — HORSE-RACES — MOUNT VERNON — ALEXANDRIA.

THE foundation of the present seat of government of the United States was one of the last national objects of the distinguished character whose name it bears. The ingratitude of a certain portion of Americans to that great and good man, is one of the foulest stains upon their character. After successfully fighting their battles, through a seven years' war, contending with the choicest troops of Europe, and gaining them independence, he resigned his commission to that Congress which appointed him their commander-in-chief, and retired to the peaceful shades of Mount Vernon. A short time only was he allowed for the enjoyment of tranquillity and domestic pleasures; for, on the formation of the federal constitution, he was called, by the unanimous voice of the delegates who ratified that compact on behalf of their fellow citizens, to fill the first post in the executive department of the state. For his military services he had already disclaimed pecuniary recompence, requesting his country to discharge only those expences which the emergencies of war had incurred. The office of the president is by law limited to the term of four years, at the expiration of which time, when Washington again looked forward for the enjoyment of his favorite retirement, his farther services were a second time called for more loudly and unanimously than before. Four years more he devoted to the service of his country; in which time he beheld the foundation of the federal city, the permanent seat of government; and he survived to see the legislators of America convened at the capitol.[1]

It was about this time that the French faction began to raise its clamors, which president Washington soon quelled, by his energetic measures; but the disaffected in secret reviled him for saving their country from the merciless fangs of a set of monsters, who would have enslaved them, under the specious pretext of liberty and equality.

They insinuated that he had pitched on a spot for the seat of government near to his estate of Vernon, in order to inhance its value, though they well knew that his private property was ten-fold greater than his private expences. His choice, I believe, was directed to one object only; the capital is built in the centre of the United States.

One man of this class alone, was hardly enough to appear the public defamer of Washington; but this man was not an American. His name is Duane,[2] — by birth an Irishman — by trade a printer; and who (as Peter Porcupine[3] alledged) had undergone *castigation* in the British settlements in India. But, that the British reader may judge of the great extent, or rather abuse, of the liberty of the press in America, I shall furnish him with a copy of one of his libels upon a character, which, for real and disinterested patriotism, has been seldom equalled, and never excelled in the annals of history. On Washington's retiring from his second presidency, the following paragraph appeared in Duane's daily newspaper, called *The Aurora*, of the 6th of March, 1797.

Lord, now lettest thou thy servant depart in peace, for mine eyes have seen thy salvation! was the pious ejaculation of a man, who beheld a flood of happiness rushing in upon mankind — if ever there was a time which could licence the reiteration of the exclamation, that time is now arrived; for the man, who is the source of all the misfortunes of our country, is this day reduced to a level with his fellow-citizens, and is no longer possessed of power to multiply evils upon the United States. If ever there was a period for rejoicing, this is the moment; every heart in unison with the

Mount Vernon, the Seat of the late President Washington.

freedom and happiness of the people, ought to beat high with exultation that the *name* of WASHINGTON from this day ceases to give a currency to political iniquity, and to legalise corruption. A new æra is opening upon us — a new æra which promises much to the public; for public measures must now stand upon their own merit, and nefarious projects can no longer be supported by a *name*. When a retrospect is taken of the Washington administration for eight years past, it is a subject of the greatest astonishment that a single individual should have cancelled the principle of republicanism in an enlightened people just emerged from the gulph of despotism, and should have carried his designs against the public liberty so far, as to have put in jeopardy its very existence: such, however, are the facts; and with these staring us in the face, this day ought to be a jubilee in the United States.

What indignation must every good man feel, upon reading this atrocious libel on the virtuous Washington! Mr. Fessenden,[4] the Hudibras of America; that same Mr. Fessenden who deceived the sage reviewers of London, in his "Terrible Tractoration," has resented the indignity in the following lines:

Step forward, demagogue Duane,
Than whom a greater rogue in grain,
Ne'er fortified by mob alliance,
Dare bid the powers that be, defiance.

Law, order, talents, and civility,
Before your worshipful mobility,
Must bow, while you their thinking man,
Lead by the nose your kindred clan.

Thou art indeed a rogue as sly,
As ever coined the ready lie,
Amongst the Catalines of faction,
None calls more energies in action.

With impudence the most consummate,
You publish all that you can come at,
To make for discord's sake, a handle,
Of private anecdote, or scandal.

Few good and great men can be nam'd
Your scoundrelship has not defam'd;
And scarce a rogue who ought to hang
Who is not number'd with your gang.

And thou, audacious renegadoe,
With many a libellous bravadoe,
Assail'dst Columbia's, god-like son.
The great, th' immortal WASHINGTON!

Dost thou remember much about a
Droll 'scape of thine once at Calcutta;
When erst invited to a breakfast,
In noose you nigh had got your neck fast?*

Sir John, however, on the whole,
Did wrong to set you on a pole;
For such a patriot ought to ride
Suspended from the *under side.*

As this man is the leader of what is termed the *Jeffersonian Mobocracy*, I shall add another note from the same pen, by way of shewing the reader the character he bears amongst the federalists.

The effects of Duane's, and of the designing and wrong-headed scribblers who labour for the *Aurora*, are ever directed to the purpose of destroying all kinds of distinction in society, except merely such as a cunning man may establish as leader of a mob. The learned professions are the constant objects of his abuse, and that of the levelling systems who dash in the Aurora. Should his strength

*"Duane is said to have set up for a patriot at Calcutta, and commenced his useful labours as editor of a newspaper, by exerting himself to foment a quarrel between the civil and military departments. Sir John Short (now Lord Teignmouth), who then commanded, paid so little regard to the *rights of man*, that he merely rewarded him with a kind of wooden-horsical promotion, which is not thought to confer any great honour on those who are the subjects of that kind of elevation. He was then sent to England, from whence he was imported, to teach Americans liberty and equality under the auspices of Emperor Jefferson. Duane says, that he was kidnapped by Sir John, having been invited to breakfast. But the man is so given to lying, that we wish our readers to place no dependance on that part of the story."[5]

succeed, *brutal strength and savage cunning* will be the only foundation for eminence. Indeed, he has laid the axe at the root of civilization; and, unless great exertions are made to counteract the influence of that vile species of poison, which he publishes, its destructive effects will for ages be felt in America.

To return to the city of Washington — I have remarked, that on my return to London, the first general enquiry of my friends is respecting this far-famed place. The description given of it by interested scribblers, may well serve to raise an Englishman's curiosity, and lead him to fancy the capital of Columbia a terrestrial paradise.

The entrance, or avenues, as they are pompously called, which lead to the American seat of government, are the worst roads I passed in the country; and I appeal to every citizen who has been unlucky enough to travel the stages north and south leading to the city, for the truth of the assertion. I particularly allude to the mail stage road from Bladensburg to Washington, and from thence to Alexandria. In the winter season, during the sitting of Congress, every turn of your waggon wheel (for I must again observe, that there is no such thing in the country as what we call a stage coach, or a post-chaise,) is for many miles attended with danger. The roads are never repaired; deep ruts, rocks, and stumps of trees, every minute impede your progress, and often threaten your limbs with dislocation.[6]

Arrived at the city, you are struck with its grotesque appearance. In one view from the capitol hill, the eye fixes upon a row of uniform houses, ten or twelve in number, while it faintly discovers the adjacent tenements to be miserable wooden structures, consisting, when you approach them, of two or three rooms one above another. Again, you see the hotel, which was vauntingly promised, on laying the foundation, to rival the large inns in England. This, like every other private adventure, failed: the walls and the roof remain, but not a window! and, instead of accommodating the members of Congress, and travellers of distinction, as proposed, a number of the lowest order of Irish have long held the title of *naked possession*, from which, were it ever to become an object, it would be difficult to eject them. Turning the eye, a well finished edifice presents itself, surrounded by lofty trees, which never felt the stroke of the axe. The president's house, the offices of state, and a little theatre, where an itinerant company repeated, during a part of the last year, the lines of Shakespeare, Otway, and Dryden, to empty benches, terminate the view of the Pennsylvania, or Grand Avenue.[7]

Speculation, the life of the American, embraced the design of the new city. Several companies of speculators purchased lots, and began to build handsome streets, with an ardor that soon promised a large and populous city.[8] Before they arrived at the attic story, the failure was manifest; and in that state at this moment are the walls of many scores of houses begun on a plan of elegance. In some parts, purchasers have cleared the wood from their grounds, and erected temporary wooden buildings: others have fenced in their lots, and attempted to cultivate them; but the sterility of the land laid out for the city is such, that this plan has also failed. The country adjoining consists of woods in a state of nature, and in some places of mere swamps, which give the scene a curious patch-work appearance. The view of the noble river Potomack, which the eye can trace till it terminates at Alexandria, is very fine. The navigation of the river is good from the bay of Chesapeak, till the near approach to the city, where bars of sand are formed, which every year encroach considerably on the channel. The frigate which brought the Tunisian embassy, grounded on one of these shoals, and the barbarians were obliged to be landed in boats. This is another great disadvantage to the growth of the city. It never can become a place of commerce, while Balitimore lies on one side, and Alexandria on the other; even admitting the navigation to be equally good — nor can the wild and uneven spot laid out into streets be cleared and levelled for building upon, for many years, even with the most indefatigable exertions.

The capitol, of which two wings are now finished, is of hewn stone and will be a superb edifice, worthy of its name. The architect who built the first wing,[9] left the country soon after its completion; the corresponding part was carried on under the direction of Mr. Latrobe,[10] an Englishman;* from whose taste and judgment much may be expected in finishing the centre of the building; the design of which, as shewn to me by Doctor Thornton,[11] is truly elegant.

The president's house is situated one mile from the Capitol, at the extremity of Pennsylvania Avenue. The contemplated streets of this embryo city are called avenues, and every state gives name to one. That of Pennsylvania is the largest; in fact I never heard of more than that and the New Jersey Avenue, except some houses uniformly built, in one of which lives Mr. Jefferson's printer, John Harrison Smith,[13] a few more of inferior note, with some public-

* Mr. Benjamin Latrobe is the second son of the late Rev. Mr. Latrobe, minister of the Moravian Chapel in Fetter-lane, London, a man highly esteemed and respected, not only by his own society, but by all to whom he was known. His maternal relations were natives of America. He received his education at the school of the United Brethren at Fulneck, in Yorkshire, and afterwards went to prosecute his studies at their seminaries at Niesky and Barby, in Germany. On his return he resided for some years in London, where he held a situation in the Stamp Office. During this interval he introduced himself to public notice as the translator of the "History of Counts Struensee and Brandt," and "Anecdotes of Frederic the Great of Prussia." Mr. Latrobe particularly excels in the art of design, and to this talent he is probably indebted for his appointment to the situation he holds in America, of which country he has been an inhabitant, I believe, about twelve years. His brother, the Rev. Christian Ignatius Latrobe, one of the present ministers of Fetter-lane Chapel, is distinguished for his knowledge of music, and their maternal uncle, Mr. John Antes, by birth an American, and now resident at Fulneck, is well known for his mechanical genius, having received several premiums for inventions and improvements, from the Society of Arts. This gentleman lived many years in Egypt, where he made a personal acquaintance with the celebrated Bruce,[12] then engaged in his expedition to discover the source of the Nile. There too he underwent the severe discipline of the bastinado, the particulars of which transaction, together with various observations on the country, were published by him, about the year 1801.

houses, and here and there a little *grog-shop*, this boasted avenue is as much wilderness as Kentucky, with this disadvantage, that the soil is good for nothing. Some half-starved cattle browzing among the bushes, present a melancholy spectacle to a stranger, whose expectation has been wound up by the illusive description of speculative writers. So very thinly is the city peopled, and so little is it frequented, that quails and other birds are constantly shot within a hundred yards of the Capitol, and even during the sitting of the houses of congress.

Ten years ago Mr. Weld, speaking of the president's house, tells us of its being then erected; and of an hundred acres of land left for pleasure-ground, and a park or mall, to run in an easterly direction towards the Capitol — that the buildings on either side of this mall, were all to be elegant of their kind, and that among the number it was *proposed* to have houses built at the public expence for the accommodation of public ministers. This traveller then proceeds with informing us that other parts of this city are appointed for churches, theatres, colleges, &c. In nearly the same state as Mr. Weld saw the city so long ago, it still remains, except indeed that some of the few houses which were then building, are now falling to ruin, the unfortunate owner having been ruined before he could get them roofed.*

Neither park, nor mall, neither churches, theatres, nor colleges, could I discover so lately as the summer of 1806.[14] A small place has indeed been erected since Mr. Weld visited Washington, in the Pennsylvania Avenue, called a theatre, in which Mr. Green and the Virginia company of comedians were nearly starved the only season it was occupied, and were obliged to go off to Richmond during the very height of the sitting of congress. Public offices on each

* In proof of this observation, a traveller need only cast his eye on what is called the twenty buildings, at Greenleaf's Point, begun by the gentleman above alluded to, Nickolson and others, first-rate speculators. A long range of houses there was so advanced before they discovered their mistake, as to be covered in, but they remain unfinished, and are dropping piecemeal.

side of the president's house uniformly built of brick, may also, perhaps, have been built subsequent to that period. That great man who planned the city, and after whom it is named, certainly entertained the hopes that it would at some future period equal ancient Rome in splendor and magnificence. Among the regulations for building were these — that the houses should be of brick or stone — the walls to be at least thirty feet high, and to be built parallel to the line of the street.

The president's house is certainly a neat but plain piece of architecture, built of hewn stone, said to be of a better quality than Portland stone, as it will cut like marble, and resist the change of the seasons in a superior degree. Only part of it is furnished; the whole salary of the president would be inadequate to the expence of completing it in a style of suitable elegance. Rooms are fitted up for himself, an audience chamber, and apartments for Mr. Thomas Mann Randolph, and Mr. Eppes, and their respective families, who married two of his daughters, and are members of the house of representatives.

The ground around it, instead of being laid out in a suitable style, remains in its ancient rude state, so that, in a dark night, instead of finding your way to the house, you may, perchance, fall into a pit, or stumble over a heap of rubbish. The fence round the house is of the meanest sort; a common post and rail enclosure. This parsimony destroys every sentiment of pleasure that arises in the mind, in viewing the residence of the president of a nation, and is a disgrace to the country.

Though the permanent seat of government has been fixed at Washington, its progress has been proved to be less rapid than any other new settlement supported only by trade. The stimulus held out by the presence of congress has proved artificial and unnatural. After enumerating the public buildings, the private dwelling-houses of the officers of government, the accommodations set apart for the members of the legislature, and the temporary tenements of those dependent on them, the remainder of this boasted city is a mere wilderness of wood and stunted shrubs, the occupants of barren land. Strangers after viewing the offices of state, are apt to enquire for the city, while they are in its very centre.

"The golden dreams of the speculator," says an American writer in describing the city of Washington, "ended in disappointment. His houses are untenanted, and going to ruin, and his land either lies a dead burthen on his hands, or he disposes of it, if not at a less price than his fond imagination had anticipated. The present proprietor is obliged to moderate his views of profit, and to centre all his hopes in the continuance of the government where it now is."*[15]

Another writer in Philadelphia says, "The increase of Washington is attributed by sensible Americans to its true cause, SPECULATION; a field for which being once opened to the land-jobbers, who swarm in the United States, they made large purchases, and bent all their resources towards running up buildings, and giving the city an eccentric appearance of prosperity. So industriously have those purchases been pursued, that in London five hundred pounds sterling was at one time asked for about the sixth part of a single lot, many of the prime of which, in point of situation, were originally purchased for twenty, and at three years credit. If this sudden increase had arisen from actual settlement alone, a more undeniable proof would be given of the prosperity of Washington, than by the magic appearance of uninhabited structures like mushrooms after a shower."

It has been asserted that a seventy-four gun ship was building on the waters of the Potomack, from which circumstance no doubt was entertained of its channel being deep

* Many English artists, enchanted with the description, given by interested writers, left their employ, which produced them a competence and happiness; in order to exert their abilities in finishing this scene of contemplated magnificence, and under the hopes of rapidly accumulating a fortune.

enough for ships of any burthen. This like most travellers' exaggerations, is not true — no ship of the line, nor even a frigate, was ever constructed on the Potomack.[16] The ship carpenters employed by government have enough to do to repair those already built, most of which are in a state of decay. I saw the plank and some of the timbers of the frigate called the United States, built at Philadelphia not twelve years ago, so rotten, that they crumbled to powder on being handled. The timber of America is not so durable as that of Europe.

The only part of this city which continues to encrease is the navy-yard, but this circumstance is entirely owing to the few ships of war which the Americans have in commission, being ordered there to be fitted out and paid off. Tippling shops, and houses of rendezvous for sailors and their doxies, with a number of the lowest order of traders, constitute what is called the navy-yard.

Among the sufferers by the Washington speculation is Mr. Thomas Law, brother to Lord Ellenborough, who, as has been already observed, invested the greatest part of the money he obtained in India, in building near the capitol, where he still resides, under the mortifying circumstance of daily witnessing whole rows of the shells of his houses gradually falling to pieces.

In November, in each year, there are horse-races in the capital of America. I happened to arrive just at this time on horseback at George Town, which is about two miles from the race-ground.[17] After an early dinner, served up sooner on the occasion, a great bustle was created by the preparations for the sport. It had been my intention to pass the remainder of the day at the far-famed city, but, stimulated by curiosity I determined to mingle with the sporting group. Having paid for my dinner, and the refreshment for my horse, I proceeded to the stable. I had delivered my beast to a yellow fellow, M'Laughlin, the landlord's head ostler. This name reminds me of an anecdote of Macklin, the English theatrical Nestor. It is said that his proper name was M'Laughlin, but dissatisfied with the harsh pronunciation, he sunk the uncouth letters, and called himself Macklin. Be that as it may, I went for my horse, to attend the race, and repeatedly urged my dingy ostler to bring him out. I waited long with great patience at the stable-door, and saw him lead out a number without discovering mine. I again remonstrated, and soon heard a message delivered to him to saddle the horses of Mr. A. Mr. B. Mr. C. and so on. He now appeared with the horses according to the recent order, leading them by their bridles. Previous to this, I had saddled my own horse, seeing the hurry of the time, yet I thought it a compliment due to me that the servant should lead him to me. I now spoke in a more angry tone, conceiving myself insulted by neglect. The Indian sourly replied, "I must wait upon the gentlemen," (that is the sporting sharpers). "Then," quoth I, "a gentleman neglected in his proper turn, I find, must wait upon you." I was provoked to knock the varlet to the ground. The horses which he led startled at the sudden impulse, ran off, and before the ostler recovered from the effects of the blow, or the horses were caught, I led out my nag, and leisurely proceeded to the turf.

Here I witnessed a scene perfectly novel. I have been at the races of Newmarket, Epsom, York, in short I have seen, for aught I know to the contrary, one hundred thousand pounds won and lost in a single day, in England. On coming up to an enclosed ground, a quarter of a dollar was demanded for my admission. Rather than turn back, though no sportsman, I submitted. Four-wheeled carriages paid a dollar, and half that sum was exacted for the most miserable single-horse chaise. Though the day was raw, cold, and threatening to rain or snow, there were abundance of ladies, decorated as if for a ball. In this year (1803) congress was summoned very early by President Jefferson, upon the contemplated purchase of Louisiana, and to pass a bill in order to facilitate his election again, as president. Many scores of American legislators, who are all allowed six dollars a day, besides their travelling expences, went on *foot* from the Capitol, above four English miles; to attend the sport. Nay, it is an indisputable fact, that the houses of congress adjourned at a very early hour to indulge the members for this purpose. It rained during the course, and thus the law-makers of the country were driven into the booths, and thereby compelled to eat and pay for what was there called a dinner; while their contemplated meal remained untouched at their respective boarding-houses. Economy is the order of the day, in the Jeffersonian administration of that country, and the members pretend to avail themselves of it, even in their personal expences.

I saw on the race-ground, as in other countries, people of every description, sharpers in abundance, and *grog*, the joy of Americans, in oceans. Well mounted, and a stranger, I was constantly pestered by these sharks; and had I been idiot enough to have committed myself to them, I should soon have been stripped of all my travelling cash.

On my last visit to the navy yard, I found six frigates, dismantled and laid up in ordinary, and one nearly equipped for sea, for the purpose of carrying back the Tunisian embassy to Barbary. A small vessel of war, pierced for 20 guns, had just been launched. Mr. Jefferson, two years ago, adopted an idea of his own, in order to raise the credit of the American navy, and for the destruction of the powers of Barbary. This is, to build a number of small vessels of about 100 tons burden, to be called gun-boats, each of which is provided with two heavy pieces of ordnance — one at the stem, and the other at the stern. Though the inutility of these mockeries of men-of-war has been manifested on many occasions, yet the president persists in riding his naval hobby-horse, even in Kentucky; where several gun-boats are building on the river Ohio. One of them was nearly lost on a voyage to the Mediterranean — being, the whole voyage, to use a sea phrase, "wet and under water." Another, *gun boat, No.* 1. (thus they are named, to No. 8,) in a hurricane in South Carolina, was driven nearly a mile into the woods. These vessels must be very unmanageable in action. It would not be amiss if the projector could invent a piece of mechanism which would quickly turn them round; for, in this case, they might as we turn a wheel, first present the head gun, and then, while it was loading, by a magic touch, in a second give a stern shot! Thus, these nimble and redoubted gunboats might chance to beat off an Algerine, or Tripoline rover.[18]

Added to these, the Americans have a frigate and two or three small vessels of war in the Mediterranean; and which constitute their navy.[19] One of their finest frigates, in attempting to bombard Tripoli, grounded and every exertion of the crew to get her off, proved ineffectual. She was taken possession of by the armed boats of the Barbarians, and the whole crew led into slavery, where they endured greater hardships, and bore heavier burthens than their own domestic negro slaves. Strange reverse of fortune; that those who from infancy have been accustomed to hold the whip, are now flogged and chained with ten-fold cruelty!

Travellers, whose only business is to view the country, and make observations on the manners of the people, generally visit Mount Vernon, once the favorite retirement of General Washington, on their progress through the United States. A description of this place by various writers is already before the public, but a correct view is difficult to be found. The accuracy of the annexed may be depended upon. There is nothing very striking in the design or execution of the building, but the situation, commanding an extensive prospect over the majestic river Potomack, where it is nearly two miles wide, added to the circumstance of its having been the seat of one of the greatest characters of the last century, renders it an object of attention. As a tribute of respect to his memory, vessels of war, and such as are armed, on passing, salute the house. The Mount Vernon estate is now in the occupation of Bushrod Washington, Esq. a nephew of the late general, and one of the associate judges of the supreme federal court. The mount is two hundred yards above the level of the water, and the house stands within sixty yards of the verge, nine miles below Alexandria, and in Fairfax county, Virginia: it is 280 miles from the sea. In front there is a lofty portico, ninety-six feet in length, and supported by eight pillars. The rear is towards the river, and it is a pleasing relief to the eye of the passenger, wearied with the succession of woods that clothe its banks. On the the other side is the state of Maryland, which renders the view from the mount more delightful. There are two wings to the house, and on the either side is a grove of trees, the choicest of the forest. The shrubberies and gardens are laid out in the English style, and through them wind serpentine gravel walks. There is a small park of deer, some of which were imported from England, and they entice the wild American herds into their company, so that they may easily be taken.

There is in the house only one large apartment, called the banqueting room, and this was finished after the general had converted his sword into a plough-share. During his absence it had fallen much to decay; devoting his whole time to the service of his country, for which he never would accept any remuneration, it was totally neglected."*

In the course of the war, three small British armed ships sailed up the Potomack as far as Alexandria, and conse-

* Throughout his campaigns he was attended by a black man, one of his slaves, who proved very faithful to his trust. This man, amongst others belonging to him, he liberated, and by his will left him a handsome maintenance for the remainder of his life. The horse which bore the general so often in battle is still alive. The noble animal, together with the whole of his property, was sold on his death, under a clause in his will, and the charger was purchased by Daniel Dulany, Esq., of Shuter's Hill, near Alexandria, in whom it has found an indulgent master. I have often seen Mr. Dulany riding the steed of Washington in a gentle pace, for it is now grown old. It is of a cream color, well proportioned, and was carefully trained to military manœuvres.[20]

quently passed Mount Vernon. I am at a loss to conjecture what object this force had in view. There were no stores, nor anything on the river worth making a prize of. They did considerable damage in their progress, but the commanders gave strict orders to respect Mount Vernon; and, to their honor, it was not molested. Their arrival at Alexandria threw the people into dreadful alarm, the seat of war being far removed from that place. They mustered in haste at the market-place, under the command of Colonel John Fitzgerald, one of General Washington's aides-de-camp, who happened then to be on leave of absence with his family, residing there. The ships displayed an intention of landing, and Fitzgerald, leaving the command to a militia-colonel, proceeded at the head of several of the citizens to Jones's point, in order to repel the invaders. Soon after the departure of this party, the ships fired a few shot at the town, upon which the commander of the militia ordered his colours to be struck; but for this pusillanimity he was chastised upon the spot. The ships never seriously meditated a landing, and these were merely random-shot to create an alarm, on their departure.

Alexandria was about eight years ago a very flourishing place; but the great losses sustained from the capture of American vessels by the French in the West Indies, occasioned many failures. In the year 1803, the yellow fever,[21] which broke out there for the first time, swept off a number of its inhabitants. These shocks have so deeply affected the mercantile interest, that the town has but two or three ships in the trade with Great Britain; and there is little prospect of its ever attaining to its former prosperity.

Alexandria, first called Belhaven,[22] is laid out upon the plan of Philadelphia; and being well built and paved, in point of uniformity and neatness it somewhat resembles that city on a small scale. Its situation is elevated, commanding a view of the river and the opposite shore of Maryland. The navigation of the Potomack, on whose banks the town is built, is very good. I question whether a line of battle ship might not come up from the sea, and lie alongside of the wharfs, which is a distance of 289 miles. Six miles higher on this river is the city of Washington, but a bar impedes the navigation up to the navy-yard of the government.

The following appropriations were made by the government of the United States for the navy for 1805, a year when they were at war with Tripoli:

Pay and subsistence of officers, and pay of seamen	$415,578.00
Provisions	227,086.40
Medicines, instruments, hospital stores	10,750.00
*Repairs of vessels	411,951.20
The corps of marines	82,593.60
Cloathing for the marines	16,536.00
Military stores for the marines	1,635.00
Medicine and hospital stores	1,250.00
Contingent expenses	8,419.00
Navy-yards, docks, clerks, &c.	60,000.00
	$1,235,799.20

or about 278,054*l.* 15*s.* 6*d.* sterling — not much more than the yearly charge of two line of battle ships in the English navy, manned, and with a year's provision. This, too, was a war year; in peace, their appropriation will hardly amount to a third of this sum.[23]

NOTES — CHAPTER XV

1. Janson errs in stating that Washington survived to see the legislators convene in Washington The seat of government removed from Philadelphia in 1800. The first Congress met at the new capital in November of that year.

2. Again Janson's prejudices lead him to distort facts, if he really knew them. William Duane was born May 17, 1760, near Lake Champlain, New York, of Irish parentage. Following his father's death in 1765, he returned to Ireland, where his mother disinherited him for marrying a Protestant. He learned the printer's trade, and went to India in 1787, where he established the *Indian World* at Calcutta. Because of his denunciation of the methods of the

* Though the American navy is scarcely twelve years old, yet the reader will perceive, by this charge, that the repairs are nearly equal to the "*pay and subsistence of the officers, and the pay of the seamen.*"

East India Company and his espousal of the grievances of army officers, he was arrested without charges, deported without trial, and his property confiscated. Returning to London, he served as parliamentary reporter for the *General Advertiser* and sought the restitution of his property through Parliament and the courts. Despairing of justice, he left England in disgust. In Philadelphia he became associated with Benjamin Franklin Bache in editing the *Aurora.* When Bache died in September, 1798, Duane succeeded him as editor and made the *Aurora* the most powerful weapon of the Jeffersonians.

3. William Cobbett, editor of the *Gazette.*

4. Thomas Green Fessenden, the most important American satirist in verse between Trumbull and Lowell. *Terrible Tractoration,* a vigorous Hudabrastic satire, was a pretended assault on the metallic tractors. Actually it ridiculed the most prominent of the skeptical physicians in England and Scotland. Although the book had small merit, it was surprisingly popular.

5. See Note 2.

6. Weld in his *Travels through the States of North America,* pp. 47-48, also complained bitterly of the condition of American roads. That from Baltimore to Washington was the worst he had seen anywhere. Abigail Adams, in a letter to Mrs. Smith, on November 21, 1800, also added her words of protest concerning the so-called roads. See *Letters of Mrs.* (Abigail) *Adams,* ed. C. F. Adams, pp. 239-40.

7. Claude G. Bowers in his *Hamilton and Jefferson,* pp. 486-89, gives a vivid description, based on contemporary sources, of Washington in 1800. W. B. Bryan, *A History of the National Capital,* I, 279-380, sketches the appearance of the city. The hotel to which Janson refers was located near New Jersey Avenue. The United States or National Theatre opened on August 22, 1800, the first regular place of amusement in Washington. A company under the management of Wignell and Reinagle came from the New Theatre in Philadelphia and remained for nearly two months. Performances were given three times weekly. Three hundred persons were considered a full house, and that number attended several performances.

8. Speculation in land began at the inception of the city and continued with increasing volume for several years. Among the investors were James Greenleaf, Robert Morris, Thomas Law, and Samuel Blodgett.

9. George Hadfield, who came to America in 1795, followed Stephen Hallet as architect of the Capitol. Like his predecessor, he was discharged, May 28, 1798, on account of disagreements with the commissioners over his desire to change Thornton's design. In 1800 when Congress first assembled in Washington, only the north wing of the Capitol was completed. In 1803 Congress provided for the erection of the south wing.

10. Latrobe's mother was Anna Margaret Antes of Germantown, Pennsylvania. In 1803 Jefferson appointed Latrobe to the newly created post of surveyor of public buildings in Washington. His first task was adding the south wing to the Capitol.

11. Dr. William Thornton, born on the island of Tortola in 1761, studied medicine at the University of Edinburgh. He practiced his profession at Tortola

and while there saw the announcement asking for the submitting of plans for a capitol building.

12. James Bruce, the African traveller and explorer.

13. Evidently Janson refers to Samuel Harrison Smith, who, on October 1, 1800, began the publication of the *National Intelligencer*. In this paper he proposed "to enlighten not only by fact but by reason."

14. Christ Church, Episcopal, occupied a small frame building in 1800. St. Patrick's Catholic Church on F Street, and St. Andrew's Presbyterian Church, both frame structures, opened their doors before 1800. In 1803 the Baptist church occupied a brick structure on the southwest corner of 19th and I Streets, N. W. Although no school which deserved the designation of college functioned in Washington at this time, various academies were in operation.

15. Allen C. Clark in *Greenleaf and Law in the Federal City* says tourists gave "overdrawn" descriptions of Washington and cites Janson as an example. However, he fails to produce proof that the specific facts as given are incorrect.

16. In the *Centinel of Liberty* of June 18, 1799, William Marbury of Annapolis, naval agent, advertised "for ship timber for a 74-gun ship to be built at the navy yard, Washington." In January, 1800, Captain Thomas Tingey was ordered to Washington to superintend building this ship and to aid in the arrangement of the navy yard.

17. Horse racing began as early as 1769 in Georgetown. In 1803 the races were held on the grounds of the Washington Jockey Club, located about four miles from Capitol Hill. The spectators numbered between 3,000 and 4,000 people of all ages and both sexes. Both houses of Congress adjourned.

18. Gunboats were authorized by Congress and approved by President Adams as a part of the naval equipment in 1798, but none appears to have been built at that time. President Jefferson presented the matter to Congress in 1804 and again in 1807. An act of March 2, 1805, provided for an appropriation of $60,000 for the purpose of building not more than 25 gunboats. Gunboat No. 7 with Lieutenant Peter Ogelvie in command sailed for the Mediterranean on June 20, 1805, and was never heard from again. The other nine made the trip to the Mediterranean successfully, "a feat requiring no little daring and skill." Gunboat No. 8 was commanded on this voyage by Lieutenant Nathaniel Harriden. These vessels played an important part in the war with the Barbary pirates. See Maclay, *History of the U. S. Navy*, I, 298.

19. On July 24, 1804, Captain Preble had collected off the harbor of Tripoli a fleet of fifteen ships, including gunboats.

20. John Hunter, a merchant of London, spent a day and night at Mount Vernon in 1785. In his diary he wrote: "Thursday 17th November (1785) . . . I afterwards went into his stables, where among an amazing number of horses, I saw old Nelson, now 22 years of age, that carried the General almost always during the war; Blueskin, another fine old horse next to him, now and then had that honor. . . . They have heard the roar of many a cannon in their time. Blueskin was not the favorite, on account of his not standing fire so well as venerable old Nelson." From this statement, it would appear that the animal owned by Daniel Dulany could scarcely have been old Nelson.

21. In 1797-98 Alexandria suffered from a very fatal epidemic of yellow fever. Governor Wood ordered a quarantine of the town.

22. The early settlers erected a large tobacco warehouse on the bluff overlooking the river and named the settlement which grew up around it Belhaven, in honor of a planter by that name. An act of the Assembly in 1748 for erecting a town gave it the name of Alexandria, because it was laid out on land of the Alexanders.

23. See the Naval Appropriation Act, *Annals of Congress, 1804-1805*, II, 1661.

CHAPTER XVI

EMBASSY FROM TUNIS — EXTRAORDINARY CONDUCT OF THE TURKISH NEGOCIATOR — DRUNKENNESS OF HIS ATTENDANTS — HIS DEPARTURE FROM AMERICA — DEPUTATION FROM THE CREEK AND OSAGE INDIANS — THEIR APPEARANCE IN THE HOUSE OF REPRESENTATIVES — THEIR SONGS — DANCE OF SAVAGES IN THE WASHINGTON THEATRE — SUDDEN DEATH OF ONE OF THE CHIEFS — PARTICULARS OF THE EXPEDITION FOR EXPLORING THE MISSOURI.

THE conduct of the Americans in maintaining the representatives of the Tunisian tyrant for so long a period, has doubtless excited the surprise, and perhaps the contempt of civilized nations.

The circumstance which gave rise to the admission of a train of barbarians into the United States, is certainly contemptible. It appears from a message of the president to congress, that during the blockade of Tripoli by the squadron of the United States a small cruizer under the flag of Tunis, which, with two prizes, (all of trifling value) attempted to enter Tripoli, was turned back, warned, and on a second attempt to enter, was taken, and detained as prizes by the squadron. Her restitution was claimed by the bey of Tunis, with a threat of war in terms so serious, that on withdrawing from the blockade of Tripoli, the commanding officer of the squadron thought it his duty to repair to Tunis with his squadron, and to require a categorical answer whether peace or war was intended. The bey preferred explaining himself by an ambassador to the United States, who, on his arrival, renewed the request that the vessel and her prizes should be restored. It was deemed proper to give this proof of friendship to the bey, and the ambassador was informed that the vessels would be restored. He afterwards made a requisition of naval stores to be sent to the bey, in order to secure a peace for the term of three years, with a threat of war in case of refusal.

This ambassador, whose name is Sadi Suliman Mala Manni,[1] was taken on board the Chesapeak frigate, at Tunis, with a numerous suite, and landed, *under a discharge of cannon*, at the Navy-Yard in the city of Washington. Carriages were ready to convey them to one of the best houses in the city, and which had been engaged for them by order of the president. The cavalcade was formidable, and the dress of the ambassador and his two secretaries was a novelty which attracted considerable attention.

The day after taking possession, a coach was in attendance to carry these three personages to Mr. Jefferson, whose plain and unassuming habits formed a striking contrast with the pompous forms of Turkish despotism. This, it appears, was merely a visit to pave the way "to better acquaintance," for the Turk was in no hurry to enter upon the subject of his credentials. He proposed to repeat his visit in a day or two, and to honor the president by drinking coffee and smoking his pipe with him. In all matters which tended to his ease, this mockery of diplomatic functions was extremely observant; but his appetite only increased with indulgence. He soon became importunate in his demands for personal gratification and public homage. A military guard, preceded by music, was ordered to do duty at his house, while carriages were ready at his command.

The charge of the embassy was defrayed by the United States; and it is the more surprising, economy being the constant "order of the day," that these diplomatic drones should be maintained so many months at the public cost. It was even whispered that the mussulman threw out hints, which could not be misunderstood, of the inconvenience he experienced from the want of his seraglio — that a few female domestics would be agreeable, &c., &c. It is beyond a doubt that he found means, in part, to gratify his inordinate sensuality; for the fact was promulgated by Mr. J. Randolph, in his place as a representative of the people.*

The repeated and increasing demands of Mala Manni began to grow extremely troublesome and expensive. His guard was removed, and his carriage no longer rolled about at the public cost. It now became evident that the cunning Turk was "nursing the job" with the utmost circumspection. In order to save a little out of the drain which he had made from the public treasury, an officer was sent to make a bargain, for a stipulated sum per week, for the maintenance of himself and his people. This was still more agreeable to Mala Manni, and the only difficulty consisted in the sum to be named for that purpose. Two hundred dollars were at length agreed upon as a weekly provision for these unwelcome visitors. Previous to this, a purveyor was constantly employed in providing for their table; but by this mode they were never satisfied, always wanting better accommodations than the country would produce.

The Turks now *condescended* to cater for themselves, and it was believed that the ambassador did the job for *one half* the sum appropriated to that purpose. He immediately observed a rigid economy; would allow no strong liquors to his followers; and, instead of two or three courses at dinner, a single dish or two was served up, and the joint so exactly proportioned, as to leave not a single fragment behind.

Under a charge of DRUNKENNESS† he drove his two secretaries out of his house; well knowing they would not be suffered to starve amongst Americans. Thus, it was by some believed, that *avarice* was his ruling passion, and that by reducing the number of his followers, leaving them thus doubly upon the public, he merely intended to multiply the

* See the extract from his speech, page 148. A. of C., 1805-7, 569, March 5, 1806.

† These disciples of Mahomet will drink almost as large a quantity of *spirits* in a day, as a London coal-heaver would of porter.

number of dollars that were to accompany him back to Tunis. Others scrupled not to say, that the old Turk was *jealous* of his young secretaries; for it was admitted on all hands that he had formed a tender connection with a frail Christian of the softer sex. I was unwilling to credit this; for a more disgusting figure, bending too under the weight of years, can scarcely be conceived; but the very dregs of prostitution appear to be emptied into the city of Washington.

One evening, during the last spring, I went to Stelle's Hotel, on the Capitol Hill, in order to secure a place in the stage-coach, or rather waggon, to Baltimore. In the bar-room I found the two degraded secretaries, and a third Turk, in the most perfect harmony with several Christians. They were engaged in trials of personal strength, such as wrestling, &c. I was informed that the Mahometans were at first very forward in introducing this athletic exercise, and prided themselves on their muscular force; but they had been so often tripped up by the agility of smaller Christians, and their breech had so sensibly suffered by suddenly coming in contact with the floor, that they now were afraid lest the feet of their opponents should effect that which could not always be done by the arm. They are great drunkards, for they were every ten or fifteen minutes drinking gin, unadulterated by water; and I found myself under the necessity of contributing towards their intoxication. They were, however, perfectly good-humored, or perhaps, in more suitable words, the barbarians were strongly inclined to sociability with the Christians. They spent their time chiefly at the little "grog shops," and at night were generally in a state of drunkenness.

About the end of the month of May this mock embassy commenced its departure from Washington, after rolling there, in luxury and sloth, between five and six months, The government having with firmness resisted the impudent demand of naval stores, no valedictory compliments passed on the occasion; on the contrary, in order to fill up the measure of the farce, his Mahometan highness hurled threats of the vengeance of his barbarian master.

The order of departure was as ostentatious and expensive as could be devised. His highness, with a few attendants, set off the first day, and on the following, the secretaries had their cavalcade set in motion. The first day's route was to Baltimore, where they *indulged* the inhabitants with a view of their sacred persons at the theatre and on the race ground. In this manner did the government, in spite of the threat, conduct the barabrians to Boston, at which port the frigate Chesapeak was ordered to receive and convey them back to Tunis. Now, as this ship was ordered from Washington to Boston for this purpose alone, it follows, that the good citizens of America were not only, at their own charge, to return them to their native land, but also, while they still breathed the threats of war, for their gratification, to escort them near five hundred miles, when they might have been shipped within as many yards of the very spot where they insulted the country.[2]

The temper of the people on this head may be ascertained from the following extract, copied from the Philadelphia *Aurora*, a daily newspaper, devoted to the measures of President Jefferson:

> The information communicated to Congress in the message from the president, respecting the state of relations with Tunis, has been for some time anticipated. When the ex-minister of Spain, Yrujo, was at Washington, it is said, he labored very hard with Mali Manni, the barbarian ambassador, to excite his enmity against our government; indeed, he is said to have so far prevailed as to draw from the barbarian the most brutal and contumelious expressions towards the United States, the citizens of which he demoninated Yerbins, or transported thieves, an appellation derived from a place called Yerbin, in Africa, to which convicts are transported.*

* From this observation, it is evident that the barbarian had been apprised that the part of the United States where he was dealing out this invective, was originally peopled with convicted felons from the mother-country.

A discourse of this kind passed in presence of an American who had been in Barbary; he rose and resented it, saying, that as they were privileged characters, he could not treat them as they merited, but that he could not stay in the company of men who disgraced the country.

In the year 1803, President Jefferson projected an expedition of discovery to explore the head of the great river Missouri, and thence to penetrate to the Pacific Ocean. For this purpose, he pitched upon two skilful and prudent officers, Captain Lewis and Lieutenant Clarke, to whom he intrusted the conduct of this interesting and dangerous enterprise. These gentlemen having previously obtained the sanction of congress, took their departure from Washington in the spring of the year, at the head of 32 picked men, well armed. The whole party were provided with every article, as well for taking astronomical observation, and ascertaining distances, as for convenience and comfort, during their contemplated journey. Arrived in the heart of the Missouri country, they prevailed upon the chiefs of the Osage nations to send a deputation to Washington. This was a master-piece of policy, as the government of the United States were in that case in possession of hostages for the safe return of their citizens through the savage territories.[3]

These Indians arrived at the seat of the American government in October 1805, about the time of the landing of the other barbarian embassy from Tunis. Their appearance differing considerably from other savage tribes, excited much curiosity; while they appeared perfectly indifferent and unmoved at the most curious object presented to them. They were grave and reserved, a conduct always observed among the higher orders of savages, who consider it beneath the dignity of a warrior to betray emotions of surprize, fear, or joy. For this reason, the most ridiculous object, which would betray an European philosopher into a broad laugh, will barely excite a smile in an Indian chief. On visiting the navy-yard, to which they were attended by the officers, they viewed the frigates and heard their guns fired without surprize. They conversed with each other on their construction, and appeared gratified with the idea of their usefulness in conveying a great number of people at a time over great waters. Thus they also regarded the military drawn out on the occasion; considering them useful in defence against the enemy. The muskets attracted not the slightest attention; but they fixed their eyes on the bayonets, which they appeared to compare with one of their implements of war.

I was present when they visited the house of representatives. The present place of meeting of that body is only temporary, until the south wing of the Capitol is finished, when they will occupy it, as the senate now does the north wing. The gallery of this temporary room is consequently small, and when the Indians approached, the seats were taken up, as usual, by Americans citizens, among whom were many genteel females, to hear the debates. The speaker, to their great mortification, ordered this gallery to be cleared; and, not aware of the reason, I was preparing to leave the house under the impression that the members were about to proceed to secret business with closed doors; a practice followed about the time of passing the Non-importation Bill with Great Britain.

The approach of the Osage Indians was announced by the jingling of little bells, such as we call hawks' bells. These were fastened to their clothes, as white men wear buttons. They were ornamented with a variety of foxes' tails and feathers, bones, ivory trinkets in different shapes, curiously-carved shells, and pieces of hard polished wood. From the nose was suspended a small piece of silver; some wore this in the shape of a heart, and others round, and the size of a sixpence; and from each ear hung a fish-bone, a piece of ivory, or some other fanciful ornament. The face of the first chief was painted all over the colour of brick-dust — that of the next in rank was half reddened; another a fourth part; others were half black, and the remainder of the natural colour.

A single lock of hair alone hung from the middle of the back of the head, to which was tied an enormous fox's tail, or a bunch of feathers of various colours; the whole forming a most grotesque, yet interesting group.

During the debate, which had begun as they were entering, they betrayed no symptoms of surprize; and seldom made a remark to each other respecting the proceedings of the house. A mission of Creek Indians[4] arrived about the time of those from the Missouri, on a treaty of trade and friendship; and they, in compliment to their far-distant brethren, attended at the same time, but each party took different sides of the gallery. The Creeks are nearly civilized, and, from the dress of the greater number, there was no distinguishing them from the American citizens — some indeed were a little darker than the inhabitants of the Southern States.

Having with much apparent attention listened to the business before the house, the chief whispered the next, the purport of which appeared to be instantly understood, as they rose with one accord, and returned in the order they came, without noticing or even seeming to observe any other person but themselves.

Doctor Mitchell,[5] a senator from the state of New York, gave an entertainment to the Osage Indians at his apartments in Washington; and in return, they amused the doctor and his friends with a specimen of their songs.

The Indians from the south of Missouri are said to have no idea of poetry, as it derives its character from rhyme or measure. Their songs are short enthusiastic sentences, subjected to no laws of composition, accompanied by monotonous music, produced from a reed or cane, either quick or slow according to the subject or fancy of the singer. Their apologues are numerous and ingenious, abounding with incidents, and calculated to convey some favorite lesson. Their tales also, inculcate, in general, some moral truth, or some maxim of prudence or policy. In one, the misfortunes of a great chief are so linked with his vices, and wind up so fatally at last, that a man of worth whom he sought to oppress, is by his own agency, made the instrument of his destruction, and established as his successor. The private virtues of this successor, particularly his respect for the other sex, the want of which was the great vice of the deposed chief, are made the foundation of his fame and prosperity. In another, the particular duties of the sex are inforced, by shewing how certain women who deviated from ordinary rules were persecuted by the Manitoo of the woods; in the progress of the story they are made to owe their safety, in various trials, to some particular act of female discretion or delicacy, which they had before neglected.

The Indians have their Circe as well as the Greeks; she is very seducing, and the fate of her votaries highly terrible. The strokes of the pencil by which she is drawn are masterly; but the tales respecting this lady are only calculated for the ears of men.

A translation of the songs sung at Dr. Mitchell's has been inserted in the American prints;[6] they are rendered into verse, which destroys the idea of the energy with which they were repeated; independent of the fact of the Missouri Indians having no idea of rhyme or measure. I have restored them to the style in which they were sung, or rather pronounced, in energetic strains:

My brave companions, and friends of high renown! hither have ye come from far distant lands, to behold your great sire of this country, (the President) and to listen to his talk!

The great master of life (the Supreme Being) hath preserved you from accidents, and from sudden death. He hath fed you, and defended you from your foes — from the cold, and from piercing winds; that you might be made happy in the sight of the father of this land!

Ye red men! Since ye came hither, ye have seen the face of your great white father. He has cherished you as his own children. He has made your beating hearts rejoice!

Great chief of the Osages! fear not to follow our steps. Leave awhile thy sylvan home. The path which we have trodden is free and clear. For thee it will grow wider and smoother!

When thou art inclined to march, we will form behind thee a lengthened file. Dauntless thus will we for awhile quit our woods and vales, to listen to the voice of our white father!

This is a delicate compliment to the government of the United States; while it conveys the real sentiments of their hearts. The following composition on WAR, is admirably calculated to inspire courage, being supposed to come from the mouth of their great chief: —

Say, my brave warriors, when of arms we sing — when every tongue proclaims our martial deeds — why intrude the thoughts of death? — Why mourn the common fate of man? — Why fancy your doom is sealed; and that, pursuing or pursued, you must fall?

Doubt not the care of *Tewàsalàgè*. He will lead you forth, and he will shew you where the enemy is concealed. With his own hand will he make the attack, drive the foe from their ambush, or destroy them on the field of battle!

Our tribes led on by me, what nation can withstand our arms, or check our course? When our enemies hear of my warlike deeds, they will be struck with terror at my name. They will fly before us, or die with fear.

The evening of the day on which the Osage Indians visited Congress, they made their appearance at the theatre in the Pennsylvania Avenue; which was announced by handbills.[7] Their performance here was by no means disinterested; for they stipulated with the managers to be paid half the net proceeds, with a supply of rum during the entertainment. Their dance consisted of stamping in procession round the stage in different figures, and screaming in horrid discord. The war-dance exhibited something of the terrific; and the scalping scene was a dreadful picture of that inhuman practice among savage nations. The act of taking off the scalp of the supposed victim, was executed with such adroitness, a false scalp being substituted, that the deception was not to be perceived. One of the chiefs eminently exerted himself on this occasion. Before the conclusion of the entertainment, the greatest part of them were intoxicated, and the audience became anxious to quit the house. Next morning, the chief, who had been the principal actor was found lifeless in the bed which government had provided for him; and his death was imputed to excess of drinking, and his great exertions during the preceding evening. His interment was attended by his tribe, with the Creeks, and a great concourse of people, among whom were several members of Congress.[8] Much curiosity was excited, from the hopes of witnessing the savage ceremonies on such an occasion; but these expectations were disappointed, very little being said or done over the grave. In order to guard against a similar catastrophe, the inhabitants were publicly cautioned against giving these strangers any strong liquors; and informed, that the allowance made them by the government was in every respect abundant.

To return, Captain Lewis, who commanded the party of discovery, was fortunate enough to fulfill the object of his mission, and to return in safety to the seat of government in October last, after an absence of two years and six months.

He reports, that on the 14th of May, 1804, his party entered the Missouri; and on the 1st of November took up their winter quarters near the Mandan Towns, one thousand six hundred and nine miles above the mouth of the river, in latitude 47 deg. 21 min. 47 sec. north, and 99 deg. 21 min. 45 sec. west from Greenwich. On the 8th of April, 1805, the party proceeded up the river in pursuance of the objects prescribed to them. During their stay among the Mandans, Captain Lewis had been able to lay down the Missouri, according to courses and distances taken on his passage up the river, corrected by frequent observations of longitude and latitude: and to add to the actual survey of this portion of the river, a general map of the country between the Mississippi and the Pacific, from the 34th to the 54th degrees of latitude. These additions are from information collected from Indians with whom he had opportunities of communicating during his journey, and residence with them.

Having been disappointed after considerable preparation, in the purpose of sending an exploring party up the river in 1804, it was thought best to employ the autumn of that year in procuring a knowledge of an interesting branch of the river called the Washita. This was undertaken by Mr. Dunbar,[9] of Natchez, who greatly aided the party with his disinterested and valuable services in the prosecution of their enterprise. He ascended the river to the remarkable hot springs nearly in lat. 34.31. long. 92. 50. west from Greenwich, taking its courses and distances, and correcting them by frequent celestial observations.

The party were on the 23d of September, 1805, at Saint Louis. They had passed the preceding winter at a place which Captain Lewis calls Fort Clatsop, near the mouth of Columbia River. They set out thence on the 27th of March last, and arrived at the foot of the rocky mountains May 10th, where they were detained until the 24th of June, by the snows, which rendered the passage over these mountains impracticable till that time. Captain Lewis found it two thousand five hundred and seventy miles from the mouth of the Missouri to the great fall of that river, thence by land passing the rocky mountains, to the navigable part of the river Kooskookee, three hundred and forty miles, of which two hundred would admit of good road, and one hundred and sixty miles over tremendous mountains, which for sixty miles are covered with eternal snows; then seventy-three miles down the Kooskookee into a southeasterly branch of the Columbia; one hundred and fifty-four miles down that, to the main river of Columbia; and then four hundred and thirteen miles to the Pacific ocean: in all three thousand and five hundred and fifty miles from the mouth of the Missouri to the mouth of the Columbia. In this last river the tide flows one hundred and eighty-three miles, to within seven miles of its great rapids.

Captain Lewis also reports, that this whole line furnishes the most valuable furs in the world, and that there is a short and direct course for them to China; but that the greatest part of them would be exported from the mouth of the Missouri. His force consisted of thirty-one men; and he observes, that he was fortunate in not sending back from the head of the Missouri any part of his force, as more than once they owed their lives and the fate of the expedition to their numbers. One man of his party died before he reached fort Mademo in the year 1804, but the remainder returned in good health.

The great Mandan chief accompanied Captain Lewis on a visit to the president of the United States. The greatest cordiality subsisted between the two leaders; and from their abilities the old world may soon hope to have a particular account of their discoveries. They left the Pacific ocean on the 25th of March last, previous to which some American vessels had arrived there. They represent the Indians near the ocean as remarkably peaceable, and the winter mild.

Mr. (now Sir Alexander) Mackenzie, many years ago explored the country from Canada to the Pacific, but his route was very diffrent from that of the present expedition; and in a latitude unfavourable to the making of discoveries. Thus, his labours have been productive of little benefit in a commercial point of view, while there is every reason to suppose that the Americans have discovered a source of trade of the utmost importance; and it is highly probable, that by treating with the Inlians, they will establish a safe communication to export their goods to the east, through the Pacific ocean.

The river Missouri had long proved advantageous to the United States, in trading with the Indians for castor;[10] peltry, hides, deer skins, tallow, and bear's oil; but this trade never extended farther than twenty-five leagues above its junction with the Mississippi, about the forty-first degree north latitude. After thus uniting, it flows twelve hundred miles before it empties itself into the gulph of Mexico. On ascending six hundred leagues, no diminution is perceived, either in its width or rapidity. The principal rivers which discharge themselves in to the Missouri, are the Gasconade, the river of the Osages, the two Charatuns, the Great river, the river Des Canips, Nichinon, Batony, the great and little Nimaho, the river Plate, the river de Sionæ, the L'Eau Qui Court, and several of inferior note. The banks of these rivers are chiefly hunting ground for the Indians; and when the United States makes a treaty with them, which, from the success of the expedition under Captain Lewis and Lieutenant Clarke, they will most probably attempt, the trade will become a national object.

The banks of the Missouri are alternately woods and *prairies*, and they seem to encrease annually from the fires which are kindled every autumn, by the savages, or white hunters, either by chance, or with a design of facilitating their hunting. The water is muddy, and contains a fine sand, which soon precipitates; but this circumstance takes nothing from its salubrity. Its course is generally west by north west.

The flats are covered with trees of an enormous size Out of the trunk of one sycamore tree a canoe has been made able to carry eighteen thousand pounds weight.[11] The poplar and the maple are also found here in abundance, as well as the wild cherry, the red and white elm, the linden tree, the Indian chestnut, the water willow, the white and red mulberry. On the shores of the Missouri are found, in abundance, the white and black oak for ship-building — the pine, the cedar, and the triacanthos, which, like the English quickthorn, forms impenetrable hedges.

The plants are still more numerous. The Indians are well acquainted with the virtues of many of them. They make use of them to heal their wounds, and to poison their arrows. They have one, which is said to be a certain and prompt cure for the venereal disease — another, which renders them for a few moments insensible to the heat of fire. By using it, they will seize a red hot iron, or a burning coal, without injury. With different woods they dye their garments of beautiful colours.

The lands on the Missouri are capable of yielding all the productions of the temperate, and even some of those of the warm climates — wheat, maize, and every other species of grain and esculent roots. Hemp seems here to be indigenous; even cotton succeeds, though not so well as in more southerly countries; its culture, however, yields a real advantage to the inhabitants, who find in the crop of a field of two acres, a harvest sufficient for the cloathing of their families.

The *prairies* afford excellent pasture. Different kinds of clay are found here among which it is believed, is the real *kaolin*, to which the porcelain of China owes its reputation. Numberless caves on the river, abound in salt-petre.

The stones are generally calcareous and grit. There is one peculiar to the banks of this river. It is of a blood red color, compact, and soft under the chissel, but it becomes hard in the air, and is susceptible of a most beautiful polish. The Indians make use of it for calumets; but, from the extent of its layers, it might be employed for more important purposes. They have also quarries of marble, streaked with red; and a species of plaster, similar to that which the Americans bring in large quantities from the British dominions on the river St. Croix. Volcanic stones are likewise found in the Missouri country, which clearly denote the ancient existence of volcanoes, though none were heard of by Captain Lewis or his party.

Mines of lead, iron, and coal have already been discovered on the borders of the Missouri; and there are, no doubt, some of tin, copper, silver, and even of gold, according to the accounts of the Indians, who have found some particles of these metals.

At about three hundred miles from the village of the

Great Osages, in a westerly direction, after having passed several branches of the river Arkansas, is a flat, surrounded by hills, of an immense extent, and about fifteen leagues in diameter, the soil of which is a black sand, very fine, and so hard, that horses scarcely ever leave a trace. During a warm and dry season, this flat exhales vapors, which after being condensed, fall on this black sand, and cover it with an incrustation of salt, very white and fine, and about half an inch thick. Rains destroy this appearance; but about eighteen miles farther are found mines of genuine salt, near the surface of the earth. The Indians, who are well acquainted with them, are obliged to use levers to raise it. About fifteen leagues from the flat, and in a southerly direction, is a second mine of genuine salt, of the same nature as the other. These two mines differ only in colour; the first borders on blue — the other on red. Farther south, and still on the branches of the Arkansas, is a *saline,* which is one of the most interesting objects in nature.

On the declivity of a small hill, there are five holes, about eighteen inches in diameter, and two feet in depth, always full of salt-water, without ever overflowing. When any is taken out the hole, it immediately fills of itself; and what is still more extraordinary, about ten feet lower, a large stream of pure and fresh water, flows from this same hill.

If this country were peopled, the working of these salt mines would be very easy, by means of the river Arkansas. This species of salt is found preferable to any other for salting provisions.

The fur trade from thc upper Missouri, hitherto neglected by Americans, is carried on by the British, and the commodities they purchase are sent by them to Canada.*

* A recent letter from Lieutenant Clarke, to his brother, General Clarke, containing further information on this subject; with an account of the great river Missouri, higher up than had hitherto been explored by a white man, appearing very interesting, I shall present it to the reader in its original state:

"DEAR BROTHER, "*St. Louis, Sept.* 23, 1806.

"We arrived at this place at twelve o'clock to-day from the Pacific Ocean, where we remained during the last winter, near the entrance of the Columbia river. This station we left on the 27th of March last, and should have reached St. Louis early in August had we not been detained by the snow, which barred our passage across the rocky mountains until the 24th of June. In returning through those mountains, we divided ourselves into several parties, digressing from the route by which we went out, in order the more effectually to explore the country, and discover the most practicable route which does exist across the continent by the way of the Missouri and Columbia rivers. In this we were completely successful, and have therefore no hesitation in declaring, that such as nature has permitted, we have discovered the best route which does exist across the continent of North America in that direction. Such is that by the way of the Missouri to the foot of the Rapids below the great falls of that river, a distance of 2575 miles; thence by land passing by the rocky mountains to a navigable part of Kooskooke, 340; and with the Kooskooke 73 miles; Louis's river 154 miles; and the Columbia 413 miles to the Pacific Ocean; making the total distance from the confluence of the Missouri and Mississippi to the discharge of the Columbia into the Pacific ocean 3554 miles. The navigation of the Missouri may be deemed good — its difficulties arise from its falling banks, timber embedded in the mud of its channels, its sand bars, and the steady rapidity of its current, all which may be overcome to a great degree of certainty by using the necessary precautions. The passage by land of 340 miles, from the falls of Missouri to the Kooskooke, is the most formidable part of the track proposed across the continent. Of this distance, 200 miles is almost a good road, and 140 miles over tremendous mountains, which for 60 miles are covered with eternal snows. A passage over these mountains is open, to the last of September; and the cheap rate at which horses are to be obtained from the Indians of the Rocky mountains, and west of them, reduces the expenses of transportation over this portage to a mere trifle.

The navigation of the Kooskooke, Lewis's river, and the Columbia, is safe and good from the 1st of April to the middle of August, by making three portages on the latter river, the first of which, in descending, is 1200 paces at the falls of Columbia, 261 miles up the river; the second, of two miles, at the long narrows, six miles below the falls; and a third, also of two miles, at the great Rapids, 65 miles still lower down. The tide flows up the Columbia 183 miles, and within seven miles of the great Rapids. Large sloops may with safety ascend as high as tide-water, and vessels of 300 tons burden reach the mouth of the Multnomah river, a large branch of the Columbia, which takes its rise on the confines of New Mexico, with the Callerado and Apostles Rivers, discharging itself into the Columbia, 125 miles from its entrance into the Pacific Ocean. I consider this tract across the continent of immense advantage to the fur trade, as all the furs collected in nine tenths of the most valuable fur country in America, may be conveyed to the mouth of the Columbia, and shipped from thence to the East Indies, by the first of August in each year, and will of course reach Canton earlier than the furs which are annually exported from Montreal arrive in Great Britain.

"In our outward-bound voyage, we ascended to the foot of the Rapids below the great falls of the Missouri, where we arrived on the 14th of June, 1805. Not having met with any of the natives of the Rocky mountains, we were of course ignorant of the passes by land which existed through these mountains to the Columbia river, and had we even known the route, we were destitute of horses, which would have been indispensably necessary to enable us to transport the requisite quantity of ammunition and other stores to ensure the remaining part of our voyage down the Columbia; we therefore determined to navigate the Missouri, as far as it was practicable, or unless we met with some of the natives from whom we could obtain horses, and information of the country. Accordingly, we took a most laborious portage at the fall of the Missouri, of 18 miles, which we effected, with our canoes and baggage, by the 3d of July. From thence, ascending the Missouri, we penetrated the Rocky mountain at the distance of 71 miles above the upper part of the portage, and penetrated as far as the three forks of that river, a distance of 180 miles further. Here the Missouri divides into three nearly equal branches at the same point; the two largest branches are so nearly of the same dignity, that we did not conceive that either of them could, with propriety, retain the name of the Missouri; and therefore called these streams Jefferson's, Madison's, and Gallatin's rivers. The confluence of these rivers is 2848 miles from the mouth of the Missouri by the meanders of that river. We arrived at the three forks of the Missouri the 27th of July. Not having yet been so fortunate as to meet with the natives although I had previously made several exertions for that purpose, we were compelled to continue our route by water.

"The most northerly of the three forks, that to which we have given the name of Jefferson's river, was deemed the most proper for our purpose, and we accordingly ascended it 248 miles, to the upper fork, and its extreme navigable point. On the morning of the 17th August, 1805, I arrived at the forks of Jefferson's river, where I met Captain Lewis who had previously penetrated with a party of three men to the waters of the Columbia, discovered a band of the Shoshone nation, and had found means to induce 35 of their chiefs and warriors to accompany him to that place. From these people we learned that the river on which they resided was not navigable, and that a passage through the mountains in that direction was impracticable. Being unwilling to confide in this unfavorable account of the natives, it was concerted between Captain Lewis and myself, that one of us should go forward immediately with a small party and explore the river; while the other, in the interim, should lay up the canoes at that place, and engage the natives with their horses to assist in transporting our stores and baggage to their camp. Accordingly I set out next day, passed the dividing mountains between the Missouri and Columbia, and descended the river, which I since called the east fork of Lewis's river, about 70 miles. Finding that the Indians' account of the country in the direction of that river was correct, I returned to Captain Lewis on August 29, at the Shoshone camp, excessively fatigued as you may suppose, having passed mountains almost inaccessible, and been compelled to subsist on berries during the greater part of my route. We now purchased seventeen horses of the Indians, and hired a guide, who assured us that he could in fifteen days take us to a large river in an open country west of those mountains, by a route some distance to the north of the river on which they lived, and that by which the natives west of the mountains visit the plains of Missouri, for the purpose of hunting the buffalo. Every preparation being made, we set forward the 31st of August, through these tremendous mountains, in which we continued until the 22d of September, before we reached the lower country beyond them. On our way we met with the Olelachshook, a band of the Tuckapacks, from whom we obtained seven horses, and exchanged eight or ten others; this proved of infinite service to us, as we were compelled to subsist on horse beef about eight days before we reached the Kooskooke. During our passage over these mountains we suffered every thing which hunger, cold, and fatigue could impose; nor did our difficulties terminate on arriving at the Kooskooke, for, although the Pollotepallors, a numerous nation inhabiting that country, were extremely hospitable, and for a few trifling articles furnished us with abundance of roots and dried salmon, the food to which they were accustomed, we found we could not subsist on these articles, and almost all of us grew sick on eating them; we were therefore obliged to have recourse to the flesh of horses and dogs, as food, to make up the deficiency of our guns, which produced but little meat, as game was scarce in that vicinity, where we were compelled to remain to construct our perogues to descend the river. At this season the salmon are meagre, and form but indifferent food. While we remained here I was myself sick several days, and my friend, Captain Lewis suffered a severe indisposition.

"Having completed four perogues and a small canoe, we gave our horses in charge to the Pollotepallors until we returned, and on the 7th of October re-embarked for the Pacific Ocean. We descended by the route abovementioned. The water being low at this season, we experienced much difficulty in descending; we found it obstructed by a great number of dangerous rapids, in passing which our perogues several times filled, and the men narrowly escaped with their lives. This difficulty does not exist in high water, which happens within the period I have previously mentioned. We found the natives extremely numerous and generally friendly, though we have on several occasions owed our lives, and the fate of the expedition, to our number which consisted of thirty-one men. On the 17th of November we reached the ocean, where various considerations induced us to spend the winter; we searched for an eligible situation for that purpose, and selected a spot on the south side of the little river called by the natives Neta, which discharges itself at a small bar on the south side of the Columbia, and fourteen miles within Point Adams. Here we constructed some log-houses, defended by a common stockade work; this place was called fort Clatsop, after a nation of that name, who were our nearest neighbours. We found here abundance of elk, on which we principally subsisted during the last winter. We left fort Clatsop the 27th of March. On our homeward voyage, being much better acquainted with the country, we were enabled to take such precautions as in a great measure secured us from the want of provisions, and greatly lessened our fatigues, compared to those we were compelled to submit to in the outward journey. We have not lost a man since we left the Mandans, a circumstance, I assure you, which is a pleasing consideration to me. As I shall be shortly with you, and the post is waiting, I deem it unnecessary to attempt to detail the occurrences of the last eighteen months. I am,

"Your affectionate brother, "W. CLARKE."

NOTES — CHAPTER XVI

1. The ambassador arrived in Washington on November 30, 1805, with two black domestics and two Turkish secretaries, and went to the house provided for him on Capitol Hill. A communication of President Jefferson to Congress on April 14, 1806, stated the case in something of the same words used by Janson. It does not go into details concerning the activities of the embassy, however.

2. The ambassador left Washington on May 24, 1806. Mr. Cathcart attended him through the principal towns to Boston, where he embarked for Tunis. His suite did not accompany him, "preferring an asylum in this free and happy country." See *National Intelligencer*, May 28-June 16, 1806.

3. The *National Intelligencer* quotes a letter from a gentleman in Indiana Territory dated May 25, 1805. It reported that six of Lewis and Clark's men and about twenty Indians who had never been to the settlements before were on their way to see Mr. Jefferson. Another item in the *Intelligencer* of December 30, 1805, announced a visit of the chiefs "to their Fathers, the Representatives of the People" at the Capitol.

4. Four Creek chiefs and three interpreters accompanied Colonel Benjamin Hawkins to Washington, where they concluded a treaty.

5. Dr. Samuel Latham Mitchell, Representative and Senator from New York.

6. See the *National Intelligencer*, March 12, 1806.

7. In the *National Intelligencer* of December 27, 1805, a theater advertisement informed the citizens that "in addition to the concert and fireworks there will be a Grand Indian Dance by a party of savages of the Missouri nation, lately arrived in this city."

8. A Ricara chief sent to Washington by Lewis and Clark with Joseph Gravelines as interpreter died there. Gravelines returned to the tribe with presents and messages from the President.

9. William Dunbar, planter and scientist, known in Mississippi history as Sir William Dunbar. After his plantation in West Florida was swept away, he established another in 1792 near Natchez. Here he applied his knowledge of chemistry and mechanics to farming. In 1798 he was appointed surveyor general of the District of Natchez. During the next year he made the first meteorological observations in the Mississippi Valley. In 1804 and 1805 he was appointed to explore the Ouichita River country and the region bordering the Red River.

10. A mineral.

11. Jedidiah Morse, *American Geography*, p. 461, mentions a sycamore tree on the bank of the Muskingum which at some distance above the ground measured 44 feet in circumference.

CHAPTER XVII

THE LAW — JUDGES — PROCRASTINATION — TERM REPORTS — BANKRUPT-LAW — FACILITY OF EVADING IT — EXAMPLE OF FRAUDULENT BANKRUPTCY — NECESSITY OF A DIFFERENT SYSTEM.

IN THE United States law is easy of access, and the expence very small, compared to that of the English courts. The people are naturally inclined to litigation, the offspring of chicanery. In the county courts, which generally sit four times in the year, it is surprising to see the numbers of people assembled in a part which you would judge to be very thinly inhabited. Most of them have a cause upon the docket, and the remainder come, as they call it, "for a frolic," which produces intoxication; and in the southern states, all those dreadful and savage combats, which will be hereafter particularly described.

The judges of the supreme courts, as in England, are appointed for life, and are removable from their office only by impeachment. A chief, and four associate judges preside in the superior court of record. They go the circuit of the Union twice a year, and in each state hold a federal, or government court, where all affairs relating to the union, and matters of great import, are determined. They are associated and assisted in these circuits by district judges. Every state has a resident district judge, and under him are courts of law and equity which take cognizance of such business, arising in their state only, as may not be of sufficient importance to be brought before the Federal Court.[1] Thus we find that each state is independent of the rest, and yet the whole are subject to the federal government.

The common law and, in short, the whole jurisprudence of the country, is grounded upon the English statutes; except where they are repugnant to a republican form of government. The distribution of property is equalized in cases of intestacy. The right of primogeniture is taken away, and the widow and the children share alike. The estate of the intestate is vested in the courts established for that purpose, and generally called the Orphan Court. A man may by will bequeath his property to his family in such shares and proportions as he may think fit, provided reason govern the deed. Instances have often occurred, where a capricious or unjust demise has been made to the exclusion of children, that such will has been set aside, and an equitable distribution decreed. In demurrer, and all questions on law, American practitioners quote, and the courts admit, the reports of adjudications of the courts of record at Westminster.*

The lawyers do the whole business of their suits, from the issuing of the writ, to final judgment. Though the proceedings for bringing a suit upon the docket are unclogged with most of the formalities which render justice so expensive in England; yet the lawyers in America can find cause for procrastination as readily as their European brethren. I cannot adopt a better method of giving the reader an idea of their proceedings, than by subjoining some selections from their Term Reports lately published at Philadelphia.

SUPREME COURT OF PENNSYLVANIA.

Monday, December 2, 1803.

Present — Judges Yeates, Smith and Brackenridge.

The attorney-general, in a speech of two hours, concluded the cause of Commonwealth, vs. Dennie. This speech might have been delivered, and the cause concluded on Saturday evening at the nisi prius, but the court adjourned at seven, and three hours were lost.

After the charge was given, and the jury had retired, Judge Yeates took up the list of trials.

Ashley v. Miller was the first cause; it had been depending six years. Mr. Rawle hoped it would be delayed for a few days, as Mr.

* At the trial of the impeachment of Judge Chase, in the court, the highest in the United States, and there operating like the house of lords in England, MacNally's Rules of Evidence, a recent authority, were frequently recurred to.

Watt, from Carlisle, one of the defendant's counsel, had not arrived in town. Mr. Ingersoll earnestly remonstrated against deranging the list, and hoped that the court would take up and dispose of the causes in their regular order, as otherwise he was sure there would be nothing but delay, irregularity, and confusion. The court, however, ordered it to be postponed till Wednesday morning.

The next cause was M'Call v. Lemaire — six years old. Mr. Hopkinson for the defendant hoped as the former action was fixed for Wednesday, this might be fixed for Thursday morning. Mr. Tilgham said there was no reason for it in this case, as there was in the other. Mr. Hopkinson replied, that one furnished a reason for the other. Judge Yeates said to Mr. Hopkinson, "Sir, the court do not concur with you as to that inference."

M'Call v. Lemaire was fixed for the afternoon. Adjourned till three P. M.

Monday afternoon, December 2.

Jury sworn in M'Call v. Lemaire, at about half past three. At seven the court adjourned — the cause unfinished — three hours lost again.

LIBERTY OF THE PRESS.

Respublica v. Joseph Dennie, Esq.

The trial of this indictment, which has been depending since 1803, for a libel on democracy, was begun on Friday last in the court of nisi prius; and we are happy to state that, after an ingenious and elaborate discussion by the counsel on both sides, which was listened to with unusual patience and attention by an upright and impartial jury, the defendant was yesterday pronounced to be "Not Guilty."

Wednesday, Dec. 4, 1805.

At the opening of the court in the morning, Ashley v. Miller, which had been fixed for this day, was continued by consent of parties.

The jury were then sworn in the cause of Sparks v. Garrigues, in which the court and jury were engaged until half past one, when an adjournment took place. At half past three, P. M. the court met. Sparks v. Garrigues was proceeded in; at half past seven, in the midst of the speech of Mr. Levy, of counsel with the plaintiff, the court adjourned. The reporter is not sure whether the proposal for adjournment came from the court or the counsel; he thinks it was from the former; two hours and a half lost. Mem. — Judge Washington* sat till ten o'clock, and even eleven, if necessary.

Thursday, Dec. 5.

In the morning Mr. Levy resumed his address to the jury in Sparks v. Garrigues, which he finished at twelve. Mr. Rawle for for the defendant (the concluding counsel) began his reply, and spoke till half past one, when the court adjourned.

Afternoon.

Mr. Rawle continued in Sparks v. Garrigues, and finished at four.

The charge was given, and the jury withdrew.

The list of trials was then taken up. Duane v. Dunlop was called. Counsel on both sides ready — only six jurymen appeared, six of those on the pannel in this cause being out in the case of Sparks v. Garrigues. Mr. Rodney, of counsel with the plaintiff, prayed the court to award a "tales." No sheriff or officer was in court. On sending to the sheriff, an officer came in; the court reprimanded him, and through him the sheriff, for neglect of duty, saying they ought always to be attended by an officer.

When the "talesmen" were about to be collected, Mr. Rodney said, the cause of Duane v. Dunlop was of a particular nature, and he was rather desirous of having the jury from the original pannel. Mr. Ingersol, for the defendant joined him in this wish. Mr. Rodney, however, said, he did not desire any other cause to be tried first, lest it should occupy the whole week, and he should lose his chance, and rather than run that risk, he would take "talesmen." The counsel in several other causes said they were ready. — The court said, if any short cause could be brought on by consent, so as to occupy the evening, they should have no objection. Mr. Dallas mentioned the case of Thompson vs. Warder, as one of that description, in which he was ready for the plaintiff. Mr. Hallowell for the defendant said, he would rather be excused from trying it out of the order of the list.The court then adjourned before five o'clock, saying they thought it right to wait till morning, in order to obtain the jurors mentioned in the pannel, and struck for the case of Duane v. Dunlop; as it was particularly circumstanced. The gen-

*A judge of the supreme federal courts.

eral sentiment seemed to be in favor of their adjournment for this purpose; and the reporter is not disposed to withhold his approbation, merely observing, that seven or eight jurors who had been summoned in Duane v. Dunlop, exclusive of those who were out in the cause of Sparks v. Garrigues, did not answer when called; that they were neither fined nor any notice taken of their non-attendance, although their absence occasioned the loss of five hours.

CIRCUIT COURT OF NORTH CAROLINA

JANUARY TERM.

Lord Carteret, devisee of
Earl Granville v. *Collins and Allen.*

This was an ejectment cause, brought forward by the devisee of Earl Granville, who claimed as proprietor of the soil, under an ancient grant from England, long previous to the American Revolution; and which came on to be tried at June term, when a demurrer was offered to the evidence of the defendants, and a joinder therein, thereby taking the trial of the cause from the jury, and referring it to the court upon the law of the case merely. When this demurrer came on for argument at this term, it was moved for the defendants that the demurrer should be withdrawn, and a repleader ordered, upon the ground that the parties demurring were in the affirmative of the propositions, and the evidence of the defendants was of a negative nature; that neither the legality of the evidence of the defendants only was embraced by the issue, and not that of the plaintiffs, and therefore a judgment upon the demurrer would not be decisive of the question, or else the issue as joined must admit the truth of the plaintiff's own evidence.

The consideration of this preliminary question the court reserved, without prejudice to either party, and ordered an argument upon the main question. This argument was opened on Thursday, by Mr. Gaston, for the plaintiffs, at great length, and with much method, perspicuity, elegance, and strength — the defence was argued on Friday by Messrs. Cameron, Baker, and Woods, with great ingenuity, skill, and force, and the argument was closed on Saturday by Mr. Harris for the plaintiffs, with much learning and ability. The court have reserved the consideration of the principal question also; and it is believed that judgment will be rendered at the next term, but for whom it will be given no hint has been dropped. The counsel for the defendants made the following points in their defence:

1st. That by the mere effects of the revolution the plaintiffs were divested of their right, and the land in question became the property of the state.

2nd. That by the 25th section of the declaration of rights, the lands in question are declared to be the property of the people of this state, and to be by them held in sovereignty, thereby destroying the plaintiff's right.

3rd. That the plaintiff's right, if not before taken away, or lost, was forfeited and divested by the confiscation and entry laws of this state.

4th. That the plaintiffs are aliens, and therefore cannot inherit lands in this state.

5th. That the plaintiffs are barred of recovery by the acts of limitation.

The points made by the plaintiff's counsel were intended to meet the objection to a recovery arising out of the points relied on by defendants.

It was said by them, that the revolution had no effect on private rights; that it occasioned only a change of sovereignty in the country; that the 25th article of the bill of rights, which speaks of the property of the soil being one of the essential rights of the collective body of the people, had relation only to the territorial rights and did not affect the title of Earl Granville; that in 1744, seven-eighths of the lords proprietors of the Carolinas having disposed of their rights and immunities to the king, the Granville family retained one-eighth share only, and that divested of all its sovereign appendages; that they therefore could be considered only as common subjects, whose property was not affected by the revolution. With respect to the confiscation-laws, they were silent respecting this property; the estates of others had been confiscated by name, but this had not been touched: that the law providing for the entry of lands had, it was acknowledged, been considered as making this land liable to entry; but though this had been the general opinion, it was no proof it was a correct one. They contended it was not, as the land had been already granted, and all granted land is expressly excepted by this law. But, supposing this property had been forfeited, either by the revolution or the confiscation-laws, the state had never become seised of it by any office found, and therefore could not legally grant it.

With respect to alienage, it was insisted that as Lord Carteret, (the present plaintiff) was born a subject of Great Britain, he could not become an alien to his fellow-subjects by the revolution; and as they considered the grant of the land in question as void, having been already granted by the king to the plaintiff, the act of limitation could not operate in its favor.

Col. A. Martin[2] spoke at some length, as an *amicus curia*, in favor of the defendants.

The decision of this cause is all important to the people of this state, two thirds of all the soil being involved in it."

A bankrupt law, modelled from those of England, passed the houses of congress on the 4th of April, 1800, and was repealed in December, 1803. The enormities committed under the cloak of this act; the inefficacy of a democratic government to carry their laws into execution; added to the facility with which villains could with impunity defraud their creditors, loudly called for its repeal.

A regular system of bankruptcy throughout so extensive a territory as the United States, was almost impracticable. The abuse was soon found to exceed the benefit. The district judge, one of whom is appointed in every state, and who is of a subordinate rank to the federal judge, issued the commissions against the bankrupts, and was supposed to preside over the business; but the first and the last proceedings were the whole that he had occasion to concern himself about. He received a fee for the commission, and another for the certificate.

The process was soon reduced to mere matter of form. For instance: — Suppose an *honest* merchant of Virginia finds it either necessary or convenient to avail himself of the bankrupt law, in a place far distant from the residence of the district judge. A couple of his *good friends* mount their horses, and post away to his honor, relate their case, take the necessary oaths, give the names of other *good friends*, as security, or rather, in this case, as pledges to prosecute. This being the whole required in the first proceeding, his honor grants a commission, bonds are filled up, and the *said friends* are to have them duly executed, and returned to him by post, with names at least as necessary as John Doe and Richard Roe, at the bottom of a declaration, *in Banco-Regis*, on an *assumpsit*, on whom, if called upon for a breach of condition, his honor would frequently find the return to his writ, "*non est inventus*."

Commissioners having been named (three more *friends* to the business) they advertise in some obscure weekly newspaper, or by notice stuck upon the court or meeting-house door, a declaration of bankruptcy against their unfortunate friend, with a notice to him to surrender, &c. These forms having been gone through, the bankrupt makes his discovery, assignees take possession, a dividend is made, the certificate signed; "all which actings and doings were had, made, done, and executed, without any lawful let, suit, trouble, denial, eviction, or interruption whatsoever." The bankrupt soon opens his "store" again, with a fresh assortment of goods.

Such is a faint sketch of the proceedings under an American commission of bankruptcy. In Norfolk, in Virginia, the evil was growing to so alarming a height, that Mr. Newton,[3] a young lawyer of good abilities, and the representative in congress of that town, at the desire of the more virtuous part of his constituents, brought in the bill to repeal the law.

A commission of bankruptcy was declared in the Norfolk *Herald*, about the end of the year 1802, to have been awarded and issued against John Proudfit, of the borough of Norfolk, merchant; and his failure was calculated to be for twenty thousand dollars. Bankrupts in America, as in England, must, *upon oath*, deliver up their whole property to their assignees, and make a full disclosure of all debts due to them, before they can obtain a certificate. In America, the bankrupt, on his effects producing a certain ratio in the pound, was allowed a small part in proportion to the dividend. Concealment of property is in England, as in the case of Bolland, a capital offence, and for which he suffered death. The law in this respect in America was severe, but very few crimes are there punished with death.

So expeditiously did Mr. Proudfit's commission of bankruptcy pass through all the legal forms, that we find him certified, and advertising a fresh assortment of goods for sale, by computation of the value of forty thousand dollars, in about six months from the time it was issued.

To his invoice of goods, wares, and merchandise, and few merchants in America could produce one much superior, must be added, a dwelling-house completely furnished, and rented of John Taylor, an Englishman, well known in Manchester, at one hundred pounds rent per annum!!!

That the above is the true amount stated in Proudfit's advertisement, Messrs. Willett and O'Conner, printers of the Norfolk *Herald*, can attest; that he became a certified bankrupt a very few months previous to the insertion of the advertisement, every inhabitant of Norfolk well knows; and, that he rented and furnished a house immediately after his bankruptcy, Mr. Taylor can prove. "How are we ruined!"

The bankrupt law being repealed, the insolvent, and such as choose to defraud their creditors, can still effect their purposes, if not so effectually, certainly with less trouble and more speed by the old law, which yet remains in force; the difference consisting in liberating the body only, leaving the goods afterwards acquired at the mercy of the creditor. To describe the mode, I shall quote the words of a Philadelphian on the subject:

> The laws of the American states are much too favorable to debtors willing to defraud their creditors. A man who owes more than he chooses to pay, in America, may transfer his property, by a secret assignment, to some confidential friend, suffer himself to be laid in prison for debt, then, after a few days' imprisonment, swear that he has nothing in the world wherewith to satisfy his creditors, come out of prison free from any claims of creditors, resume the property of which he had made a trust-transfer, and renew his business, a

richer and more flourishing man than before.* This laxity and facility of the laws of insolvency in America have proved fatal to the reputation of American commercial faith. It is certain that a very large proportion of the bankruptcies in London are occasioned by disappointments of remittances from America. An English merchant, known to trade largely with America, would at that moment be judged to be, and for that reason alone, of very suspicious solvency. It is astonishing that the legislature of the United States should not perceive that it is of the greatest importance to make the commercial credit of their country as good as possible; and that it is utterly impossible for any country to be very rich in commercial credit, unless its laws be severe against insolvent debtors, and afford the utmost facility to creditors, especially to foreign creditors, in the recovery of their debts. Should the merchants of America, in general, persist in giving the same trouble, as of late, to English merchants trusting them, the necessary consequence must be, that within a very short time, no American will be able to procure one sixpence worth of goods to be shipped for him from London, unless he shall have previously paid the price. America will thus be, in effective commercial wealth, some millions poorer than it is at present. For to the honest, sensible, industrious merchant, and especially to every commercial nation, credit is more than even ready money; it is the very lever of Archimedes, capable of moving the world from its foundation. To the man who has failed in his wild speculations, to the spendthrift, and to the swindler, it is amply the means of fraud and ruin. We exhort the patriots of America to render their bankrupt laws more rigorous, that their public and private credit may become more worthy of a great commercial nation.

NOTES — CHAPTER XVII

1. Janson has confused the functions of the Federal and State courts, and fails to recognize that the importance of the case does not determine the question of jurisdiction. This confusion is easily understood when one remembers that he was not familiar with the idea of divided sovereignty.

2. Governor Alexander Martin of North Carolina.

3. Thomas Newton, Jr., except for one term Representative from Virginia from 1801 to 1833.

---

* Close imprisonment is always dispensed with, on giving bonds for prison bounds, which are generally of considerable extent. Thus, men may carry on their business while the law considers them in prison, merely by removing within prison bounds; nor can they resume their property without its being subject to seizure by their former creditors. This, however, seldom happens, for the same cloak which covers one iniquity, generally conceals the other — as a lie often requires an hundred to clear it from imputation.

Drawn under the direction of the Author, and Engraved by M. Marigot.

Philadelphia Theatre, in Chesnut Street.

CHAPTER XVIII

THE DRAMA — ITS RISE AND PROGRESS IN PHILADELPHIA — MR. COOPER — THE NEW YORK THEATRE — MR. HODGKINSON — POVERTY OF AMERICAN MANAGERS — CHARLESTON, THE GRAVE OF AMERICAN PERFORMERS — MRS. WRIGHTEN — MISS BROADHURST — MISS FONTENELLE — MR. VILLIERS — EMINENT LIVING ACTORS — INDECOROUS BEHAVIOUR OF AN AMERICAN AUDIENCE — THEATRICAL CRITICISM.

THE first dramatic representation in the then colonies of America, was performed in Philadelphia, by a small company from England under the management of Mr. Douglass,*[1] father-in-law to the present theatrical veterans, Mr. Hallam,[2] of the New York Theatre, and our favorite, Mrs. Mattocks.[3] Some few years before the commencement of the revolutionary war, Douglass had erected a regular theatre in Philadelphia,[4] but that event drove him to seek his fortune in the West India islands.

Peace being restored, Mr. Hallam, in right of his father-in-law, claimed the theatre, and went to London for per-

* Williams,[5] who acquired considerable literary notoriety in London under the assumed name of Anthony Pasquin, and who has since been reduced to the drudgery of editing a Boston newspaper, in his late publication intitled "The American Drama," shews that he possessed but little information on the subject. He erroneously asserts that "the first theatrical company on record, who enacted in North America, is a little troop who came from the West Indies, the management of which devolved upon a performer of the name of Hallam, who travelled and performed in all principal towns."

With somewhat more correctness he reprobates the custom of smoking segars, and drinking, in the American theatres. The *filthy* custom is now somewhat abated — the *beastly* practice increases. The lobbies of all American theatres are provided with bar-rooms, to which the men resort between each act to drink, and from which the ladies are regaled in their seats with glasses of their favorite beverage. Thus, on the fall of the curtain, the *dashing* fellows are in a state of intoxication. Smoaking is a still greater evil in a crouded house, to prevent which, the managers are constantly making unavailing remonstrances.

formers. He there acted Hamlet, I believe at Drury-lane,[6] and with some success. Having formed a connection with Mr. Henry,[7] who about that time unsuccessfully attempted the arduous part of Othello at Covent-garden, they made up a small company, among whom were Mr. and Mrs. Kenna of the Manchester theatre, Mr. and Mrs. Morris, Mr. Harper, a young gentleman of promising abilities, and a few recruits from strolling companies.[8] The theatre in Philadelphia was fitted up and embellished in a good style; the scenery, dresses, and decorations, being far superior to what Douglass had exhibited. The astonishment of the Americans at the first representation of a tragedy which required magnificence may easily be imagined. The theatre immediately became a place of fashionable resort, to the great emolument of the performers.

In the company was a favorite actor of the name of Wignal,[9] who, aspiring to management, had the address, in concert with Mr. Reinagle, a musician, and a monied man, to obtain a large subscription towards erecting a new and more spacious theatre. He saw the foundation laid, then embarked for England, in order to form a company which might excel that from which he had lately seceded. The other managegers were not idle in counteracting his plans. — Mr. Henry arrived before him, and engaged Mr. and Mrs. Hodgkinson (late Miss Brett) of the Bath company, the celebrated Mrs. Wrighten[10] of Drury-lane, who at that time was under some unhappy domestic embarrassment, Mr. Prigmore, of the Rochester theatre, and a few others of established reputation in the provincial companies. This formidable reinforcement arrived, and performed with unbounded applause a whole season before the new theatre opened. Wignal was long delayed in England, but in the summer of 1793 he arrived in the river Delaware, with a company which would have done credit to a theatre-royal. At this time the yellow fever first broke out in Philadelphia, and raged to a most alarming degree. The actors were landed at Wilmington,

30 miles below the seat of contagion, and, in the winter, opened their campaign in an elegant new theatre in Chestnut-street.[11] The other theatre, with what was called the Old American Company, had also commenced the season and at no period during the management of Garrick at Drury-lane, and Rich at Covent-garden, was rivalship carried on with more spirit.[12] The inhabitants flocked alternately to each, and the comparative merits of the companies formed the principal subject of the day.* Mr. Hodgkinson had become deservedly very popular, and to oppose him, Mr. Fennel,[13] as the champion of the new company, came forward in Othello, and was received with bursts of applause. In comic operas Mrs. Wrighten had delighted the audience, supported by Mrs. Hodgkinson, also a first-rate singer. To these were opposed Mrs. Oldmixon,[14] late Miss George, of Drury-lane, Miss Broadhurst, from Covent-garden, and Mrs. Seymour, from the Portsmouth theatres; and thus both houses gave a rich musical treat, alternately with comedy and tragedy, every night during the season, and to overflowing houses. In Wignal's company were also Chalmers, formerly the harlequin at Covent-garden, but now a first-rate comedian; Darley, from the same theatre; young Blisset, from Bath; Warren, Francis, Biddle, Green, Finch, &c. all eminent in their line of acting.[15] Tragedy, from the support of Mrs. Merry,[16] was decidedly in favour

* Mr. Weld says, "that it is only a few years past, since 1779, that any public amusements have been suffered in this city (Philadelphia); the old corporation, which consisted mostly of the Quakers, and not of the most liberal-minded of the city, having always opposed the establishment of any place for that purpose." This gentleman's information on this head is extremely defective. The year he mentions was in the very height of the American war, when the mind of every individual was engrossed by the momentous transactions of the day — when Philadelphia was alternately in possession of the contending armies. It was this event which, previous to 1779, drove the comedians out of Philadelphia, whence they embarked for Jamaica. There they remained until the United States acquired their independence, and were settling into tranquillity. They had *then* been permitted to perform theatricals many years previous to the war.[17]

of the new company, the other house having no actress to stand in competition with her. On the other hand, with the lively acting of Mrs. Hodgkinson, Mrs. Henry, Mrs. Hallam, and Mrs. Morris, comedy seemed to incline to the Old American company. The ballet-dances at the new theatre had a powerful attraction. They were led by Byrne, from Covent-garden, assisted by Francis, a good dancer, and a favorite comic performer.[18] Philadelphia, notwithstanding the fever in the summer, was a scene of gaiety in the winter. Besides the attraction of the theatres, Rickets[19] and Lailson* had each amphitheatres, where rival horsemanship and Burlettas were also well attended.

The next season, the old company being called for in New York, and, it is said, willing to decline a farther contest, left the field to their opponents. This circumstance by no means abated the zeal of Wignal. He brought forward new pieces and fresh performers. Among the latter was Mr. Cooper,[20] whose abilities are known in London, and who far eclipsed all competitors of the buskin; but, as a general actor, Mr. Hodgkinson was the best perofrmer I have seen in America. His death which shall hereafter be particularly noticed, was a great loss to theatrical amateurs. Mr. Cooper had a high opinion of his own merit. He would not enter into a regular engagement with any of the American managers; and thus he lays them all under contribution, migrating as it were in a short space of time from north to south, and dividing the profits of the theatre in which he may condescend to perform. As a proof of this gentleman's industry, after acting his limited number of nights last season at Philadelphia, he set off in his phaeton on a Saturday morning, and arrived at Baltimore on Monday, where he performed on that stage the same evening. He now contemplated a journey to Charleston, where Placide,[21] formerly a rope-

* I have been informed that both these men, at different times, were drowned in returning to Europe with the property acquired by their exhibitions in America.

dancer at Sadler's Wells, has an elegant theatre. Having performed three nights at Baltimore, for the trifling consideration of a *free* benefit, he proceeded on his route to Richmond in Virginia, where he performed the same number of nights, and on the same terms. He arrived in Charleston in ten days, a distance of between five and six hundred miles; and after skimming the theatrical cream there, he returned with equal expedition, to the north, ready for the opening of the Boston Theatre.[22] The greatest part of this rapid travelling he performs with his own horses, and drives himself. His horses fell sick at Baltimore — he sent them to pasture, and purchased a fresh set. At Charleston he sold his new purchase at an advanced price, bought others, and on his arrival again in Baltimore, he took the former, being favorites and now refreshed, and disposed of those he had last driven. Thus is this theatrical hero amassing a fortune.

In the New York company, or, as it is still called the Old American Company, there has long been a kind of theatrical inter-regnum. On the death of Henry, the co-partner of Hallam, his place was filled by Hodgkinson, who became joint-proprietor and acting-manager, and for some time the theatre was jointly governed by them; but Hallam growing old and inactive, Mr. Dunlap,[23] celebrated as a dramatic writer, purchased of Hallam, and entered upon an active part in the management. He soon took the ostensibility upon himself, the funds being below par, and Hodgkinson's extravagant manner of living rendered him unable to maintain his ground as a manager. We now find the theatre under the sole controul of Dunlap, and Hodgkinson once more merely a player. With the pen Dunlap did much, but, totally unacquainted with the interior regulations of a refractory company, he soon failed in his speculation; and at length was obliged to give up the whole to his creditors and the renters, who had subscribed to the building of a large theatre in the park of New York, in which the company performed but a few seasons. These proprietors and creditors deputed Tyler and Johnson, two of the performers, acting managers,[24] Hodgkinson[25] having left the company, and joined that at Charleston. They recalled Harper, who had been some years manager of the theatres in Boston, Providence, and Newport in Rhode Island. Mr. Harper is a good performer, a great favorite, and in his manners and dealings a gentleman; but unequal to supply the want of Hodgkinson. Sully, Bailey, young Darley, and his wife, were drawn from other theatres. With these performers, added to the remains of the company, among whom was Mrs. Melmouth,[26] whose name was a powerful attraction, the theatrical campaign of 1805 was opened in New York. They had not the Philadelphia company to contend with; all opposition to them in the same city, except in respect to Mrs. Melmouth, would now have been in vain.

It appears that, notwithstanding the exertions of the newly-deputed managers, and their company, matters did not turn out to the expectation of the proprietors. Overtures were sent to Hodgkinson, who accepted the sole management, and in consequence left Charleston to prepare for the next season. He arrived late in the summer in New York, and entered upon his office. From that place he set off in quest of performers, and a theatre being then open in the city of Washington, and another in Fairfax county, Virginia,[27] he arrived at the former place to make engagements. It is supposed that he had inhaled the pestiferous air of the month of August in New York, as, on his arrival at the former place, he was seized with the symptoms of the yellow fever, which in three days put a period to his life. At this time it raged in New York with dreadful malignity. The people at the hotel where he lodged fled his chamber in affright. Mr. Hopkins, one of the performers at Washington, who had agreed to follow his fortune in New York, with Dr. May, his physician, alone attended to him. Thus perished John Hodgkinson, a man most eminent in his profession, and highly respected by the first characters in America.

His remains were wrapt in a blanket by some negroes, who were induced by a considerable reward to perform the office, thrown into a waggon, and conveyed to an obscure burial ground on the Baltimore road, where they were left *unattended*, till a shell of a coffin was made, and a grave hastily dug, when the same negroes returned, and consigned him to the earth.[28]

Some of the most eminent physicians in New York and Philadelphia contend that the yellow fever is not infectious when the patient is removed from the tainted atmosphere where it is generated. A proof to the contrary of this opinion is demonstrated in Hopkins, who accompanied Hodgkinson. There was no fever — no sickness, in Washington; yet in a few days Hopkins sickened, was attacked with the same symptoms with equal malignity, and died in nearly as short a time as the friend he had attended.

From the encouragement given to theatrical exhibitions in Philadelphia, it would be concluded that Messrs. Wignal and Reinagle, the managers, must have accumulated large sums of money. I cannot define the cause, but it is very certain that the contrary is the case. They were ever involved in debt, and finally availed themselves of the bankrupt laws; thus giving up the theatre to their creditors. They were, however, soon re-invested with the management, and after their "white-washing" appeared as before; a common circumtsance in America. It appears that all the American managers are losers. We have already instanced those of New York and Philadelphia. At Boston, Powell,[29] with great encouragement, made nothing — Harper could barely keep his ground, and was often much reduced — West, of the Virginia company, is greatly in debt, so as to prevent the opening the theatre at Alexandria for several years; and Placide, at Charleston, says, that he can barely support himself by his theatre.

Charleston has proved a grave to the theatrical corps in America. The high salaries given there, from the great plenty of money, and riches of the principal inhabitants, who are great amateurs, drew thither numbers of performers on the expiration of their engagements with the northern managers. Among those of eminence who fell a sacrifice to an unwholesome climate, we have to lament Mrs. Wrighten,[30] then married to Mr. Pownal, a druggist in New York, and one of her daughters, who was following the mother in the same line of stage business. Miss Broadhurst's death was attended with melancholy circumstances. Viewing with dread the havock made among the performers, she intreated her mother to spend the sickly months with her on Sullivan's Island, a place at those times of great resort, and to permit her to decline a proffered engagement as first vocal performer in the concerts at the public gardens. The parent refused to acquiesce, and the victim prognosticated the fatal consequences. She entered upon the duties of her engagement — sung a few nights — was then taken ill, and in a few days expired. To this young and accomplished female must be added Miss Fontenelle, who first appeared in Moggy M'Gilpin at Covent-garden, and whose remains are interred at Charleston. In the list of deaths in this place are also the names of Mr. Williamson, and Mr. and Mrs. Jones, from the Salisbury theatre, Mrs. Kenna, and her son, a rising young actor.[31] Mr. Jones, had risen to eminence in the late Mr. Edwin's style, and was acting-manager under Placide.

Jones was succeeded in his management by Mr. Villiers,[32] a young man of superior address and education, who, from his own account, left a very genteel family and good connections to become a player in America. His real name was not Villiers, and, from the same motives which probably influenced him to conceal that of his family, I decline making the discovery. He was a good low comic actor, studying nature in all he attempted; and he was a great favorite. In the summer of 1805 he came as far as New York on the business of his theatre, and was proceeding up the Hudson river to Albany, where the Old American Company were performing, when he was suddenly seized with sickness, and landed at a small town called Esopus, where he died, with the most violent symptoms of the yellow fever, imbibed during his short stay at New York.

From this mortality, the American stage is at present somewhat depreciated, and it is not to be expected that England can spare a supply of such performers as have been last named, with the celerity with which a Carolina climate may carry them off. At New York, Cooper has lately been invested with the theatrical command, having rented the theatre of the proprietors:[33] from his taste in selection, added to his abilities in performance, much is expected.

The death of Wignal has thrown the direction of the Philadelphia company into the hands of Warren, who is well qualified for the arduous undertaking. Wignal was also cut off suddenly. He had recently married Mrs. Merry, and in a very few months she was left in a state of second widowhood.[34] The performers brought forward last season at Philadelphia were Mr. and Mrs. Woodham, and Mr. Bray, late of the York theatre. The lady possesses a fine figure, and is easy in genteel comedy. Mr. Woodham is a good singer, and a musician. Bray is one of the laughter-loving sons of Momus, and manages his business in the manner of Emery, and with considerable effect; his figure and *phiz* being well calculated to pourtray the Yorkshire clown.*

While I am treating of this subject, I may be permitted to add an anecdote relative to the demeanor of an American audience during the representation of one of Shakespeare's tragedies. I was present, in the month of May last, at the performance of Coriolanus in the Baltimore theatre, by the Philadelphia company. I took my seat in the pit, an invariable custom with me when I go for the purpose of giving my whole attention to the performance. I was early in my attendance, and on my entrance, I found the back row in the

* The public prints have just announced that Mr. Hallam, who is mentioned in the beginning of this chapter, after having been fifty-four years a faithful dramatic servant to the public, at Philadelphia, is dismissed the theatre, and obliged to sell his property in it for bread.

pit taken up by a number of boys, many of whom were in an uniform of blue faced with black. I was afterwards informed, that this dress became a fashion from Mr. M'Henry,[35] the late secretary of war, thus cloathing his sons. This, methought, looked something like a puerile badge of Aristocracy in the land of democracy. As the house filled, these urchins set up a violent clamour, beating with sticks, stamping with their feet, and the house echoed with their shrill pipes for the music — "Yankee Doodle, Jefferson's March;" and thus uncontrolled, they practised all the routine of the gallery, which, in fact, could not keep pace with them. The occupiers of the boxes appeared to admire this juvenile spirit of liberty.

Behind me was placed a vulgar, noisy, squat figure, dressed, it is true, somewhat better than the lower order of republicans. He was the oracle of three or four more, to whom he attempted to act the critical buffoon. He too was extremely clamorous before the curtain drew up, uttering the most coarse and vulgar phrases, and ending each with a loud and hoarse laugh. He soon succeeded in interrupting the serenity I had assumed; and as the tragedy began, the critic made his comments in a tone of voice louder than the performers. Often did I turn and in vain intreat his silence. In London, a common disturber is soon turned out — not so in a land of liberty, where every man tells you that he will do as he may think fit; and it was this fellow's pleasure to damp my evening's entertainment. Had I seized the noisy intruder, instead of finding support, I might have had the whole pit upon me. I repeat nothing but what I saw and felt, neither do I "set down aught in malice;" but I will, upon all occasions, speak the truth, and "nothing extenuate."

This buffoon I found to be a bookseller of the name of Hill, who continued his loud and rude observations till the the fall of the curtain. The inferiors of the theatre, who swelled the processions, he called "chaff and bran." The plebeian mob who elected Coriolanus to the consulship, he termed "dirt and straw." The chaste acting of Mrs. Melmoth in the Roman matron, was in a great measure lost to me in his noise. When Coriolanus was killed by Tullus Aufidius and the Volscian chiefs, he roared out, "that's not fair, by G—d, three to one is too much; let him get up again and have a fair chance; one at a time, I say, by G—d."

I should not have descended to repeat such grossness, had not this man borne a nominal rank among those who are deemed respectable people; and, what made this outrage more reprehensible, was, that one of the joint proprietors of the house, Reinagle, the musician, who presided in the orchestra during the performance, was a lodger in his house. Nor is this a singular instance of the kind; interruption by loud talking around you is common in all the American theatres. I mentioned my situation next day to some of the actors, with whom I had formed an acquaintance. They had long been mortified with such kind of interruption, and were well acquainted with Hill's enmity. A single dissatisfied churl in the English theatres must keep his disapproving vociferation to himself, or feel the resentment due to the disturber of others.

The following strictures, from the Norfolk *Herald*, Virginia, while they afford a specimen of American criticism, also display the conduct of the performers during the time of representation, on any disapprobation on the part of the audience.

The opera of the Highland Reel was performed on Tuesday evening, and very fortunately for the credit of the town and the reputation of the performers, to a very thin house — for never in my life did I behold such a performance. It set at defiance all the rules of propriety, and puzzled criticism to find out where to begin, and where to end its strictures. The play is certainly pleasing, entertaining, and instructing, and one which should have called forth all the abilities of the performers, if any they possess. But, with the solitary exceptions of Mrs. Hopkins, in Moggy M'Gilpin, and Mr. Sully, in Shelty, who kept alive the drooping spirits of the audience, the rest were weary, stale, flat, and unprofitable in the extreme and it is ardently to be hoped that we never shall look upon the like again. The play was succeeded by the entertainment of the Sailor's Garland, or a Family Picture, but owing to some disturbance which took place in the gallery, the audience was unable to appreciate the merits of the piece. 'Tis said that a person present found fault with some part of the performance, for which he was seized by the door-keepers, and kicked down stairs, and that this *laudable exertion* to screen the *performance* from *censure* was seconded by some of the PERFORMERS. I always thought, till now, that the performers were employed only as *buffoons* behind the scenes, and not as *bullies* before them. At any rate, 'tis a new way of commanding attention. The manageress* will do well to look to this evil — and the performers had better exert themselves to merit attention by the *correctness of their performance*, than to silence censure by the strength of their arms, or their dexterity in the *pugilistic art*.

In their private capacity, the performers are treated by the Americans with an assumed contempt. They will neither associate with, nor notice them off the stage. Mr. Harper, whose company I always found interesting, one day amused me with an account of a journey of the Old American Company, some years before, to Richmond in Virginia. He said the people were assembled when the performers arrived; at first they were stared at as though they were so many wild beasts; but at length the gaping croud discovered them "to be men and women, formed and dressed like other folks!"

* The company at this time was under the management of a lady of the name of West,[36] who made the annual theatrical circuit of Virginia — Norfolk, Fredericksburg, Richmond, Petersburg, and Alexandria. At these towns she owned a part of the theatres, from which she had an exclusive right of performance.

NOTES — CHAPTER XVIII

1. Janson entirely disregarded the facts, if they were available, that a theatre had been built at Williamsburg, Virginia, in 1716, one in New York by 1732, and another in Charleston, South Carolina, in 1736. Even in Philadelphia it seems "the New Booth on Society Hill" may have been in existence by 1724. In August, 1749, a company led by Walter Murray and Thomas Kean played in a large warehouse owned by William Plumsted. Lewis Hallam and his "Company of Comedians from London" were in Philadelphia in 1754, four years earlier than David Douglass's coming to the northern colonies.

2. Lewis Hallam, the younger, son of Lewis Hallam who came to America in 1754. For many years he was the most popular actor on the American stage.

3. A daughter of Lewis Hallam, the elder.

4. In April, 1759, Douglass secured permission to build a theatre on Society Hill, just beyond the city line. At the end of that year, however, he with his company left Philadelphia and did not return until 1766. In that year, calling themselves the American Company, they built a permanent theatre, the New Theatre at Southwark, which opened by November 14, 1766. The company remained in the colonies until 1774, its last appearance in Philadelphia being in November, 1773.

5. John Williams, a prolific writer of the late eighteenth and early nineteenth centuries.

6. Hallam acted Hamlet at Covent Garden on January 3, 1775. He returned to Philadelphia in 1784, and opened the Theatre in Southwark between April and June 9. He resorted to borderline performances to avoid the legal restrictions in force at this time.

7. John Henry went to England in the summer of 1792 and secured the services of Mr. and Mrs. Hodgkinson, Mr. King, Mr. Prigmore, Mr. West, and Mrs. Pownall.

8. The Kenna family arrived from England in May, 1786. Mr. and Mrs. Owen Morris had played with the Old American Company before the Revolution. Joseph Harper later became manager of the "New Exhibition Room" in Boston and for years was associated with the theatres of Boston and Providence.

9. Thomas Wignell left the Old American Company in 1791 and joined with Alexander Reinagle as manager of the New Theatre. The following year he went to England to secure players.

10. Mrs. Wrighten or Mrs. Pownall became the grandmother of the famous Placide family of actors.

11. Wignell brought back a company of 56 men, women, and children. He took the players to Sandtown, New Jersey, until the danger of yellow fever passed. Finally the "New Theatre" on the north side of Chestnut Street above Sixth, opened on February 17, 1794.

12. The Old American Company spent the season from November 11, 1793, to June, 1794, at the John Street Theatre, in New York. It returned to Philadelphia and played at old Southwark from September 22 to December 4, 1794, its last appearance in that city. Researches do not show that both companies played in Philadelphia at the same time.

13. James Fennell.

14. See Chapter XII, note 26.

15. It has been impossible to secure a complete list of the christian names of all these actors. Evidently the author refers to John Darley, Francis Blisset, William Warren, William Francis, and William Green.

16. Ann Merry, daughter of John Brunton, manager of a provincial theatre in England, left the stage to marry Robert Merry. She lived in retirement until 1796, when because of her husband's reduced fortune, she signed with Wignell. She first appeared on the American stage at the Chestnut Street (New) Theatre on December 5, 1796.

17. On March 2, 1789, the act prohibiting theatricals in Philadelphia was repealed.

18. James Byrne and William Francis.

19. John Bill Ricketts opened the Art Pantheon or Ricketts's Ampitheatre just opposite the New Theatre on October 19, 1795. From 600 to 700 persons attended the daily performances. Lailson opened a still larger circus on April 11, 1797. The following year he sold it and returned to France.

20. Thomas Abthorpe Cooper, who first appeared at the Chestnut Street Theatre in Philadelphia on December 9, 1796. He had previously played at Baltimore in November. Wignell induced him to come to America with the offer of a three year contract at $25 weekly and benefits.

21. Alexander Placide, father of the famous Placide actor family.

22. A consideration of the distance and travelling conditions makes this feat seem improbable. No other references to Cooper's playing in either Charleston or Richmond at this time have been found.

23. William Dunlap became manager of Park Theatre in New York in 1798, and remained in that capacity until 1805. Hodgkinson went to Boston and formed a company which performed at the Haymarket, but at the close of the season hopelessly in debt, he was again engaged by Dunlap.

24. The Park Theatre was under the direction of Johnson and Tyler, who officiated as presidents for a commonwealth of players. This arrangement lasted only a short time, and in 1806 Cooper undertook the management of it.

25. Hodgkinson went to Charleston in the summer of 1803 for two successful seasons.

26. Mrs. Charlotte Melmouth.

27. Evidently at Alexandria, where the Liberty Hall Theatre had been built in 1797.

28. In the spring of 1805, Dunlap having become bankrupt, Hodgkinson obtained the lease of Park Theatre. He went South to secure actors and to fulfill an engagement at Washington. On the way he was seized with yellow fever and died in a tavern near Bladensburg, Maryland, on September 12, 1805.

29. Charles Stuart Powell, manager of the Boston or Federal Street Theatre.

30. Mrs. Mary Ann (Wrighten) Pownall died on August 12, 1796, according to rumor overcome by her daughter Caroline's marriage to Alexander Placide. Another daughter, Mary Wrighten, died on August 24, 1796, of grief following her mother's death.

31. Mrs. John B. Williamson, formerly Miss Fontenelle, died in 1799.

32. Thomas Clarendon Villiers died at Athens, New York, in September, 1803.

33. See note 24.

34. Thomas Wignell married Mrs. Merry in January, 1803, and died on February 21. William Warren and William Wood became acting managers of Chestnut Street Theatre.

35. James McHenry, Secretary of War in John Adams's cabinet, 1796-1800.

36. Mrs. West was still proprietor of the theatre at Norfolk in 1806.

CHAPTER XIX

ARTIFICES AND FRAUDS OF LAND-SPECULATORS—METHOD OF COOKING LAND — DIFFICULTIES OF NEW SETTLERS IN KENTUCKY — THE NEW MISSISSIPPI BUBBLE — GRANT OF LAND BY THE STATE OF GEORGIA — INFAMOUS FRAUD PRACTISED ON THE PURCHASERS — ALTERCATION BETWEEN GENERAL JACKSON AND A PRINTER — PROCEEDINGS IN CONGRESS RELATIVE TO THE MISSISSIPPI COMPANY'S CLAIMS.

THIS species of swindling, since the peace with America, has been fatal to the emigrant. Placing confidence in the reports of interested men, he was led to believe, that the dismal swamps, barren desarts, and pine woods of the new world, flowed with milk and honey — that a fortune would soon accumulate from the production of "some dunghill fowls, a cow, and a breeding sow."

It is no easy matter to undeceive those who, like myself, have formed a determination to visit a foreign land. They readily give credit to every high-wrought tale; which, while it intoxicates the imagination, creates a momentary dislike to their present situation. I never conversed with an emigrant who did not admit the truth of this observation, and confess some disappointment. Even those who had successfully courted fortune in the new world, yearned for that which they had left. It is, indeed, unnatural not to love the country which gave us existence.

Soon after the peace, a number of adventurers who had rioted in the spoils of war, as royalists, finding their resources exhausted, associated themselves, and commenced the nefarious practice of land-jobbing. In this confederacy it was necessary that some one should assume the character of a considerable land-owner in the United States of America. This man set several pens at work to produce travels, anecdotes, and varnished descriptions of the glorious country containing the lands to which he pretended to have a legal title. The infatuated Englishman, ever a dupe to specious advertisements, instantly swallowed the bait, and gave his cash to the London agent for this *rus in nubibus*. He crosses the Atlantic, with money to purchase the fowls, the cow, and the sow, which he soon expends in searching for his land. In many instances he might as well look for "the philosopher's stone." Numbers of Frenchmen have also suffered in this way, from the arts practised upon them by the Paris confederate.

The following luxuriant description of one of the embryo cities, I found copied into an American newspaper, from an European publication:

> It is proposed to build public edifices in the angles within the lines forming the circus and crescents, and the other public buildings with suitable cupolas, and built with a sufficient degree of uniformity to give those structures a handsome appearance. Common sewers, aqueducts, market-places, granaries, piers, and landing-places, paving the streets, planting the vistas with trees corresponding with their names, embellishing the circus and crescents, planting the public garden, lighting, watching, cleansing, &c.

This magnificent city was to be called (a dozen years ago) Franklinville, but the spot set apart for those spacious buildings, is still tenanted by wild beasts.

How very beautiful a city Washington appeared when laid out — on paper!

To enumerate the different frauds, and to lay open the arts practised upon deluded Englishmen by these gangs of coalesced adventurers, would alone exceed the limits of these sheets. To such a pitch of barefaced deceit did they arrive, that the American government was at length obliged to be its own land agent, and to open offices for retailing land to English settlers.[1] To the disgraceful and villainous deeds of land-speculators, Dr. Priestley,[2] and indeed most of the recent English settlers, could bear testimony. False titles, forged grants, fictitious patents, and deeds of bargain and sale of land in the clouds were daily imposed upon the unwary. Sometimes, indeed, the conspirators would discover a tract, which was under some indispensable necessity of being sold, of which they would make a *bonâ fide* purchase, and under this cloak have they conveyed it, again and again, perhaps a dozen times. In other instances, the land granted was described to begin at a *sycamore* tree on such a point; from thence running in a parallel line till it struck a *mulberry* tree; from thence running due south till intersected by an *oak*. In short, the described portion comprised the most valuable timber, and rich, clear land, and all for one dollar per acre. In these cases the purchaser would often find his land, and the remains of the trees described; but alas! instead of rich meads, fertile plains, valuable forests, and meandering rivers, he found a barren desart, not producing a single shrub. The trees had been planted for deception only, and the navigable rivers had found another course. Colonel Michael Payne,[3] of North Carolina, marshal of the state, informed me that he was obliged to attend a sale of land in the interior part of the state, which had been levied upon under an execution issuing out of the Federal Court, and that upon his journey over one of the most barren and rocky countries he had ever travelled, he observed a party of men planting trees. So strange an employment in so dreary a spot induced the colonel to enquire of the laborers what benefit they expected to derive from their labor. He also observed two or three carts, loaded with young trees, and a man at a little distance, surveying the ground, who said, in answer to the colonel's questions, that the land was advertised for sale in London at half a guinea per acre, and that they were "cooking it up a little." This cookery consisted in planting a few young trees, the choicest growth of a far distant forest, as divisional lines and marks. The cook proved to be a confederate land-speculator, and a *ci-devant* congressman. The colonel added, that from the nature of the soil, and unpropitious situation of the land, a colony of English farmers could not make it worth a shilling.

The new state of Kentucky is more extravagantly described and extolled than any other part of the United States. From the accounts I have collected from such as have explored that country, the land is certainly of a superior quality to some of the states, and well watered by large rivers. It has increased much in population since the peace of 1783, but that it does not equally allure all who visit it to settle there is certain. Many have returned, after struggling against the numerous difficulties of subsisting in a new country, one, two, and three years before they could make their daily bread. A new settler should have what is here termed "plenty of force;" that is, he should not attempt the planting and farming business without about a dozen laborers. This assistance, with two or three hundred pounds, may in a few years complete the clearing of a few hundred acres of land, the erecting of log-houses, and other necessary work. This land, thus cleared, will produce tobacco, hemp, wheat, barley, oats, clover, and most European fruits and vegetables. But, while we mention the quality of the land, another question naturally arises; namely, how is the superfluous produce to be carried to market? It is at present above a thousand miles to export produce from the extreme parts of Kentucky, Ohio, and Tennessee, by water to the commercial cities in the United States, and a great many hundred by land! We find none of these difficulties fairly demonstrated by the writers and compilers of American voyages, history, and travels. The corn of these states could not, without great loss, be sold in Philadelphia, at the rate of the grain grown in its vicinity.

We have now before us, reader, a state fraud — land speculations by wholesale — a scene of chicanery and iniquity hitherto unknown in the history of nations — a scene which has excited in Congress more odium, and created more discord and intemperate warmth in that body, than any question before them since the adoption of the federal constitution.

In the year 1795, "the free, sovereign, and independent state of Georgia," under the great seal of the state, and signed by the governor and commander in chief, for certain considerations to be paid in Spanish milled dollars, granted and sold to certain individuals associated in companies, under the names of "The Georgia Company," — "The Georgia Mississippi Company,"[4] and the "Tennessee Company," a vast tract of land lying within the boundaries of that state.

As this nefarious transaction raised a clamour through the United States, equal to the bursting of the South Sea bubble in London; and what is much more material at present, as a short history of it will prove useful to those who may hereafter wish to hold land within the Untied States, by putting them on their guard, should they even purchase of a state; I shall give a copy of the patent, and the *wiles* thrown out to purchasers in order to advance the value of the purchase. This document I unluckily became possessed of, from being myself a considerable sufferer in the Georgia Mississippi Company: a *name*, however, is all they hold at the present day. The other two grants from the state of Georgia ran in the same words, with the alteration of names and parcels:

COPY OF THE PATENT

THE Georgia Mississippi Company having purchased from the government of the state of Georgia, that part of its western territory, lying between the rivers Mississippi and Tom Bigby, and extending from thirty-one degrees eighteen minutes to thirty-two degrees forty minutes north latitude, computed to be, at least, one hundred and eighty miles in length, and ninety-five miles in breadth, did obtain a grant for the same, under the great seal of the said state, bearing date the twenty-sixth day of January, one thousand seven hundred and ninety-five, in the following words:

STATE OF GEORGIA,

By His Excellency GEORGE MATHEWS, Captain-General, Governor and Commander in Chief in and over the said State, and of the Militia thereof.

To all to whom these Presents shall come, Greeting,

KNOW ye, That in pursuance of the Act of the General Assembly intituled, An Act supplementary to an Act intituled, An Act for appropriating a part of the unlocated territory, of this state, for the payment of the late state troops, and for other purposes therein mentioned, declaring the right of this state to the unappropriated territory thereof, for the protection and support of the frontiers of this state, and for other purposes, passed at Augusta, on the 7th day of January, in the year of our Lord one thousand seven hundred and ninety-five, and, of the sovereignty and independence of the United States of America the Nineteenth, and by virtue of the powers in me vested, I have given and granted, and, by these presents, in the name and behalf of the said state, do give and grant, under and by virtue of the before-mentioned supplementary Act, and securing to the state, according to the directions, reservations and stipulations therein contained and expressed, unto Nicholas Long, Thomas Glascock, Ambrose Gordon, and Thomas Cumming and their associates, their heirs and assigns for ever, in fee simple, as tenants in common, and not as joint tenants, all that tract or parcel of land, including islands, situate, lying and being within the following boundaries, that is to say, beginning on the river Mississippi, at the place where the latitude of thirty-one degrees and eighteen minutes north of the equator intersects the same; thence a due east course to the middle of Don or Tom Bigby river; thence up the middle of the said river, to where it intersects the latitude of thirty-two degrees and forty minutes north of the equator; thence a due west course along the Georgia Company's line, to the river Mississippi; thence down the middle of the same to the place of beginning, together with all and singular the rights, members and appurtenances whatsoever, to the said tract or parcel of land, including islands, belonging, or in any wise appertaining; and also all the estate, right, title, interest, claim and demand of the state aforesaid, of, in, to, or out of, the same; reserving, nevertheless out of the said tract of land, six hundred and twenty thousand acres, to be subscribed by, and for the use and behoof of other citizens of the said state, who shall choose to do the same, at such time, at such rates, and to such effect, and in such form and manner as are pointed out and expressed in the before-mentioned Supplementary Act; provided also, that the said Nicholas Long, Thomas Glascock, Ambrose Gordon and Thomas Cumming and their associates, shall not be entitled to dispose of the said territory, in part or in whole, in any way or manner to any foreign king, prince, potentate or power whatever; to have and to hold the said tract or parcel of land, and all and singular the premises aforesaid, with their and every of their rights, members and appurtenances, unto the said Nicholas Long, Thomas Glascock, Ambrose Gordon and Thomas Cumming and their associates, called the Georgia Mississippi Company, their heirs and assigns forever in fee simple, as tenants in common, and not as joint tenants.

Given under my hand and the great seal of the said state, this twenty-sixth day of January, in the year of our Lord one thousand seven hundred and ninety-five, and in the nineteeth year of American Independence.

GEO. MATHEWS.

Signed by his Excellency the Governor,
the 26th day of January, 1795.
"EDWARD WATTS, *S. E. D.*"

Under such a title — the faith of a free state, little doubt or suspicion was entertained. No wonder, therefore, that monied men stepped forward as purchasers.

The Georgian government having received into their exchequer the full stipulated consideration in specie for their Mississippi lands, proceeded at the usual time of election, to the choice of a new governor and assembly of representatives. The sovereign people, at this time, fermented by French politics, chose men of congenial principles, and appointed one Jackson,[5] a subject of the king of Great Britain, in the place of governor Mathews. He commenced his career with a bill declaring the grant of the Mississippi lands illegal and void; and procuring an *ex post facto law* for this purpose, seized the records, with which he marched in triumph, attended by his majority of assembly, and burned *them before the court-house!*

In vain the defrauded purchasers remonstrated. Georgia being "free, sovereign, and independent," no redress could be obtained; and this fair and promising structure of speculation, which had cost many hundred thousand dollars in erecting, was thus in an instant demolished. The whole of the purchase-money still remains in the treasury of the state!

The sufferers were immediately persecuted by the importunites of those of whom they purchased. Many joined issue upon record in courts of law, and the question was there agitated in various forms without their obtaining relief. Others compromised, and got up their securities; while the greater number were plunged into ruin.

Mr. Thomas Hutchins,[6] geographer to the United States, having at a former period surveyed this land, made a very favorable report of the many natural advantages it possessed. It was printed, with other allurements, in the form of a pamphlet, and put into the hands of such as were inclined to become purchasers. The whole tract of land sold as stated, contained many million acres, of which the author, at the sacrifice of several thousand dollars, purchased a considerable portion; and still holds his claim.

Soon after the *bonfire frolic*, the state offered the *same land to* Congress. A bargain was struck, and fresh conveyances were made, with a reservation of five million acres "to quiet any claims on the state of Georgia." Thus this land is now held by the United States, and a bill is pending before Congress to make restitution to the purchasers. Commissioners, consisting of the secretary of state, and of the treasurer of the United States, with the attorney-general, were appointed to enquire into these claims, and reported in favor of the purchasers; yet the bill for the two last sessions has met with great opposition from the democratic party, while it is supported with much firmness by the federalists.[7]

These proceedings consequently gave rise to much political rancour. The transaction was not only reprobated by the federalists, but condemned by every moderate man in the country. One of the leading characters instrumental in the sale of the lands, was General Gunn,[8] who became an object of the persecution of Jackson's party. The printer of a newspaper at Savannah, the capital of Georgia,[9] was prevailed upon by two of Jackson's aids-de-camp, for he was a general of militia to insert an extract from the Philadelphia paper, called the *Aurora*, libelling the character of Gunn. This produced an answer from a friend of the injured party, retorting the scandal upon those by whom it was propagated, which he also admitted into his publication. The young aids took umbrage, and insisted on the printer's giving up the author of the reply, but this he resolutely refused to do. Printers in America have the virtue to keep authors' names, where necessary, a profound secret. On the same day the printer being at the post-office, there met Jackson, who began an harangue on the blessings of democracy, which he ended, to use the printer's words, "by praising his own exploits during the American revolution, and declaring that the country, and this state in particular, (Georgia) was indebted to him for its independence." He then observed, that he, the printer, was a good republican when he came to Savannah; to which the latter replied, that his principles were then what they had ever been. The redoubted hero denied this, and charged the *man of letters* with being in *British pay;* for which falsehood he was by the other denounced a *liar.* This produced a little blustering, and thus the matter ended. Next day the two young *men of war,* instigated, as the printer alledged, by their commander, again called on him for the name of the author who had vindicated General Gunn. A denial was still persisted in, when one of them made a blow with a loaded whip, which the printer seized, and applied it to the owner's shoulders, with considerable effect. — "After this," continues the printer, "they collected a mob, presented their pistols to my breast, threatened to pull down the printing-house, and to throw the types into the river, if I did not give up the author's name; but they were soon opposed by more than an equal number of citizens, which occasioned them to disperse in a terrible rage. They collected a third time, but finding the respectable part of the inhabitants determined to protect me, they moved off, still swearing vengeance."

The following day Jackson procured a meeting of his party, where it was resolved, "*That no printer in the state of Georgia should be allowed to publish any thing against the President of the United States.*" The democratic chief was appointed a committee to draw up rules and organize a society in each county of the state, for the purpose of carrying such resolution into effect.

The career of this turbulent character, was arrested by death about a year ago, at the city of Washington, where he was attending as a senator for the state of Georgia. He was the idol of his party, as may be seen from the following disgusting speech on his death, pronounced in the house of representatives by John Randolph. It will also give the reader an idea of the proceedings of that house during the reign of democracy. A bill had originated in, and passed the senate, making compensation to the defrauded purchasers of the Georgia lands, for what was called the Yazoo claim, and which was rejected in the house of representatives; on which Randolph sprang up and exclaimed — "I shall live ten years longer. Mr. Speaker, a few days ago we adjourned to pay the last mournful tribute of public respect to one of the best men that America has known — I move that we now adjourn to do honor to his apotheosis — His last words to me were, 'Could I but survive to see Yazoo annihilated, I should then die in peace; and, should it be annihilated after my death, I shall at least not have lived in vain.' I move that we adjourn to honor the deceased hero, General James Jackson, and to triumph in the salvation of our country from corruption." — The house did accordingly adjourn![10]

This claim, which in common honesty should have been satisfied many years ago, was several times before the house, and on each question, a majority of the members voted in favor of the claimants.[11] On the present, Randolph contrived to maintain a very small majority, and took the above method of shewing his exultation. The question will be renewed in the present sitting of Congress. It has become a national question of great importance; and, if finally determined against the claimants, many of whom are distinguished characters in New England, it is conjectured that very serious consequences may ensue.

NOTES — CHAPTER XIX

1. This statement is misleading. The American government became "its own land agent" in 1785, when the first ordinance for the disposal of the public lands of the United States was passed on May 20. This action was taken, not because of the speculation but in order to raise revenue and to dispose of the western lands to settlers. Later modifications and new laws changed the methods and finally the principles upon which this ordinance had been based. The United States land offices were open to *all* settlers who could pay the price. Janson evidently had in mind the Land Act of 1800 under which large quantities of public domain passed into private hands. P. J. Treat, *The National Land System*, gives an outline of the various laws dealing with the land question.

2. See Chapter 14, note 10.

3. Colonel Michael Payne of Chowan County, North Carolina, was a captain during the Revolution, and later served in the State Senate for a number of years.

4. A copy of the grant given to the Georgia Mississippi Company signed by Governor George Matthews on January 26, 1795, may be found in *The Contract for the Purchase of Western Territory made with the Legislature of Georgia in the Year 1795*, Augusta, 1799, pp. 90-92, or in Abraham Bishop, *Georgia Speculation Unveiled, Second Part,* Hartford, 1798, pp. 43-45.

5. James Jackson, United States Senator, resigned his office in order to become a candidate for the Georgia Legislature on the land fraud issue. He was elected Governor in 1798. The author speaks of him as "a subject of the King of Great Britain" because he was born in England.

6. See Chapter 9, note 2.

7. John Randolph led this opposition to the Yazoo settlement.

8. James Gunn, brigadier-general of Georgia militia, was born March 13, 1753, served in the United States Senate from March 4, 1789, to March 3, 1801, and died July 30, 1801.

9. Savannah ceased to be the capital in 1786, when the seat of government removed to Augusta.

10. House of Representatives, March 29, 1806. *Annals of Congress, 1805-1807*, p. 921.

11. The author, in his enthusiasm for the claimants of whom he apparently was one, overlooked the fact that he contradicted a statement just previously made.

CHAPTER XX

CONJECTURES ON THE EXISTENCE OF THE MADOGIANS OR, WELCH INDIANS — NARRATIVE OF MAURICE GRIFFITH — EXPEDITION OF THE SHAWNESE TO EXPLORE THE MISSOURI — DISCOVERY OF A NATION OF WHITE INDIANS — NATURAL ABILITIES OF THE INDIANS — DIALOGUE BETWEEN AN INDIAN CHIEF AND AN AMERICAN AGENT — ADOPTION OF A WARRIOR BY THE CANADIAN INDIANS.

VARIOUS writers have asserted the existence on the American continent of a race of Indians, descended from the ancient Britons. There are traditions of a number of people from Wales landing on the continent of America, as far back as the year 1170; whose descendants are said still to form a distinct tribe, and to speak the Welsh language. Though this conjecture is supported by no certain proofs, yet it is believed that there are civilized Indians possessing a large tract of land west of the Mississippi. From the state of the arts, and from the manners and customs of these tribes, I have reason to suppose they are of European origin.

Many attempts have been made to ascertain the truth or falsehood of this conjecture. The extent of territory, impenetrable forests, obstructions of rivers, and the worse opposition from unfriendly natives, have hitherto rendered them abortive.

In the year 1795, Mr. Evans, a Welchman, went up the river Missouri in search of this settlement.[1] The Spanish commandant at St. Louis arrested him, and confined him in prison; where he might still have lingered, had not Judge Turner interested himself in his behalf. By his influence Mr. Evans obtained his liberty — he also procured him a passport to go up the river, and promised him a reward of two thousand dollars on his return, provided he discovered the Pacific Ocean.

About the same time a merchant of the name of Mackie,

went up the river Missouri to trade with the Indians. He was met at a place called Cincinnati, by a gentleman, who furnished him with a Vocabulary in Welch and English. The merchant promised, if possible, to see Evans, and give him the book, with every assistance in his power; but nothing hath been since heard of either of them.

Conjecture on this point has a vast extent to traverse, in order to reconcile the reports of travellers, Indian traders, and interpreters, on the existence of the tribe called the Madogians; for if proved to be a fact, it will place the discovery of America, many centuries before the voyages of Columbus. The distance between the river Mississippi and the Pacific Ocean is supposed to be about two thousand miles, and from the source of the Missouri about half that distance. This being the tract supposed to be occupied by the Welch Indians, their ancestors must have landed or been shipwrecked on the coast of New Albion, which was visited by Sir Francis Drake. The land in the greatest part of America is the most barren next the sea-coast; we must therefore suppose that the strangers, finding no opposition, nor human inhabitant, advanced till they found the richest ground and the best climate. Their bark, perhaps dashed to pieces, and all hopes lost of returning to their native land, they might have formed themselves into a little commonwealth; and their offspring, cut off from all intercourse with civilized nations, may have degenerated into the savage state, retaining the language of their ancestors, which is said nearly to resemble that still used by the common people of Wales. That they also excel all other tribes in the arts, is accounted for upon the same principle. It is probable that their ancestors had some mechanical implements, and some of them might have been complete masters of their use. The country might also favor the cultivation of the arts, which in an encreasing population is an object of the highest importance. Ore of various kinds has been discovered in the western states, and even iron is manufactured in large quantities in many parts of the Union. Thus we account for the specimens of mechanism said to come from the country of the Madogians.

These observations were made some years previous to the expedition of Captain Lewis and Lieutenant Clarke, to explore the source of the Missouri, and from them no light is thrown upon the subject. We must therefore conclude that the accounts are fabulous, or that those gentlemen did not chance to meet with their settlements; and yet the following account, published by Mr. H. Toulmin,[2] a gentleman of respectability at Frankfort, in Kentucky, is worthy of consideration in the investigation of this subject. He observes, that he had it from Mr. John Childs, of Jessamine county:

Maurice Griffith, a native of Wales, which country he left when about sixteen years of age, was taken prisoner by a party of Shawnese Indians, about forty years ago, near Vosses' Fort, on the head of Roanoke river, in Virginia county, and carried into the Shawnese nation. Having staid there about two years and a half, he found that five young men of the tribe had a desire of attempting to explore the sources of the Missouri. He prevailed upon them to admit him one of the party. They set out with six good rifles, and six pounds of powder apiece, of which they were of course very careful. On reaching the mouth of the Missouri, they were struck with the extraordinary appearance of the muddy waters of the Mississippi. They staid two or three days amusing themselves with this novel sight; they then determined on the course which they should pursue, which happened to be so nearly in that of the river, that they frequently came within sight of it, as they proceeded on their journey. After travelling about thirty days through good farming woodland, they came into the open prairies, on which nothing grew but long luxuriant grass.— There was a succession of these varying in size, some being eight or ten miles across, but one of them so long, that it occupied three days to travel through it. In passing through the large prairies, they were much distressed for water and provisions, for they saw neither beast nor bird; and though there was an abundance of old springs, fresh water was very scarce. In one of these prairies, the salt springs ran into small ponds in which, as the weather was hot, the water had sunk, and left the edges of the ponds so covered with salt, that they fully supplied themselves with that article, and they might easily have collected bushels of it. As they were travelling through the prairies, they had likewise the good fortune to kill an animal which was nine or ten feet high, and of a bulk proportioned to his height. They had seen two of the same species before, and they observed four of them afterwards. They were swift footed, and had neither tusks nor horns. After they had passed through this prairie, they made it a rule never to enter on one which they could not see across, till they had supplied themselves with a sufficiency of venison to last several days. After having travelled a considerable time through the prairies, they came to very extensive lead mines, where they melted the ore, and furnished themselves with what lead they wanted. They afterwards came to two copper mines, one of which was three miles through, and in several places they met rocks of copper, as large as houses.

When about fifteen days journey from the second copper mine, they came in sight of white mountains, which, though in the heat of summer, appeared to them to be covered with snow. The sight naturally excited considerable astonishment, but on their approaching the mountains, they discovered, that instead of snow they were covered with immense bodies of white sand. They had, in the mean time, passed through about ten nations of Indians, from whom they received very friendly treatment. It was the practice of the party to exercise the office of spokesman in rotation: and when the language of any nation through which they passed was unknown to them, it was the duty of the spokesman, a duty in which the others never interfered, to convey their meaning by appropriate signs.

The labor of traveling through the deep sands of the mountains was excessive, but at length they relieved themselves of this difficulty by following the course of a shallow river, the bottom of which being level, they made their way to the top of the mountains with tolerable convenience.

After passing the mountains, they entered a fine tract of land, which having travelled through for several days, they accidentally met with three white men in the Indian dress. Griffith immediately understood their language, as it was pure Welch, though they occasionally made use of a few words with which he was unacquainted;

however, as it happened to be the turn of one of his comrades to act as spokesman, or interpreter, he preserved a profound silence, and never gave them any intimation that he understood the language of their new companions.

After proceeding with them four or five days journey, they came to the village of these white men, where they found that the whole nation were of the same color, having all the European complexion. The three men took them through the village for about the space of fifteen miles, when they came to the council-house, at which an assembly of the king and chief men of the nation was held. The council lasted three days; and as the strangers were not supposed to be acquainted with their language, they were suffered to be present at their deliberations. The great question before the council was, what conduct should be observed towards the strangers. From their fire-arms, their knives, and their tomahawks, it was concluded they were a warlike people; it was conceived they were sent to look out a country for their nation; that if they were suffered to return, they might expect a body of powerful invaders, but that, if these six men were put to death, nothing would be known of their country, and they should still enjoy their possession in security. It was finally determined that they should be put to death. Griffith then thought that it was time for him to speak. He addressed the council in the Welsh language. He informed them that they had not been sent by any nation — they had no hostile intentions — that it was their wish to trace the Missouri to its source, and that they should return to their country satisfied with the discoveries they had made, without any wish to disturb the repose of their new acquaintances. An instant astonishment glowed in the countenances not only of the council but of his Shawnese companions, who clearly saw he was understood by the people of the country. Full confidence was at once given to his declaration; the king advanced and gave him his hand. They abandoned the design of putting him and his companions to death, and from that moment treated them with the utmost friendship. Griffith and the Shawnese continued eight months in the nation, but were deterred from prosecuting their researches up the Missouri, by the advice of the people of the country, who informed them they had gone a twelvemonth's journey up the river, but found it was as large there as it was in their own country. As to the history of the people, he could learn nothing satisfactory. The only account they could give was, that their forefathers had come up the river from a very distant country. They had no books, no records, no writings.

They intermixed with no other people by marriage; there was not a dark-skinned man in the nation. Their numbers were very considerable. There was a range of settlements on the river for fifty miles, and there were, within this space, three large water courses, which fell into the Missouri, on the banks of each of which they were likewise settled. He supposed there must be fifty thousand men in the nation capable of bearing arms. Their clothing was skins well dressed. Their houses were made of upright posts, and the bark of trees. The only implements they had to cut them with were stone tomahawks. They had no iron: their arms were bows and arrows. They had some silver, which had been hammered with stones into coarse ornaments, but it did not appear to be pure. They had neither horses, cattle, sheep, hogs, nor any domestic or tame animals. They lived by hunting. He said nothing about their religion.

Griffiths and his companions had some large iron tomahawks with them. With these they cut down trees, and prepared a canoe to return home in; but their tomahawks were so great a curiosity, and the people of the country were so eager to handle them, that their canoe was completed with very little labor. When this work was accomplished, they proposed to leave their new friends, Griffiths, however, having promised to visit them again. They descended the river with considerable speed, but amidst frequent dangers from the rapidity of the current, particularly when passing through the White Mountains. When they reached the Shawnese nation, they had been absent about two years and a half. Griffith supposed that when they travelled, they went at the rate of about fifteen miles a day. He staid but a few months with the Indians after their return, as a favorable opportunity offered itself to him to reach his friends in Virginia. He came with a hunting party of Indians to the head waters of Coal river, which runs into the New river, not far above the falls. There he left the Shawnese, and easily reached the settlement on the Roanoke. Mr. Childes knew him before he was taken prisoner, and saw him a few days after his return, when he narrated to him the preceding circumstances; Griffiths was universally regarded as a steady, honest man, and a man of veracity. Mr. Childes has placed the utmost confidence in his account of himself and his fellow travellers, and has no more doubt of the truth of his relation, than if he had seen the whole himself. Whether Griffiths be still alive or not, he does not know.

Mr. Toulmin investigates this subject with great assiduity. He says,

that by recurring to a passage in history, it appears that several years before the discovery of America by Christopher Columbus, a certain Welsh prince embarked from his native country, with a large party of emigrants; that after some time a vessel or two came back, with the account that they had discovered a country far to the westward, and that they set sail again with a fresh reinforcement, and never returned any more. The country which these adventurers discovered, it has been supposed, was the continent of North America, and it has been conjectured, that they had landed on this continent somewhere in the Gulph of Mexico, and from thence proceeded northward, till they got out of the reach of the hostile natives, and seated themselves in the upper country of Missouri. Many accounts accordingly have been published within the last thirty years, of persons, who, in consequence, either by accident or the ardor of curiosity, have made themselves acquainted with a nation of men on the Missouri, possessing the complexion of Europeans, and the language of Welshmen. Could the fact be well established, it would afford, perhaps, the most satisfactory solution of the difficulty occasioned by a view of the various ancient fortifications with which the Ohio country abounds, of any that has hitherto been offered. These fortifications were evidently never made by the Indians. The Indian art of war presents nothing of the kind. The probability too is, that the persons who constructed them were, at that time acquainted with the use of iron: the situation of those fortifications, which are uniformly in the most fertile land of the country, indicates that those who made them were an agricultural people, and the remarkable care and skill with which they were executed, affords traits of genius of a people, who relied more on their military skill than on their numbers. The growth of the trees upon them is very compatible with the idea, that it is no more than three hundred years since they were abandoned.

We are equally ignorant of many other nations of Indians, in this unexplored part of America. The nation of the Snake, the Gnacsitaries, the Padoucas, the Kansez, the Macoutens, and numerous other tribes are known only by name.

Many Indians chiefs have displayed talents in oratory, and are men of considerable natural abilities.* The following conversation on a religious subject, inserted the official paper, printed at Washington is worthy of notice:

In the year 1797, Istehoche (called by the white people the adjutant) visited the agent for Indian affairs. This old man was esteemed

* Among many examples that might be adduced to corroborate this assertion, I shall content myself with mentioning the Mohawk chief, Teyoninhokerawen, or as he is likewise denominated, John Norton. This interesting Indian about two years ago visited England, where numerous traits of an amiable disposition and a vigorous intellect produced the most pleasing impressions on all who were introduced to him. A proof of his possessing, in a high degree, the qualities of a good temper and great mental quickness, occurred at the Upper Rooms, at Bath, where he appeared in the dress of his country. A young Englishman, who had been in America, accosted the chief with several abrupt questions respecting his place of abode, situation and the like. To these Norton returned answers at once pertinent and modest. The inquirer, however, expressed himself dissatisfied with them; and hinted, in almost plain terms, that he believed him to be an impostor. Still the American preserved his temper, and endeavored to convince the *Gentleman* that his account of himself might be depended upon. "Well but," returned the other, "if you really are what you pretend to be; how will you relish returning to the *savages* of your own country?" "Sir," replied Norton with a glance of intelligence, "I shall not experience so great a change in my society as you imagine, for I find there are *savages* in this country also." Animated with the spirit of genuine patriotism, this generous chieftain was unweariedly occupied, during the intervals of his public business, in acquiring every species of useful knowledge, for the purpose of transporting it to his own country, for the benefit of his people; and, what the friends to the happiness of men will hear with still greater admiration and pleasure, he was also engaged, under the auspices of Mr. Wilberforce and Mr. Thornton,[3] in the laborious employment of translating the gospel of St. John into his native tongue.

Teyoninhokerawen appeared to be about forty-five years of age; his person is tall, muscular, and well-proportioned; his countenance fine and intelligent, illuminated with "an eye like Mars to threaten and command." His mother being a Scotch woman, and he himself having spent two years of his life (from thirteen to fifteen), in Edinburgh; he has acquired sufficient knowledge of the English to read it with ease, and speak it with fluency; the French language also is equally familiar to him. Assisted by great natural sagacity, and habits of deep reflection, he appears to have *generalised* more than could have been expected from the circumstances of his place of birth, and the state of society in which he has spent his life, and has not only worked out, by the energies of his own mind, many schemes for the improvements of *his* country, and the benefit of *ours,* but also acquired a very considerable share of moral, political, and philosophical information. His wife is a female of his own tribe, by whom he has two children.

by all who knew him, being an honest man, communicative and jocular, and when a boy, was appointed by the chiefs of the Creek nation to make the fire of welcome for General Oglethorpe, on his first arrival to take possession of, and establish the colony of Georgia. There were then at the residence of the agent, the principal chiefs of the twelve towns of Lower Creeks. Their object was to prevail on the agent to give up the plan of civilization, and conform himself in the management of Indian affairs to the caprice and insolence of the Indians. Their conversation on this subject lasted three days, and became insolent in the extreme on the last day. Istehoche remained on his bearskin, a silent hearer till the evening of the third day, and then had the following dialogue with the agent.

Istehoche. Father, have not you white people a book which tells when you were created, and where: there are two of them, a small one attached to a large one, which I remember to have seen when a boy?

Agent. Yes, go on.

Istehoche. Is it true that when Esaugetuh Misse (the master of breath) made you white people, that he made two of you, a man and a woman, and he made a garden for them, and put all the good things in it, and gave it to these two white people, and is this in the book?

Agent. Yes, go on.

Istehoche. When he made these two people, and everything for them, he called up the woman, and gave her a *talk.* Woman, says he, I have made all these things for you, and they are all good, but the grapes are not ripe, you must not eat them, and then Esaugetuh Misse left her. Is this in the book?

Agent. Yes, go on.

Istehoche. When Esaugetuh Misse left her, and went off, the snake came up, and asked: What! did he say that the grapes are not ripe? Woman, they are ripe, they are good, eat them; and the woman ate them. Is this in the book?

Agent. Yes, go on.

Istehoche. Bye and bye, Esaugetuh Misse came back, and looking round him, exclaims: Ha! ha! who has spoiled my tables? The woman replied, the snake has spoiled your tables: he told me the grapes were ripe, advised me to eat them, and I did eat them.. 'Did he spoil my tables? Go then, woman, and mash his head, and tell your children to mash his head.' Is this in the book?

Agent. Yes, go on.

Istehoche. Ever since I heard this story, I have remembered it, and that you white people when you see a snake you kill it. The talk was not given to me or my people: I never killed a snake. In my hunting or travelling if I see them, they generally give way to me, and if they are cross I give way to them, I suppose something has vexed them; I leave them; there is room enough for me and them. I am now an old man as you see, can just creep about, and my greatest pleasure is to crawl here, to see and converse with you, and take a dish of coffee with you. Your plan of civilization I think I comprehend, and I believe it is for the good of my nation. I am very old, as you see, and was a hardy lad when General Oglethorpe first came to Savannah; then I was appointed by my father to make a fire for him, and welcome him to our land; and when I grew up to manhood, I accompanied him in his attack on St. Augustine against the Spaniards, and from that day to this I have associated much with white people, am greatly attached to them, particularly those in authority, from whom I have received many acts of kindness, and it is a pleasure in me to be able to say to you, that I never stole a skin's-worth of property in my life, or did any injury to a white man. I am old as you see, and have seen more than any chief in my land. I have listened to your plan, I am pleased with it, and if I was young, I would soon prove to you that there would be no other difference between us than the color of our skin. I am old as you see; and I firmly believe that Washington, like Esaugetuh Misse, has given a talk for the salvation of us red people, that you have brought and delivered this talk to us; that these people are playing the snake, and that unless you take and mash their heads (clenching his fists and knocking his knuckles together repeatedly) you will not succeed in your plan.

After this speech the old man laid himself down on his bear skin, the listening chiefs sat in silence for a few minutes, then rose up, and went off without saying one word.

In quitting this subject I am unwilling to neglect Mr. Lang's extraordinary account of the adoption of a warrior by the Canadian Indians. He says that he himself underwent the ceremony:

A feast is prepared of dog's flesh, boiled in bear's grease, with huckleberries,* of which it is expected every one should partake. When the repast is over, the war song is sung in the following words — "Master of life view us well! We receive a brother warrior, who appears to have sense, shews strength in his arm, and does not refuse his body to the enemy."

After the war-song, if the person does not discover any signs of fear, he is regarded with reverence and esteem — courage in the opinion of the savages, being considered not only as indispensible, but as the greatest recommendation. He is then seated on a beaver robe, and presented with a pipe to smoke, which is put round to every warrior, and a wampum belt is thrown over his neck. When the pipe has gone round, a sweating-house is prepared, with six long poles fixed in the ground, and pointed at the top; it is then covered with skins and blankets to exclude the air, and the area of the house will contain only three persons. The person to be adopted is then stripped naked, and enters the hut with two chiefs; two large stones, made red hot, are brought in, and thrown upon the ground; water is then brought in a bark-dish, and sprinkled on the stones with cedar branches, the steam arising from which puts the person into a most profuse perspiration, and opens the pores to receive the other parts of the ceremony. When the perspiration is at the height, he quits the house, and jumps into the water. Immediately on coming out a blanket is thrown over him, and he is led to the chief's hut, where he undergoes the following operation: Being extended on his back, the chief draws the figures he intends to make with a pointed stick dipped in water in which gunpowder has been dissolved; after which, with ten needles dipped in vermilion, and fixed in a small wooden frame, he pricks the delineated parts; and where the bolder outlines occur, he incises the flesh with a gun-flint; the vacant spaces, or those not marked with vermilion, are rubbed in with gunpowder, which produces a variety of red and blue; the wounds are then seared with pinkwood to prevent their festering.

This operation, which is performed at intervals, lasts two or three days. Every morning the parts are washed with cold water, in which is infused an herb called Pockqueeregan, which resembles the English

* These berries grow in abundance in all parts of the United States. They are small and black, resembling those which grow on moors and waste lands in England. They are a pleasant and wholesome fruit, and when taken with milk, cool and refreshing.

box, and is mixed by the Indians with the tobacco they smoke, to take off the strength. During the process, the war-songs are sung, accompanied by a rattle hung round with hawk's-bells, called cheesaquois, which they keep shaking to stifle the groans such pains must naturally occasion. Upon the ceremony being completed, they give the party a name; to Mr. Lang, who submitted to undergo this cruel operation, they allotted the name of Amik, or Beaver.

NOTES — CHAPTER XX

1. There must have been considerable discussion during this period concerning the Welch Indians. In 1797 a London firm published a small pamphlet of thirty-five pages entitled *The Welch Indians or a Collection of Papers Respecting a People whose Ancestors Emigrated from Wales to America in the Year 1170, with Prince Madoc,* (*Three Hundred Years before the First Voyage of Columbus*), and who are said now to inhabit a beautiful Country on the West Side of the Mississippi. Dedicated to the Missionary Society by George Burder. The author of this collection brought together many statements which had found their way into print before that time.

2. Reverend Henry Toulmin, a Unitarian clergyman, native of England, emigrated to Kentucky in 1791. In the following year he published a pamphlet in England, *Description of Kentucky,* inviting emigrants to that State. He served as Secretary of State for Kentucky from 1796 to 1804.

3. William Wilberforce, English philanthropist, crusader in the anti-slavery movement in England and a leader in the Church Missionary and Bible societies.

4. Henry Thornton, English philanthropist and economist, associate of Wilberforce in the Missionary and Bible societies.

CHAPTER XXI

ORDER OF THE CINCINNATI — SATIRE ON THIS INSTITUTION — IMAGINARY ADVENTURES OF ONE OF ITS MEMBERS — THE EAGLE — BURLESQUE ON AMERICAN ELECTIONS — BADGE OF THE ORDER.

THE order, or society of the Cincinnati, is composed of officers who served in the American war, and honorary members.[1] The honors and advantages are hereditary in the eldest sons of the officers, and in default of issue male, in the collateral male heirs; but this does not extend to honorary members, and the latter are limited not to exceed the ratio of one to four of the officers and their descendants.

This institution was projected and carried into effect upon the banks of the Hudson or North river, a short time previous to the disbanding of the American army on the conclusion of the war in 1783. They fixed on Cincinnatus, the Roman dictator, by way of their titular saint, and divided themselves into state societies. Their annual meeting is on the 4th of July, the day of commemoration of the Declaration of Independence. To perpetuate the memory of the cause in which they had served, and to maintain the bonds of friendship and union between the different states, appear to be the principal objects of this institution. They have also a fund for the relief of the widows and orphans of officers who fell in the war.

No sooner had peace been proclaimed between England and America, than the latter began to feel the defects of their government, and was torn by intestine broils and civil commotions. Jealous of power, and suspicious even of those who, at the hazard of life and fortune, had been the more active agents in confirming the independence of the thirteen states, the institution of the order of the Cincinnati was viewed with distrust and envy. The officers were charged with an attempt to create an hereditary aristocracy, by dignifying themselves with rank and title. The press teemed with invective, and nothing could exceed the odium which for some time prevailed against the men who had saved their country. They were violently opposed in congress, when they presented their resolutions for the sanction of the legislature. The officers of government, seconded by men of liberal education, and possessing sentiments of gratitude, by argument and persuasive means appeased the heated imagination of the mass of the people, and obtained the act of incorporation. This institution, which was magnified into the great foundation-stone of despotism in a different shape from that they had recently shaken off, has no features resembling those of the horrid monster which existed in the minds of the people. So little is it esteemed as an object of power or gain, that many officers never applied for their admission, nor attended their annual meetings. It is little more than a yearly meeting in the form and nature of a society, for the purpose of partaking of a good dinner and a social glass; over which they may be permitted, like Alexander, "to fight all their battles o'er again, and thrice to slay the slain!"

Though the Cincinnati prevailed against the clamour excited by their institution, they are still the sport of the humourist, and the object of satire. — This is evinced by the following burlesque, from the pen of the Hon. H. H. Brackenridge, composed at a period when smarting under political disappointments.[2] He has since been elevated to the dignity of a Judge of the superior courts of Pennsylvania, and likewise enjoys a seat in congress. It not only serves to illustrate the subject under review, but also affords evidence that, in political tergiversation, the statesmen of America are not behind certain great men on this side of the Atlantic:

A gentleman travelling on horseback, attended by an Irish servant, overtook one of the Cincinnati on his route to attend the yearly meeting, with the Eagle, the emblem of his order, at his breast. The gentlemen entered into conversation, and alighting at the same inn, they agreed to sup together. The people of the inn had not seen the badge before, and prompted by the never-failing curiosity of the country, eagerly enquired of Teague what was the meaning of the ornament appended to a ribbon worn by one of the guests. Teague, it seems, was also ignorant, but unwilling to betray his want of knowledge, and, like the clown in the pantomime, ever ready to turn each circumstance to the advantage of his stomach, replied that it was a goose; and that the meaning was, that the gentleman preferred a roast goose for supper to all other dishes! This was delivered with an affected sagacity, and accompanied with many hints of the merit, rank, and consequence of the guests. The landlady was greatly perplexed at Teague's reply, declaring she had not a goose in her house; but requested his opinion whether a couple of fat roast ducks would not be a good substitute. He replied in the affirmative; and while the good woman ran to deprive the devoted birds of life, Teague anticipated the idea of the legs, wings, or breasts, that might fall to his share. Supper being ready, the landlady entered with the ducks, followed by Teague with a shoulder of boiled pork and potatoes, in case of short allowance. The good woman having decorated her table to the best advantage, turned to her guests, and with an obesiance began her apology for producing ducks, assuring the gentleman in the ribbon that she was not able to procure him a goose. The toils and perils by which the officer obtained his eagle, did not more mortify and astonish him than did the address of the landlady. 'A goose, madam! What mean you, madam?' then casting his eye upon his fellow-traveller, which only increased his confusion, the distressed warrior, choaking with pride and mortification which instantly seized him, made several efforts before he could articulate —'S'death, madam, do you take me for a goose? — You cannot, mean it — one animal preys not upon another of its own species — dog will not eat dog. I cannot, therefore, be a goose if I eat one!'

The good woman was undue similar embarrassment — she craved his honour's pardon, but assured him, that though his servant had informed her of his great partiality for a goose, and which she found to be true, (pointing significantly to the Eagle) yet she was not given to understand that his honour could not endure to have it mentioned to him. 'It has been many a poor woman's case,' said she,—'The signs of longing are different.'— again looking with a smile at the Eagle.

— . . . By this time the mystery began to unfold, while Teague retired towards the door to avoid his master's horsewhip, which he saw him preparing to apply to his shoulders. It was also highly necessary to interrupt the lady, who would probably have given the symptomatic longings of all the pregnant women in the neighborhood. Teague vowed by St. Patrick that what he had done was purely to get their honours a good supper, and not to give offence to the *gemman* with the bird at his breast. This excuse, confirmed by the evidence of two fine ducks on the table, was admitted; and the captain, while he washed them down with a glass of old madeira, gave Teague an unlimited licence to use his *Eagle* for such purposes, as long as he travelled with his master. The Hibernian stared when he heard the name of the bird he had mistaken for a goose; but observed, that as an eagle's flesh must be tough and black, he should never call it by its proper name in the kitchen of an inn, as he thought geese, turkies, ducks, chickens, or even pigeons, more delicate food than eagles.

Good humor being restored, the officer, notwithstanding the irritability of his nervous system when he thought the honour of his Eagle at stake, was a man of liberality and some humor.— He began to relate the trouble he had recently had with a clergyman, who took the Eagle for a *graven image*. He insisted that it was contrary to the injunction of the decalogue, which prohibits any such representation for the purpose of worship; and he alleged this to fall within the meaning of that part of holy writ. The officer, in answer, declared that so far from worshipping the image, he seldom prayed at all, and never discussed religious tenets except now and then with some deistical chaplains of the army, when, finding the world to be of no longer duration than the period fixed by Moses, they recurred to the Chinese, and found the flood had never reached them, and consequently the story of the ark, the dove, and the other engines and agents of inspiration, were rendered extremely doubtful;— that what he thought a graven image was nothing more than a hieroglyphic, being the effigy of a bald eagle, a native of America, and which designates the cause in which he had successfully served. The clergyman, who was as much the slave of fanaticism as the captain was free from the shackles of religious austerity, appearing to demur, the Cincinnati gentleman continued: — Was not the eagle the standard of the Roman legions; and does it not remain the arms of several European nations? Are not the lion and unicorn the arms of England, as is the thistle of Scotland, and the harp of Ireland? The eagle therefore had been chosen by the Cincinnati for their badge, and being of this order, he wore the device, and for no other reason.

It was admitted by the holy man that in rigid strictness it might not be a graven image, as the term certainly meant engraving on wood or metal with the point of an instrument; and therefore the wearer might, under this exposition, say it was not a graven image. It was, at all events, continued the priest, a molten one, and therefore was doubtless for the purpose of idolatry. It was the representation of a bird, the emblem of some heathen deity. The eagle was sacred to Jupiter, and perhaps was now worn in honour of that false god. In vain the officer maintained his position; the priest persisted that it was an idol; shewing from scripture that in the last times idolaters were to spring up, and concluding by an insinuation, that this order of the Cincinnati might be the Gog and Magog of the Apocalypse!

The captain rising early next morning, and setting out on his way, had arrived at a place where a number of people were convened, for the purpose of electing persons to represent them in the legislature of the state. A weaver, who was a candidate for this appointment, seemed to have considerable interest among the people; but another, who was a man of education, was his competitor. Relying on the elocutionary talents which he thought he possessed, he thus harangued the multitude: —

Fellow citizens, I pretend not to any great abilities; but am conscious within my own mind that I have the best good-will to serve you. But it is very astonishing to me that this weaver should conceive himself qualified for the trust; for, though my acquirements are not great, yet his are still less. The mechanical business which he pursues must necessarily take up so much of his time that he cannot apply himself to political studies. I should therefore think it would be more compatible with your dignity, and conducive to your interest, to be represented by a man at least of some letters, than by an illiterate handicraftsman like this. It will be more honorable for himself to remain at his loom and knot threads, than to come forward in a legislative capacity; because, in the one case he is in the sphere where God and nature have placed him, in the other he is like a fish out of water, and must struggle for breath in a new element. Is it possible that he can understand the affairs of government whose mind has been concentrated in the small objects of weaving webs? The feet of him who weaves are more occupied than his head; and therefore the whole man must be, at least, but half accustomed to use his mental powers. For these reasons, setting aside every thing else, the chance is in my favour with respect to information. However, you will decide, and give your suffrages to him or to me, as you shall judge expedient."

The captain, hearing these observations, and looking at the weaver, could not forbear advancing and undertaking to subjoin something in support of what had just been said. He had not uttered many words before he heard a bustle among the crowd. Honest Teague, hearing so much about elections and serving the government, took it into his head that he could be a legislator himself. The thing was not displeasing to the people, who seemed to favour his pretensions, owing in some degree to there being several of his countrymen in the crowd; but more especially to the fluctuation of the popular mind, and a disposition to what is new and ignoble.

The captain, finding this sudden turn of the tide, was greatly chagrined at not having been able to give the multitude a better idea of the importance of a legislative trust, but more so from an apprehension of losing his servant, again harangued the electors, telling them that they were making the matter worse — that they had better choose a weaver than a bog-trotter, who, so far from being competent to enact laws, could not understand a single letter of the language in which they ought to be written. "A free government," continued the captain, "is a noble possession to a people; and this freedom consists in an equal right to make laws, and to have the benefit of the laws when made. Though, doubtless, in such a government, the lowest citizen may become chief magistrate, yet it is sufficient to possess the right, not absolutely necessary to exercise it. Or even should you think proper now and then to claim your privilege, and exert, in a signal manner, the democratic prerogative, yet it is not descending too low to filch away from me my hireling, whom I cannot well spare, to serve your purposes? You surely are carrying the matter too far, in thinking to make a senator of this stable-boy! to take him from an employment to which he has been bred, and put him to another, to which he has served no apprenticeship! to set those hands which have been lately employed in currying my horse to the draughting of bills, and the preparation of business for the legislative assembly!"

The people, however, were tenacious of their choice, and insisted on giving Teague their suffrages; nay, the frown upon their brows seemed to indicate resentment at what had been said, as indirectly charging them with want of judgment, or calling in question their privilege to do what they pleased. "We will empower him," said one who spoke for the rest, "and we had rather trust a plain man like him than one of your highflyers, who will make laws to suit themselves."

Finding that it answered no end to expostulate with the multitude, he called Teague aside to try how argument would work upon him. Having explained the nature and difficulty of filling the character of a statesman, and touched him upon the point of honour, as to quitting an honest calling to become a member of congress; declaring he would rather see him digging turf again in Ireland than passing laws which he knew nothing about, Teague conquered his ambition, and told the electors, that, upon considering the matter, he found it would not do to leave a good place for the sake of going to congress. The weaver was therefore elected by a large majority.

The captain having thus rescued his servant, proceeded on his journey. He had not gone many miles before he overtook a man driving a horse loaded with two kegs or half-barrels. The captain took him for a pack-horse man carrying something to market. A person of a philosophic turn of mind never hesitates to enter into conversation with any character whatever, because human nature is the field from which he gathers thoughts and expressions. The captain therefore accosted this man; they entered into conversation, and he soon found, to his great mortification, that another election was about to take place a little distance forward; that this man was a candidate; and that the two kegs contained whisky for the voters. The captain was thrown into a reverie, and began to reflect within himself on the nature of a republican government, where canvassing, by such means as this, can work so great an evil as to elevate the most unqualified persons to a seat in the highest deliberative assemblies. But in the mean time recovering himself a little, he had the presence of mind to recollect the danger in which he was likely to be again involved with his man Teague; whom, looking round, he saw about forty yards behind him. It would have been advisable to have turned off from the road, and taken a circuitous route to avoid the election, but the lane would not favor the attempt. There was no alternative than either to proceed or to leap the fence, and strike off across the country. To the latter, his sober nag was by no means competent. Besides, if Teague could not leap after him, he would be left exposed in the lane to the populace, who might again solicit him to be their representative. To turn back, would appear indecorous, and unless he could drive Teague on before him, which was not customary,* and to which he might not immediately submit, his situation would be of course in the rear, where he might himself be picked up and sent to some public body.

In the midst of this dilemma, looking up, he saw the immediate approach of danger; the people appeared in view, convened to choose their representative; it was therefore too late to avoid them. He advanced, keeping a sharp look-out upon Teague, the principal cause of this concern.

Meeting one of the electors near the ground where the election was to be held, he communicated to him the delicacy of his situation, and the apprehensions he had on the part of Teague. The elector assured him that he might be under no concern on that head, as there remained no doubt that the man with the two kegs would be elected. "There is no resisting good liquor," continued the elector, who was of a superior order of beings; "it has a wonderful effect on the judgment in the choice of a representative. A man that has a distillery or two in this country cannot want suffrages. He has his votaries about him, like the heathen gods, and because the fluid exhilarates the brain, they revere him who makes it, as a deity."

The candidate who opposed the man with the two kegs, was a person of gravity, sense, and experience. The judgment of the people was in his favor, but their appetite leaned against him. Teague, seeing a second instance of the contest to be a member of congress, began to repent his former conduct in declining, at the very moment his election was secure. He had begun to make a bustle among the electors before the captain observed him, and was actually gaining their attention, when fortunately the kegs were tapped, and the man who brought them was immediately elected.

* The scene of this satire is in Pennsylvania, where the manners and customs of the people differ as widely from the southern states, as those of France and Spain. In North Carolina, in travelling, the servant goes *before* the master. The reason assigned to me for this deviation was, that the flies in summer followed the foremost horse.

Caligula made his horse a senator. A man was made a knight,* in modern times, for stuffing birds. A Scotch university has been charged with granting diplomas to any applicant who could pay their fees; and also, with making bishops for America. A man was pensioned for writing a book which contributed to set Europe in flames.† Where, then, would have been the joke in Americans sending an honest Irishman to congress?[3]

The device of the medal of the order of Cincinnati is, Britannia represented as a fine woman, with her bosom bare, affrighted; and Cincinnatus, an accoutred knight, attacking her thus unarmed, as Saint George did the dragon; the eagle, the bird of Jove, meanwhile grasps the lightning in his claws; an image that would seem unnatural. The eagle might be represented in the clouds of Jove, where the lightning might be left to work its forked course, without the intervention of the bird; and in the other figure, Cincinnatus might raise his lance against the lion that supports the crown, and not against the defenceless goddess of the island.

The motto of the badge is, *Omnia reliquit servare rempublicam.* The infinitive is here used instead of the gerund with the preposition, *ad servandam;* as if it was intended to express his motion, or change of place, and not the object. But, in fact, the motto does not at all express that in which the merit of Cincinnatus really consisted. It was not in his leaving every thing to accept the commission of the Roman senate; but in resigning his commission, when he had achieved the salvation of his country, and going back to his plough again. His praise would have been better expressed by the phrase, *Victor ad aratrum redit.* In fact, it cannot apply well to the American army, most of the officers not having much to leave when they accepted their commissions; but discovering a Cincinnatus-like disposition, in returning, after the war, to the employments of civil life. It is true,

* Sir Aston Lever, knighted by King George the Third.[4]

† See Mr. Strutt's speech in the house of commons, Nov. 23, 1795, respecting Burke's then recent publication.

there would have been less tinsel, and more bullion, in the patriotism of retiring without a badge, as Cincinnatus did; but it is a thing that can do little harm, and it is pleasing to indulge a whim.

It may doubtless be said, that there were officers that left the plough, and fought, and returned to it, as well as those who are within the limitations of the institution, and are as justly entitled to a badge; that troops who had served a short enlistment, and militia, who have, at least, fought a little, were not wholly destitute of some claim to the badge of merit. Even those who lost property might be said to suffer, and advance pretensions to the reward of honour. Not that all of them should claim gold medals, or even silver; but some brass, some copper, pewter, a bit of tin or pot metal, just as the specific value of their services might entitle them. Perhaps, while some wore it at the breast, others might be enjoined to wear it at the breeches pocket; and thus, as well by the point from which appendant, as by the bob itself, designate the proportion of their honour.

Passing from gay to grave, it may not be amiss here to give the reader some idea of the constitution of the legislative assemblies of the American republic. The congress of the United States consists of two houses of legislators, the senate, and the house of representatives. They exercise certain functions delegated to them by the people, resembling those of the lords and commons of Great Britain. Acts of congress must pass both houses, and either house can throw out a bill, as in the English parliament. When the act has passed both houses, it is left for the *fiat* of the president; in short, in the manner of conducting their public business, the rules laid down in debate, and the standing orders of the house, they are modelled after the usage of their mother country.

The senate is composed of two members from each state; and as there are already seventeen states, that house consequently consists of thirty-four members, with the vice-president of the United States, who sits as their president; and who, on an equal division on a question, has the casting vote.

The house of representatives are elected by the free and uninfluenced voice of the people; every freeman having a right to vote at the elections, which take place every second year. Care was taken to guard against every species of corruption in this, as well as every part of the federal constitution, which was formed under the auspices of the man who was the principal agent in securing their independence; I mean — Washington.

By this constitution, thirty-three thousand freemen are entitled to elect one of themselves, as a member of the house of representatives. The following is the proportion of members sent by each state, arranged in geographical order.

1*	From	New Hampshire	5	11*	From	Virginia	22
2*	"	Massachusetts	17	12	"	Kentucky	6
3	"	Vermont	4	13*	"	North Carolina	11
4*	"	Rhode Island	2	14	"	Tennessee	3
5*	"	Connecticut	7	15*	"	South Carolina	8
6*	"	New York	17	16*	"	Georgia	4
7*	"	New Jersey	6	17	"	Ohio	11
8*	"	Pennsylvania	18		"	Mississippi Ter'ry	1
9*	"	Delaware	1		"	Indiana Territ'ry	1
10*	"	Maryland	9				143

The states marked* composed the British colonies previous to the American war.

The territories of Indiana and Mississippi had not, on the taking of the last census, a sufficient population to entitle them to be added to the federate body. From the great emigration to those parts of the country, there is little doubt that, on the next enumeration of citizens, they will be declared independent states. Estimating the population according to the number of representatives, it does not make the whole population equal to what I have already stated. This is easily explained: — for instance, the above territories might have *nearly* numbered an amount, entitling them to return each another representative; and a large surplus over the 33,000 votes were found in other parts of the Union. On this account, I have no reason to alter my calculations of the population in the third chapter.

NOTES — CHAPTER XXI

1. A sympathetic outline of the history of the Society of the Cincinnati is to be found in a review by Winthrop Sargent in the *North American Review*, October, 1853, of a book printed in 1851 for the use of the members of the New York Society, entitled *The Institution of the Society of the Cincinnati.* In 1859 Winthrop Sargent edited *A Journal of the General Meeting of the Cincinnati in 1784*, by Major Winthrop Sargent, later governor of the Mississippi Territory. An example of the attacks on the Order may be found in the work by Count de Mirabeau, *Considerations on the Order of Cincinnatus* (Translated from French), London, 1785. The review by Sargent gives a compact history of the Order in the United States and abroad.

2. H. H. Brackenridge, jurist, author of Revolutionary propaganda, satirist, and a Republican, lived in Pittsburgh, Pennsylvania. *Modern Chivalry*, his best known writing, is a satirical picaresque novel.

3. The quotations from *Modern Chivalry* as given by Janson represent the most flagrant of all attempts to *pad* his work. They are in no sense direct quotations. He often skips paragraphs in his resumé, and the sequence is unpardonable.

4. Sir Ashton Lever was an English sportsman and collector. He first collected live birds, and his aviary was reputed to be the best in the kingdom. Stuffed birds next occupied his attention, and ultimately he became interested in all kinds of natural objects as well as in savage costumes and weapons. He was knighted by George III on June 5, 1778.

CHAPTER XXII

DEPLORABLE EFFECTS OF THE UNCONTROLLED LIBERTY ALLOWED TO YOUTH IN AMERICA — SMOKING — AN ACADEMIC FROLIC — SLINGERS — ELEVENERS — GOUGING — BITING — KICKING — PICTURE OF A CAROLINA LOG-HOUSE.

ONE of the greatest evils of a republican form of government is a loss of that subordination in society which is essentially necessary to render a country agreeable to foreigners. To the well-informed this defect is irksome, and no remedy for it can be applied. The meaning of liberty and equality, in the opinion of the vulgar, consists in impudent freedom, and uncontrolled licentiousness; while boys assume the airs of full-grown coxcombs. This is not to be wondered at, where most parents make it a principle never to check those ungovernable passions which are born with us, or to correct the growing vices of their children. Often have I, with horror, seen boys, whose dress indicated wealthy parents, intoxicated, shouting and swearing in the public streets. In the use of that stupefying weed, tobacco, apeing their fathers, they smoke segars to so immoderate a degree, that sickness, and even death, has been the consequence. This is fully elucidated by the following paragraph, copied from a late newspaper, printed at Salem, in Massachusetts.

> Died in Salem, Master James Verry, aged twelve, a promising youth, whose early death is supposed to have been brought on by *excessive smoking of segars!!!*

That this pernicious custom was habitual in an infant, not four years of age, I was myself a witness. This little boy is the son of Thomas Taylor, a segar-maker, in Alexandria, near Washington. While conversing with the father, I observed the son smoking a large segar, made of the strongest tobacco. I expressed my astonishment; on which the infatuated parent, with an exulting smile, replied, that the child had contracted the habit above a year ago, and that he smoked three, four, or more daily, which he was regularly supplied with, "or he would cry for them." In addition, he would steal them when opportunity offered, and, in fact, he was seldom without a lighted segar in his mouth. What was most surprising, the child was fat and healthy; thus for a time, and at this early age, proving that "habit is second nature."

When children are thus indulged, we need not wonder at an evening's frolic of some young students of William and Mary College, at Williamsburg, in Virginia. The particulars of that abominable transaction found their way into the public newspapers.[1] The first intimation was in the Norfolk *Herald*, a paper of extensive circulation, at that time conducted by Messrs. Willett and O'Connor. The perpetrators of the outrage were, soon after the publication, *proved* to be students of the college. I shall dismiss this unpleasant subject by adding a copy of the paragraph alluded to. The subsequent public comments on the transaction I have not preserved:

Norfolk Herald, April 15, 1803.

A gentleman of veracity who has been lately at Williamsburg, informs us, that on the first of April, some youths of that place perpetrated some of the most wicked acts that human imagination could invent. A party of them broke into the church, played on the organ for nearly two hours, and then went to the church-yard, dug up the body of a female that had been buried for many months, took it from the coffin, and placed it on the floor of an empty house in a situation too shocking to describe!!! The coffin being found, led to the discovery. It surely could not be any of the students of William and Mary College, for it is impossible, one would imagine, that they would attempt so atrocious and villainous an act under the eyes of their preceptors. Certainly that college must be under better moral government; yet we are told that strong suspicions lurk toward that seminary. It is an old saying, "give a dog a bad name, and hang him"; it will therefore behove the governors of that institution, to endeavor, by all means, to discover the offenders, bring them to justice, and rescue the college from the reproach that will otherwise attach. It is the duty of every parent and guardian that have youths educating there, to probe this matter to the quick; for if the rules and regulations at William and Mary cannot keep its students within the pale of decency, then education will rather be a curse than a blessing to them.

There is a numerous set of people in the Southern States, called *slingers,* and another, styled *eleveners.* It is strange to reflect on the effects of habit, when we give way to indulgences. Our very appetites become vitiated, and the most unnatural propensities degrade the character of man.

I know of no custom more destructive than that which is practised by slingers and eleveners. The European learns with astonishment, that the first craving of an American, in the morning, is for ardent spirits, mixed with sugar, mint, or some other hot herb; and which are called *slings.* If those who have unhappily adopted this pernicious practice, would but for a moment consider the effects of strong liquors on the stomach, it would soon be exploded. A celebrated physician says:

> No kind of poison kills more certainly than ardent spirits. Sometimes, by destroying the nervous energy, they put an end to life at once; but in general their effects are more slow, and in many respects similar to those of opium.

Such is the opinion of the faculty, with reference only to those who indulge with the bottle in the evening, or, at any rate, after a hearty dinner; a custom prevalent in Britain. No idea was entertained by this author of *morning* drinkers, because *his* countrymen never drink wine or spirit until the *afternoon.* But, if ardent spirits produce such dreadful effects among them, how much more certain and speedy must they prove to those who swallow slings upon an empty stomach. It is giving the poison a double chance of proving fatal —

it is like throwing aqua fortis upon steel. Englishmen, in some measure, counteract its effects by laying a foundation for the spirits they take to work upon; but the Virginians, Carolinians, and Georgians suffer it to prey upon their very vitals.

A second-rate consumer of distillations from the sugar-cane, the grape, and the juniper-berry, is the *elevener*. Sometimes I have found both these vile habits in one unfortunate fellow-creature; to such, admonitions are in vain. These eleveners are generally found strolling about the corners of streets, or other public places, at the eleventh hour, A. M. After the common-place conversation, they adjourn, and take more spirits.

The delicate and entertaining diversion, with propriety called GOUGING, is thus performed: — When two boxers are wearied out with fighting and bruising each other, they come, as it is called, to close quarters, and each endeavours to twist his fore-fingers in the ear-locks of his antagonist. When these are fast clenched, the thumbs are extended each way to the nose, and the eyes *gently* turned out of the sockets. The victor, for his expertness, receives shouts of applause from the sportive throng, while his poor eyeless antagonist is laughed at for his misfortune." Such are the very words of Morse,[2] in his American Geography, under the head of North Carolina.

That the European reader may give immediate credit to the existence of this most horrible practice called *gouging*,[3] I have quoted the words of a native author. It is in vain for later writers to gloss over the subject; to pretend that this custom was *once* practised in America; or that such was the revenge which *once* prevailed in the breast of civilised man. It is my avowed purpose to paint "the manners living as they rise;" and upon this point, with pain am I compelled to declare, that this more than savage custom is daily practised among the lower classes in the southern states.

Though Mr. Morse gives frequent occasion to differ from

him on many points, yet I admit that he did travel through the different states of the Union to collect materials for the work above-mentioned. I farther admit a belief that Mr. Morse did not write to serve any dishonorable purpose — that he meant to instruct, and not to mislead. And, were he divested of that strong prejudice, so prominent a feature in the works of most American authors, when speaking of their country, his Geography might be pronounced an acquisition to the British reader.

It is therefore evident that *gouging* is a barbarity still continued in America; but, as an author, posterior to Mr. Morse, and an Englishman, has attempted to insinuate that it is now no longer practised, I shall relate a few recent instances of its existence, and a painful description of an ocular demonstration of the horrors of its execution.

Passing, in company with other travellers, through the state of Georgia, our attention was arrested by a gouging-match. We found the combatants, as Morse describes, fast clenched by the hair, and their thumbs endeavoring to force a passage into each other's eyes; while several of the bystanders were betting upon the first eye to be turned out of its socket. For some time the combatants avoided the *thumb stroke* with dexterity. At length they fell to the ground, and in an instant the uppermost sprung up with his antagonist's eye in his hand!!! The savage crowd applauded, while, sick with horror, we galloped away from the infernal scene. The name of the sufferer was John Butler, a Carolinian, who, it seems, had been dared to the combat by a Georgian; and the first eye was for the honor of the state to which they respectively belonged.

The eye is not the only feature which suffers on these occasions. Like dogs and bears, they use their teeth* and feet, with the most savage ferocity, upon each other.

* During the author's residence in North Carolina, Mr. Standen, the post-master, and a merchant of Edenton, had a part of his cheek bitten off in an affray with O'Mally, a tavern-keeper in that town.

A brute, in human form, named John Stanley, of Bertie county, North Carolina, sharpens his teeth with a file, and boasts of his dependence upon them in fight. This monster will also exult in relating the account of the noses and ears he has bitten off, and the cheeks he has torn.

A man of the name of Thomas Penrise, then living in Edenton, in the same state, attempting at cards to cheat some half-drunken sailors, was detected. A scuffle ensued; Penrise knocked out the candle, then gouged out three eyes, bit off an ear, tore a few cheeks, and made good his retreat.

Near the same place, a schoolmaster, named Jarvis Lucas, was beset by three men, one Horton, his son, and son-in-law. These ruffians beat the unfortunate man till his life was despaired of, having bitten, gouged, and kicked him unmercifully. On the trial of an indictment for this outrageous assault, a Carolina court of justice amerced them in a small fine only.

In the county of Pitt, upon Tar river, in North Carolina, lived a family, by name Dupray; of such extraordinary propensity for mischief, that it could not be determined whether the father or his sons were most wicked. These ruffians long lived upon plunder, and the principal object in committing their depredations appeared to be amusement. Falling into company one evening with an Irish taylor, at a small publichouse, they insisted on his joining them at a game at cards. On his refusal, they began to quarrel; when, dreading the consequences, the Hibernian adroitly put out the candle, and crept under the table. The younger ruffians seized their father, whom they mistook for the taylor, and, from the severity of beating, gouging, biting, butting, and kicking, actually killed their parent. This horrid outrage, connected with the mischief and depredations committed by this family, drove the parricides out of the state, to the great joy of the more peaceable inhabitants.

Another bestial mode of assault used by men in North Carolina, is properly called butting. This attack is also copied from the brute creation, and is executed nearly in the same manner as practised in battle between bulls, rams, and goats. A traveller has endeavored to confine butting to the negroes; but he must excuse my implicating the white man in this brutal act.

That the reader may become a little familiar with these Columbian accomplishments, I can assure him that disputes terminated in England by fair blows, are *generally* there maintained by the practice of some, and often all of these dreadful stratagems, should opportunities offer during the combat.

An American pugilist is equally dexterous with his feet, which are used, not only against his antagonist's shins, but are applied, with the utmost violence, against those parts which the contending beasts of the field never assail. Hence ruptures, loss of eyes, mutilated noses, and indented cheeks so frequently surprise and shock the traveller. A fellow named *Michie*, in my presence, boasted "that he could kick any man, six feet high, under the chin, and break his jaws."[4]

But let us conclude this odious subject, which should never have stained these pages, had not the author first alluded to, proclaimed to the world the cruel and unnatural facts, by observing, that these barbarities appear not to have been the genuine growth of American soil. No such practices would be endured by an English mob; no such disgraceful revenge ever entered the breast of a Creek, a Cherokee, or a Kicapoo Indian.

The lower class in this gouging, biting, kicking country, are the most abject that, perhaps, ever peopled a Christian land. They live in the woods and desarts, and many of them cultivate no more land than will raise them corn and cabbages, which, with fish, and occasionally a piece of pickled pork or bacon, are their constant food. This land, on which, prior to their settlement, no human step had ever marked a path, required clearing of trees, whose tops almost reached the clouds, before a spot could be found large enough to erect a shelter for the women and children. Their habitations are more wretched than can be conceived; the huts of the poor of Ireland, or even the meanest Indian wig-wam, displaying more ingenuity and greater industry. They are constructed of pine trees, cut in lengths of ten or fifteen feet, and piled up in a square, without any other workmanship than a notch at the end of each log, to keep them in contact. When this barbarous pile is raised between six and seven feet, they split the remainder of their logs to the thickness of two or three inches, and by laying them over the whole in a sloping direction, form the roof. The chimney is, if possible, worse than Dr. Johnson describes the hole in the roof of a house in Scotland, through which the smoke found a passage. The summer's scorching sun, and the bleak winds of winter, are accessible to this miserable dwelling. The interstices between the logs are often left open to the elements, and are large enough to give admission to vermin and reptiles, which abound in this part of the world.

Amid these accumulated miseries, the inhabitants of log-houses are extremely tenacious of the rights and liberties of republicanism. They consider themselves on an equal footing with the best educated people of the country, and upon the principles of equality they intrude themselves into every company. In the taverns in this part of the United States, there is generally no other accommodation than a large sitting-room, in common, where the governor of the state, and the judge of the district, in travelling, must associate with their fellow-citizens of every degree.

NOTES — CHAPTER XXII

1. A communication to the *Georgia Republican and State Intelligencer* of May 5, 1803, dated the occurrence April 1, 1803.

2. Jedidiah Morse, *The American Geography,* London, 1792, p. 418n.

3. In his *Travels* Weld gives a description of gouging and adds that ". . . in some particular parts of these states (Virginia, the Carolinas, and Georgia), every third or fourth man appears with one eye."

4. Many westerners, or frontiersmen, became very dexterous at this art of kicking.

CHAPTER XXIII

BEE-HUNTING — ADVENTURE OF AN AMERICAN QUARTER-MASTER SERJEANT — ALLIGATORS — ESTABLISHMENT OF A CAROLINA FARMER AND INN-KEEPER — THE LOCUST — THE COCK-ROACH — ANTS.

IN THE Carolinas, there are innumerable commonwealths of bees, subject to no control from man. They build their hives in the hollow parts of large trees, and as near the summit as they can find a convenient cavity. The hunting of these industrious societies, is an object of both profit and pleasure to the inhabitants. When their retreat has accidentally been discovered, it is marked by cutting notches in the trees to the nearest habitation, and a day is appointed for a bee hunt. Half a dozen men or more, assemble, each provided with a gun, for the double purpose of killing game in their expedition, and for defence against the beasts of the forest. They also carry axes to cut down the tree.

On an occasion of this nature, as the party cautiously approached the marked spot, they were surprised to find the proprietors of the hive in great wrath flying over their property; and on a nearer view, they witnessed the cause of the tumult. A bear, of enormous bulk, attracted by the smell of the ripe honey, of which those animals are extremely fond, had scented the tree some minutes before the arrival of the two-legged plunderers. Bruin was in the act of lapping the honey, which he obtained by thrusting his paw through a hole in the centre of a knot, which the bees used as the entrance to their cell. The insects, in their defence attacked him by swarms, and darted their stings into the most vulnerable parts of his face; to guard which, he applied one paw full of honey over the annoyed parts, and ate the next, in swallowing which he would give a few strokes amongst his antagonists, and then proceed to another scoop of honey.

A ball from a rifle, brought Bruin, in the midst of his repast, to the ground, and great was his fall. The hunters quickly felled the tree, and, being prepared to resist the darts of the owners, soon secured the remainder of the honey, the comb of which had been dreadfully mangled by the paw of the bear, but his carcase made them ample amends.

Mr. Andrew Nilson,[1] of Philadelphia, a native of Ireland, who served under General Washington in the American army during the whole of the war, and who is now a major, informed me, that at the time Lord Cornwallis was pursuing the Americans through the Carolinas, at which time he was a quarter-master serjeant, he had, during a day's rapid retreat, marked a hive of bees. At night, whilst both the pursuers and the pursued were obliged to halt and rest, he privately singled out a file of soldiers, with whom, carrying a barrel for the purpose, he retrograded some miles to attack the bee-hive, which was then at an equal distance between the two armies. He arrived with his party at the tree, which they felled without creating alarm; and the moon afforded them light to secure the honey, which was slung upon a pole. After proceeding with it two or three miles, they were surprised by an armed reconnoitering party. To escape was impossible; and resistance, having no arms, was in vain. Convinced that his rashness had thrown him into the hands of his enemy, he prepared to surrender himself and party as prisoners of war. He was hailed — the parole and countersign were demanded, and Nilson repeated those given out for the night by the American commander; which, to his great joy, proved satisfactory. It was a party from the American army watching the early approach of their pursuers; and the commanding officer proved to be the major of the regiment to which the offending serjeant belonged. Being interrogated as to the motive of the honey-men being from their quarters, Nilson told the truth, with an humour peculiar to his country, which so pleased the major, that he ordered the delicious banquet to be brought forward, and both parties sat down and regaled themselves on the fruits of the industrious bee. The canteens of the armed men contained spirituous liquors, which operating on the honey, produced a pretty mellow effect. The major, however, got his party off; but Nilson continued so long upon the spot, that his men could not reach their friends with their booty, and were obliged to leave what remained in the barrel, a prey to the pursuing British.

On the great Alligator river, which branches out of the large waters of Pamlico and Albermarle Sounds, in North Carolina, the country appears congenial to the bee. The natives derive great profit from their labour; every family having a number of hives in their gardens. Many families even depend upon their honey and wax to barter for winter stores and clothing. About midsummer the bees begin to swarm. The owner attends, and by gently striking on a tin pan, hastens the important business. Having secured the young bees, he proceeds to take the honey from the hives which they have left; in effecting which, he destroys the old ones with sulphur.

At this time a number of trading boats arrive from Edenton, Nixenton, Windsor, and the adjacent places, with merchandize, tobacco, and large supplies of rum, in order to exchange their commodities for honey and wax. A scene of drunkenness and riot ensues; the traders' boats drawing the people from a distance, like a country fair. They are here, as in most parts of the southern states, dissipated and lazy; great cheats and horrible blasphemers.

This large river was named "Alligator River," from the quantity of those dangerous animals found there, on its being first explored. When I was there in the year 1798, a young one was caught, which I had an opportunity of examining. It was of the same species as the crocodile of Egypt, from which it differed very little. It seized a stick, and with its sharp and monstrous teeth, severed it into three pieces, leaving it shorter by a foot, and holding the middle piece in its mouth, while the end dropped on the ground, and the remainder continued in my hand. In this manner, though deemed very young, it could have treated the limb of a man. I am informed that it was sold, and exhibited in different parts, to the great emolument of the purchaser.

On a branch of the river lived in the year I have already named, a wealthy planter, by name John Foster. With this man I remained several days; and in him I learned something of the character of a Southern planter. He cultivated about two hundred acres of land, had built a tolerable house, which he converted into a tavern, and thus he acted in the double capacity of farmer and landlord. He was of a most tyrannical and cruel disposition to his dependents — imperious and quarrelsome with his guests, as intoxication proceeded — a great bully, and, of course, a great coward. The force* of his plantation, consisted of a decent well-behaved white man, who was the overseer, two civil, humble men slaves, and four or five wenches.† His kitchen was attended by a cook-wench, and two or three young wenches, who were yet unable to endure the slavery of the field.

I was greatly surprised to see these younger wenches going about their domestic business naked — literally in *puris naturalibus.* Mine host had led me over the plantation, and we arrived, almost exhausted from the effects of a scorching sun at the hour of dinner. Our meal consisted of venison, and a variety of vegetables, which we diluted with apple-brandy and water. This is a most detestable beverage. I had no choice of spirits; and to drink water undiluted, is often of dangerous tendency. Thus is an "Alligator tavern" provided with liquors; and, in fact, it was as well supplied as any other place of public resort in the district.

A different circumstance, produced in me, while at dinner,

* Force, is here applied when speaking of the number of slaves employed in field labour on each plantation.

† Female slaves, in this part of the world are uniformly called wenches, and are bought, sold and exchanged.

more disgust than even the fumes of the deleterious drink: this was the officious attendance of two wenches, three parts grown, without even the covering our first mother made for herself after her expulsion from paradise. The effluvia arising from the body of a negro in the month of July, are by no means odoriferous; hence I could have dispensed with one of these being placed in compliment behind my chair. To complete the scene, Mr. Foster's daughter, a fine girl of sixteen, dined at our table, and gave her orders to the naked creatures of her own sex, with the most perfect *sang froid.* She did the honours of the table, her father being a widower. In order to avoid being pressed after dinner to drink the trash before me, in which my landlord was freely indulging himself, I proposed another walk, when I expressed my displeasure at the appearance of our attendants. My host, with a tremendous oath, replied, that he could not make the b——s wear clothes; and that he had two months ago given out their summer suits, which they tore to pieces in a few days, to avoid the incumbrance of wearing them. This is common in most young negroes here, till the more advanced marks of puberty render the wearing of garments rather a compulsion, than a voluntary act.

In that neighbourhood, I observed an unusual number of locusts, which make a long creeking noise, extremely unpleasant to the ear. Being of the same colour with the leaves of the trees in which they take shelter, they are seldom to be seen, though their noise appears very near. I have, with difficulty, succeeded in catching them. They are four times the size of the dragon fly, their bodies are plump, and as large as the smallest of the feathered race. It is said by an American philosophical writer, that about the middle of the seventeenth century there were such swarms of these insects, that, in New England, for the space of two hundred miles, they destroyed all the trees. Innumerable holes were seen in the ground out of which they had broken forth in the form of larvæ, or maggots. These being turned into winged insects, had a kind of tail or sting, which they struck into a tree, and thereby envenomed and killed it. The females pierce the tender branches of trees with the dart at the posterior extremity of their bodies, depositing their eggs in the holes thus formed. But it is the great voracity of these insects in actually devouring the foliage that does most harm.

Another destructive insect peculiar to America is the cock-roach — the *Blatta Americana* of Linnæus. They are described to be so flat, that they creep into every chest, or drawer, where there is the least crevice. They gnaw woollen cloths of every kind, but especially such as have had hair-powder on them: what is very remarkable, they will not touch silk of any kind. They frequently throw off their exterior skin; and after every change of this kind, they appear fresh and young. The Americans know of this species by the name of *kakkerlac*. It is sometimes brought over alive among clothes or merchandize from the West-Indies into Europe. In the houses of many parts of America they often commit great depredations by gnawing and devouring both clothes and provisions, and it is extremely difficult to guard against their ravages. With respect to provisions, every thing that they run over, contracts from them so nauseous a smell, as to be scarcely eatable.

According to Reaumur,[2] these cock-roaches have a formidable enemy in a large species of sphex. He says, that when one of the latter encounters a cock-roach, he seizes it by the head, pierces its body with his poisonous sting, and afterwards carries it off into his hole. Here the female has deposited her eggs; and the bodies of the cock-roaches serve the *larvæ* for food till they attain their winged state.

In North Carolina, I also observed a curious species of the ant; very diminutive, and in prodigious numbers. If undisturbed, they will completely cover a piece of meat, bread, or sugar, and in a short time carry it to their nests, to which they are constantly going and returning by different tracks. They are chiefly to be found in houses, from which it is impossible to exclude them. It is said, that when tasted, which often happens, from their being concealed in victuals, they are an agreeable acid; and I have seen people eat them rather than brush them away. These very small insects are of different colors, red, and black; so far from associating with each other, a severe battle is fought, whenever they meet; and thus, one house will be pestered with the black, and another with the red ant.

The swamps produce a variety of what may be denominated land turtle. The natives call them loggerheads, tarapins, snappers, and hawsbills. In the summer, the slaves catch them in abundance, and bring them to market. On this account they are but little valued by their masters; but I pronounced them the greatest luxury of the dog-days in this burning climate. When well cooked, they are a tolerable substitute for the sea turtle; though I cannot say that there is in the former any great appearance of the green fat so highly prized by the epicure. Yet they make an excellent dish; and, in fact, reflecting at this moment, I think that I could scarce have found a substitute for fresh meat in the scarcity of summer, had it not been for loggerheads and tarapins. I have purchased them from ten to fifteen pounds weight, for an English shilling a piece; and the females would frequently yield a score or more eggs, several larger than the yolk of an hen's egg, and of nearly as good a flavour.

NOTES — CHAPTER XXIII

1. The author must have given an erroneous spelling of this man's name, for no one by the name of Nilson is listed in F. B. Heitman's *Historical Register and Dictionary of the United States Army.*

2. Rene Antoine Ferchault de Reaumur, *Memoires pour servir a l'histoire des insectes.* Paris, 1734-42. 6 vols.

CHAPTER XXIV

MIRANDA'S EXPEDITION — HIS OPERATIONS IN AMERICA — JUDICIAL PROCEEDINGS AGAINST MR. OGDEN, PROPRIETOR OF THE LEANDER — TYRANNICAL CONDUCT OF JUDGE TALLMAGE — SPIRITED DEFENCE OF MR. OGDEN'S COUNSEL — SINGULAR NOTIONS OF LIBERTY DISPLAYED BY A REPUBLICAN JUDGE — FAILURE OF MIRANDA'S ENTERPRIZE — PARTICULARS OF HIS EARLY LIFE.

THE expedition fitted out at New York by General Miranda during the last spring, has been a matter of much surprise in Europe, and was the cause of great animosity in America. Early in life, this officer entered the American army during the revolutionary war, as a volunteer; and, after the peace, still continuing for some time to reside there, and to visit every part of the United States, he became well acquainted with the disposition of the inhabitants.

The active part which he took in France, being second in command to Dumouriez, together with the cause of his leaving that service, are well known. I shall, therefore, for the present, confine myself to his last daring enterprise, and then shew the restless and ambitious spirit which prevails in this singular character.[1] Having served in America and France upon the same principles, his revolutionary visions were turned upon his native country, Spanish America. It has appeared, since the death of that great statesman, that Mr. Pitt had employed him in the affair of Nootka Sound, and had listened with attention to his plans of operation against the province of Caraccas, where he was born. Hence, it may be supposed, that had Mr. Pitt survived, this adventurer would have received his assistance. Deprived of his patron, he boldly determined alone to attempt the enterprize, and for that purpose embarked for New York, where he intended to lay the foundation of his future operations.

To this end, he engaged a small fleet, among which was a large ship called the *Leander*, mounting ewtnty-four guns, the property of Mr. Samuel Ogden, a merchant in New York, in which he carried his revolutionary flag. He then proceeded to Washington, the seat of the American government; and though his object was known, he was received by, and had an audience of the president, who is charged with being privy to his schemes, and is said to have been cautioned to beware of him. He was also cordially received by Mr. Madison, the secretary of state; and he had long and frequent conferences with that minister, as well as the president. On the day previous to his departure from Washington, Mr. Madison gave him a grand dinner; and it is asserted, that previous to the breaking up of the company, they were closeted together for a considerable time. No orders were given to the collectors of the different sea-ports — no step was taken to prevent his carrying his plans into execution; nor was any communication made to the Spanish diplomacy.

On Miranda's return to New York, he found his little fleet nearly ready for sea. The *Leander* had lately returned from a contraband trip to St. Domingo, for which purpose she was armed, with several other ships, against the cruizers of France, and thus were the revolted negroes supplied with provisions and warlike stores.* She was consequently, ready

* This trade was not only inimical to the views of the American government, but attended with imminent danger to the individuals that embarked in it. The dreadful example of Mr. Tate, the mate of an American vessel called the *Pilgrim*, could not curb the rage of speculation. The story of this unfortunate man is deserving of notice.

While the *Pilgrim* lay at one of the ports in St. Domingo, occupied by the negroes, two Frenchmen and some mulattoes, to preserve life, fled on board, and were placed by the crew among the cargo under the deck. The commander of the vessel, Captain Gibson, and Mr. Lynch, the supercargo, were on shore; and it does not appear that the unfortunate victim to negro ferocity, was even privy to the concealment. Christophe, then commander of the black army, received information of this circumstance, and immediately detached a guard to search the *Pilgrim;* who tore up the deck over the heads of the unfortunate fugitives, and, together with Mr. Tate, they were forced on shore. On their landing, the for an enterprise of the nature planned by that officer. On his departure, all communication between the Spanish ambassador, the Marquis d'Yrujo, and the president, was suspended, by an order for his removal from the seat of government.

The great expence attending the fitting out of this armament was defrayed by Miranda. He appeared to have a plentiful stock of cash: and this circumstance has added to the suspicions entertained in America respecting those who aided his proceedings.

A number of American adventurers proffered their services to Miranda; and he found no difficulty in acquiring his complement of men. Every military equipment, stores of provisions, and even a printing press, with compositors, were put on board the *Leander*. Several young men, of respectable families, were volunteers in his service. It yet remains a secret from what source he derived the means of making these formidable preparations. The president was charged with having received information of his proceedings; and a request is said to have been made him, upon Miranda's sail-

wretched victims saw but too plainly the fate which awaited them. Tate, addressing himself to some of his terrified countrymen who had been on shore, and were assembled on the alarm, in agony, exclaimed: "Americans! will you see me dragged to execution like a dog, without proof of my guilt? — will no one step forward to assert my innocence?" "I will," replied the noble-hearted Mr. Smith, of Baltimore, a supercargo of a vessel from that port. A centinel was instantly ordered to bayonet the humane man, who fortunately escaped, by springing into his boat. The unfortunate Tate, with the two Frenchmen, were led to a public place; halters were placed round their necks; not a single moment was allowed them to make their peace with heaven; and they were instantly launched into eternity.

On mounting a platform a little raised from the ground, which served as a scaffold on this murderous occasion, Tate, in a most heart-rending fit of agony, called out, "Americans! — friends! — Americans! I die this ignominious death for duly executing my orders!"

The Frenchmen had been pinioned; but Tate's arms remained unconfined. In his efforts to preserve life, the sufferer laid hold of the cord by which he was suspended, and by repeated efforts removed it from his throat. As he grew weaker, it remained round his chin and the back part of his neck. In this manner he long writhed in agony before life was extinguished, to the great satisfaction of his murderers.

ing, to send the *Hornet* sloop of war, then lying ready for sea, to bring him back; and hence it is affirmed, that the government connived at, if not furnished the means necessary for the expedition.

On the other hand it was alledged, that there is not any law of the United States, by which Miranda could have been molested, or brought to account for his subsequent conduct in the Spanish colonies, even if it had been of a dishonourable nature. If the government had been acquainted with his designs, they could not interfere with any man's pursuits that were not hostile to the country: they had no power to arrest Miranda, or to prevent the equipment of vessels, the destination of which was decidedly for a port to which it was legal to sail. In answer to the charge of not communicating Miranda's designs to the Spanish ambassador, the friends of government observed, that his conduct had been so long of such a nature, as to forbid any respect due to the quality of an ambassador; that it had been insolent and contumacious in various instances; and that it could not be presumed that such a man so conducting himself, could be deemed worthy of confidence; that it could not be expected by Spain, that the conduct her government encouraged on the frontiers of Louisiana, should be returned by any confidential act; and that, finally, her minister, the Marquis D'Yrujo, had been dismissed from the exercise of his diplomatic functions. The discovery of Miranda's interviews with the president, and his being closeted with the secretary of state, if such took place, was insinuated to have been made by the spies of the Spanish ambassador.

One of the democratic prints, the *Aurora*, of the 7th of July, 1806, on this subject, contains the following observations: — "SPANISH INCENDIARY. In the Philadelphia *Gazette* of Saturday, there is an article, which, on the face of it, bears the impression of this little, malicious, political incendiary* — whom the indulgence and liberality of the people

* Alluding to the late Spanish ambassador, the Marquis d'Yrujo.

whose government he abuses — of whose hospitality he is unworthy — and who would have been served like his countryman *Sancho* in any other country than this, for one twentieth part of the unworthy conduct in which he indulged in the United States."

No sooner had Miranda with his fleet sailed, than the danger likely to result from the expedition being fitted out in a port of the United States, was discovered in New York. It became a question whether it was sanctioned by the government: one party charged them with an underhand dealing with Spain — and the other denied the accusation. The charge was founded upon the declaration of Colonel Smith, who asserted that he had sent a letter, written by Miranda, to the president, communicating the nature of his enterprize. The New York *Gazette* published the charge, and on being called upon to verify the truth, in the next paper, the editor says: "The substance of the information relative to the destination of the *Leander*, which was on Monday communicated through the medium of this *Gazette*, is correct. We were only mistaken as to the channel through which the secret was divulged; instead of inserting the name of Samuel G. Ogden, we ought to have said that the evidence implicating the government, came through Colonel Smith, and we are since informed that the evidence has been corroborated by another gentleman of the first respectability."

These circumstances so greatly agitated the public mind that, at length, a rigid investigation of the affair was commenced. The district judge, Tallmage, a son-in-law to Clinton, the present vice-president of the United States, directed his attorney to prosecute Samuel Ogden, the owner of the *Leander*. They had been previous to taking this step, some days employed in examining into the law, and collecting proofs whereon to ground a prosecution. Writs were finally issued, to hold him to bail; and Mr. Ogden, alarmed at their proceedings, shut up his counting-house, and stopped payment. The following is a copy of his address to the public upon this occasion: —

It is well known to the public, that for some time past a prosecution has been depending against me, touching the expedition of my ship, the *Leander*.

I am sensible that it would be improper for me to discuss the merits of that case in an extra-judicial manner; or to make suggestions, which, by any construction, might be deemed to interfere with the course of justice. It is far from my intention to adopt any such measure. On the contrary, I am, and always have been, ready to submit to the laws of my country; in confidence that they will be administered upon pure and proper principles: and if my conduct shall be found to have been legally criminal, I know that I am bound to abide the legal consequences. But yet, whatever may be the event of the depending prosecution, it is a duty which I owe to my friends and myself, and which I can never lose sight of, to vindicate my motives. And if it shall appear that I have acted in good faith, that nothing has been done but with the knowledge and implied approbation of the present administration: I trust that my vindication will be complete — though political motives may have induced a change in the ideas of our rulers.

Be that as it may, as the ultimate result of the present prosecution cannot be foreseen, and the consequences of it may be productive of serious injury to my mercantile concerns, I have determined, for the present to suspend all my payments, and wait the issue with as much tranquillity as possible.

I am governed in this decision, also, by other causes of the utmost importance, which in my mind render this measure for the present indispensible. Any assistance that I might have required as to pecuniary matters, I have been offered in the fullest extent by my friends, but I have thought it my duty, under existing circumstances, to decline their offers.

The inconveniences which this measure may cause to those who hold my paper, will, I confidently hope, be but of short duration; and with a view of more fully explaining to them my particular motives, and of making them acquainted with the state of my affairs, I request they will meet me at my house, No. 120, Greenwich-street, on Wednesday evening, the 16th inst. at seven o'clock, when the necessary explanation shall be given.

SAMUEL G. OGDEN.

New York, April 7, 1806.

The form of the writ which held him to bail was novel. It stated that, "whereas there was strong reason to suspect that Samuel G. Ogden had been concerned in preparing and providing the means of fitting out a certain ship called *Leander*, upon an enterprise hostile to some foreign nation (name unknown) at peace with the United States, the marshal was therefore to take the said Samuel G. Ogden, and him forthwith bring," &c.

Mr. Ogden was taken into custody at nine o'clock in the morning, and he was not permitted by the marshal to speak with any person whatsoever; but was told that the orders of the judge were to bring him before him instantly, without suffering him to communicate with his friends. He was accordingly brought before Judge Tallmage, whom he found attended by the district attorney, and the clerk of the court. Mr. Ogden addressed the judge, and said that he was desirous of having a friend present, or sending for counsel: when he was answered that he must send for nobody.* The district attorney then told Mr. Ogden, that he was brought before the judge in a two-fold quality — as a party charged with a crime — and as a witness — and that he must undergo an examination in both capacities. A long string of questions, ready prepared, were now propounded; some of which he answered, and refused to reply to others, alledging that he could not be compelled to criminate himself. The answers which he gave as far as concerned himself, were reduced to writing. He was then informed that he must be sworn as a witness against others, and in that capacity he must answer all questions put to him on pain of imprisonment. The oath was accordingly administered, and questions were put to him relative to the cargo and destination of the *Leander*. These he refused to answer, alledging that he was owner of the ship, and they might tend to criminate himself, and on this he was threatened with commitment. An order, on his per-

* This savors something of a star-chamber proceeding in a republican government.

sisting in a refusal, was actually made out; when, as the prisoner alledged, rather than suffer the inconvenience and disgrace of imprisonment, he answered all the questions that were put to him. His examination was then read to him, and he was ordered to swear and sign it. This he positively refused, until he was again threatened with imprisonment. He was then ordered to find bail for his future appearance.

Another warrant was issued against Colonel Smith, who being also afterwards brought forward in a similar manner, deposed, that he was apprehended about nine in the morning, and detained in a room, without being permitted to see or communicate with any person, till six o'clock in the evening, when he was carried before the judge, and told that he must be sworn to answer all such questions as should be put to him; and on refusal he should be imprisoned. The colonel answered by declaring his ignorance of the law, but observed, that in case the judge was empowered to inforce his examination, he would tell what he knew at once; to which this second Judge Jeffries answered, that he had such power, nay more, in case of a refusal, to punish him by imprisonment. Colonel Smith's examination was not gone through until midnight, and at that unseasonable hour he was compelled, in order to obtain his liberty, to send for friends to become sureties for his future appearance.

I have little doubt that every reader must have become interested in the issue of the proceedings of this inquisitorial court: and more especially as they display the manly opposition of Mr. Ogden's counsel, in supporting the law against the oppression of power: I shall therefore continue a brief narrative of this singular business.

Mr. Ogden being liberated on giving bail, immediately resorted to the advice of counsel. The gentlemen of the law, upon the affidavits of the facts of Messrs. Ogden and Smith, moved the court, that the depositions extorted from those gentlemen be filed with the proper officer. They told the judge that they had been taken in a manner tyrannical, unjust, and unprecedented — extorted by threats which a judge had no right to make, and which he should not have dared to put in execution — that the parties had been refused the benefit of counsel, which every man, in such a case, could claim as a matter of right. Attended by counsel they should not have answered a single question so propounded — and in case the judge had been hardy enough to have committed them to prison, he would have been liable not only to an action for false imprisonment, but to an impeachment. "The manner," continued the counsel, "in which this business has been conducted is so glaring, so palpably wrong, that it is in vain to seek for the cause of it in ignorance. In no instance has it been known, that in order to extort confession from a man under examination, and to criminate himself, was he made to change forms as the prosecutor might direct — now a party — now a witness." The counsel concluded by telling the judge it was altogether a mockery of justice, dishonorable to those concerned in it — disgraceful to the country.*

The answer of the district-attorney was in unison with the conduct of the judge. He said, that the examinations spoken of were not in court — that he had a right to lay such evidence before the grand jury as he thought proper, without being controlled by the counsel for the defendant — that the application was novel, and this reason alone was sufficient for the refusal of the court, and that the manner of making it was both an insult to him, and to the judge who then sat upon the bench.

The counsel for the defendants replied, that the examinations ought to have been in court, and that it was the duty of the magistrate before whom they were taken to have duly returned them; a neglect for which he would hereafter become answerable.

The application was refused.

The circuit-court of the United States was soon afterwards

* Had the learned judge acted uprightly, would he not have committed the counsel? — *Norfolk and Portsmouth Herald,* April 19, 1806.

opened. Judge Patterson, of the supreme court, then on the circuit, was taken sick, and it was therefore opened by Tallmage, the district judge for the state of New York, alone, who had already taken so decided and active a part against Mr. Ogden.

The grand jury having been sworn, the counsel for Mr. Ogden immediately rose, and stated, that in behalf of his bail he had to move the court to surrender him in discharge of their recognizance. This the district-attorney consented to, and the surrender and discharge of the bail being entered, he moved the court for the commitment of Mr. Ogden to the custody of the marshal. This was opposed, on the ground that the motion could not be granted unless some reason was then shewn to support it — that the defendant being now in a very different court from that in which his recognizance was taken, this court could act alone upon information now before it, without regard to what had happened elsewhere — and that it was inconsistent with the principles of liberty that any citizen should be imprisoned without knowing the specific charge made against him.

In answer, the district-attorney said, that as the original recognizance had been taken before the same judge who was then on the bench, and was therefore perfectly acquainted with all the facts, it would be absurd for him to call for new information to govern his discretion. The judge ordered the commitment of Mr. Ogden. His counsel then applied for a habeas corpus, which his honor* allowed; and the marshal immediately made a return thereto, stating the commitment and other particulars. Mr. Ogden's counsel then moved for his discharge, on the ground that it did not appear on the face of the return that he was confined upon a charge of having committed any crime; and that his commitment could be considered in no other light than a *general commitment*, which was odious to the law of the land, and dangerous to the liberty of the citizen — that the court had

* Judges throughout the United States are addressed — *your honors.*

no power to remand him to prison unless it appeared that he was charged with a crime upon oath.

This republican judge determined to this effect — "I know well what the prisoner is confined for, and that is cause enough for me to remand him. Liberty, to be sure, is sweet; but, as the court will sit but a few days, an imprisonment for that time will be no great hardship!!!"

It was then moved to admit Mr. Ogden to bail, to which the judge replied: "Yes, if he can find security for his appearance in twenty thousand dollars." His counsel then objected to it as excessive; but there was no alternative, and bail was actually given to that amount!*

It was during this state of the proceedings that I quitted the country. Private letters inform me that another judge admitted Mr. Ogden to bail on a smaller recognizance; and on his trial before a jury, and a judge somewhat differing from Tallmage, he was acquitted. On this memorable occasion, my letters farther observed, that Counsellor Emmett,† late of Dublin, was retained by Mr. Ogden, and acquired great credit for the animated speech he made in his behalf.

To return to Miranda. — I have stated that he was at sea during the persecutions against the owner of the ship in which he floated. During the equipment of his fleet, the Marquis D'Yrujo placed spies over his proceedings, from whose reports the ambassador was convinced that the armament of Miranda was destined against Caraccas. He secretly dispatched a swift-sailing pilot-built vessel to La Guira, a principal port there, with information of the hostile armament, and thus the resistance and defeat he experienced are sufficiently accounted for.

* During my long residence in the United States, and my knowledge of some of the courts, I have not heard of a similar instance of such excessive bail — in fine, of such proceedings.

† This gentleman is brother to the Mr. Emmett who was executed in Dublin for treason. He was also implicated, and pardoned on condition of leaving the kingdom.

It appears that Miranda arrived off Ocumare, on the coast of the province of Caraccas, and fourteen leagues west of La Guira, where he made an unsuccessful landing. The Spanish government being apprised of his motions, attacked him with two vessels of war. The *Leander* sought her safety in flight, leaving two smaller vessels, manned by Americans, a prey to the Spaniards, who, it has been reported, put the crews to death. It has also been said that the British Admiral Cochrane assisted this adventurer with a small British vessel of war, but still his force was entirely inadequate to carry his plans into execution.

The last accounts from America state, that Miranda arrived at Barbadoes in the British sloop of war *Melville*, on the 9th of November last; and that he will remain there till he hears the result of some dispatches which he has forwarded to England. It is conjectured that the government of Great Britain have some intention to take this adventurous officer into their employ.

I have already observed that Miranda was born in Caraccas, a province of South America belonging to Spain. He cannot, therefore, be considered in any other light than as a Spanish subject, and consequently a traitor to his native country. He is of an ancient and noble family, his grandfather having held the important office of captain-general of the Caraccas. Before he had arrived at the years of manhood, he formed the resolution of exploring the vast continent of America, and to this end he set out on foot and unattended. He was disguised in mean apparel, a circumstance which ensured his safety among the different hordes of savages through whose country he passed unmolested. The savage will very seldom put the passing stranger to death, being stimulated to that barbarous deed either by war or the hope of plunder. No suspicions were entertained that Miranda was either rich or a warrior, and he received many proofs of kindness from the Indians. It was on these his first travels that he joined the American army. His courage and his adventurous spirit gained him the esteem of some French officers, who were engaged in the same cause under Rochambeau. He accompanied, or soon followed them, to France, and was introduced at the Court of Versailles. He made the tour of France, then visited England, and afterwards Italy. Old Spain was the last country which he traversed in Europe. It has been asserted that he went to St. Petersburgh, and was introduced to the late Empress Catharine, with whom he soon became a favorite, and actually found means to obtain from her money to the value of four thousand pounds sterling. During these different journies, Miranda carefully gained every possible political information respecting South America. From this circumstance, it is evident that he long had it in contemplation to make his own country the goal of his ambition.

It appears that he returned to his native land with a view of comparing the intelligence obtained in Europe with the nature of things on the spot. He noted the towns, fortifications, military strength of the country, and the disposition of the inhabitants. Possessed of this information, he obtained an interview with Mr. Pitt, who, I have already said, employed him in the dispute between this country and Spain respecting Nootka Sound. We next find Miranda high in command in the French army early in the revolution. He was second in command to Dumouriez at the battle of Jemappe. The event of that business, with the circumstance of the commander making prisoners of the deputies sent by the convention to apprehend him, have often been related. Miranda was, however, secured, and sent to Paris, where he stood his trial, (a dangerous ordeal in those times) and as that archfiend Thomas Payne, in a recent publication in America, would lead the world to believe, was acquitted chiefly through his evidence. This renegado says: "He summoned me to appear to his character, and also a Mr. Thomas Christie, connected with the house of Turnbull and Forbes of London. I gave my testimony as I believed, which was, that his leading object was and had been the emancipation of his country, Mexico, from the bondage of Spain, for I did not then know of his engagements with Pitt. Mr. Christie's evidence went to shew, that Miranda did not come to France as a necessitous adventurer, but believed that he came from public-spirited motives, and that he had a large sum of money in the hands of Turnbull and Forbes. The house of Turnbull and Forbes was then in a contract to supply Paris with flour."

Since that period, Miranda has not been an object of public notice, till this recent enterprize drew upon him the attention both of the Old and New World.

NOTES — CHAPTER XXIV

1. The author has stated with a fair degree of accuracy the facts concerning the fitting out of the expedition by Miranda in New York, with, of course, the usual exaggeration due to prejudice or to reliance upon gossip and public discussion contemporary with the events. The whole story is told in William Spence Robertson's *Life of Miranda*, which gives probably the latest and most critical account of the activities of this Latin-American hero. Robertson brings out facts which tend to lend color to Janson's intimations that the high officials of the United States government winked at the whole affair until Spain protested and then took measures to punish those who aided him in New York. These men were acquitted.

CHAPTER XXV

NORFOLK, IN VIRGINIA — THE GREAT DISMAL SWAMP — LAKE DRUMMOND — DEER-HUNTING IN THE SWAMP — EXTRAORDINARY DILEMMA — LITTLE DISMAL SWAMP — THE PANTHER — DREADFUL CONFLICT BETWEEN PLANTERS AND BEARS — CANALS — CULTIVATION OF TOBACCO — FRAUDS OF AMERICANS IN THAT COMMODITY — NATURAL BRIDGES IN VIRGINIA.

THE passage from Alexandria to Norfolk is generally made by sea, on account of the distance by land; and it was in a regular packet that I proceeded to the latter place. The situation of Norfolk, in a commercial point of view, is one of the best in the United States; for health, one of the worst. Though it has been rebuilt since the year 1776, when Lord Dunmore ordered it to be burned,[1] yet the houses are in general mean, wooden buildings, and the streets unpaved; in summer covering you with dust — in winter, nearly impassable from mud and filth.[2] In the winter of 1800, returning to Mrs. Paterson's boarding-house, after dark, it was necessary to cross the main street. I was directed where to *ford the mud;* but after deliberately taking my observations, I lost my bearings, and nearly opposite to the spot where the Borough Tavern[3] then stood, I found myself almost knee deep. I plunged and labored some time to extricate myself, which I could not effect without the loss of one of my "shoe boots." Here, the gentlemen find it necessary to wear *thick shoes over their boots;* and even thus fortified, it is often a matter of difficulty to wade through the mud. Next morning I employed a black man to seek my shoe, for I had worn it only twice, and went to shew him the spot where I had sustained my loss; but after much *raking* and *dragging,* we were obliged to give up the search. The streets, except Main and Church Streets, are narrow, and even these are irregular. Those near the water were so filthy, that even in winter the stench was often offensive in passing. In the hot months of the years 1801 and 1802, contagion made dreadful havoc in this quarter of the town;[4] but the next year a fire destroyed nearly every house where disease had been engendered, and thus also purifying the air, the town has become less dangerous to the constitution. New houses, built of brick, have been erected upon the site of those which were burned, and more attention is paid to cleanliness.

The town is in a low situation, adjoining to swamps and marshes. It contains about six hundred and fifty houses; and, with these disadvantages, a great deal of business is done, both with the West India Islands, and in the exportation of tobacco and flour. Here are two episcopalian churches, one of which has been lately built, and is attended by the most respectable of the inhabitants. A handsome church was about the same time erected by the presbyterians, where I was present when it was crowded, to hear a sermon preached by Doctor Smith,[5] provost of Trenton College. This worthy divine travelled through Pennsylvania, Maryland, and Virginia, raising contributions to replace the library of the college, which had been consumed by fire. I never heard more exalted pulpit eloquence, more true piety, or more sound doctrine. There is also a church for the methodists, and a Roman Catholic chapel. Two banks have of late years been established in Norfolk; the first, a branch from that of the United States, and the other from the bank of Virginia.

In the vicinity of this town is the Dismal Swamp, a natural curiosity, of an extent unequalled in any part of the world. It reaches from Albemarle Sound, in North Carolina, to the neighborhood of Portsmouth, which is on the opposite side of the harbour to Norfolk, and contains about two hundred and fifty square miles, or one hundred and fifty thousand acres. It is a vast plain, slightly inclined, the greatest elevation being about thirty feet. About the middle is Lake Drummond, which is formed from the drainings of this vast tract of useless land. For centuries undisturbed by man, the lake is crowded with fish of great size and variety. Surrounded by lofty trees, it is unruffled by the wind, and so transparent, that its numberless inhabitants are seen in shoals by those who have resolution and perseverance sufficient to visit them. Mr. Moore,[6] the elegant translator of Anacreon, and author of Little's Poems, who recently visited America, has, in a volume of his compositions, published since his return, given a beautiful little ballad on the subject of a story which he says is current in this neighborhood, though I must confess that it never came within the circle of my observation. It is entitled "THE LAKE OF THE DISMAL SWAMP." "In the neighborhood of this dreary track," says Mr. Moore, "which lies about twelve miles distant from Norfolk, in America, the inhabitants have the following story, which forms the subject of this ballad: — A young man losing his senses upon the death of a lady, to whom he paid his addresses, imagined that she still lived upon the above lake; thither he repaired, and probably perished in some of its dreadful morasses, as he was never heard of afterwards by his family."

BALLAD

THEY made her a grave too cold and damp,
For a soul so warm and true;
And she's gone to the Lake of the Dismal Swamp,
Where all night long, by a fire-fly* lamp,
She paddles her white canoe.

And her fire-fly lamp I soon shall see,
And her paddle I soon shall hear;
Long and loving our life shall be,
And I'll hide the maid in a cypress tree,
When the footstep of death is near!

* The fire-fly is an insect common in this part of the country. In its flight, at short intervals, it sheds a beam of apparent fire, or lightning — brighter than the glow-worm. It is so perfectly harmless, that children amuse themselves in following and catching it.

Away to the Dismal Swamp he speeds—
His path was rugged and sore;
Through tangled juniper-beds of reeds,
Through many a fen where the serpent feeds,
And man ne'er trod before!

And when on the earth he sunk to sleep,
If sleep his eyelids knew,
He lay where the deadly vines do weep
Their venomous tears—and nightly steep
The flesh with blistering dew!

And near him the she-wolf stirr'd the brake,
And the rattle-snake breath'd in his ear,
Till he starting cried—from his dream awake—
"Oh! when shall I see the dusky lake,
"And the white canoe of my dear?"

He saw the lake, and a meteor bright
Quick o'er the surface play'd—
"Welcome," (he said) "my dear one's light!"
And the dim shore echoed for many a night
The name of the death-cold maid!

Till he form'd a boat of the birchen bark,
Which carried him off from the shore;
Far he follow'd the meteor spark,
The winds were high, and the clouds were dark,
And the boat return'd no more!

But oft from the Indian hunter's camp,
This lover and maid so true,
Are seen by the hour of midnight damp,
To cross the lake by a fire-fly lamp,
And paddle their white canoe.

Near Lake Drummond the land is firmer than in any other part of the swamp, and has afforded shelter for fugitive negroes; but, *that wild men have been found in it, who were lost, as it is supposed, when children,* as related by Mr. Weld, is a mere joke—nor do cattle go much farther than the skirts of the wood in quest of food.7 This is the effect of a natural instinct, as we find that the dread of snakes prevents cattle from penetrating; for, in such case, they would inevitably become a prey to the wild beasts, with which the desart abounds.

I was induced to accompany Mr. Wm. Carter, of Edenton, in pursuit of the deer, into this swamp, a temerity which I had reason to repent before I regained the cleared ground. This gentleman was a great sportsman, and derived infinite satisfaction from toiling the whole day in pursuit of game. He had with him a couple of dogs, which started and ran the deer till they came within shot. The sportsmen are placed at certain breaks in the underwood, through one of which the deer will pass at full speed. They sometimes bound past so suddenly, that a young sportsman is either startled, or cannot seize the moment to fire with effect. I was not put to the test, for we had started no game when the morning lowered, and presently the wind and rain rendered farther pursuit impracticable. We had, however, penetrated far enough to alarm me greatly, and to puzzle my guide as to the direction to be taken for the purpose of reaching the open country. My fears were greatly heightened by the knowledge of the following circumstance: — my companion loved his joke, but, like many other jesters, often carried it too far, having designedly led some of his acquaintance into the swamp; and, under pretence of following game in another direction, left them in the labyrinth, where they were actually obliged to pass just such a night as that now approaching threatened to be. His doubts were so evident, that with some agitation I mentioned the trick he had once played his friends, and threatened him with vengeance if he dared to repeat it upon me. He assured me I was perfectly safe, but for some time appeared at a loss in which direction to proceed; and such was the effect produced on my mind, that I fancied every five minutes we had come to the spot we had just left, and even challenged trees by certain marks my eye had caught, charging Mr. Carter with having lost the way. I observed him walk round several large trees, surveying them with great attention. He would then climb one of them, and as the seaman from the maintop looks out for land, so he appeared to be looking for some known mark to guide his course. My fears were increasing, and the tales I had heard of men perishing in the swamp, and of others being many days in extricating themselves, in which time they were nearly famished, drove me almost to a state of desperation. All this time my companion in silence was apparently employed in fixing upon our course; at length he called out that he had discovered it. He then pointed to a large tree, the bark of which, in the direction in which we stood, was incrusted with green moss. "This," said he, "is the north side of the tree; I now know our course; I was in doubt only till I ascertained this point, and the trees we have lately passed did not fully convince me."* On going round the tree, I found the other sides free from the mossy appearance. He observed, that but few of them clearly shewed it in the swamp, but I have since observed the effect on all trees less exposed to the air, as well as upon old houses and walls. He said that he was rarely obliged to recur to this guide, as he never ventured into the swamp but when the day promised to be fair, as he could work his way by the sun. Few men will venture, like Mr. Carter, but experience had made him regardless of the consequences of being lost in this desart.

I found in many parts of it good walking ground, the lofty trees being at some distance from each other, and the underwood by no means so thick as to impede our road; but

* I have since been informed that the Indians, by this observation, work their way through immense forests, when the sun is obscured by thick clouds. Mr. Jefferson, in his Notes on Virginia, mentions a circumstance of some Indians, on a mission, suddenly quitting the public roads, and striking through the woods, in order to visit some old Indian graves, at a considerable distance. A century, he observes, must have passed since that part of Virginia, where the graves were made, had been inhabited by Indians; and therefore these travellers must have found their way from a description of its situation handed down by tradition, and by their observations of the sun, and the mossy side of the trees.

after thus proceeding a few miles, the pursuit of game is impracticable. Sometimes we had to cross where it was knee deep, but my companion had in this case generally marked a place where we could pass over on a fallen tree. I had mounted one of these, of a monstrous size, and was proceeding heedlessly along, when I suddenly found myself sink up to the middle in dust; the tree having become rotten, though it retained its shape. This was a good joke for my friend, but a sad disaster for me; for I had great difficulty in getting out of the hole into which I had fallen; the tree, like ice, being more rotten in some parts than others, I was compelled to break my way till I came to a part sound enough to bear me, and having fallen between two knots, I could not conveniently get out of the trunk into the swampy ground beneath, had I been so inclined. With fearful steps I advanced to the end, but was very wary how, in future, I trusted to a bridge formed by a fallen tree.

During the last summer, a tremendous fire raged for several days in the Dismal Swamp, consuming all the timber, and destroying large quantities of staves and shingles, collected for sale, for many miles. The navigation of the new canal was stopped by monstrous half-burnt branches of trees falling against it, to the ruin of many families. In clearing land, the planter often sets fire to the woods; sometimes the conflagration passes the intended limits, and is productive of much damage; threatening, from the extent and thickness of the woods, destruction to the adjacent country.

In North Carolina there are a number of swamps of this description, but very inferior in extent. I crossed one in Alligator county, called the Little Dismal. It was about five miles across, which saved fifteen in going the high road; but this difference of distance was not so much my object, as a desire to penetrate into the interior of this desart. I was on horseback, and had for my guide a negro man on foot, belonging to a planter of my acquaintance, who went before me, guided by notches cut in the trees. My horse had frequently gone the road, and appeared conscious of the difficulty, recognising the marshy places; and trusting to his judgment, he avoided many broken pieces of ground with a sagacity inherent in that well-trained animal. I carried my gun in my hand, loaded with slugs, and more ammunition slung across my shoulders. About midway, and about two hundred yards before me, I saw a large quadruped nimbly climb a tree. The negro, looking in a contrary direction, did not perceive the motion, and, eager to fire, I did not inform him. We went a foot's pace, and when within gun-shot, I discovered the beast through the foliage of the wood, and immediately fired. The shot took effect, and my astonishment was great to see a monster, of the species of the tiger, suspended by his fore feet from the branch of a tree, growling in tones of dreadful discord. The negro was greatly terrified; and my horse, unused to the report of a gun fired from his back, plunged, and was entangled in mire. Losing the reins, I was precipitated into the morass, while the negro vociferated "Massa, Massa, we are lost!" Recovering, I beheld the ferocious brute on the ground, feebly advancing towards us. By an involuntary act I presented my empty gun, at sight of which, conscious, no doubt, that the same motion had inflicted the smart he felt, the creature made a stand, gave a hideous roar, and turned into the thickest part of the swamp, while, in haste and great agitation, I reloaded my piece. The poor slave, whose life to him was as dear as mine could be to me, held up his hands, and thanked the God he worshipped for his deliverance. I was unconscious of the danger I had courted till he told me that the beast I encountered was a panther, larger than any he had ever seen despoiling his master's flocks and herds, and that when pursued by man, those animals rally with great ferocity. Had I been apprised of this, I should have sought my safety in flight, rather than have begun an attack; but I conjectured the creature to be of no larger dimensions than a wild cat, when I fired.

This leads me to a story related by my friend Carter.—A planter, who frequented the Edenton market, resided on the other side of the Great Dismal Swamp, where it is only eight or ten miles broad. He had spent an evening freely, that is, in these parts, not without copious draughts of grog or toddy; and, inspired by these with fool-hardy temerity, he determined to cross the Great Dismal, instead of going the usual, but longest road. Few were bold enough to proceed, even in the daytime, by the route he had rashly adopted; but this man was of uncommon strength, and of a daring mind. Resisting the entreaties of his friends, he sallied forth about midnight from Edenton, on foot, and with a trusty stick in his hand. About the middle of the forest, the moon shining bright, he perceived the cub of a bear before him, at which he threw his stick, with an effect which caused the young inhabitant of the woods to roar; and this brought the enraged, yet tender mother, to its relief. The man had recovered his stick, and was proceeding to secure the cub, (delicious eating as a young pig) when *Mrs. Bruin* advanced. A battle immediately commenced between the savage matron and the incautious man. The latter had, however, recovered from the stupidity occasioned by drinking ardent spirits, yet, though he abandoned the possession of the cub, he could neither pacify the mother nor avoid her embraces. The man survived the bloody conflict, and the account he gave of the battle is yet current in the district of Chowan. He related, that, having delivered up the cub, he wished to evade a contest with the dam, but she pressed so closely upon him that he was obliged to prepare for battle. For some time he defended himself with his stick, in which interval the bear merely tore his jacket. She fought upon her hind legs, and thus the combatants were nearly of the same height. While the stick served him, he evaded the bite, as well as the hug of the bear; but on making a desperate blow, the weapon was shivered, and then they came to closer quarters. He now substituted his fists, and with lusty sinews dealt his blows upon the hard head and tough hide of the bear. — They closed, and, in the struggle which ensued, the man suffered most dreadfully from the hug of his enraged opponent.

Some philosophers assert, that the animals of the forest are superior to man in his primeval state, in cases of defence and hunger, the natural instinct of every animal. I am not inclined to discuss this proposition, conceiving the case in point decisive. The man in question was illiterate, and in faculty, perhaps, inferior to the wily matron of the forest on her own ground; and yet, in the height of contest, when acquired endowments are for the moment lost, the biped conquered the quadruped of twice his size and strength, and with nature's weapons alone. The first onset, with the stick, I consider merely defensive — it was soon rendered useless without in the least degree disabling the enemy. It appeared, from corroborating circumstances, and the "ploughed ground," as it was termed by those who viewed the scene of action, that they had wrestled with various success — sometimes the bear, sometimes the man, being undermost. The latter, almost exhausted, dreadfully bitten, torn, and squeezed, by the light of the moon observed a fallen tree, just such another as I met my disaster in, but in a sounder state; over this tree, with a desperate effort, he threw his antagonist, and falling on her, stifled the brute so that she opened her jaws for breath, into which the animal-man thrust his hand, and choaked the monster. Faint with loss of blood and uncommon exertion, he reached his home towards morning, when the neighbours assembled, and proceeded by the sick man's directions to the scene of the contest, where they found the old bear, attended by two of her cubs, mourning her fate. They secured the young ones, and dragged home the immense carcase of the mother. The different weights of the combatants were ascertained by the astonished countrymen, The bear weighed, on being brought to the conqueror's house, 305, and the man, when recovered, 191 pounds.

Another combat of this nature was thus related by Mr. Lawson of Philadelphia: —

A farmer, named Wayborne, in Ovid township, went out one afternoon through the woods in search of his horses, taking with him his rifle, with the only load of ammunition he had in the house. On his return home, about an hour before dusk, he perceived a very large bear crossing the path, on which he instantly fired, and the beast fell; but immediately recovering his legs, made for a deep ravine a short way ahead. Here he tracked him awhile by the blood; but night coming on, and expecting to find him dead in the morning, he returned home. A little after day-break the next morning, taking a pitchfork and hatchet, and his son, a boy ten or eleven years of age, with him, he proceeded to the place in quest of the animal. The glen, or ravine, in which the bear had disappeared the evening before, is eighty or ninety feet from the top of the banks to the bottom of the brook below: down this precipice a stream three or four yards in breadth is precipitated in one unbroken sheet, and, forming a circular basin or pool, winds away among thick underwood below. After reconnoitering every probable place of retreat, he at length discovered the bear, who had made his way up the other side of the ravine, as far as the rocks would admit him, and sat under a projecting cliff, steadfastly eyeing the motions of his enemy. Wayborne, desiring his boy to remain where he was, took the pitchfork, and, descending to the bottom, determined to attack him from below. The bear kept his position until he got within six or seven feet, when, on the instant of making a stab with the pitchfork, he found himself grappled by Bruin, and both together rolled down towards the pond, at least twenty or twenty-five feet, the bear munching his left arm and breast, and hugging him almost to suffocation. By great exertion, he forced his right arm partly down his throat, and in that manner endeavored to strangle him, but was once more hurled headlong down through the bushes, a greater distance than before, into the water. Here, finding the bear gaining on him, Wayborne made one desperate effort, and forced his head partly under water; and repeating his exertions, at length weakened the animal so much, that, calling to his boy, who stood on the other side, in a state little short of distraction for the fate of his father, he sunk the edge of the hatchet, by repeated blows, into his brain. Wayborne, though a robust muscular man, was with great difficulty able to crawl home, where he lay upwards of three weeks with his wounds, his arm being mashed from the shoulder to the elbow into the bone, and his breast severely mangled. The bear weighed upwards of 420 pounds.

These swamps contain vast quantities of timber, but it can never be brought from the interior. On the margins, abundance of shingles are made from the juniper and cypress tree; and staves of every description of the oak. The shingles are for the West-India market, and for home-consumption; the houses in America, with a few exceptions in large towns, where slate is used, being covered with them.

A canal, which has been several years in finishing, was lately opened at Norfolk. It is cut through the Great Dismal Swamp, thus connecting the waters of Pamlico and Albemarle sounds with the harbour, and removing former impediments to the trade between North Carolina and Virginia. The color of the water is a deep red, occasioned by the roots of the trees through which it passes; but it is perfectly clear, the taste by no means disagreeable, and very wholesome. Labouring people who reside near swamps, drink it in preference to spring water, attributing to its virtue the prevention of agues and bilious fevers. It is of a diuretic quality, and those who drink it are generally healthy, while others, at a distance from the swamps, in the fall of the year, are suffering under those complaints. This canal was cut by an incorporated company, who are the owners of about one half of the swamp, and are called "The Dismal Swamp company."[8] The shares in this concern were at one time, when the plan was by some conceived to be impracticable, of very little worth, but they are now become valuable property.

The tobacco for the British market is chiefly raised in Virginia. Its cultivation, but for the enemies which attack the young plants, would be attended with little more trouble than raising cabbages. In spring, the seed, which is very small and black, is sown upon a rich piece of ground, on which they strew ashes, in order to kill the insects which devour the young plants, but with little effect. It was a matter of surprise to me to find from many planters, that they knew of no remedy against the devastation produced by the "*tobacco-fly*," which is of the beetle species, black, and large enough to be seen committing its depredations as you pass the plant. As soon as the tender leaves shoot forth above the ground, they are immediately attacked by the fly, and though negroes are constantly attending to pick them off, yet they seldom save more than one in a score, and sometimes they are wholly cut off.

When the surviving plants have acquired some strength, they are drawn out of the bed, and planted out nearly as we plant cabbages, but farther apart; and of course on a much larger scale. I have seen a tobacco-field of fifty, and seldom less than five acres. In their new situation, the young plants, relieved from the fly, become a prey to a worm, which is called the "*tobacco-worm*." It is of the caterpillar kind, green as the leaves, which renders it difficult to be discerned, though it grows to the length of three inches, and is thick in proportion. In addition to this, small flies of different sorts, with which the country swarms, deposit their eggs among the leaves, which alone often prove fatal to the plant. The same hill is frequently occupied by three or four plants successively before one of them survives its numerous enemies. These insects constitute the principle trouble; for when out of their power, little more attention is required than to keep down weeds, to top the plant, and to break off the suckers, which draw the strength from the large leaves. I planted in my own garden alternately a tobacco and a cabbage plant. The fly would not touch the latter, but I have sometimes observed it attacked by another insect, and both would often fall at the same time by their different natural enemies. The cabbage-plant was, however, rarely destroyed, while the tobacco-hill was frequently replanted from the seed-bed. The cabbages which were thus raised acquired a strong taste, as though they had been preserved through a severe winter in a dark cellar; while those out of the same seed-bed, planted by themselves, were of the usual flavor.

In August, the tobacco-plants are cut down, having then arrived at maturity, though still of a greenish colour. They are hung up in houses built for the purpose of drying them, but I have seen them dried in the sun, spread out on rails and boards. In this mode of curing, care must be taken that they are not exposed to the rain. When perfectly dry the leaves are of a brown colour, and are tied up, ten, twelve, or fifteen together, which are called hands of tobacco. In this state they are carefully packed in hogsheads, and sent to the nearest tobacco-inspection.

These warehouses of inspection belong to the state, and officers are appointed by government to inspect and receive into the store-houses all merchantable tobacco. They then give the owner a certificate, distinguished by marks and numbers of inspection, and safe custody. These certificates are called tobacco-notes; and being payable to bearer, are current payment, and frequently an object of speculation.[9]

These hogsheads are sometimes of a prodigous size. I have known them of eighteen hundred pounds weight, rolled by horses two hundred miles. In order to effect this least expensive mode of conveyance, they drive pieces of oak into the head of the hogshead, to which are fastened a pair of shafts, and thus the hogshead is rolled over rocky grounds and mountains to a sea-port. The hoops and staves are sometimes worn even to the tobacco, which, however, remains firm, having, from pressure, become one solid mass.

Shippers of tobacco should be very particular as to the quality and weight of their shipments. The growth of Maryland is not in equal estimation in England with that produced in Virginia, though they are adjoining states, and though the first is clearly the finest and mildest. There is great deception in weight, for the hogsheads seldom in Britain prove of the weight marked on them at the American inspection-houses. In bargaining for tobacco for exportation, the purchaser should stipulate to have it re-weighed, and to pay at that rate. In three hogsheads only of those I brought with me, being advised to remit money in this shape, the loss, according to the marks, was as follows: —

				C.	Q.	L.
WG.	No. 3.	Philadelphia, mark of Barker and Annesley		15	3	10
	No. 6.	Ditto	Ditto	17	0	21
AK.	No. 8.	Ditto	Ditto	11	1	20
				44	1	3
British custom-house mark,	No. 3.			14	2	0
	No. 6.			15	1	0
	No. 8.			9	3	0
				39	2	0
Making a loss of				4	3	3

This tobacco, with other shipments, cost in Philadelphia eight cents per lb. — four-pence halfpenny sterling; and by the deficiency above stated, there was a loss of upwards of eight pounds British money in only three hogsheads! I certainly was aware of this species of deception; but, in haste to fill up a vacancy in the hold of the ship, and relying on the integrity of the *Quakers* of whom I purchased, I did not attend to the business. I also suffered in another way in this unlucky transaction. Being pressed for time, (which is always the case when a ship is about to sail) I employed the inspector, Thomson, to chuse for me the prime tobacco; and for this service I gave him a dollar per hogshead. He made a great many flourishes of his rhetoric in order to convince me that he had procured some of extraordinary quality — such as seldom came to the British market — and that no man was so good a judge of tobacco as himself. It proved to be the worst of the whole cargo.

The greatest curiosities in the large territory of Virginia

are two natural bridges, which may be ranked among the most sublime works of nature in America. Rockbridge has been described some years ago by Mr. Weld, in the account of his travels through part of the United States.[10] The natural bridge, over a stream running from Stork Creek, which rises in Clinch Mountain, in the western part of this state, is far more stupendous. It is three hundred and thirty-nine feet in height, while Rockbridge, according to Mr. Weld, is only two hundred and thirteen; but from recent observations, the other exceeds it by one hundred and thirty-four feet. I never had an opportunity of examining this wonderful production of nature, but in an account of it which I met with, its summit is described to project eighty-seven feet over its base, fronting the south-west, and to be arched as regularly as if formed by the hand of art. The arch in front is about two hundred feet high, and slopes off to sixty feet, at the distance of one hundred and six feet from the entrance. From its mouth in a straight direction, it measures four hundred and six feet; thence, at right angles, three hundred feet. The roof is regularly arched, and gradually descends to eighteen feet, which is the lowest part at the intersection of the second angle; it then rises to twenty, thirty, forty, and seventy-five feet, which is the height of the northeast entrance. The stream of water is from forty to fifty yards wide at its common height, but it is sometimes suddenly swelled by rains to ten or twelve feet perpendicular. There is a waggon-road over the bridge, which is never used but in times of freshets, and then it is the only part where the water can be crossed. The approach to the south-west front produces the most pleasing and awful sensations. The front is of a solid rock of lime-stone; the surface very smooth and regular, formed in a semi-circle, the rock of a bright yellow colour. The arch is partly obscured by a spur of the ridge which runs down the edge of the creek. Across the creek are several lofty trees, which add to the beauty of the scene. The view from the verge fills the mind with horror. From the level of the summit of the ridge, where the road passes, to the verge of the fissure, the mountain descends about forty-five degrees of an angle, and is from forty-five to fifty feet in perpendicular height. The rock is covered with a thick stratum of earth, which gives growth to many large trees. To the west of the arch about four hundred yards, the ascent to the verge is much more level. This bridge may be passed without the traveller's noticing it, from the thick surrounding wood, unless his attention be attracted, in the time of freshets, by the roaring of the water below.

The French frigate *Magicienne* was, during several months in the year 1801, blockaded in the harbour of Norfolk by the English frigate *Boston*. The first was a heavy ship of 44 guns — the other one of the smallest in the British navy of her rate, mounting only 32. On board the Frenchman embarked Jerome Buonaparte, and Miss Paterson of Baltimore, whom he had recently married, in order to escape to France.[11] They pursued Adet's plan, and in a gale of wind got through Hampton Roads, having received information that the *Boston* had left the coast; but before they could double Cape Henry, they espied her bearing down upon them under a press of sail. The French thought it prudent to return, having, without doubt, orders to avoid an engagement, from the brother and sister-in-law of Napoleon being on board.*

During the blockade of Norfolk, a riot took place in the public streets between part of the crew of the *Magicienne* and some English and Irish seamen belonging to merchant ships; and so much was the scale of politics now turned, that they were aided by American sailors. It happened on a Sunday, and I rose from the dinner-table to witness the cause of an alarm which ran through the town. The heat

* Recent accounts state that this *most amiable youth* is about to be again married to a Princess of Saxony. I could wish, should this take place, to have him arraigned for bigamy in the American courts of justice.

of the battle was over before I arrived at the scene of action, and the unfortunate Frenchmen were pursued in all directions. They were chiefly marines, and had come on shore full-dressed, and with their side-arms, to visit the town. The moment the British tars perceived them an attack was meditated. They hastily procured a few sticks, and on their road were asked by some American seamen the cause of their proceeding; when, being told it was to drub the French, they followed. A gentleman who saw the attack made, told me, that the assailants were headed by a little Irishman, who was conspicuously active in spiriting up the Americans against those whom he called every man's enemy. The Frenchmen had received notice of their approach, and assembling together, drew their swords. This was declared by the sailors a challenge, and, in defiance of their arms, they rushed upon their adversaries with an intrepid desperation which astonished my informant. Several of the assailants were dreadfully cut at the onset, but in an instant the Frenchmen gave way, though at the time superior in numbers, the sailors seizing and breaking their arms. A panic struck them, and they fled in every direction. I was in time to witness three or four pursued by one sailor, with a stick in his right hand, and a sword, wrested from the adversary, in his left. This flight and pursuit continued up the main street of Norfolk, a considerable distance from the place of action, in Water-street.

At this time the French frigate was moored in the middle of the harbor between Norfolk and Portsmouth, and could in a short time have reduced both those towns to ruins. The account of the attack was consequently very soon received on board, when the French instantly manned their boats, and filled them with armed men. The town was also in alarm, and the citizens collected upon the wharfs, to view the proceedings on board the ship. The armed boats, three in number, soon approached the shore; they were cautioned not to land, but to send an officer with a small party to state their grievance. This was not relished by the French. who were upon the point of giving hostile information to the ship, when the officers recognised Mr. Moses Myers,* their agent, standing near Mr. Wm. Vaughan, the mayor, and other magistrates. This brought on an explanation; and the officers hearing, as the fact really was, that it was a riot made by the sailors, and which ended before the officers of the peace could interfere, they appeared satisfied. After waiting above an hour the return of their companions who had been put to flight, they returned on board. Some of the Frenchmen had been dreadfully beaten and bruised, but I saw no wound that could have been inflicted by a sword. It was reported that one or more of them were killed, but no public account of such circumstance transpired. The officers had imprudently, at different times, permitted a number of their men to come together into the town with their side arms; and this class of Frenchmen, since the adoption of liberty and equality, are generally ferociously insulting. On the part of the sailors, this was alledged, and instances were adduced, in which they had conducted themselves with insult towards some of their own body, as well as to the inhabitants. Matters were, however, compromised without farther bloodshed, and when the Frenchmen in future came on shore, they were accompanied by an officer.

Jerome and his wife, driven back by the sight of the *Boston,* were landed at Hampton, about fifteen miles from Norfolk, whence they returned to Baltimore; and at length escaped the vigilance of the British cruizers by embarking in an American ship, in which they passed unsuspected. The tyrannical prohibition of Napoleon against this unfortunate woman's landing in France or Holland, and the asylum she found in England until her return to her unhappy parents, are circumstances which must be known to every reader.

* This man is a Jew, and by French agency, added to benefits received from the acts of Virginia, in cases of insolvency, has contrived to hold considerable property. He sports his carriage, and is a colonel of the militia.

NOTES — CHAPTER XXV

1. See Margaret V. Smith, *Virginia, 1492-1892*, p. 198. Weld estimated the loss at £300,000 sterling.

2. Weld's *Travels*, pp. 99-100 corroborates Janson's description of the condition of the streets.

3. One of the old taverns, the scene of many celebrations of a patriotic nature during pre-Revolutionary days.

4. Norfolk was practically swept away by a series of conflagrations, the first occurring in 1799. On February 22, 1804, another fire swept over the district from Market Street to Town Point, south of Main Street. In 1805 a third destroyed part of the town. Yellow fever first appeared in 1795. Again in 1802 it claimed victims by the hundreds. From that time the city was practically free from this plague until 1821.

5. Dr. Samuel Stanhope Smith, a graduate of Princeton, became president of Hampton-Sidney in 1775 and of Princeton in 1795. The school was burned during the Revolution.

6. Thomas Moore, the Irish poet, travelled in the United States in 1804 and wrote a number of poems about American scenes and stories. While at Trinity College, Dublin, he translated Anacreon in metrical form.

7. See Weld's *Travels*, pp. 102-03 for his description of the Dismal Swamp.

8. The North Carolina legislature in 1790 incorporated the Dismal Swamp Canal Company, as the result of a movement started in 1786. The second canal mentioned seemingly was first planned in 1797. For a full discussion of these projects, see C. C. Weaver, *Internal Improvements in North Carolina previous to 1860. Johns Hopkins University Studies in History and Political Science*, XXI, 3 and 4. Baltimore, 1903.

9. This practice had been followed much earlier, and in all probability it continued until the period during which Janson lived in the United States.

10. The description referred to by Janson may be found in Weld's *Travels*, pp. 127-29.

11. Janson's dates are incorrect. Jerme Buonapart married Elizabeth Paterson of Baltimore on Christmas Eve, 1803. This marriage aroused the displeasure of Napoleon, then First Consul. In October, 1804, Jerome embarked for France on a brig which was wrecked at the mouth of Chesapeake Bay. In March, 1805, he again embarked at Baltimore and proceeded to meet his brother, now Emperor, at Allessandria. He left his wife at Lisbon, from which place she went to Amsterdam and later to England. Napoleon attempted to have the marriage annulled by the Pope so that the son of Jerome and Elizabeth, born in England on July 7, 1805, might not have any future claims. The Pope refused to accede to Napoleon's wishes, and this probably marked the first step towards a rupture between the Emperor and Pius VII. A civil divorce terminated this American union, and Jerome later married Catherine of Wurtemberg. For a full discussion of this matter see A. H. Atheridge, *Napoleon's Brothers*. London, 1909.

CHAPTER XXVI

THE MOCKING-BIRD — THE RED-BIRD, OR VIRGINIA NIGHTINGALE — THE WOODCOCK OF THE SOUTHERN STATES — THE WOODPECKER — THE WHIP-POOR-WILL.

OF THE great variety of the feathered race in America, but few excel in note and melody of song. In this respect, if we could except the mocking bird alone, the musicians of the forest in Britain have a decided preference; nay, even the nightingale has been frequently set up in competition with that first of American songsters.

At the president's house, I was highly gratified, by hearing a mocking-bird in full song. It was the favourite of a little aviary belonging to the steward. Mons.——,* a Frenchman, who acts in this capacity, with a politeness and attention worthy a more dignified office, took great pains to encourage his wonderful warbler to go through the full variety of his melodious medley. As it changed its imitations, he would announce the name of the original songster of the forest, when we appeared to be unacquainted with the note. Thus we heard, and generally in an elegant, if not a superior style, the strains of the favorites of the woods; and the mocker then descended to the brute creation, giving us the mewing of the cat, and the barking of the dog. Thus far, Monsieur informed us, we had heard the natural acquirements of the bird; it could, on hearing any tune, give a perfect imitation, in a very short time. He then led it to follow him in some French airs; and this was a prelude to another piece, consisting of a variety of Scotch airs, and American popular tunes. During the whole of this concert, which for variety and execution, excited our wonder, the performer appeared

*I forget this gentleman's name; he was introduced to me by M. Labille, of Georgetown.

to be proud of our attention, and still anxious to detain us; for he had begun anew as we left the house.

The colour of these birds, as though nature had done enough in the song, is mean; they are something like the English hedge-sparrow, but larger. They are delicate when young, and therefore difficult to be raised; but when grown into full song, they may be sent to any part of the world, by attending to the nature of their food, and other precautions.

Before I dismiss this subject, having already mentioned the nightingale, the only competitor of the mocking bird in Britain, I shall add a few observations on their comparative merits.

The full song of the nightingale is from fifteen to twenty parts — or beginnings and closings; but these are varied with a sweetness and judgment unequalled. Its tone is more mellow than that of any other bird; and, as an elegant, or if we may be allowed the term, a scientific warbler, superior to the natural notes of the mock-bird. It is too, an original — and such an original as the other must fail in copying. The latter appears to have no will of its own, being impelled to relinquish a melodious strain, to follow the lowings of a cow, or the grunting of a hog rooting below the tree on which it may have perched. In order to try their comparative abilities, it would be well to have a mock-bird within the hearing of the nightingale, and to confine it to this object only. By frequent repetition, the imitator would follow the nightingale, and by practice, their merits might be decided upon.

In the southern states, there is a bird of both beautiful plumage and fine song — the Virginian nightingale, or, as the natives call it, the red-bird. Its form is something like a paroquet in miniature; and it is of a bright red colour, with a tuft or crown on the head of the male. It must be the colour alone, however, that obtains it a preference; for it is far excelled in song by the English sky-lark, and some of the linnets; while the goldfinch, in both, may vie with the red-bird.

A traveller has confounded the mocking-bird with the Virginia nightingale, and speaks of them as the same bird by different names; but they are very different, both in colour and song. The red-bird of Virginia and the Carolinas, is by the English called the Virginia nightingale, a name not given by Americans to any bird of the woods. In plumage, a bird of the species of the woodpecker, misnamed in the southern states, the woodcock, is the most beautiful. It has the golden hue of the English goldfinch, variegated with crimson, back and white. On its head it has a beautiful tuft, but its notes are harsh and discordant. It is of the size of the dove, and is generally seen on decaying trees, in quest of insects. The woodpecker is smaller, of a greenish tint, and the noise occasioned by its bill against a tree, is like the quick strokes of a blacksmith's hammer on his bare anvil, beginning loud and gradually dying away. The flesh of both these birds is black, tough, and ill-flavored. If the name of nightingale were to be given to any of the feathered race in the southern states, that called the "*Whip-poor-Will,*" is best entitled to it. This bird sings a plaintive note almost the whole night long, resembling the pronunciation of the words by which it is named. It has been said to be so very wary, that it is seldom seen, much less taken; and that many have imagined the noise does not proceed from a bird, but from a frog. This is a wild conjecture. The bird it not otherwise shy, than because nature has assigned to it the task of watching in the night, when certainly it can seldom be seen; but its existence is as well known, as that of the mocking, or other rare birds.

CHAPTER XXVII

ECCENTRIC ADVERTISEMENTS — OF A PUBLICAN — A LOTTERY-OFFICE KEEPER — A HAIR-DRESSER — A NEGRO OYSTER MERCHANT — A POETICAL FRISSEUR — A POLITICAL BARBACUE — PORTER-SELLER — ITINERANT PARSON — MATRIMONY — DIVORCE.

IN THE early part of my residence in the United States, I had frequent opportunities of observing sarcasms thrown out in the newspapers there against those of England for eccentric advertisements, and particularly respecting quack medicines. In the course of a very few years I found the American journals even outdoing, in this particular, those of the mother country The arrival of the self-created Dr. Church, an obscure quack from London, and a few others of the "cure killing" tribe, engrossed many of their columns. At the present day, almost all the nostrums and never failing specifics, so fatal to the incredulous in Britain, are advertised in America, with the addition of those of a numerous host of French, German, and native quacks. The reader there is constantly pestered with a column dedicated to the worm lozenges; while others hold out infallible cures for every incurable disorder in the catalogue of human infirmities. Venereal doctors also, rise up in print like mushrooms, asserting cures, from the Indian weed, up to Dr. Solomon's Balm of Gilead. To give a specimen of these ingenious impositions, would be merely a repetition of the style of our own immaculate quackeries. I shall, however, subjoin a few local curiosities of the advertisement kind, which, for eccentric folly, stand pre-eminent. In all countries they are in some measure characteristic of the people, and from them alone we gain some idea of their manners and customs.

MODERN PHILOSOPHY!!

What is a name?
That which we call white,
By any other name would look as fair.

MY OWN.

JOSEPH PILGRIM, in conformity to his whole life, viz. the convenience and happiness of his fellow-creatures, has erected a booth, the second on the right hand turn of the corner, on the Race Ground, Govan's Town; but to prevent any mistakes, (not with the least reference to *himself!*) he has affixed over his tent, the figure of the celestial goddess of Wisdom!

It has been the contest of ages, What can most conduce to the happiness of Man? — The grave tenant of the pulpit, and the deeply researching philosopher, have in vain advanced their different theories. The discovery was left alone to immortalize the name of Joseph Pilgrim: the depth of whose experience and observation for many years, has convinced him beyond a doubt, that nothing can insure and perpetuate the happiness of man but deep libations to the rosy god, whose rubic nose and bloated eye, look with scorn at the sallow and meagre visage of care. The ancients may boast of Lethean springs as the antidote of anxiety; but in their days of darkness and superstition, they knew nothing of good cool *punch,* and were equally ignorant of the enlivening qualities of *brandy and water!* Those beverages, in their best style, together with their requisite concomitants of boiled ham, and well-seasoned relishes, are to be had in the greatest profusion, at the booth of the Moral Philosopher, on the race-ground as above described, from this day until the close of the races.— *Baltimore Advertiser.*

Is She Rich? an Extract.

Since the question now asked concerning a lady is not, Is she handsome? Is she accomplished? or, Is she amiable? but, *Is she rich?* It is of the greatest importance to the sex, that this question should be answered in the affirmative. Now there has been no shorter method yet discovered, (not even by Sir Isaac Newton) of becoming rich, (for saving industry is not only very slow and tedious, but is now becoming quite unfashionable) there is no shorter method than that of becoming adventurers in the Precincts Market-house Lottery, now drawing, in which, notwithstanding scarcely four thousand tickets are yet drawn, the wheel has gained the astonishing sum of six thousand eight hundred and thirty seven dollars, neither of the capital prizes being yet drawn.— *New York Papers.*

Much wanted. — A neat well-behaved female, to do kitchen-work in a small family, in Charlestown, near Boston. She may pray, and sing hymns, but not over the dish-kettle; may go to meeting, but not to believe in the divinity of Elias Smith; nor belong to the whining congregation of midnight worshippers. — Inquire at the Repertory Office, near Boston. — *From a Boston Paper.*

The following advertisement, taken from the United States' *Gazette*, is republished not for the purpose of exposing a plagiarism, but of circulating so delicate a compliment to Mr. Jefferson, as is here conveyed by our ingenious frisseur, in picking up the identical phrases of that great philosopher and superb writer, from his various speeches, replies and messages, and adapting them to the humble purpose of an advertisement. That the reader may distinguish at once how much is borrowed from Mr. Jefferson, all that part is printed in italics. — *New York Post.*

FASHIONABLE INTELLIGENCE

John Richard Deborous Huggins, ladies hair-dresser, from New York, takes the earliest opportunity to inform the ladies of Philadelphia, that in compliance with earnest and reiterated entreaties, he has arrived at this city, and intends to make it the place of his *residence* long enough to *develope character and design;* or, in other words, he means to devote some days to the best employment of his talents in the line of his profession. *Of the various duties of a* hair dresser of eminence, *none excites more anxious concern than that of* turning his abilities to the most profitable account for himself, and most for the happiness of others.

THE SUBSCRIBER

Most respectfully acquaints his friends and the public generally, that on the 1st day of next month he intends to open an Oyster House, where he at present resides, in King-street, a few doors west of Washington-street, where gentlemen can be supplied at any time with Oysters, served up in whatever manner they may think proper to order them — and

> Where is there, by land or water,
> A nicer morcel than an Oyster.

He also intends to entertain generally, for which purpose he will at all times be supplied with liquors of a superior quality, and the best provisions the market will afford; and as it is his determination to use every effort to give satisfaction.

> He hopes the color of his face *
> Will his calling never disgrace,
> But that his conduct and attention
> Will be a means to gain him custom.

The public's most humble servant,

Alexandria, September, 28, 1805. JAMES HAMMOND.

N. B. As a new beginner, I hope gentlemen will not expect credit. My capital is very limited, notwithstanding which, it is my determination to go in debt to no person, I consequently cannot afford to credit.

> My art can lend new beauties to the face,
> And spirit give to ev'ry native grace;
> The magic of the mine 'tis I impart;
> But for my skill in the cosmetic art,
> What were the proudest dame?

The brilliant talents and acquirements of Henry J. Hassey, whose residence is at No. 128, Front-street, and whose unrivalled merits, like the blaze of a comet, throws a glory round the general prospect which renders visible the common herd of frizzeurs, are universally acknowledged; but the visibility of that herd is very evanescent; and when seen, are no more to be regarded by the side of the grand luminary, than the constellation of smaller lights, encircling the moon, when in full-orbed splendor. In the classical language of ancient Rome, Henry J. Hassey shines among the candidates for notoriety in his profession,

> Velut inter ignes Luna minores.
> With me, presumptuous miscreants, do ye vie,
> The brush and razor only doom'd to ply?
> Or, haply, to revive the rotten locks
> Of paltry caxons, mounted on your blocks.

BARBACUE.

The citizens generally of all parties both in town and country, are respectfully invited to partake of a Barbacue on Saturday next,

* The advertiser was a negro.

the 17th inst. at the spring, on Monocasy, near Stoner's White House Tavern, two miles from Frederic, on the Lancaster road. The candidates are all particularly requested to attend, as it is expected there will be a political discussion, that the people may then have an opportunity of being fully informed on public subjects, by hearing both sides face to face, in a fair and open manner.

Pennsylvania, Sept. 10, 1805.

A political discussion over the fumes of whiskey, is perfectly American.

PORTER

Deep draughts of grog makes your life shorter,
Live long and drink deep draughts of good porter.
On the charms of the hop 'tis needless to dwell,
For none but those who taste, are able to tell.

A fresh supply of Philadelphia brown stout, just come to hand, and delivering at my store, at eighteen pence per bottle. Also, a few dozen of Hibbert's London porter, may be drank at 2s. the bottle.

THOMAS DANIEL.*

Cheapside, Fredericksburg. At the Free Horse Pound.
The finest sifted meal, corn, oats, hay, and fodder, in any quantities.
Genuine Spanish segars, at 18d the quarter hundred.
Punch (for the play-house) at 1s. 6d a bottle.

The following is worthy of a conspicuous place for the *elegance* of its diction, and *correctness* of its orthography: the author, we are told, is a candidate for the incumbency of Lynhaven parish, in the county of Princess Ann, where, (as the church-wardens say) a minister of *talents* is wanting!!!

Messrs. Willet and O'conor,

Be plesed to ensert thee within and oblige

Your most humble St,

RICHARD EDWARDS.

[Yes, Mr. Edwards, we will oblige you by inserting it *verbatim et literatim.*]

* This man is the son of the late Mr. Daniel, a goldsmith, and one of the livery of the city of London; and who failed there in the business to which he succeeded his father. Notwithstanding his curious *puffs*, he also became bankrupt in Fredericksburg.

This is to give notice to all the people in this County that is frinds to the protistant Episcopal Church that I intend if I am weel wilt gods leve to read prayers and Read a small pice of archbishop Tillotsons advice a Bout religion and I should be very glad the people is friends to the Church wauld meet me at the Brick Church, 2 Sunday in August 3d Sunday at the Eastern Shore 16th august — the foth Sunday at Pungo august 23 and I weel teel you all what is Reason of so many decenters in this Country. This from your most humble Sarvent RICHARD EDWARDS.

Norfolk Herald, Virginia.

MARRIED,

In George Town, on Sunday last, by the Rev. Mr. Balch, Mr. Nicholas Hingston, botanist and merchant, of Alexandria, to Miss Elizabeth Bloomfield, sister to the celebrated author of the 'Farmer's Boy.'

Lo! I have seen a tender flower
In winter rais'd, which yet surpass'd
The child of spring: and in the bower
Amongst the sweetest might be class'd.
Thus may this couple whom love has join'd,
Tho' in the fall of life they be,
In their endearments unconfin'd,
Bring up the sweetest progeny.

This loving couple had arrived at that period of life when the procreative faculty becomes equivocal.

Elizabeth Laywell doth hereby give public notice to all whom it may concern, that she will petition the next general assembly of the state of Virginia, for a divorce from her husband, Abraham Laywell, he having, a number of years ago, left her in a destitute situation, and without support; since which he hath intermarried with another woman. And she doth hereby give the said Abraham Laywell notice, that she will proceed on the 29th day of November next, at the tavern of James Edmondson, in the town of Staunton, to take the depositions of sundry witnesses, to be read in support of said petition, when and where he may attend to cross-examine such witnesses, if he thinks proper.*

* Divorces through this medium are readily obtained in many parts of the United States.

Augusta County, Oct. 4, 1800.

CHAPTER XXVIII

SOUTH CAROLINA — VALUE OF PLANTATIONS — HOUSES OF THE PLANTERS — SLAVES — THEIR TREATMENT — PLAN FOR IMPROVING THEIR CONDITION — SLAVE-TRADE — DANGERS TO BE APPREHENDED FROM ITS PROSECUTION — INTENDED INSURRECTIONS OF THE SLAVES — INFLUENCE OF SLAVERY ON THE POLITICAL REPRESENTATION OF THE STATES — PROPENSITY OF THE INHABITANTS OF CAROLINA TO DUELLING — GOLD-MINES DISCOVERED IN NORTH CAROLINA — GOLD COMPANY — CULTIVATION OF COTTON — INDIGO.

THE state of South Carolina produces abundance of rice, tobacco, cotton, and indigo, for exportation; and contains more slaves, for the number of square miles, than any other part of the United States. It is, indeed, the only one which admits the horrid traffic,[1] and thousands of these miserable people are dispersed over the adjoining states, through the port of Charleston, where there is a greater slave-market than, perhaps, was ever known at one place in the West India islands.

The richest planters in the United States are to be found in South Carolina, some drawing a yearly revenue from the labor of their slaves to the amount of forty or fifty thousand dollars, and many enjoy an income of from twelve to twenty thousand from the same source. A planter in moderate circumstances is in the receipt of from three to six thousand; while others, so capricious is fortune, drag on a miserable existence with large families, on the wretched pittance of eighty or one hundred dollars a year.

The best lands are the tide-swamps, where cotton and rice are grown, and which, in high cultivation, have sold as high as one hundred and seventy dollars per acre; — an enormous price, when it is remembered that land, capable of producing corn, may be had, and in good situations, too, from five to fifteen dollars — while uncleared land, that is, land in its original state, inhabited by the beasts of the forest alone, is selling at one third of the last-mentioned price. The value, in short, rises as the land is cleared, while in England we estimate our estates in proportion to the quantity of timber upon them. In general, the tide-swamps command from seventy to one hundred — inland swamps twenty to fifty — while such as bear corn, sweet potatoes, &c., fetch from six to forty dollars, and high uncleared land from one to six dollars per acre, in South Carolina.

The buildings on the plantations are in proportion to the value of the latter — from the cost of thirty thousand dollars, to a miserable loghouse. The best houses consist generally, of not more than a ground-floor, with bed-chambers above; and many of them of a ground-floor only; but in this case, they cover a considerable space. At the southfront it is an invariable rule to attach a piazza, which impedes the extreme heat of the sun from penetrating into the sitting and lodging-rooms; and in the evening it affords an agreeable walk. The kitchens and out-offices are always at the distance of several yards from the principal dwelling. This is done as well to guard against the house-negroes through carelessness setting the houses on fire, for they generally sit over it half the night, as to keep out their noise. Negroes are great and loud talkers; and in this warm climate, having wood for the trouble of fetching it, they often sit up, after their work is done, over a large fire, in the summer, when I could scarcely endure the excessive heat of the night in the open air.

The masters here, as in the other southern states, regard their slaves, as English farmers do their live stock. The men are valued, like horses, for their superior properties — the females, for their fecundity. The infant slave is generally valued at a year's service of the mother and as she is compelled to work, three parts of the time she is breeding and nursing, planters are very attentive to this mode of enhancing the value of their estates.

The swamps and low lands are so unhealthy, that they cannot be cultivated by white persons. Here, however, the negro is compelled to work, uncovered, through the sun's meridian heat, and labor till evening, often up to his waist in water, for these lands are generally overflowed with stagnant pools; while his pampered master can barely support himself in the shade in such a relaxing atmosphere. If he be employed in the rice-grounds, he must toil all day long in soft mud, ditching and draining the ground; while to a white person such an occupation would, in a few days, prove certain death. The punishments they often undergo are inflicted with savage ferocity, and frequently at the caprice of a cruel overseer. What else can be expected from the natural brutality of man, in a country where the murder of a slave is only punished by a fine of fifty pounds, and if wilfully perpetrated, or, as the law terms it, "with malice aforethought," then the fine is only doubled — but, in fact, the bloody deed, when committed, is seldom looked into.

Though I execrate the treatment of this unfortunate race of human beings, yet, as they have been brought into the country, I would not advocate an unqualified emancipation; for such a step would be attended with fatal consequences. The cultivation of the staple commodities of the country would, in all probability, not only be neglected, but the galling injuries inflicted on them by white men since they were stolen or forced away from their native country, might stimulate them to break entirely the bonds once loosened, and deal destruction upon the heads of their oppressors. Yet I would have their condition ameliorated by law — their food and clothing should be nourishing and comfortable — and as our soldiers and sailors live well, and conquer the enemies of their country on the rations and cloathing provided for them by government — so might these unhappy people, by a similar mode, and the same quantity and quality of food and raiment, be rendered fit, in bodily strength to undergo the hard tasks imposed upon them. I deprecate the end of this slave-trade, which continues to be followed with an eagerness which the thirst for gold ever stimulates: no matter through what unworthy means it may be obtained. All the other states have prohibited the admission of fresh slaves, while South Carolina alone, regardless of the stigma, continues the importation with double exertion. The following advertisements, which appeared *the same day*, and in the order they are placed, in one of the Charleston newspapers, will shew to what a disgraceful height the *slave-trade* has arrived in *a land of liberty:*[2]

☞ The sale of the ship Margaret's cargo of 250 prime Congo slaves, will commence on board the said ship, at Geyer's South Wharf this day, the 9th inst. and will be continued every day (Sundays excepted) until the whole are sold.

GIBSON AND BROADFOOT.

Sept. 9, 1805.

CONGO SLAVES.

☞ The sale of the ship Ariel's cargo of 260 very prime Congo slaves, is continued on board said vessel, at Vanderhost's wharf.

WILLIAM BOYD.

August 14.

CONGO SLAVES.

☞ The sale of the ship Esther's cargo of 370 very prime Congo slaves, is continued on board said ship, at Vanderhost's wharf.

WILLIAM BOYD.

Thus these three cargoes make together 880 fellow- creatures on sale, like beasts in a pen on a fair-day, in the small city of Charleston!!! This slave market is open every day in the year, except Sundays, as Messrs. Gibson and Broadfoot piously observe by public auction, private contract, or by way of barter. A horse for a man, or a man for a horse, is a common exchange; and thus these miserable objects are driven about from owner to owner, at the caprice of their fellow-men. Nay, they even become the stake of the gamester, who, with unconcern, attaches their fate to the cast of a die, or the turn of a card.

It was the eager and boundless prosecution of the African trade, which, in St. Domingo, filled with negroes every situation which ought to have been occupied by men of the same complexion as the planter — that stationed a conspirator wherever an ally ought to have been found — that crowded with enemies every avenue through which succour could arrive in time of alarm and danger. It was in St. Domingo that the standard of revolt was first reared;[3] that it waved over the most flourishing colony, and gave the signal to her mass of blacks to attack and butcher the whites. They instantly set at nought her twenty thousand militia; bade defiance to her regular forces, and the shipping in her harbours; ravaged her fruitful fields, demolished her commercial towns, and left her inhabitants weltering in their blood. Such were the dire effects of the African trade on St. Domingo; and in the Leeward Islands it menaces the same horrors; nor are the southern states of America free from the apprehension that it will one day overwhelm them. For it is this trade, with its dangerous facility of procuring slaves, and the treacherous submission of their demeanour, that has multiplied the lurking assassins, till they swarm wherever the planter turns his eyes. It is this trade that has excluded from his employment, and driven from his society his white brethren; it is this trade which has cut him off from succour and from hope, when destruction is at hand, when death stares him in the face, and remorse of mind, worse even than death itself, haunts him the short remnant of his life.

When we contemplate the cruel treatment which the wretched negroes so often receive, it cannot be matter of astonishment that they should pant for an opportunity of regaining that liberty, of which they have, in general, been unjustly deprived. A white man — a monster in human shape — a few months ago, at Charleston, compelled one of his negroes to cut off the head of another, while the master *superintended* the horrid deed! He was tried for the offence, and convicted. The judge, in a speech which did honor to him as a man, lamented the inefficacy of the law with respect to the punishments apportioned to such a crime. The murderer was fined, and then liberated.* The commission of such a deed is alone sufficient to stimulate the whole of the color of the sufferer, to revenge. The seeds of revolt were sown with information of the massacre in St. Domingo, and their growth needs not such dreadful acts of barbarity to quicken it. Seven years ago, a dangerous insurrection was planned by the negroes in Virginia,[4] which would have certainly deluged the capital of the state with the blood of the white inhabitants, had they not been betrayed by one of their own people just time enough for the governor, Mr. Munro,[5] the present ambassador in London, to muster the military, who took the insurgents by surprize, on the very eve of the intended attack. The leaders of this dangerous revolt were hanged, as well as a mulatto, at Norfolk, convicted of conspiring to set fire to that town and harbor.† Yet even these dreadful lessons are not sufficiently impressive to teach Americans the danger of continuing this abominable traffic.

In this boasted land of freedom there are, according to calculation, nearly one million slaves for life; besides some

* This transaction, with the charge of the judge, was given in the London papers in the month of September last.

† Still more recent is the contemplated insurrection of these people at Savannah, in Georgia. *The True American*, a daily paper, printed at Philadelphia, says, "that on the 14th and 15th of October last, an insurrection was apprehended at Savannah, in Georgia, among the negroes. Several meetings had taken place among them, and an attack upon the town was determined on. They had appointed generals and other officers. According to their plans they were to make three distinct landings; namely, one at Wayne's wharf — one at the Coffee-house wharf — and one at the fort. They were then to set fire to the town, and massacre the whites. But a difference existed between two of their leaders, and one of them divulged the secret; in consequence of which, the different companies of volunteers were stationed under the Bluff, and the militia at Spring Hill, where twelve of the leaders were taken prisoners." The negroes are in proportion to the whites as eight to one in the town of Savannah.

thousand European emigrants, sold for a certain term of years, to defray the expense of bringing them across the Atlantic. After what has been already said on this subject, the reader will be yet more surprised when he learns that this unfortunate race of men are actually represented in congress, being enumerated with the white men in a certain ratio. Thus Virginia, with 40,160 *free* people *less* than Massachusetts, sends five representatives, and five electors for a president and a vice-president, *more* than Massachusetts; and this great influence arises from the *enumeration of the slaves* in Virginia, while Massachusetts admits *no kind of slavery.*

The states which contain nine tenths of the slaves in the United States are, Georgia, South Carolina, North Carolina, Virginia, Kentucky, and Maryland. Of late years, Georgia has *doubled* her number of slaves; South Carolina has increased in the ratio of 146 to 107; North Carolina, in that of 133 to 100; Kentucky, in that of 40 to 12. Maryland has increased but in a smaller proportion, being the farthest from Charleston, where the nefarious traffic is exclusively carried on. In the New England states, slavery is nearly abolished. In Pennsylvania and Delaware the number of slaves has decreased; and in New York it is nearly stationary.

"The day is not far off," says an American writer, "when the southern and western states will have more representatives in congress, and electors for president and vice-president, for slaves only, than the northern for all their free people." This is another reason for the opinion I gave in the former part of this work, that the time was fast approaching, which will sap the foundation of the present government of the United States, and sever New England from the Federal Compact.

While such is the condition of slaves in South Carolina, their owners in some cases entertain such high and strict notions of what they call *honor,* and *a good name,* that duels frequently take place among them. In one of these rencounters fell the son of a departed friend of mine, and what rendered the circumstance more afflicting was, that his conduct to his antagonist was of such a nature as to preclude commiseration for his death. The story may prove a lesson worthy of remembrance.

Mr. Rutledge,[6] a gentleman of South Carolina, of considerable property, and a member of Congress, left his house, with his wife and childen, on the approach of the hot months, to enjoy the salubrious air of Rhode Island. At Newport he became acquainted with the son of my respected friend, the late Doctor Senter. This young man succeeded to his father's business, and had commenced the practice of physic. Mr. Rutledge having staid at Newport as long as he had intended, returned to his home, without any suspicion to the prejudice of his new acquaintance. Soon after their departure, the young doctor likewise made his appearance in South Carolina. Without entering into the cause of this step on the part of the latter, and unwilling to wound the feelings of the survivor, suffice it to say, that the Rhode Islander was so near being detected by his injured friend, in a clandestine visit to his wife, as to owe his safety to immediate flight. Mr. Rutledge pursued, and overtook him at or near Charleston, where they fought. The guilty man fell, being badly wounded in the thigh, and he died under amputation. This unfortunate event should not have found its way into these pages, had it not already passed the comments of American editors.

Another memorable duel took place at Charleston during my residence in America, between two "stage-struck heroes;" the subject — all subduing love! The theatrical duellists were Placide,[7] the manager of the Charleston company, who formerly was a tight-rope dancer at Sadler's Wells, and one of his troop, named Douvillier, a ballet-dancer. The manager kept a lady, of whom the performer was also enamoured; on which the "green-eyed monster" took possession of the breast of Placide, who, however, was uncertain as to the actual commission of the injury he suspected. At length, caution was lulled into security, as it is in all such cases, sooner or later, and the commander had demonstration of his being *brutified.* A challenge was given by the aggrieved party, and being both expert swordsmen, in fact, acting occasionally as fencing masters, it was determined by Placide to wipe away his disgrace by the sword. A place was appointed, and the next day, *at noon,* fixed for the combat. Before the time arrived, half of Charleston were apprised of the circumstance; and the combatants went to the ground, attended by multitudes to witness the event. The attack was begun by Placide, who furiously rushed upon his antagonist, determined to put him to death in an instant. I learnt from those who were present, that the science displayed by Douvillier in defending himself from this imminent danger, added to his coolness and activity, interested the spectators for the moment, though he was known to be the offender. Having parried the deadly thrusts, and sustained the shock of the onset, he maintained his ground, and the science of fencing was, in good earnest, displayed for some minutes, without intermission, till Placide was disarmed. He affected now to smother the disappointment of revenge, and to hide his chagrin, until suddenly springing upon his antagonist, he recovered his sword, and before the other could put himself on his guard, he was run through the body. There was said to be something of foul play in this; however, Placide returned to his lodgings in triumph, and immediately turned the frail fair one into the street, from whence she proceeded to her vanquished lover, whose wound she dressed, and who recovered to live many years with her for whom he had fought. Shortly after this, Placide married one of the daughters of the late Mrs. Wrighten, of Drury-lane, who were then performing in Charleston. By this lady he has children, and is yet manager of that theatre.

Independent of the valuable vegetable productions of North and South Carolina, it has recently been discovered that some parts of the former state are no less rich in the most precious of metallic substances. In the year 1804 a bed of gold ore was discovered in North Carolina,[8] in a creek running through the land of Mr. John Read, a native of Hesse Cassel, in Germany, which promises to prove a source of great wealth to the proprietor. Some of it was coined at the mint of the United States in Philadelphia, a few months after the discovery, to the amount of eleven thousand dollars, and a much larger quantity has been found. It appears that the children of Mr. Read, having been fishing in the creek, were attracted by the shining metal, and brought home several pieces as a curiosity, totally ignorant of their real value. On being tried, the ore was found to contain gold of a very pure quality. Since this discovery, these little boys have picked up daily from one hundred to one hundred and twenty pennyweights; but Mr. Read himself found a lump of the ore weighing twenty-eight pounds, which it was supposed, when fluxed, would be worth fourteen hundred pounds British money. At the mint it was regretted that the gold had been melted into very small ingots, for the convenience of carriage, it being many hundred miles from Cabarrus to Philadelphia. Thus, a considerable portion of it was wasted. The finest particles yet remained, the large lumps alone being sought after.

In consequence of these promising appearances, a company has been formed for the purpose of exploring the lands supposed to possess the largest portion of these natural treasures. It is entitled the North Carolina Gold Company, and has purchased 35,000 acres for 110,000 dollars. An agent, Mr. W. Thornton, was sent last summer by the company to visit these lands, and, from the success of his experiments, he reports very favorably of the probable productiveness of the speculation. From his account the following particulars were extracted: —

The season of 1806 was one of the most unfavourable that could have been selected for examining the runs of gold, as they were all dry, so that it was necessary to carry the sand and gravel sometimes above a mile before water could be found. Some fine specimens were thus obtained, one of about two penny-weights, and some smaller; but after obtaining about twenty dollars' worth, the want of water to wash for more obliged him to desist. While thus engaged in the lands adjoining to the mine of Mr. Read, one of the proprietors of that concern observed, that he thought the prospect of the company as good as their own. Mr. Read and his partners possess about 400 acres, and they are said to have obtained already, from this small place, between 30 and 40,000 dollars' worth of gold. That found on the company's land requires no purification.

Mr. Thornton visited Mr. Read's mine, and found that by amalgamation with quicksilver a great quantity of gold is obtained from the sand, after picking out all the lump gold. He was informed that they obtained about six or seven ounces at a distillation, several times a week, from a very small still. He afterwards visited the mines of Mrs. Parker and Mr. Harris. They lie in a hill that intersects the company's land. Mr. Harris, in ploughing across a small branch in his land, turned up a good-sized piece of gold. Having no regular weights, he tried it in a pair of scales against a pewter plate and spoon, which it outweighed. He then searched the run, and was successful in finding gold. This little branch runs immediately into the company's land, lying between it and Mrs. Parker's. But as it was dry, Mr. Thornton made no search in it, nor in any of the branches on that side, though he was informed that gold had been found in several.

Mrs. Parker's mine was discovered in a very unexpected manner. Hearing of several discoveries, she said in a joking manner to some company, while drinking tea with her, "I wish, gentlemen, any of you could find a gold-mine in my land," — on which one of the company replied, "I will go, madam, and search for you." He went, and in a little time returned with a very good specimen. After this, they found six hundred dollars' worth, and in the season of 1806 three hundred more, though they had not yet prepared any apparatus for even washing the gravel and sand.

From this examination, Mr. Thornton judges that some of the hills are rich in gold. He is of opinion that it is not carried far by the currents, but only falls down into the small hollows and little branches, as it has been met with in considerable quantities in the smallest depressions on the hills, as well as in the deeper runs and branches. From the number of these runs, branches, springs, and depressions, in which gold has been found in the premises of the company, he is confident that it may be computed to possess 160 miles of gold land.

There are three sorts of cotton raised in the Carolinas, viz. *Nankeen*, *green-seed*, and *black-seed* cotton.

Nankeen cotton is principally grown in the middle and upper country, for family use. It is so called from the wool resembling the colour of Nankeen cloth, which it retains as long as it is worn. It is not in much demand, the white cotton having engrossed the public attention. Were it encouraged, however, cloths might be manufactured from it perhaps not inferior to those imported from the East Indies, the cotton being probably of the same kind; as, from experiments which have been made, nankeens have been manufactured in South Carolina, of good colour, and of very strong texture.

Green-seed cotton produces a good white wool, adhering much to the seed, and of course it is difficult to be ginned. Its produce is greater, and its maturity is more early, than the black seed, for which reason it is principally cultivated in the middle and upper country, as the favorable seasons of those districts are shorter by several weeks than those of the lower country, and the frosts are more severe.

Black-seed cotton is that which is grown in the lower country, and on the sea-islands, producing a fine white cotton of silky appearance, very strong, and of good staple. The mode of culture is the same with all these species, and rich high land is the soil on which they are generally planted. In the middle country, however, the *high swamp* lands produce the green seed in great abundance; and some tide lands and salt-water marshes, after being reclaimed, in the lower country, have also made excellent crops of this valuable article.

This plant is raised from the seed, and is managed in nearly the following manner—About the latter end of March, or the beginning of April, commences the season for planting cotton. In strong soils the land is broken up with ploughs, and the cotton is sown in drills, about five feet from each other, and at the rate of nearly a bushel of seed to the acre; after which, when the plant is a few leaves high, the mould is thrown up in a ridge to it on each side by the plough, with a mould-board adapted to that purpose; or, in the first instance, beds are made rather low and flat, and the cotton is sown in them. By some it is sown in holes at about ten inches distance; but the more general practice is to sow the seed in a drill, along the length of the bed, after which it may be thinned at leisure, according to its growth. In rich high-land soils, not more than fifteen of these beds are made in a quarter of an acre; but in inferior lands, twenty-one beds are made in the same space of ground. When the plants are about four or six inches high they require a thinning, at which time only very few plants are left at each distance where the cotton is intended to grow; and from time to time those plants are again thinned, till two, and sometimes one only is left at each distance, which is from eighteen inches to two feet, and the rows three or four feet apart. At the time of thinning also the first hoeing is generally given, which is repeated every two or three weeks. With some planters, the practice of topping the main stalk has been used, when the plants are too luxuriant; but as it throws out in this case an abundance of suckers, and thus increases the toil of the negroes to pull them away, the custom has been discontinued. Towards the middle of September, however, it may be advantageous to top the plant to the lowest blossoms, as from that time no blossoms will produce cotton. By this treatment also the sun has a greater influence on the plant, the pods open sooner, and its strength is not unnecessarily drawn from those pods which are likely to come to maturity.

Towards the middle of June, the plants begin to put forth their beautiful blossoms, and continue in flower and forming pods till the frosts set in; at which time all the pods that are not well grown are destroyed. Early in August the harvest of cotton begins on the Sea Islands, and in September it is general throughout the state, continuing till December. The cotton-wool is contained in the pod in three or four different compartments, which bursting when ripe, presents the cotton full blown to the sight, surrounding its seeds. It is then picked, and carried to the cotton-house, and thence taken out in a very few days, and spread upon a platform to dry, after which it is soon ready for ginning.

For this purpose, various kinds of *gins* are used for extricating this valuable staple-commodity from its seed. The most common gin, because of the simplest mechanism, is called the *foot-gun.* It is worked with cranks, by a foot-board, almost resembling a turner's lathe. It is composed of two small rollers, about three-fourths of an inch in diameter, which, by pullies, are made to pull contrary ways. At each of these gins is placed a negro, who applies seed-cotton, as it is called before ginning, to the rollers, which, by their motion, draw the cotton from the seed. It then falls into a bag, and the seed is discharged on the ground. Thus, a negro will gin from twenty to twenty-five pounds per day, amounting to above a thousand weight during the cotton-harvest.

Private families gin their cotton by the hand, which is called *picking*, and this work is set apart for the evening. The whole family of a small planter sit round the fire in a winter's evening, without any other light than what proceeds occasionally from a pitch-pine knot over their task of picking; and this is practised among the better class of country-people. Sometimes they invite their acquaintance to what they call "a picking frolic," at which, after the visitors have duly performed their task, they are regaled with a supper, and the evening concludes with a reel or country dance.

After the cotton is ginned, a number of hands are employed in picking from it any dirt or pieces of broken seed; it is then packed up in bags containing 250 or 300 lbs. and thus made ready for market. As the carefulness of its preparation is the principal object with manufacturers, it is well worth the planters, while to pay attention to have it gathered clean from the field, and if possible, to have every speck of dirt or even stained parts, which may remain after it has passed through the gin, picked out. Cotton, thus prepared, will assuredly command a ready sale and a good price, as, in the extensive spinning machines in the United Kingdom, the smallest particle of trash, or fragment of the seed, breaks the thread, and interrupts the progress of the manufacture.

Indigo is produced from a plant indigenous in America, and is made in large quantities, though of an inferior quality, in South Carolina. A botanical author says, that indigo is a precipitated fecula, dried and reduced into a solid mass, light, brittle, and of a deep azure colour. This substance is of great utility in the arts. Great use is made of it in dying, painting, bleaching, and other processes of different manufactures.

The vegetable which produces this colouring fecula, is termed the indigo plant, *indigofera*. It is a polypetal plant, of the family of the leguminous, and has much resemblance to the *galegas*.

There are twenty-seven species of the indigo: the best is termed *indigo franc, indigofera anil*. In the islands of the Antilles, is found a variety of the best species of indigo, which grows to twice the height of the indigo franc. It is termed the wild indigo plant, or maron, and is mixed with the indigo franc, in order to obtain a more considerable and better produce.

Though indigo has been manufactured for nearly a century, its preparation is still so imperfect, that, even with the best manufacturer, generally ten, fifteen, and even twenty-five tubs, fail out of a hundred which he undertakes. Sometimes, inexperience, or the contrarieties of temperature, cause the failure of a much larger number of the tubs, and thus entail ruin on the proprietor who reckons on large profits: — hence, in part, arises the high price of indigo.

In order to obtain this colouring substance, the indigo plant is cut when it has arrived at maturity. The whole is put to macerate in a bason of brickwork, which is termed the tub. To complete the maceration, requires from fifteen to thirty, and even to thirty-six hours, according to the temperature of the atmosphere; it is also necessary to consider the quality of the plant, the nature of the soil, and of the water in which it is immersed.

The first indication that the maceration begins to approach its ultimate point, is the sinking of the scum, that rises in the space of about half a foot, which has been left empty in the tub. When this scum has become a kind of crust of a copper blue colour, the plants will soon be sufficiently macerated. However, this indication is insufficient, and often even fallacious. A certain method of ascertaining this is, by accurately observing the water poured into a silver cup. Five or six minutes after it has been poured into the cup, it forms round the sides a ring, or hedge of fecula, which is at first of a greenish colour, and afterwards becomes blue. As long as the maceration is imperfect, this ring detaches itself with difficulty from the sides of the cup. But, at last, it is seen to precipitate and concentrate itself at the bottom of the vessel, always touching the centre under the water, which has become limpid, with a yellowish tinge.

These appearances indicate the success of the first operation. The water is then drawn off into a second tub, placed beneath the first. Its use is for heating the water still charged with the fecula. In order that it may separate quickly, it is agitated. This operation is performed by the hands, or in the largest tub by a mill. It is of consequence not to agitate it too long: excessive agitation mixes anew the fecula with the water, from which it does not separate any more, and the tub fails. Instead of indigo, nothing is produced but muddy water.

This latter inconvenience may easily be obviated by a little attention. When it is discovered that the fecula is sufficiently united, the water should be drawn off into a third and smaller tub. The bottom of the *batterie* is then covered with a liquid blue paste, which is received into bags of coarse linen cloth, in the form of inverted cones, which suffer the watery part to run off. These bags are afterwards emptied upon tables in the drying rooms, where the blue paste is kneaded; and after it has acquired a denser consistence, it is spread out and cut into small square cakes, that it may dry the sooner. The manufacture of the indigo is now completed, and it is soon sufficiently dry to be introduced into commerce.

NOTES — CHAPTER XXVIII

1. In 1803 South Carolina repealed the law which had prohibited the slave traffic and became the only State to legalize it at that time. See W. E. D. DuBois, *The Suppression of the African Slave Trade to the United States of America, 1638-1870*. New York, 1896.

2. So many pages have already been consumed in discussions of the various phases of the slavery question that it seems unnecessary to make any further comments here. It suffices to say that these advertisements are representative of those current in the period during which Janson lived in America.

3. Janson evidently refers to the revolt which broke out in 1791. See Sir James Bashett, *History of the Island of St. Domingo*. London, 1818.

4. A negro insurrection occurred at Richmond in 1800. A thousand or more slaves armed themselves with guns, knives, scythes, and other weapons. They appointed a night in August as the time for the massacre. After gathering at different places, they expected to unite outside the city. A violent storm came up, and for hours rain fell in torrents. Streams overflowed, and the roads became impassable. According to accounts, a young negro, awed by the storm, repented, swam a creek, and warned his master of the plot.

5. James Monroe, governor of Virginia from 1799 to 1802 and minister to England from 1803 to 1805.

6. John Rutledge, Jr., a Federalist, served as Representative from South Carolina from 1797 to 1803. He fought a duel with Dr. Horace Senter of Newport, Rhode Island, in January, 1804. Dr. Senter died at Savannah, Georgia, on January 19. Contemporary accounts of the duel and its circumstances may be found in the *Newport Mercury*, February 11 and 18, 1804.

7. Alexander Placide married Caroline Wrighten in August, 1796. According to rumor, Mrs. Pownall, mother of Caroline, grieved herself to death because of her daughter's elopement with a man whom she had thought already married. The Placides were the parents of the famous actors, Henry, Thomas, Caroline (Mrs. Blake), and Jane Placide.

8. John H. Wheeler in his *Historical Sketches of North Carolina*, Philadelphia, 1850, pp. 63-64, gives "a Sketch of the discovery and history of the Reed Gold Mine, in Cabarrus County, North Carolina, being the first gold mine discovered in the United States," Statement by George Barnhardt, January, 1848. This statement recounts the story of the discovery and of Reed's learning that the nugget found by his son was gold. A company which developed the mine was formed.

CHAPTER XXIX

TREATMENT OF SLAVES — BARBARITIES EXERCISED ON THEM — PUNISHMENT INFLICTED ON A NEGRO FOR A RAPE — SINGULAR MODE OF CURE ADOPTED WITH ANOTHER — THE DYING NEGRO — OBSERVATIONS ON SLAVERY, BY JEFFERSON AND DR. MORSE.

HAVING shewn the great benefits which slave-owners derive from the labour of this miserable race of their fellow-creatures, we naturally turn our thoughts to the treatment they receive to enable them to undergo the drudgery of the field. When we see men toiling in rice and indigo grounds, which are generally overflowed with stagnant water; enduring the scorching rays of the sun, in raising tobacco, and different kinds of grain, to supply luxuries for their master's tables, we should naturally conclude that their food is of the best quality, and their raiment adapted to their respective employments. I wish any thing could be advanced to palliate the hardship of their lot — but on this subject we only find the horrors of slavery too often aggravated by the neglect of the owner, and the savage ferocity of an overseer.

An opportunity once offered, which gave me full demonstration of the treatment of negroes in North Carolina. — I had hired a small sailing boat to convey me from the island of Mattamuskeet, on Pamlico Sound; the wind proving adverse, with the appearance of an approaching summer squall, the boatman proposed to make a harbour in a small creek which he observed led to a new negro quarter belonging to Mr. Blount,[1]* of Newburn; adding, that as he was acquainted with the overseer, I might there find shelter till the weather proved favorable. This I gladly agreed to, as these summer gusts, which they call "white squalls," are

* This man is, at this time, a member of the House of Representatives in Congress for the district of Newburn, in North Carolina.

often so sudden as to upset a vessel before the sail can be handed. From the head of the creek a canal had been cut to the quarter, and from thence it was intended to communicate with the Great Alligator river, for the purpose of transporting lumber, with which the country abounds, to a sea-port. For this purpose, Mr. Blount had placed there a gang of about sixty negroes, whose daily work was in water, often up to the middle, and constantly knee-deep. The overseer was a man of some information, and he gave us a hearty welcome to his log-house, which was a few hundred yards from the huts of the slaves. He said, that no human foot had trod upon the spot till his arrival with the negroes, who had penetrated about a mile into the forest with the canal, through the haunts of wild beasts. There was an unusual number of children in proportion to the working slaves; and on my noticing this circumstance, the overseer replied, that but few of them belonged to the gang, being sent thither 'to be raised in safety.' From the situation of the place, there was no chance of their escaping; and being fed at a very small expence, and suffered to run wild and entirely naked, he observed, that their encreased value, when the canal was finished, would nearly defray the expence attending it. An infant slave, when born, is computed to be worth thirty or forty dollars; of course, every year increases his value, and a stout 'field fellow,' is worth three or four hundred dollars; a 'field wench' a fourth part less.[2] He had already been two years in this desolate place, and calculated upon remaining three more before the canal would be finished.

The day of our arrival happened to be on Saturday, when the week's allowance is given out. This consisted of *salt herrings*, of an inferior quality, and a peck of *Indian corn in the cob*, to each, the grinding of which occupied the remainder of the day. Such was the daily food, without variation, of these wretched people, and even of this, the allowance was extremely scanty. No such luxury as salt pork, or beef, had they been indulged with for many months; and Mr. Overseer, with perfect indifference, observed, that he did not expect any fresh supply for some time after what was brought them should be consumed. A few barrels were at first allowed, by way of reconciling them to the place; and so accustomed were they to drag on this miserable existence, that I observed no repining, each receiving his pittance without a murmur. The overseer, however, took special care of himself. His residence was surrounded with turkies and fowls, and his cupboard was supplied with excellent bacon. These provisions were set before us, together with a bottle of brandy. During our repast, we were attended by a stout negro boy, entirely naked, whom the overseer had selected to be about his person. The poor fellow's attention was so riveted on the victuals, that he blundered over his employment in a manner that extorted a threat of punishment from his master, who would not attribute his momentary absence of mind to the cause from which it sprung. As soon as an opportunity offered after dinner, I cut off, unobserved, a piece of bacon, and gave it to the boy, who snatched at it in an extacy, and instantly ran off to the negro huts. On his return, I questioned him what he had done with it, when the grateful and affectionate creature replied, that he had given the morsel to his poor mother, who was sick, and could not eat her herrings. Hear this, ye pampered slaveholders! contemplate the virtues of this boy; and while you teach your own off-spring to follow his example, treat his unfortunate race as human beings!

The day proving boisterous, we remained all night with the overseer. He described, with much apparent satisfaction, the means he employed to keep *his gang* under subjection, and the different modes of punishment which from time to time he inflicted on them. Some months ago, it appeared, that he missed some of his fowls; and being convinced they had been stolen by the slaves, he ordered them all into his presence, charged them with the robbery, and ordered them to point out the perpetrator. This not producing the desired effect, he threatened to flog them all, observing, that by so doing he should get hold of the thief without confession; and he actually put this threat into instant execution. The job, he continued, occupied the whole day, as he took his leisure, that it might be complete, and serve as a warning in future. Thus suffered the whole of those innocent miserable people, by way of punishing one, who might have been guilty.

The first week in the year, in this land of slavery, is a kind of fair for the disposal of negroes, some for life, and others for a limited time, by public auction, the sheriff of the county generally acting as auctioneer.

Here is often exhibited a spectacle which would soften the most obdurate heart, that had never participated in the horrid traffic. At these times slave-dealers attend from a distant part of the country, making a trade of their fellow-men. Husbands for ever separated from their wives; mothers torn from their children; brothers and sisters exchanging a last embrace, are subjects of mirth to the surrounding crowd of bidders. Indulgent nature equally formed this sable group; yet, it would seem, that while the exterior of the Ethiopian is tinged with the darkest hue, the heart of the white man is rendered callous to all the finer feelings, which are said to give him rank above the other creatures of the Almighty. Often have I witnessed negroes dragged, without regard to age or sex, to the public whipping-post, or tied up to the limb of a tree, at the will of the owner, and flogged with a cow-skin,* without pity or remorse, till the ground beneath is dyed with the blood of the miserable sufferer. These punishments are often inflicted for an unguarded expression of the slave, while groaning under an oppressive task — for neglecting to do homage as his master passes by — and too often to indulge private resentment or caprice. Sometimes they are fastened on a barrel, the hands and feet nearly meet-

* This instrument of punishment is made of the skin of an ox or cow, twisted hard when wet, and tapering off like a riding whip; it is hard and elastic, inflicting dreadful wounds when used with severity.

ing round it, are tied together; thus the breech is presented, and in this position they endure their torments. Shocking cruelties of this nature have been practised, even in the more enlightened state of New York.

An account of some of these barbarities appeared in New York newspapers, so late as the year 1805. They related the circumstance of a female slave, the property of a fellow at Brocklyne, on Long Island, coming to a house in Pearl street, New York, to beg for food. She was observed to exhibit symptoms of much pain, and to have something concealed under a handkerchief, which she held to the side of her head. On an examination of the circumstance, it was found that, amongst other diabolical modes of punishment and torture, her owner had gratified his brutality by hacking off a part of one of her ears, and cutting a gash in the other, through which he suspended a large iron padlock. In this situation the unfortunate girl was left, and thus she had crossed the ferry; and wandered through the streets of New York, begging a morsel of bread.

A man of the name of C. A. Hoffman, was thrice arraigned at the bar of justice, in New York, for abusing a child who unhappily was his slave. The facts proved against him exhibited horrid scenes of more dreadful cruelties, than perhaps ever disgraced human nature. Though I learnt upon the spot every particular of this savage treatment, yet I shall here repeat only as much as was published on the monster's conviction.

A witness proved that Hoffman tied the hands of the child together, drew them up above his head with a rope attached to the wall, and fastened his feet by another rope to a staple in the floor. He then stripped the boy, and applied a horsewhip with such violence, that the first blow drew forth a quantity of blood. The strokes were followed up with the same violence to the number of one hundred and forty, when the rope broke, and the sufferer fell to the floor. Not having yet glutted his fury, he gave forty more while the victim lay prostrate at his feet. So great was the quantity of blood which issued from the mangled body, that a woman was called in to mop it up. To encrease the poor creature's torture, he applied a mixture of salt and brandy to the wounds.

A second witness testified, that having on an another occasion beaten the child in a most barbarous manner, he forced down his throat two table-spoonfuls of salt, in order to excite thirst, and then confined him in a small, uncomfortable, dreary apartment, without food or drink, during forty-eight hours.

By way of punishment, this monster was fined two hundred and fifty dollars, and put under a recognizance of two thousand dollars to treat the boy with more humanity. What aggravated these cruelties was, that the child was of years too tender to have given cause for them, nor was he conscious of having committed any fault deserving of punishment. Notwithstanding these penalties, and in open violation of the security given, Hoffman continued his cruelties, till the grand jury again found a bill of indictment against him; but he chose to manumit the boy, rather than stand another trial, and thus the case was dismissed.

An American editor, in commenting on this foul business, says: "The reiterated occurrence of such barbarous transactions demands legislative interference. Unless the strong arm of government interpose, the evil will not be corrected. Sympathy may weep, and pity supplicate for mercy — but vain will be the attempt to awaken the seared conscience to a sense of justice. As easily could you rouse the feelings of humanity within the cold and obdurate marble. Such unfeeling wretches, possessing power and forgetting right, will still indulge their savage resentment — will torture and mangle a fellow-creature, because, forsooth, they find him guilty of having a skin not colored like their own. That such beings should be found amongst civilized men, is a fact deeply to be lamented — and that they are to be found in this region is a truth humiliating to the feelings."

In the district of Chowan, in North Carolina, a negro man slave, in the absence of his master and mistress, knocked at their door, and demanded admission. The parents having gone on a visit to their friends a few miles distant, had left their daughter at home, who having before received improper conversation from the fellow, and fearing to inform her father, apprehensive of the dreadul punishment he would inflict on him for his presumption, refused to open it. The negro persisted, and finally broke it open, seized the terrified female, and satiated his lust. He immediately fled to the woods, and the object of his brutality, exhausted with resistance, lay helpless till the return of her parents. The distracted father fled to his neighbors, and related the horrid circumstance. The inhabitants quickly mustered, and went in pursuit of the villain, with burning light-wood, the knots of the spruce pine-tree. He was after a long search, discovered. The enraged pursuers tied him to tree, collected wood around him, and immediately consumed his body to ashes.

Another instance of punishment, for an attempt only, of a negro to commit the like crime, in the same state, was related to me by Doctor Frederic Ramcke, of Edenton: — Calling on a wealthy planter, whose family he had long attended as a physician, but whose name, though then repeated, I have now forgotten, he observed, that he had a dangerous negro fellow, who had made attempts on the chastity of his white female neighbors, and who had been heard to boast that he never would cohabit with those of his own color, if he could, by any means, possess a white woman. The whole of the planter's conversation, while they drank a glass of grog together, turned on this subject, and he concluded by swearing, that he would give him up to the white men, unless he, the doctor, could cure him of this cursed propensity. Speaking in plainer terms, he entreated the doctor to perform an operation which would answer his purpose. The doctor hesitated — the planter offered an hundred dollars — entreated — and was violent. The doctor demanded an indemnity, which was immediately given.

The planter now ordered the libidinous slave into his presence, and at the same time directed his overseer, a white man, already privy to his crimes, to attend. When in the room where the doctor sat, the planter tripped up the heels of the slave, and this being the signal for the overseer, he rushed into the room, and assisted in binding the prisoner, who conceived that he was on the point of receiving an ordinary punishment, which he was conscious of meriting. Thus bound, they placed him on a table, and the doctor, in a few minutes, with his pocket instruments, performed the operation of castration. The fellow, when released, was told that he had received the punishment due for his abuse and insults to white women.

The doctor added, that he would not touch a single dollar by way of recompence, and was soon informed that his patient had become a *cool orderly* slave. About three months after the operation, visiting a patient on the road near the dwelling of the planter, the emasculated slave suddenly appeared before the doctor. We may conclude that no pleasant sensations pervaded the mind of the operator, for the fellow had on his shoulder a wood-cutter's axe. To turn back, or to risk a meeting was the question. The doctor checked his horse, to view the physiognomy of the slave, and finding it tolerably gentle, he boldly enquired after his health, though at a cautious distance. The negro replied: "Tank ye, massa doctor, you did a me much great good; white or blackee woman, I care not for." This expression, the doctor said, was more acceptable at the moment, than the planter's offered fee of an hundred dollars would have proved at any period of his life.

The following lines I met with several years ago, in some American publication. Though I do not think the condition of this unfortunate race by any means a subject for sport; yet as this little piece affords a true picture of that levity which they evince even on the most awful occasions, I have thought it worth preserving:

THE DYING NEGRO

Old Cato on his death-bed lying,
Worn out with work, and almost dying,
With patience heard his friends propose
What bearers for him they had chose.
There's Cuff and Cæsar, Pomp and Plato;
"Dey do bery well," quoth Cato —
And Bantam Philips; now for t'other
We must take Scipio, Bantam's brother.
"I no like Scip," old Cato cries,
"Scip rascal, tell about me lies,
And get me whipp'd"— ki, 'tis all one,
Scip shall be bearer, Scip or none.
"Mind me," quoth Cato, "if dat cur,
Dat Scip, come bearer, I wont stir."

Mr. Jefferson, the present president of the United States, in his Notes on Virginia, on the subject of slavery in that state, says:

There must doubtless be an unhappy influence on the manners of our people, produced by the existence of slavery among us. The whole commerce between master and slave is a perpetual exercise of the most boisterous passions, the most unremitting despotism on the one part, and degrading submission on the other. Our children see this, and learn to imitate it, for man is an imitative animal. This quality is the germ of all education in him. From his cradle to his grave, he is learning to do what others do. If a parent could find no motive either in his philanthropy, or his self-love, for restraining the intemperance of passion towards his slave, it should always be a sufficient one that his child is present. But generally it is not sufficient. The parent storms, the child looks on, catches the lineaments of wrath, puts on the same airs in the circle of smaller slaves, gives a loose to his worst of passions, and thus, nursed, educated, and daily exercised in tyranny, cannot but be stamped by it with odious peculiarities. He must be a prodigy who can retain his manners and morals, undepraved by such circumstances. And with what execration should the statesmen be loaded, who permitting one half of the citizens thus to trample on the rights of the other, transforms, those into despots, and these into enemies; destroys the morals of the one, and the *amor patriae* of the other. For if a slave can have a country in the world, it must be any other in preference to that in which he is born to live and labor for another: in which he must lock up the faculties of his nature, and contribute, as far as depends on his individual endeavors, to the debasement of the human race, or entail his own miserable condition on the endless generations proceeding from him. With the morals of the people, their industry is also destroyed. For in a warm climate no man will labor for himself, who can make another labor for him. This is so true, that of the proprietors of slaves, a very small proportion indeed are ever seen to labor. And can the liberties of a nation be thought secure, when we have removed their only firm basis, a conviction in the minds of the people that these liberties are the gift of God? That they are not to be violated but with his wrath? Indeed I tremble for my country when I reflect that God is just; that his justice cannot sleep for ever: that considering numbers, nature, and natural means only, a revolution in the wheel of fortune, an exchange of situation, is among possible events; that it may become probable by supernatural interference! —The Almighty has no attribute which can take side with us in such a contest.[3]

Doctor Morse,[4] an American divine, and author of several geographical works, adopts the following observations on slaves, which he tells his reader he took from the works of an European writer.

If there be an object truly ridiculous in nature, it is an American patriot, signing resolutions of independence with one hand, and with the other brandishing his whip over his affrighted slaves.

The doctor next, speaking for himself, says:

Much has been written of late to shew the injustice and iniquity of enslaving the Africans, so much as to render it unnecessary here to say any thing on that part of the subject. We cannot, however, forbear introducing a few observations respecting the influence of slavery upon policy, morals and manners. From repeated and accurate calculations, it has been found, that the expence of maintaining a slave, especially if we include the purchase-money, is much greater than that of maintaining a free man; and the labour of the free man, influenced by the powerful motive of gain, is at least twice as profitable to the employer as that of the slave. Besides, slavery is the bane of industry. It renders labour, among the whites, not only unfashionable, but disreputable. Industry is the offspring of necessity rather than of choice. Slavery precludes this necessity; and indolence, which strikes at the root of all social and political happiness, is the unhappy consequence.

These observations, without adding any thing upon the injustice of the practice, shew that slavery is impolitic. Its influence on manners and morals is equally pernicious. The negro wenches in many, perhaps I may say in most instances, are nurses to their mistresses' children. The infant babe, as soon as it is born, is delivered to its black nurse, and perhaps seldom or never tastes a drop of its mother's milk. The children, by being brought up, and constantly associating with the negroes, too often imbibe their low ideas, and vitiated manners and morals; and contract a negroish kind of accent and dialect, which they often carry with them through life. A mischief common, in a greater or less degree, in all the southern states, at which humanity and decency blush, is the criminal intercourse between the whites and blacks. "The enjoyment of a negro or mulatto woman," says a traveller of observation, "is spoken of as quite a common thing." No reluctance, delicacy, or shame, appear about the matter. It is far from being uncommon to see a gentleman at dinner, and his reputed son a slave, waiting at the table. "I myself," says the writer, "saw two instances of this kind; and the company would very facetiously trace the features of the father and mother in the child, and very accurately point out the more characteristic resemblances. The fathers neither of them blushed, nor seemed disconcerted. They were called men of worth, politeness and humanity. Strange perversion of terms and language! The Africans are said to be inferior in point of sense, understanding, sentiment, and feeling, to white people; hence the one infers a right to enslave the other. The African labors night and day to collect a small pittance, to purchase the freedom of his child; the white man begets his likeness, and with much indifference and dignity of soul, sees his offspring in bondage and misery, nor makes one effort to redeem his own blood. Choice food for satire! wide field for burlesque! noble game for wit! sad cause for pity to bleed, and for humanity to weep! unless the enkindled blood inflame resentment, and vent itself in execrations!"

NOTES — CHAPTER XXIX

1. Thomas Blount served as a representative from North Carolina in the United States Congress from 1805 to 1809.

2. Again, there seems to be no reason for entering into the slavery controversy. The incidents related by Janson could be paralleled many times from the literature readily accessible in practically any library. His point of view, of course, is quite typical of that expressed by many English travellers.

3. *Notes on Virginia* in the *Writings of Thomas Jefferson,* edited by H. G. Washington. Philadelphia, 1871. VII, 403-04.

4. Jedidiah Morse, a clergyman, graduated from Yale in 1783 and in the same year opened a young ladies' school at New Haven. Later he studied for the ministry. His interest in civilizing the Indians led to his appointment by the Secretary of War in 1820 to visit the tribes on the border. He was interested, also, in geography and adapted from larger books a text, *Geography Made Easy,* the first work of the kind published in the United States. This and other works on the subject earned him the title of "Father of American Geography."

CHAPTER XXX

AGRICULTURE — PROSPECTS FOR THE EMIGRANT FARMER — HISTORY OF MR. GILPIN — YELLOW FEVER — SYMPTOMS AND TREATMENT OF THAT DREADFUL COMPLAINT — LAND-JOBBERS — SQUATTERS — A LOG-HOUSE — FENCES — THE CULTURE OF INDIAN CORN — JOURNEY TO THE BLUE RIDGE — ORANGE COURT-HOUSE — THE DANCING SCHOOL — MADISON COURT-HOUSE — ALARM OF AN INSURRECTION AMONG THE NEGROES — NIGHT EXPEDITION IN PURSUIT OF THEM — THEIR PUNISHMENT.

THE descriptions of the back country of the United States, which, during the *mania* of land speculation, were most industriously circulated through Great Britain and Ireland, by fatal experience have been proved illusive; and, like the ingenious effusions of our lottery-dealers, calculated to lead you to the end of those who made them. On the faith of interested reporters, the English farmer has taken a sudden disgust to his native soil, and imbibed the ideal sweets of a distant world. Intoxicated with the prospect, he hastily disposes of his paternal farm, and all his property. He cannot wait to reap the crop already growing, considering every hour a loss, till he arrives at the consummation of his desires.

My friend, Mr. John Bernard Gilpin,* with whom I became acquainted soon after his arrival in Norfolk, is an instance of the difficulties and dangers attending a scheme of

* This gentleman is a lineal descendant of that celebrated and pious man, John Bernard Gilpin, archdeacon of Durham, denominated THE NORTHERN APOSTLE. He was doomed to martyrdom in the reign of religious terror, and was ordered to London, where he would in all probability have met the fate of Bishop Latimer, and the other pious preachers of the reformed religion. Within a stage or two of the capital he fell from his horse and broke his leg, which delayed the completion of his journey till the death of Mary. Queen Elizabeth restored him to his church preferment, and offered him the bishopric of Carlisle, which he declined.

this nature. He possessed an estate in Westmoreland, which had descended from heir to heir for many generations, and which he sold under the influence of a scheme of emigrating to America; and there becoming the proprietor of some of those immense and rich tracts of land, so luxuriantly described on the banks of the Ohio. He engaged the cabin of a large vessel at Whitehaven, and provided himself with every implement of husbandry, and whatever might contribute to the execution of his intentions. His family consisted of an amiable wife, and two young children; a widowed sister, her three daughters, and a son. Being a man of an ancient family, and greatly esteemed, several neighbors, equally restless at home, and yearning for a sight of the new world, intreated permission to accompany him. Thus the ship obtained a cargo of respectable English emigrants; among whom were some husbandmen, who had bound themselves to Mr. Gilpin for a term of years, to assist in the settlement of his contemplated domain. Mr. Gilpin was one of the most wary and frugal of his countrymen, and from this inherent disposition, he withstood the temptation of purchasing lands in America previous to his departure from England, though allured by the most specious offer.

The passage to the United States is seldom performed under five or six weeks, and sometimes adverse winds have extended the irksome voyage to three months. Mr. Gilpin described the horrors of the sea, the sufferings of the passengers, not one of whom had ever been upon salt water, and the effects of the August sun on the coast of Virginia, with the most poignant sensations. On the American coast his sister expired, from the effects of the fatigue endured in the voyage, and the heat of the latitudes they had approached; and her remains were committed to the bosom of the deep. After being becalmed till the situation of the passengers was almost insupportable, the ship arrived in Hampton roads.

The port and town of Norfolk I have already mentioned as being one of the most unhealthy on the coast. Mr. Gilpin procured a house in the upper part of the town, called the Old Fields, and near to that where I then resided, to which he immediately removed his numerous family. The yellow fever was then raging, and I was at that moment under its baleful influence. To describe the misery of the sufferer afflicted with this horrible disease, is impossible. The symptoms by which I was attacked, were sudden. I had supped with an appetite, slept as well as the heat would permit, and was rising at my usual time in the morning, when I felt a most singular sensation, accompanied by a chill. I lay down again, and soon felt a nausea at my stomach, which produced vomiting of bile, in color and quantity which astonished me. This relieved me so much, that I ascribed the cause of my sickness to a foul stomach, and had dressed myself before I perceived new symptoms. A lassitude hung about me, and was accompanied with a depression of my faculties, an acute pain at the back of the head, and an aching through my limbs. Medical assistance was now procured, but on the third day I felt so weary that I could not remain a minute in the same posture; a sensation not to be described — worse to be endured than acute pain, and more irksome than the smart of a festering wound. During this time the fever had made great progress, and the thirst it occasioned could not be appeased, though I drank large quantities of the juice of limes, with water, which was permitted by my physician. My stomach, however, soon refused the grateful beverage; the vomiting continued often so long, and with such violence, that I was exhausted, and found a temporary relief in the deprivation of my mental faculties. In this state I suffered several days, the greatest part of which I was insensible of my situation, and the intervals of reason were horrible. My bones felt as if they were disjointed; a burning pain was seated in the spine, while the throbbing and tormenting sensation in my head drove me again into a state of delirium. The treatment of my physician was judicious; by his aid, and that of a good constitution, I struggled through the dreadful disorder. I was copiously bled in the first instance, and blisters were applied to my legs, my feet, and the back of my neck. This regimen, with the good effect produced by strong doses of calomel, and afterwards of bark, effected my cure. During this severe trial, in my intervals of reason I readily complied with the prescriptions of my doctor, and the directions of my black nurse: but was informed, that in my delirium I was most refractory, and evinced great bodily strength in attempting to escape from the chamber — a common symptom in the yellow fever.

By this malignant disorder, were Mr. Gilpin and several of his family seized. In a short time it deprived him of his wife, and reduced himself and one of his children to a very low state. The fever was now raging in a most alarming manner in Norfolk. A part of a common was inclosed, and called Potter's Field, for the interment of its victims. Here lie the remains of Mrs. Gilpin, and here my bones would have been at rest, had I met her fate. The dead were hurried to this cemetery, often without coffins,* in carts, or upon drays, by negroes, in the dead hour of night; and most of the sea-port towns in the United States, even as far north as Portland, in the province of Maine, since the year 1793, have occasionally been visited by this infection.

This misfortune, added to the intense heat of the summer, had nearly clouded the fair prospects of Mr. Gilpin, when other obstacles presented themselves, which entirely frustrated his plans. The husband-man, on whom he had

* During my stay at Edenton, in North Carolina, a New England man, of the name of Johnson, from Marblehead, arrived there with a number of speculative articles for sale, there called "Yankee notions." Among these were *a number of coffins* of all sizes, one within the other, as apothecaries buy their pill boxes. This fellow had heard of the ravages of the fever at Norfolk; and Edenton being only sixty or seventy miles distant, he calculated on a market; but the fever having never visited the latter place, the coffin speculation failed.

Another curious Yankee speculation was made by a merchant of Newberry Port. He sent as an adventure to the West Indies a large quantity of *warming pans;* and, strange to tell, they found as good a market as could be expected for such an article in Lapland. They were converted into molasses ladles!

depended for the management of his farm, and whose passage he had paid, breaking at once his bond, and the ties of gratitude, absconded. This is the common trick played by Redemptioners, who, allured by the prospect of high wages, run away on the first opportunity; and for that reason but few emigrants have found their way of late in the United States, through this medium.

I shall not suppose that any emigrant arriving in the United States on agricultural projects will make any considerable stay on the coast, the land there being mostly under cultivation, of inferior quality to that in the back country, and higher in price. The first step to be taken is to purchase land, and in order to do this, you must apply to a land-jobber, the very name of whom makes my pen recoil from the paper. He will produce plans out of number, and titles, if you choose to believe him, indisputable. Your route will lie probably to Kentucky or Tennessee, countries from which I have seen very many return disappointed and impoverished. It will be no more than common prudence to visit the land previous to the purchase, which will of course be attended with considerable expence and loss of time. Should you find the chosen spot free from *squatters*,* and from prior claims, you return and pay an exorbitant advanced price for it to the jobber, — from twenty to fifty dollars per acre for good land on a navigable river or creek.[1] There are, indeed, tracts daily offered at a dollar or less — but they are good for nothing to the emigrant.

These difficulties surmounted, I will suppose the English farmer in possession of his land by a good title. He will then

* Families of white people, who have taken possession, and have held by this usurped right for many years. It is often impossible to oust them: hence they are called Squatters. The author purchased some hundred acres of land in the district of Maine that was nearly covered with squatters, and which he was, however, fortunate enough to dispose of to another unlucky purchaser, without loss. The jobbers will seldom warrant the land free from this disagreeable incumbrance; and should they do so, it is ten to one whether they prove of sufficient responsibility on a forfeiture of the covenant.

have to conduct his family, with people to clear his ground from the mass of heavy timber with which he will find it covered. If he brings them with him, he will be subject to their desertion, and if he depends on hiring them in America, vain will be his hopes, unless he offers wages which will absorb his profits. In either case he will have to transport them many hundred miles through dreary forests, across swamps, and over tremendous mountains. For this purpose he must purchase waggons and horses, or hire them, and in either case the expense will be great.

Mr. Gilpin expressed a great desire to make an excursion towards the long chain of mountains called the Blue Ridge, about three hundred miles on the road, but not half the distance, to some parts of the Ohio, and I agreed to accompany him. We resolved to proceed by the way of Federicksburg on account of my former acquaintance in that town. From Norfolk to that place is near two hundred miles, which we had an opportunity of going by water, through Hampton Roads, up the river Rappahannock. The charge of this distance by water-carriage, in most parts of the United States, is ten dollars each passenger. Fredericksburg is a gay commercial town, beautifully situated on the high banks of the river, and at the head of the navigation. Tobacco is brought hither in large quantities from an extensive back-country, and conveyed thence down the river to Hobbs' Hole, where ships in the European trade lie ready to receive them. We were here advised to proceed to Orange Court-house, as a healthy country, and where we might recruit our health and spirits, which had greatly suffered by the attacks of the yellow fever. A waggon with five horses, which carries thirty hundred weight, costs, including the unconscionable quantity of whiskey which the driver will consume, about two shillings British money per mile. A traveller in this country must mount his waggon or walk—there is no alternative—no post horses or carriages are to be hired—no stages ever travel the road we were destined to pursue. Over rocky grounds were this family jolted for three successive days, but that inconvenience I escaped in a great measure by walking. Some parts of the road, however, compelled me to mount this unwieldly machine, to avoid wading through swamps and runs of water. Here I had an opportunity of making some observations on the country. The labour of the field is entirely performed by negroes, and the business of the farmer and planter, is carried on in a very slovenly manner. The fences are temporary, being put up on tilling and planting the ground, and after harvest suffered to fall, or perhaps burned, to avoid the trouble of cutting fuel, with which every plantation is surrounded. They are composed of the wood of the pine-tree, split into pieces, eight or ten feet in length, and laid in a transverse manner on each other. These fences require little trouble, which the Virginians particularly abhor, and are so slight that a high wind often blows them down. The wheat-harvest was over, but the majestic stalk of the Indian corn waved in yellow leaf, denoting its near approach to maturity. The wheat is generally cut down with the scythe, just as the English farmer cuts his hay, and the grain is frequently trodden out by horses on the clay floor of the barn. It is far inferior to English wheat, and if a judgment were to be formed from inspection alone, a stranger would be induced to suppose it of a different species. It is small and dark-coloured, yet makes excellent white flour, which is exported to the West Indies, and, in years of scarcity, to Europe. Indian corn is very easily raised, but it is an uncertain crop, requiring the whole summer's heat to ripen it. From the great height of the stalk, the boisterous winds and torrents of rain often lay fields for miles prostrate with the earth, and in an earlier state, the corn hills are washed away, or the seed scratched up and devoured by racoons, squirrels, crows, and birds of various descriptions. The planting is simply performed by running the plough over the ground, then with a hoe making holes three or four inches deep, and dropping four or five grains in each, which is chiefly done by children.

The seed is then covered, after which, no farther attention is required till the stalk is about a foot high, when the ground is cleared of weeds, and the plants are earthed or hilled up. At first hoeing it is usual to drop fresh grains where the first have failed; they will all ripen before the time of harvest arrives.

As we advanced up the country, the land became of a better quality. It was sandy near the coast, but now I observed many places to be rich argillaceous earth, on which were planted vast fields of tobacco, and the quantity of stubble ground indicated the large crops of wheat which had been reaped. A second crop of clover in some places had a good appearance, but three-fourths of the land was still in a state of nature.

On our arrival at Orange, we found an old wooden building, which is used both as a court-house and a place of divine worship, a tavern, and half a dozen mean dwelling-houses. We could procure no accommodation. A dancing-master occupied the tavern by his quarterly attendance to teach the Virginian mountain-misses the graces of his art. His school was numerously attended, and every corner of the house was filled by the parents of the pupils. We were now in an awkward dilemma, for the waggons were only hired to this place, and no entreaties or extravagant offers could prevail upon the drivers to proceed; they were, as they alledged, under the obligation of a penalty to go elsewhere. They were proceeding to discharge our baggage in the street, when I enquired what punishment I should incur, or what sacrilege would be committed, were it to be put into the court-house. I was referred to the clerk of the peace, but he was not to be found, and dire necessity impelled me to commit a trespass. The door was not locked, and in a short time we were in possession; which proved a seasonable relief to the poor children, whose tender joints had barely escaped dislocation by the jolting over the rocks and stumps of trees which had impeded our progress. Fortunately we arrived in the forenoon, but we were covered all over with dust. Having changed my clothes, and refreshed myself with the remnant of our travelling stock of provisions, I went to the dancing-school. The gravity of my friend, contracted from the study of theology, for he had been educated for the church, would alone have caused his declining to accompany me to such a place. I was agreeably surprised at the order and the systematic mode with which this part of polite education was conducted, amid the woods, and on the rising ground of the vast mountains called the Blue Ridge.* There were upwards of fifty scholars, though, from the *view* of the country, I could not have supposed the existence of fifty houses within the circumference of as many miles. Some of the pupils I was informed came from a great distance, and the carriages used for their conveyance formed the strangest and most uncouth collection of travelling vehicles perhaps ever collected together. A number bore such strong marks of antiquity, and so coarsely were they put together, that I could compare them only to my ideas of antediluvian machines. They however conveyed a number of pretty little modern-dressed misses, dressed and ornamented to a ridiculous pitch of extravagance. They had made great progress, performing the minuet, country dance, and reel, correctly, though this weekly school had been opened only four or five times. After the lessons were finished, a number of grown masters and misses joined in six-handed reels, the favorite dance in the southern states, and, as though I had not already undergone of late sufficient fatigue, I could not resist the desire of joining them, upon an invitation, given with Parisian politeness, by the master. Thus, in the heat of summer, and not a month out of the yellow fever, was I capering among the girls; an act of imprudence which, happily for me, was not attended with any ill consequences.

* These mountains begin almost at the extremity of the northern boundary, and extend, with little variation, to Georgia, nearly through the middle of the United States.

On my return to the Court-house, I found that Mr. Gilpin had been making provision for retaining the slender title we had acquired to it. He had made up one bed in the jury-box, and another on the table, round which the counsel sit, and had composedly seated himself, reading a Greek author, in the chair of justice. On my entrance, he was compelled to relax a little of his serious mood, and to brighten his features with a smile — the first I had observed. The loss of his wife, and disappointments resulting from the failure of his plans, had plunged him in a state of mind little better than that of settled melancholy. A partition which ran across the court-house formed a jury-room. American jurymen seldom fail to retire from the court, be the case ever so plain, to agree upon their verdict. This room had been reserved for my occupation, and accordingly I spread my mattrass on the floor, upon which, being greatly fatigued, I soon fell asleep. In the morning I endeavored to procure waggons to convey us to Madison Court-house, distant between sixteen and eighteen miles, without success. I wondered what caused my friends in Fredericksburg to advise us to proceed to this dreary place; but I afterwards found little choice in any part of the country, as to accommodation. We were favored if any of the neighbors would *sell* us a fowl, or a dozen eggs. I had attended to the whistling of the quails all around me the day after our arrival, and being always provided with an excellent English fowling-piece, I went out in the afternoon, attended by two youths, who appeared anxious to see an Englishman pursuing game. I had no dog, and the luxuriant, but coarse herbage of the cleared land was unfavorable to my pursuit. The young Virginians, conversant with the haunts, soon sprung the game, and were surprised at my success, two or three birds falling at each shot. The coveys had not been broken, and they took flight together at the same instant. Americans do not accustom themselves to shoot game upon the wing; but they are the best marksmen in the world with a rifle gun at a fixed object. The produce of my gun was very acceptable in the court-house; the girls soon prepared the game for cooking, and having with us every necessary material, without which no traveller must attempt to penetrate into the interior of this immense country, we made a delicious repast.

Here we were obliged to remain nine days, and, fortunately, during that time, our habitation was not wanted for the dispensation of law; but the gospel was twice expounded in it during our occupancy. At length we procured one waggon, which was appropriated to Mr. Gilpin and a part of his family, while I remained with his nephew, waiting the uncertainty of another conveyance. This presented at the expiration of the second day, and on the third, I arrived at Madison Court-house. My friend had already hired an unfurnished house, and to my surprise, for the long term of six months, though the contemplated extent of the tour was not to exceed six or eight weeks. I soon found that he had determined to remain during the winter among the rocks and woods; a situation, at all events, well suited to the contemplative mind.

In this small place we found some society. There was a doctor and a lawyer; but neither parson nor parsonage-house. A jolly justice of the peace, however, supplied the place extremely well; being a moral, upright man, whose advice often reclaimed the offender, when the inforcement of the law might have rendered him incorrigible. In such company occasionally, and with my gun, being in a fine sporting country, I had passed three weeks with advantage to my health, when a circumstance occurred which greatly interrupted our peace of mind for some time.

Passing the door of Mr. Alexander Hunton, the magistrate above alluded to, I was surprised at hearing his voice elevated, and the strokes of the cow-skin applied to one of his negroes; while at every blow he urged the obstinate creature to confess something which he appeared anxious to discover. In a short time we found that a conversation had been heard among his negroes of a very suspicious tendency, and he was endeavoring to extort the meaning of it from the man by whom the expressions had been used. From what was collected, there was every reason to believe that the negroes were planning an insurrection; and Mr. Hunton privately requested every white inhabitant to meet him, well armed, on the same evening, at a certain time and place. A negro was lying in the gaol under sentence of death for murdering a white man, and we supposed that a rescue, if nothing more, would be attempted. With the insurrection at Richmond present to every mind, our fears were wrought up to a high degree of alarm. I attended with my gun, and a large supply of ball cartridges, with which I was supplied, among other inhabitants, by the corporation of Norfolk, a few months before, on a similar occasion.* I did not expect my friend would have mustered, and more especially as he was not provided with fire arms; but I was greatly surprised to find him among the foremost, armed with a bayonet, which happened to be among his travelling equipage, fixed to a long pole, which he had cut down from the woods, making a very formidable weapon. A thousand such, however, would have availed but little against the determined opposition of the slaves. We counted our ranks at twelve or fifteen; they could form a phalanx of as many hundreds within the circle of a few miles.

Of our small force, six were selected to make an excursion of about two miles to a negro quarter, where we had intelligence that some of the leaders were assembled to deliberate upon the measures to be pursued, and I was one of the detachment. The night was very dark, and I found it difficult to keep pace with my companions, who were well acquainted with every step of the road, to which I was an entire stranger. It was intricate, lying across ploughed fields, and over waste

* On that occasion the leaders were apprehended, tried, and condemned to suffer death. They were accordingly carried to the place of execution, in the Old Fields, at Norfolk; but only one was hanged, as an example to the rest.

lands; so that it was no wonder that I lost my feet and fell; and had not my companions made a halt on a near approach to the enemy, I should neither have overtaken them, nor found my way back. The party was headed by Mr. Hunton, armed with a pair of my pistols. We surrounded the log-house; and he entered, with three more, while I was stationed on one side without, and the sixth on the other side. I soon heard a scrambling about the upper part of the inside of the house; in a moment the loose boards which served as a roof appeared to be removing, and a large negro man was making his escape. I called to him to surrender, and levelled my gun, and gave notice to those within. Happily I did not fire, for instant death would have ensued; though we had the orders of the magistrate to that effect. The unhappy slave leaped from the roof, and ran towards the woods. In his flight he was fired upon by the man on the other side and by others of the party as they came out of the house, without effect. The other slaves found there were two old people and their daughter, who denied all knowledge of any conspiracy; and their assertions that the man who had escaped was the lover of the girl, being admitted, we returned to the Court-house, where we found many of the slaves bound in fetters, who had been apprehended by the other parties, together with the man who had escaped from us. They underwent a strict examination before the magistrate, but nothing appeared to confirm our suspicions. On being asked why they were out at such an unreasonable hour, some said they had been hunting the racoon and opossum; and others replied that they had been visiting their friends and relations, which they could not do in the day-time. I really believed the poor wretches; but the justice differed in opinion, observing, that he had never known an instance of so many being out of their quarters at such a time. It was between two and three o'clock in the morning, and, perhaps, no search of this nature had ever been made before. He found them guilty of being out of their quarters at an unseasonable time, and ordered them all to be severely flogged, which sentence was executed by the white men, in turns. I was excused partaking in the disagreeable office, and thus the matter ended. The house which Mr. Gilpin had hired was at the extremity of the little town, which consisted of but ten or twelve houses, and it stood at some distance from the rest. About four or five nights after this punishment had been inflicted, while my friend and myself, after supper, were very moderately indulging ourselves with a glass of apple brandy* and water, we were greatly alarmed by an uncouth singing of the negroes, apparently about a mile distant. We listened attentively, and fancied the noise drew nearer. The remainder of Mr. Gilpin's family were in bed, and in great consternation we sallied out, myself with my loaded gun, and Mr. Gilpin with his mounted bayonet. We first ascended a rising ground, to determine with more precision from what quarter the alarm proceeded. Convinced that our surmises were just, apprehending an attack, and conceiving that it was the negro-war song, we hastily proceeded to the tavern, where we found a party playing at cards, the constant custom here in the evening. They were greatly surprised on seeing us enter, armed as we were the night of the general search; and, upon our mentioning the cause of our alarm, they burst into a laugh, informing us that it was only a harvest-home of the negroes, in one of the quarters. We now felt ashamed; but they greatly commended our activity, and thus we became more respected by our neighbours. The remainder of the time I passed here was free from molestation, and I left my friend, who remained at Madison nearly two years, during which a correspondence by letter continued. The last I received from this worthy man informs me of his determination to visit Canada, and then to return to England.

On my return from this excursion I met with Colonel

*This is the common drink of the country. It is only half a dollar per gallon. Peach brandy, distilled entirely from that fruit, and of greater strength, may be purchased for less than a dollar. Fowls were here three-pence British each; a fine fat turkey or goose, half a dollar; butcher's meat three-pence per pound; and good uncleared land is from five to twenty dollars per acre.

Thomas Butler,[2] who was then upon his journey as a prisoner, in order to take his trial before a court-martial, at Frederick town, in Maryland.

This gallant officer, who had with honor served his country through the whole revolutionary war, and shed his blood in its service; in the decline of life was convicted of an offence hitherto unknown in military service—*of refusing to cut off his hair;* a sentence which his feelings sunk under, and he died, much lamented, — of a broken heart.

At the commencement of the American war, Mr. Butler was a student of law under the late Mr. Wilson, then an eminent barrister, and since one of the judges of the supreme federal courts. He joined the army of the congress, as a subaltern officer, and soon rose to the rank of captain. Four of his brothers were engaged in the same service, all of whom, as well as the subject of these anecdotes, acquitted themselves with courage and good conduct. He was in almost every action which took place in the middle states; and at that of Brandywine, he received the thanks of the commander in chief, General Washington, through his aid-de-camp, the lamented Hamilton. He there rallied a detachment of retreating Americans, and greatly annoyed the British troops. At the severe battle of Monmouth, he defended a defile against the heavy fire of his enemy, and thus covered the retreat of his brother's, Colonel Richard Butler's regiment. For this gallantry he received the public thanks of General Wayne.

The war being ended, like many of his brother officers, he retired to private life, and assuming the character of a farmer, he cultivated a small plantation, sufficient for the support of his family. In this rural retirement, and in the midst of domestic happiness, he was again called by his country into the field of battle, and ordered to join the army then raising under the unfortunate General Saint Clair, for the purpose of subduing the confederate tribes of hostile Indians. That commander, from an ill-judged contempt of his savage enemy, incautiously marched into their country, and fell into an ambuscade, which they had with great judgment and secresy prepared for his army. The slaughter made among the Americans was great; and being taken completely by surprise, a great part of them fell victims to savage fury. Major Butler, lately appointed to that rank, was dangerously wounded; and his brother, Capt. Richard Butler,[3] at the imminent hazard of his life, carried him off the field of battle. The eldest brother, General Butler, was numbered with the slain. Having recovered from his wounds, he was continued on the establishment as a major, and, in the year 1794, promoted to the rank of lieutenant-colonel commandant of the fourteenth sub-legion. In the Whiskey insurrection he commanded Fort Fayette, at Pittsburg, and by his address, for he had a very small garrison, prevented the deluded insurgents from storming the fort. In 1797 he was appointed by General Washington, under whom he had long served, to the chief command in the new state of Tennessee, and ordered to dislodge some American citizens who had possessed themselves of land belonging to the Indians. He accordingly marched at the head of his regiment, and by that prudence and good sense which had ever marked his conduct, prevailed on them quietly to abandon their project; for which he received the thanks of that state. On the reduction of the army, which took place soon after Mr. Jefferson had become president, he was appointed colonel of the second regiment of infantry, on the peace establishment.

It seems Colonel Butler[4] had incurred the displeasure of General Wilkinson, the American commander in chief; but the cause, if any, does not appear. On the 30th of April, 1801, the general issued the following order:—"For the accommodation, comfort, and health of the troops, the hair is to be cropped, without exception, and the general will give the example." It appears that Colonel Butler remonstrated against this order; that he held his locks, now grown grey in the service of his country, as the gift of nature; and that he thought no power on earth had a right to take them from him. To be deprived of those hairs which he had so often worn in the battle's front, was an indignity which the veteran could not submit to. The reasons which he alleged against submitting to the order obtained him, for a time, the exclusive privilege of retaining his hair; and an order to that effect was given by the general. Two years afterwards, Colonel Butler was, by name, called upon to conform to the first order, with which he refused to comply. He was immediately ordered under arrest by the commander in chief, while commanding at Fort Adams, on the banks of the Mississippi.

To the charge of disobedience of orders, two were added for neglect of duty, in the following order: —

1st. For disobedience of the general order of the 30th of April, 1801, regulating the uniform of the hair.

2d. For disobedience of the order of the president of the United States, communicated on the 8th of June, 1802.

3d. For neglect of duty in not descending the Mississippi to take the command of Fort Adams, and organise the troops, agreeably to the peace establishment, and according to the orders of the president, but proceeding to Pittsburgh with a military command on his private business, and without permission.

To these charges the colonel made an able defence. To the first, he pleaded a justification that the order was illegal; and in support thereof he advanced various instances where an officer was not bound to obey the orders of his commander; but these cases implied a supposition that the orders were notoriously illegal.

He underwent many mortifying circumstances before he could obtain a trial. He was ordered from Fort Adams to Frederick town, in Maryland, a distance of many hundred miles, without any reason being assigned for putting him to this tedious and expensive journey. Upwards of six months expired before a court-martial sat in judgment on his case, and from the honorable manner in which he was acquitted of the two last charges, accusing him of neglect of duty, it becomes evident that they were added to magnify in the eyes of the world, the offences which he had committed. This circumstance, added to his being so long harassed before he was brought to trial, reflects little honor on the present commander in chief of the American army. The following is a copy of the sentence: —

The court, after mature deliberation, are of opinion that the prisoner is guilty of disobedience of the general order of the 30th of April, 1801, and (taking into consideration the long and faithful services, and his general character as an officer) do hereby sentence him, under the 5th article of the second section of the articles of war, to be reprimanded in general orders.

The court are also of opinion, after due investigation, that the prisoner is not guilty of the second and third specifications, and that he did according to the true intent and meaning of the orders of the 9th of April, 25th of May, and 8th of June, faithfully perform his duty, and do therefore acquit him.

(Signed) J. BURDECK, *President.*
JAMES HOUSE, *Judge Advocate.*

From this sentence Colonel Butler appealed, by memorial, to the president of the United States. The following extract from the letter accompanying such appeal, will be interesting to military readers, while it displays the abilities of this persecuted old officer.

I feel sensible, Sir, how delicate this subject is, and I, with every military man, must intimately feel how unfortunate it is that any general order should render its discussion indispensable. Yet I hope and trust that it will never be conceded, that any citizen entering into the military service of his country, thereby puts himself out of the protection of the laws; that his honor, his conscience, his moral principles, his private and natural rights are no longer under his own guardianship, but surrendered up to whomsoever may be his military superior. With deference, Sir, I have at all times believed that the power given to every officer by his commission, is the authority of the laws and constitution of his country, vested in him as a legislative organ. The expression, then, of the superior officer's will, whilst confined to subjects over which the laws have given him authority, is the command of the law itself, and must be implicitly and promptly obeyed. But if directed to subjects over which the laws have given him no authority, but which, on the contrary, the laws and constitution of the United States have ensured as inviolable to every citizen, whether in a civil or military capacity, then I contend, please your excellency, that the order of the 30th of April, 1801, being unsupported by legal authority, contains not the essence of a military command. And had the court entered into an investigation of the legal merits of that order, they would not have held it in any higher point of view than the expression of will from one individual to another, which no duty requires him to respect, and no power compels him to obey.

This appeal was answered by the secretary at war. It shews how far the power of the president could in such cases be extended, and the regularity with which the war department of the United States is conducted:

Sir,

THE memorial accompanying your letter, was, in conformity with your request, presented to the president of the United States, who referred it to the secretary of war for his decision thereon. It therefore becomes his duty to make such observations as the nature of the case requires. Presuming it to have been your intention that your memorial should be considered in the nature of an appeal from the sentence of a court martial, to the president of the United States, which sentence has been approved of by the proper officer, it will only be necessary to observe, that there exists no law, custom, or usage, within the knowledge or recollection of the secretary at war, by which the president is authorized to take cognizance of such an appeal; although the president of the United States has by law ultimately to decide on proceedings of courts martial in certain cases, it does not appear that he possesses any legal control over the sentence of any court martial duly approved by the proper officer, except by interposing the constitutional power confided to him of pardoning offences.

Signed by the secretary at war, H. Dearborn, and directed to Colonel Thomas Butler.

During these proceedings, Colonel Butler was deprived by death of the consolements he would have found in an affectionate wife, by whom he had three sons and a daughter. This unfortunate circumstance increasing his mental sufferings for this fatal stab to his honour as an officer, brought him to his grave a few months after the promulgation of the sentence of the court-martial.

It is certainly a matter of surprize to reflect upon the severity of these proceedings towards a veteran who had passed the greatest part of his life in the service of his country. I attribute his misfortunes to a strict adherence to the maxims of Washington; all the followers of his steps being obnoxious to the ruling party.

NOTES — CHAPTER XXX

1. The various States had laws which protected squatters. As a typical example, the law passed in 1778 by North Carolina gave preference to any settler who had lived upon and improved land for a period of seven years.

2. Colonel Thomas Butler of Pennsylvania was a Revolutionary soldier. He received severe wounds at St. Clair's defeat. He died in 1805.

3. Richard Butler served with the rank of Ensign in the Fourth Sublegion in 1793, received promotion to the rank of Lieutenant in 1794, and resigned from the army on March 2, 1799. There is some confusion here, for the "General Butler" appears in Heitman's *Historical Register of the United States Army* as Major-General Richard Butler, a Revolutionary soldier, Indian agent in 1778, Major-General of the United States levies in 1791, and killed in action with the Indians near Fort Recovery, Ohio, on November 4, 1791. It seems scarcely probable that two sons in the same family bore the name of Richard. One would, therefore, assume that Janson confused the names or that they were not of the same family.

4. Colonel Butler had his headquarters for a time at Southwest Point on the Indian boundary. The attempts by the United States government to remove the settlers who had established themselves on Indian lands in violation of treaties between the tribes and the Federal government had a great influence in alienating the people of the frontier and especially of the Southwest from the Federalist party. The removals from Powell's Valley and other Indian lands in Tennessee by the troops under the command of Colonel Butler aroused great opposition to the Federal government. This opposition was not allayed by subsequent accessions of land through the treaties secured by the Federalist administration of Adams.

CHAPTER XXXI

INDIAN CORN — PRECARIOUS PRODUCE OF THAT GRAIN — HUSKING FROLIC — BREEDING OF SHEEP — PROSPECT FOR THE EMIGRANT MECHANIC IN AMERICA — THE HAW — PHYSIC — THE CHURCH — OBSERVATIONS ON MR. TOULMIN'S PLAN FOR PURCHASING AND STOCKING A FARM IN KENTUCKY — GERMAN SETTLERS — STATE OF LITERATURE IN AMERICA — BOOKSELLERS — TYPOGRAPHICAL SOCIETY — BOOK-FAIR — ARTS AND SCIENCES — STRICTURES ON AUSTIN'S LETTERS FROM LONDON — FUNERAL OF GEORGE WASHINGTON.

THERE is always an uncertainty of raising a plentiful crop of Indian corn, though it is the daily bread of the people. In those states where wheat is raised, a great majority of the inhabitants, in preference to the superior grain, eat bread made of corn-flour, which is coarser food, and has some resemblance to oatmeal. Indian corn would be easy to raise, were it not for the numerous enemies it has to encounter. Should the seed escape being scratched up after sowing, by the birds, and the lesser quadrupeds, a nipping and unexpected frost will sometimes destroy the tender blade, and oblige the farmer to begin his work again. In the middle of summer, when the stalk has attained its full height, often ten and twelve feet in rich ground, sometimes fifteen feet, a storm of wind and rain, accompanied perhaps by hail-stones as large as marbles, will sometimes lay waste the fields in particular directions for many miles. The people call these unseasonable and destructive storms, summer gusts, or summer squalls; but they are generally whirlwinds, with deluges of rain. In the Carolinas, and farther southward, these are more frequent, and about once in five or seven years a dreadful hurricane, similar to those of the West-Indies, totally destroys the grain, tears up the loftiest trees, drives the ships from their anchors, and carries them often a great distance into the woods, or on the beach, destroying the unfortunate mariners. While the corn is yet growing, it is attacked by a destructive insect, which they call the Hessian fly, absurdly pretending that it was originally imported with the Hessian soldiers during the revolutionary war. This insect insinuates itself into the joints of the stalks where it deposits its eggs. When the young ones are hatched, they feed upon the sap, and generally destroy the plant. Some ears in particular directions on the surface of the earth, will be destroyed by amazing swarms of caterpillars. This happened the very last spring in several parts of Maryland and Virginia, to the great loss of the planter.

In some provinces of the United States, the farmers, on getting in the corn harvest, give a rural fete, in imitation of the ancient English custom of harvest home. This they call a *husking frolic.* After the Indian corn is gathered and brought into the barn, the neighbouring youth of both sexes repair to the farm to husk it — that is, to strip it of the outside leaves in which it is enveloped. This done, the grain is in a state of preservation, in what is called the *cob;* in which it will keep much longer than when the grains are separated, as, in the latter state, it is liable to heat and become damaged.

I was particularly struck with an account given some years ago, of one of those husking fetes, by Mr. William Baxter, a considerable farmer at Quincy, the residence of the late president Adams, near Boston. This account was concluded by a copy of the lines of the rustic bard, upon the occasion, which I preserved, and now give them to my reader, not doubting that they will be perused with pleasure by such as admire this vein of poetry.

HUSKING DAY

AUTUMN with his golden sheaf,
Kindly gives to care relief;

Now the village task is done —
Now the laughing sport's begun.

Venus, smiling planet, leads,
Printless o'er the fields and meads,
(While the western rays oblique
Linger on Monadnock's* peak,

The Moon, from ocean rising, throws
Her lustre on Watchuset's* snows)
Frolic youth the country round
Nimble stepp'd, to beat the ground.

Lo! the hills of corn appear —
Damsel's seize the blushing ear,
Laughing seize, and slily hide,
Towards the favour'd lad to slide,
When the basket borne away
Gives the hint to sportive play.

Clear the floor and now advance —
Youth and manhood form the dance,
Gay and brisk the measure beat,
Age with transport shakes his seat,
Till the herald of the morn,
Crowing, warns him to be gone.

Antic gambols then succeed —
This, to hide along the mead,
Those, in secret paths to slide,
These upon their steps to glide;
By her mimic fear betray'd,
Ev'ry youth o'ertakes a maid:
Dalliance soft, and fav'ring grove,
Ripen fancy into love;
Hymen lights the torch, and gay
Pleasure crowns the Husking Day.

The mutton in the southern states is very indifferent, but little attention having hitherto been paid to the breed of that valuable animal.

* Two high mountains in Massachusetts.

Mr. Custis,[1] a grandchild of the late Mrs. Washington, and to whom the general left a considerable part of his estate, has lately become eminent as an agriculturist. In laudable imitation of many distinguished characters in England, he gives an annual premium, and an agricultural feast at his seat at Arlington, on the banks of the Potomack, near the city of Washington, for the best yearling lamb. The following account of the last meeting, will give the English farmer an idea of the breed of sheep in Virginia:

Mr. Custis's agricultural meeting and annual sheep-shearing took place at Arlington, and was attended by gentlemen from the adjoining counties. The annual premium for the finest ram lamb of one year old, was adjudged to a lamb bred by Ludwell Lee, Esq. of Belmont, in the county of Loudoun. The judges were very minute in their inspection, and we hope succeeding years will produce increasing exertion in the improvement of this valuable race of domestic animals.

The prize lamb possesses fine proportions, with a fleece of good quality, close and well packed, though rather short. His gross weight 161 pounds; weight of fleece seven pounds three quarters. Fleeces weigh very light this season, owing to the mildness of our winter. Arlington prime ewes average five pounds.

The annual premium will continue for eight years yet to come, together with a valuable privileged annexed, viz. Any person obtaining a premium has a right, within the time just mentioned, to demand a lamb of the improved stock, free of charge.

The science of agriculture, whatever perfection it may have attained in England, will not prosper in America. Emigrating farmers and husbandmen from this country conceive that they are perfect masters of all the knowledge that can be required for tilling the earth in the imaginary paradise which they have adopted.* In this they will find them-

* Settled lands are very far from being much cheaper in America than in England. It very often happens that a man does not suit himself at the first state he touches at, and then he has either to remove his family, in a wandering and expensive search, or else to leave them behind him in a strange place, whilst he is running about to find a home for them, which, from his hurry, he generally

selves woefully deceived, and that they have to acquire a new and totally different mode of farming, extremely repugnant to the principles in which they have been educated. It will be in vain for the emigrant to continue the English practice; he will soon find that the sooner he not only conforms to the mode of the country in this respect, but the more speedily he adopts even the manners and customs of the people among whom he has chosen to take up his final residence, the sooner will they cease to treat him as a stranger, whom, and especially the English, they look upon with a jealous eye. They are extremely tenacious of being thought inferior to the ancient stock, and every comparison of this nature will excite their hatred; for, however you may *know* to the contrary, they *think* themselves a superior order of beings.

The Americans may be considered as a commercial people, displaying a spirit of enterprise and perseverance, which, though it may be said they commenced their career without capital, has greatly enriched the country. Several adventurous merchants, whom fortune has favored, have acquired large properties, but a great number have failed in their speculations. The greatest part of commerce is still carried on by a kind of superficial capital, so that the failure of a single voyage often renders the owner of the cargo incapable of taking up the securities which he has given for his adven-

does to his disadvantage. I have known several who have never taken their families from on board the ship which brought them over; not finding their expectations answered, they returned the same way they came.

"In the purchase of back lands, nothing can be more infatuated than the practice which has prevailed with emigrating persons, of purchasing lands of British agents, previously to their sailing. A man is shewn a plan of a tract of land, with, of course, a varnished description of the fertility of its soil, and the variety of its production, plenteous streams, mill-seats, &c.; and thus the *freehold* of the land may become his own at four or five shillings per acre. True: but then it never cost the proprietors as many pence; and from natural causes, such as its distance from any settlements, or of navigable streams to communicate with any market, however distant, it will be worth little or nothing to the settler, even if its soil was exuberance itself."

Information respecting emigration to North America.

ture. I found no business done without long credit, if I may except the slave trade, in which they generally require prompt payment. Even in this disgraceful traffic, barter is sometimes made the circulating medium. I was privy to a negociation of this kind, where General Bembury, of North Carolina, gave a fine young negro woman, and who was an excellent house-servant, for a horse, on which I have seen him reviewing the militia. In every other transaction, not excepting the produce of agriculture, the farmer is obliged either to dispose of the surplus of his crop by way of barter, or he must sell it upon a long credit.

This circumstance also bears hard upon the emigrant. Having surmounted the difficulties already pointed out, which may have reduced him to his last dollar, and with great labour raised some grain for market, he must yet wait sixty or ninety days before he can realize the produce of his industry.

Doctor Franklin laboured hard in his writings to encourage emigration. He drew a fascinating picture of his country wherever he found an opportunity of offering it to the European. He expatiates upon the salubrity of an unfriendly clime, and he urges the facility of forming a settlement among his countrymen. It was his interest to do so; the doctor was conspicuous for his *amor patriæ*, which is generally carried even to enthusiasm. It is true that contagion had not visited America, nor was the summer's heat so fatal, when the doctor treated on the subject. That it is a country where great labour under a burning sun must be endured, particularly in the pursuit of agriculture, we find from his own words: — "America is the land of labour, and by no means what the English call *lubberland*, and the French *pays de cocagne*, where the streets are said to be paved with half-peck loaves, the houses tiled with pancakes, and where the fowls fly about ready roasted, crying, *come eat me!*"[2]

Having now sketched the prospects before the emigrant on an agricultural plan, I shall address a few lines to the mechanic and labourer who may pant to behold the new world.

The same cause which takes the farmer into the interior of the country, I mean employment, will keep the mechanic fixed to the spot where he may chance to land. The latter cannot expect work in the woods, and the former must penetrate into them before he can find work. Man chuses the spring of the year for emigration — birds, the fall of the leaf. The spring, comprehending all the delay unavoidable in such an undertaking, passes, and summer is advanced, before he arrives in America. He lands at New York, Philadelphia, Baltimore, Norfolk, or Charleston, in the very jaws of the yellow fever. The husbandman may perchance avoid it by speedy flight, but the more unfortunate mechanic is doomed to face death in all his terrors. I can aver, and I may do so without offence to the natives, because I speak the plain truth, that not one European in one hundred ever survived of late years two summers, without undergoing the dreadful ordeal of the fever, now attached to the climate. This fever always partakes of the nature of the bilious; sometimes it assumes not a more dangerous aspect, but too often arising from local contagion, it proves fatal. The New England States, indeed, are much more healthy, but there the land is mostly under cultivation, and consequently bears a high price; and almost every branch of labour is sufficiently supplied with hands. The mechanic, then, having survived this probation of his constitution, remains in the port where he landed, or removes to another, follows his trade by which he may undoubtedly earn a dollar and a half every day he is able to work. The climate in summer, far different from his own — the violent perspiration he must undergo to keep in health, (and this must be supported by a constant recourse to ardent spirits) — and still worse, the exposure to the rays of the sun, in a few years debilitate his constitution, and bring on a premature decay. 'Tis now he seriously curses his folly — now he sighs and pants to return to that genial clime which gave him birth, and generally in vain. He is married, and his family are a barrier to his wishes; — or, he is embarked so far in business, that he finds it impracticable to retire without sacrificing a large portion of the produce of many years' toil and labour. These are the principal reasons that so few English emigrants, who outlive the immediate effects of the climate, ever return to their native land. The labourer's wages are a dollar per day, as long as he can toil twelve hours in the burning sun of August, or the pinching frosts of January.

Of the learned professions, I am certain that very few indeed will quit their native country, the region of taste, science, and literature, for the sole purpose of following their respective avocations in America. My admission to the bar, and practise in the law, was a circumstance unlooked for when I landed in the United States. That pursuit was not attended with pecuniary remuneration adequate to my labour in the profession; and had I depended alone upon my exertions in this capacity, my situation would have been by no means enviable. The lucrative business of the courts is chiefly engrossed by natives who have extensive connections. A young practitioner there has not the ample field before him which the courts of Westminster afford; and, as in the case of Mr. Lincoln, great interest will leave little to superior abilities without patronage. For these reasons, the profession with me was from the first a secondary object, which I never should have embarked in but for the ill-judged solicitations of a gentleman then at the bar, with whom I had formed an intimacy, John Faxon, Esq.[3] of the state of Rhode Island.

The practice of physic is easier of attainment. Gentlemen of that profession have opportunities of pushing themselves forward by methods which lawyers cannot adopt. A medical man, with tolerable address, may plant himself in any town in the United States, without undergoing the probation required from the lawyer. His diploma is not necessary — it will not be asked for; nor will it be enquired whether he has undergone a regular course of study, and been admitted to the royal college in London, or that of Leyden; nay, a self-created quack, like those pests to the human race who deliver their invitations to the unwary at the corner of almost every street of the British metropolis, will find no impediment in this country to the practice of physic or surgery. Of late years, this profession has in Philadelphia been placed on a more respectable footing.[4] In that city is established an institution somewhat resembling a college of physic, and a surgeons' hall, attended, in the winter season, by about two hundred pupils, who come from the distant states. I have, however, witnessed the commencement in practice of one of these medical collegians, and one who had a few years served a country practitioner, at the same time, and in the same town; and their respective increase of business depended alone upon friends or fortuitous circumstances. The large cities, as in London, swarm with quacks, who disseminate their poison in all directions, and fill the newspapers with their filthy falsehoods.

The church, in this republican country, is also open to all who chuse to enter it as preachers; upon whom there are no restrictions — who are not under the necessity of adducing any qualifications previous to an attempt to expound the scriptures. An enthusiast, should he not immediately obtain a footing in a pulpit already fixed, may, if he has a little money, soon find some dissaffected to their place of worship, who will join him, and in a short time he is enabled to build himself a meeting-house. Until a traveller from the north reaches the Carolinas, he will find the United States the very hot-bed of religion — but I have already devoted a chapter to this subject.*

* In treating of the Shakers, the author omitted to mention that Anna Leese, whom these fanatics styled the Elect Lady, asserting that she was the woman spoken of in the twentieth chapter of Revelations, died in 1784, notwithstanding all her predictions to the contrary. She was succeeded by James Whitaker, who also died in 1787, and their present leader is Joseph Meacham, who has obtained among them the reputation of a prophet.

No man of independent fortune, who is not an enemy to his country, will, it may now be presumed, emigrate to America. Some few, indeed, may be found willing to make a sacrifice, in order to indulge a desire to visit remote countries. It is, notwithstanding, the pride, the boast of its native inhabitants, a large majority of whom, happily for them, believe themselves the first people upon the earth.

On a shooting excursion in the skirts of the Blue Ridge, so called from the blue tint appearing at a distance over them, I met a German inhabitant, who invited me to refresh myself, with a draught of cyder. I gladly accepted his invitation, and over the glass he informed me, finding I was an European, that he came to America with the corps of Hessians that composed a part of General Burgoyne's army. He proved very communicative, observing that instead of being sent by the Americans to Boston to be embarked for Europe, according to the terms of capitulation, he was marched to Frederick Town in Maryland, which proved, eventually, a fortunate circumstance for his future prospects in life. The industrious among the prisoners quickly found employment, and the whole, in a short time, obtained their freedom. The Germans applied to agriculture, land being then easy of attainment, and he had become a man of considerable property.

On this subject, one Richard Dinmore,* who resides in

* This Dinmore left his country, as common report states, at a time when so many fled to avoid the punishment which awaits traitors. Like Callender, Duane,[5] Anthony Pasquin, and a horde of British scribblers in America, he has the direction of a petty newspaper at Alexandria, which he calls the Expositor; wherein he vents his rancor against his offended nation. Dinmore was an apothecary at Walton, in the county of Norfolk, in England; and a greater enemy to the British constitution is not in existence. Not content with slandering his country through his own press, he has found the means of publishing his observations in one of the most respectable London monthly publications. They appear under the shape of Letters to the Editor, and are pompously called a Tour through the United States of America. He labors to impress the reader with the idea of his being an American. This TOUR is a dull account of a journey from Alexandria to Kentucky. Speaking generally of the present place of his residence, he says, *we Americans, our country, my fellow-citizens,* and the American war he calls, *our revolutionary war.* He certainly has abundant

Alexandria, near the city of Washington, in a letter published in London, says: "In Alexandria, there are now resident several of those Hessians, whom the English paid for, and sent to conquer this country. They staid here after the war, and some of them are now among the wealthiest men in this place."

Literature is yet at a low ebb in the United States. During my stay in Philadelphia, where the small portion of genius is chiefly to be found, I heard of very few literary characters, superior to the political scribblers of the day. Joseph Dennie,[8] and Mr. Brown,[9] of that city, with Mr. Fessenden,[10] of Boston, are men of genius. The former is editor of a literary periodical paper, called "The Port-Folio," a publication which would do credit to the most polished nation in Europe. Its contemporary prints make politics their principal object;

reason to value the country which has adopted him, for America not only proved to him an asylum, but the present government, ever rewarding democratic bawlers and apostate Englishmen, actually employed him on some internal negociation, in the execution of which he gives a tedious detail of his journey over the Blue and Alleghany mountains.

There is scarcely a number of his newspaper which does not contain malignant paragraphs, and infamous falsehoods respecting the British nation; but in a style so wretched, that its circulation even with democratic support, is very limited; and were it not for the advertisements and favor of the government, Mr. Dinmore's editorship would long ago have yielded to the smarting strokes of poverty.

Among the vile scurrility of his "Expositor," last summer was the following.—After noticing the introduction of the American minister, Mr. Munroe, to the king, he adds: "For once an honest man has appeared at the court of St. James's." Another paper printed by Mr. S. Snowden,[6] in the same town, but in the federal interest, makes this observation upon the paragraph. "It is no doubt difficult for an honest man in the doctor's (Apothecary Dinmore's) estimation of the word, to get admission there; yet he cannot have forgotten that he himself was within a cable's length of having his name announced to his Britannic majesty — not by Sir Stephen Cotterill, but by the recorder of London, and ordinary of Newgate, as joint masters of the ceremonies."

The following will shew the principles and the style of writing of this man, in his letters, published in London:

"Should the present administration of Great Britain pursue towards the United States the same conduct as was practised by the last, this nation will take such steps as will be severely rued in *yours*. Believe, and I wish your politicians the Port-Folio embraces the belles lettres, and cultivates the arts and sciences. The editor, when he touches upon the state of his country, speaks in the cause of federalism; and, from his great abilities, he is consequently obnoxious to the ruling party. The government had long endeavored to control the federal prints, and had already ineffectually prosecuted some of the editors. At length, they denounced Mr. Dennie, who was indicted and tried at Philadelphia, for publishing the following political strictures: —[11]

A democracy is scarcely tolerable at any period of national history. Its omens are always sinister, and its powers are unpropitious. With all the lights of experience blazing before our eyes, it is impossible not to discern the futility of this form of government. It was weak and wicked in Athens. It was bad in Sparta, and worse in Rome. It has been tried in France, and has terminated in despotism. It was tried in England, and rejected with the utmost loathing and abhorence. It is on its trial here, and the issue will be civil war, desolation, and anarchy. No wise man but discerns its imperfections; no good man but shudders at its miseries; no honest man but proclaims its fraud; and no brave man but draws his sword against its force. The

to believe me, that the sense of this nation is against *you*, more especially since the aggression and murder of Pierce, by one of *your* commanders. It is true *we* deprecate war, for *we* know if it will not actually make *us* miserable, it will retard the progress of *our* national happiness; but sooner than permit *our* free citizens to be murdered and impressed, their property plundered, and *our* national character dishonored, *we* will, in the first instance, cease to deal with you, next (cry havock and let slip the dogs of war) let loose *our* privateers, and enter into the unprofitable, detestable, and impious contest of *trying which nation can do each other most harm*."

It is a very old but a very just observation, that when an unprincipled man injures another, he instantly becomes the inveterate enemy of the party aggrieved. This maxim may be extended farther than the ordinary intercourse of individuals. Have we not seen Englishmen who have injured society, who, to avoid the punishment due to their crimes, or the just demands of their creditors, have either crossed the Channel or the Atlantic, exceeding in political rancor those who would naturally be expected to shew the most decided hostility to the interests of Britain! 'Tis this feeling that has impelled a Payne, a Dinmore, and a large discontented phalanx in America to aim their envenomed shafts at the country which gave them birth; 'tis this that causes a Goldsmith,[7] a Dutton, and other expatriated traitors at Paris to surpass in the virulence and scurrility of the Argus, even the effusions of Napoleon's own official Moniteur.

institution of a scheme of polity, so radically contemptible and vicious, is a memorable example of what the villainy of some men can devise, the folly of others receive, and both establish, in despite of reason, reflection, and sensation.

This paragraph was copied into the federal papers throughout the union, and it became extremely obnoxious to the democratic party. The trial greatly interested all ranks; but, after much time being consumed, and much party spirit evinced by the contending advocates, Mr. Dennie was acquitted. He gives a sketch of the trial in the Port-Folio, and thus concludes: — "The causes of this prosecution, the spirit of the times, and the genius of the commonwealth, must be obvious to every observer. The editor inscribes *vici* on the white shield of his innocence, but is wholly incapable of vaunting at the victory!" [12]

Mr. Brown is editor of the Philadelphia Literary Magazine,[13] a work greatly resorted to by the compilers of some of the London monthly publications.

Printing and bookselling have of late years been extended to the most remote parts of the country. Several newspapers are printed in Kentucky;[14] and almost every town of more than a few score houses, in every state, has a printing-office, from which the news is disseminated. There is no tax whatever on the press, and consequently every owner of one can print a newspaper with little risk, among a people who are all politicians. These sheets are the utmost limits of literature in most country towns, and they furnish ample food for disputation. Several hundred different newspapers are daily distributed by the public mail, in all parts, to subscribers, at the small charge of one or two cents, at most, for postage;* but printers exchange their papers with each other, by that mode, free of any charge. I have often seen a printer receive as many newspapers by one mail, as would fill the room of several hundred letters.

* The post-towns in the United States, and which are rapidly increasing, in the year 1804 amounted to 1,159.

English publications are reprinted in various parts of the United States; but in order to make them "cheap editions," they are generally on an inferior paper, contracted and garbled. In this state they are issued from the press, often at one-fifth of the price of the London editions. A work recently published here at the price of two pounds, five shillings, in the last Philadelphia papers is advertised at two dollars. A book of the desription of these sheets, with views to illustrate the subject, will there appear divested of those ornaments, and the whole matter in explanation of the plates suppressed. If works of great extent, such as the Encyclopædia Britannica, in which a London publisher will expend many thousand pounds before a single copy can be offered for sale, are attempted there to be copied, many months are passed in procuring subscribers; and for this purpose riders are sent to every large town, by which means almost every inhabitant is solicited to lend assistance.[15]

In some instances, however, much typographic spirit is to be met with. Matthew Carey,[16] an old established bookseller in Philadelphia, has announced the accomplishment of his attempt to keep one of his quarto editions of the Bible, standing, in the type; and he advertises for sale, eighteen different priced quarto Bibles. In his advertisements he says that "he trusts it will be borne in mind that it is the first attempt that has ever been made to keep the quarto Bible completely standing. The paper, type, printing, engravings, and binding, are all American."

In Philadelphia the printers have instituted a typographical society, of which Mr. John Childs is the president.[17] This society consists of one hundred and twenty members. They have stated meetings, and an anniversary on the first day of November. The trade contribute towards a fund for the relief of the sick members, and the burial of such as depart this life in distressed circumstances. The last report mentions only one death in the fraternity during the last four years. They profess the principles of Franklin, who is revered by them as the father of the typographic art in America.

This trade have an annual book fair,[18] upon the plan of that at Leipsic, in Germany. It is held in the month of June, at Newark, in the state of New Jersey, twelve miles from New York. Here the principal booksellers meet from all parts of the United States, or send a representative, to arrange the general business, enter into regulations, announce intended publications, and exchange with each other those already on sale. Matthew Carey, above-mentioned, is the secretary; but Matthew has threatened to attend no more, unless the fair is alternately held in the vicinity of Philadelphia, where the booksellers consider themselves as taking the lead of any other place in the Union.

In a country presenting agriculture and trade in their most advantageous points of view, there is still less encouragement for the arts and sciences. Few individuals have yet amassed a fortune sufficient to enable them to indulge in elegant luxuries; and where that may have occurred, the possessor, of mean origin, remains still sordid, or is devoid of taste. Except the public buildings, there is little employment for the artisan. Half a dozen of our best portrait painters would not find employment in the United States, unless, like lawyers on a circuit, they travelled from one city to another. As many engravers obtain a bare competence in Philadelphia and New York. Mr. Edwin,[19] son of the late comedian, the best engraver in the first of those cities, informed me that he was paid with parsimony, was obliged to give long credit, and was undetermined as to his longer residence among them. Mr. Haynes,[20] another artist in the same branch, after some perseverance in the execution of his business, was obliged to return, little more than a year ago, to London.

Before I quit the subject of literature I cannot forbear taking some notice of a publication which recently made its appearance in Boston, under the title of "Letters from London, written during the year 1802 and 1803, by William Austin." [21] Were I to pass it over in silence, it might perhaps be construed in America into an admission of the justice of the remarks contained in that volume. Unwilling, however, to afford Mr. Austin occasion for such a triumph, I here, in the most unqualified manner declare, that his book is throughout a tissue of falsehood, misrepresentation, prejudice, and scurrility. In support of this opinion I shall introduce a few passages, which, I think, will prove quite sufficient for every English reader.

Speaking of monarchical governments, our republican says: "Kings and nobles are the severest libel which any people can suffer; they had their origin in the *weakness* of mankind, at length usurped an hereditary authority, and now have their continuance through the *baseness* of mankind. And when these orders are once instituted, it is their constant policy to discourage every advance to former virtue."

His observations on the relations between masters and servants in England, furnish not only a corroboration, but also a contrast to what has been said in a former part of this volume concerning those of America. "What do you imagine is the tye," says he, "which restrains the English servants in this ready servility to their masters? You observe I use the terms *servants* and *masters*. A servant is not offended if you ask him where his master is. In the United States (a country where triumph the purest principles of legislation which ever adorned civil society — a country in which the human character is already elevated to a superior species of man, compared with the miserable wretches of Europe[22]) should one ask a person where his master was, he would, doubtless, meet with a rough reply: for, in truth, there are no such characters in the United States, as masters and servants. I will now tell you the reason why the English make such *excellent* servants. They have three things before their eyes: servitude for life, Botany Bay,[23] and the gallows. Servitude they most commonly esteem the least of the three evils. But servitude has its terrors: for if their masters dismiss them without a character, they are undone. Their habits and education, or rather want of education, rendering them useless, they are forced to enter the lowest class of that great body of men who live at the public expence in England."[24]

The author then proceeds to display his wit, as he doubtless imagined, though it is obvious that he borrowed his ideas from the degraded situation of the wretched slaves in the favored land of republican equality: "The servants in England are not exactly what they ought to be: where the fathers and sons for many generations are likely to be servants during their lives, it is of great consequence they should possess as little as possible either of the dress, manners, form, or feelings of men. They should be bred in the most profound ignorance, and they should be taught from their infancy to consider themselves a distinct species. To impress this more deeply, they should be disfigured as much as might be consistent with their usefulness: both of their ears might be spared; so might their noses. It might injure their healths to paint them, but it is a pity that a certain dye-stuff could not be invented, through which perspiration might pass. In short, they should in all respects be treated like beasts of burden!!"[25]

With such ribaldry has this scribbler contrived to fill upwards of three hundred octavo pages, for the amusement of his Yankee brethren across the Atlantic. Not even the most solemn subjects can claim an exemption from his scurrility. He makes himself extremely merry at a funeral, describing it as the most humorous sight which, after a residence of four months in London, he had yet beheld. He mistook it, he says, for a shew, and in the fulness of his simplicity, no doubt, enquired of an honest Englishman what the shew was. The latter, it seems, with becoming indignation, gave this blunt reply: "You may know one day, if you do not come to the gallows." The American would persuade us that he took the hearse for a baggage-waggon, and so delighted is our Yankee with this idea, bright as that of Polonius, who pretended to fancy a cloud to be a camel or a whale, that he constantly calls this vehicle a waggon. Now for my part, friend William, I must protest that this is scarcely more ludicrous than your black boxes on wheels, with sculls and thigh-bones on the sides, in which you convey your dead, and not much worse than dragging them on the shafts of an old buggie, or in an open cart.

The greater the decency observed in paying the last tribute of respect to a departed relative or friend, the more profound is the impression which the awful scene is calculated to produce. Had our contemplative traveller followed the funeral to the grave, which I suppose he did not, he would there have witnessed the performance of the last solemn rites, which perhaps would have furnished a new subject for his satirical talents, because the English have not yet adopted the enlightened custom of consigning their dead to the parent earth, like some fanatic sects in America, in fields and gardens, without a burial service, or even a prayer.

Each observation of this author concludes with a comparison. On the last-mentioned occasion, he adds: "I believe our funerals in New England are conducted much in the manner as they were in ancient Rome."[26] If this be the case, I wonder how they came by this *manner*, as this land of fanaticism was peopled by malcontents from Old England, and ignorance, the handmaid of superstition, prevented them from distinguishing the manners of Rome from those of Grand Cairo.

The truth is, that no people upon earth make a greater parade in the burial of the dead, than Mr. Austin's countrymen. On such occasions what they call "warnings," is the day before, or early in the morning, given of the funeral. This is a notice or warning of the event in writing, which is regularly carried from house to house, and shewn or read to some of the family. Some hours previous to the procession being put in motion, the neighbors assemble, and the tenement of the deceased is soon filled; to whom wine, punch, toddy, and cakes, are handed round. During this time some dissenting minister is frequently haranguing those within the house, in what is called a funeral sermon, while the great body of those who mean to swell the procession gather together on the outside. In some places they have a vehicle which may be called a hearse, but as rude in comparison to that which diverted the Yankee in London, as their stage-waggons are to the elegant and comfortable public coaches met with on the high roads of Britain. It is in fact, as I have already said, a kind of black box on wheels, and sometimes decorated, not with nodding plumes of feathers, but with miserable daubings, meant to represent human sculls and crossed thigh-bones. This vehicle is, however, seldom to be found; carrying dead bodies upon men's shoulders, the most usual mode, is certainly attended with less expence.

The sermon ended, which generally consumes an hour, and sometimes two, the procession, if the subject of the ceremony has died rich, is conducted in the following order: — First comes the undertaker, in a scarf and hatband of black silk or white linen, according to the state of the deceased, then follow, side by side, the parson and the doctor, personages deemed necessary on those occasions, and who are also complimented with the insignia of mourning; the other clergy of the town; the body, when no hearse or chaise wheels are used, carried by four inferior republicans, without the smallest trappings of woe, while the pall is borne by six of their superiors, in hatbands and scarfs similar to those of the parson and doctor;* but which are generally put over a drab or other coloured coat, presenting a motley view; then follow the inhabitants, two and two, beginning with those who arrogate to themselves in this land of liberty a

* The British Aristophanes, Foote,[27] in one of his dramas, introduces a doctor and a taylor. The former has just returned from a funeral, and Snip from carrying to a customer a new garment; upon which he observes to the doctor that they have been both on the same errand, "carrying home their work!"

superiority over the others, until the whole is brought up by the slaves of the deceased. These processions, such is the usage, are sometimes the whole length of a large town; and the surviving relatives are gratified in proportion to the number of attendants.

The interment of inferior persons is also generally attended with a procession. Instead, however, of scarfs and hatbands, the mourners content themselves with a piece of black ribbon or crape, tied round the arm above the elbow; and on these occasions, the parading of the priest and the doctor, for reasons which need no explanation, is omitted, and the corpse is committed to the grave without the reading of a prayer, or the singing of a psalm.

From these customs it would seem that Mr. Austin's *admiration* should have been excited, at witnessing the superior solemnity of a funeral in the metropolis of Britain. A touch of *envy* must have rankled in his breast when he mistook the procession for a *shew*; especially when he compared with it the barbarous imitation of his countrymen, which has already been described. Such is their propensity to parade, especially on these occasions, that they would certainly adopt this *shew* were the *means* of making it in their possession. If any proof of this is yet wanting, I shall adduce the circumstance of their burying General Washington *in effigy* in most of their large towns.[28]

NOTES — CHAPTER XXXI

1. George Washington Parke Custis was a son of John Parke Custis and Eleanor Calvert. He grew up on the Mount Vernon estate and lived there until the death of Mrs. Washington, when he moved to Arlington. In 1803 he inaugurated an annual convention for the promotion of agriculture and especially for the encouragement of the wool growing industry.

2. In the *Works of Benjamin Franklin,* Published with a life of the author, by Jared Sparks, Chicago, 1882. II, 470-71: "Information to those who would remove to America."

3. According to the *Civil and Military List of Rhode Island 1647-1800,* compiled by J. J. Smith, a John Faxon served in Newport as Justice of the Peace from 1791 to 1793. This gentleman may have been the author of the "ill-judged solicitations" which caused Janson to enter the legal profession. On

January 7, 1790, a John Faxon married Lydia Gardiner Champlain, widow of Captain Robert Champlain. At this time Faxon was listed as an attorney. Later he and his wife moved to Lubec or Machias, Maine, where he died on May 22, 1826, aged 65 years. See *Vital Records of Rhode Island, 1636-1850, Marriages,* p. 76; *Deaths,* p. 490. Also see *The Narragansett Historical Register,* Hamilton, R. I., I, 213.

4. The first approach to a medical school in Philadelphia was Dr. William Shippen's Anatomical Theatre, in which the doctor gave lectures in 1762. He continued them for three years, after which he and Dr. John Morgan established the Medical College of Philadelphia. He held a professorship in the college and in its successor, the University, until 1806, or for more than forty years. Dr. Benjamin Rush, born in 1745, was the real founder of medical science in this country. When not yet fifteen years old, he graduated at Princeton College and then gave attention to the study of medicine under tutors in Philadelphia. He continued his medical education in Edinburgh, where he received his doctor's degree in 1768. He returned to Philadelphia and served as professor in the new medical school continuously until his death in 1813.

5. James Thomas Callender and William Duane.

6. In 1800 Samuel Snowden assumed control of the *Columbian Mirror and Alexandria Gazette,* established in 1792. In 1800 a daily paper, the *Alexandria Advertiser,* also was being edited by S. Snowden.

7. Evidently Lewis Goldsmith, a political writer and journalist. In Poland during the war of independence, he attacked the powers which repressed the revolution in *The Crimes of the Cabinets,* in 1801. By an arrangement with Bonaparte, he established in Paris *The Argus, or London Reviewed in Paris,* in 1802.

8. An essayist and editor born in Boston and graduated from Harvard. After being associated with several other magazines, he and Asbury Dickins, a bookseller, established *The Portfolio* in Philadelphia on January 3, 1801. Published weekly, it was devoted to literature and politics. During the period of its greatest popularity from 1802 to 1805 it had a distinguished list of contributors and even printed from manuscripts some of the poems of Campbell, Moore, Leigh Hunt, and Monk Lewis. The magazine continued publication in various forms until 1827.

9. Charles Brockden Brown, novelist and journalist, the first person in the United States to make authorship a profession and the first American novelist to win an international hearing.

10. Thomas Green Fessenden, the satirist. He wrote virulent assaults on Jefferson and minor Democratic leaders. In 1805 he published *Democracy Unveiled: or Tyranny Stripped of the Garb of Patriotism.*

11. See *The Portfolio,* April 23, 1803, p. 135.

12. Dennie's attacks upon the democratic system became so violent that upon the instigation of William Duane, Dennie was indicted by the Grand Jury in 1803 for uttering "inflammatory and seditious libel." Aided by his friends among whom were Judge Hopkinson, Charles Ingersoll, and William Meredith, all able lawyers, he was found not guilty when the case came to trial in 1805. See *The Portfolio,* December 7 and 28, 1805, for reports of the indictment, trial, and verdict.

13. Charles Brockden Brown edited and contributed to the *Literary Magazine and American Register* from 1803 to 1807.

14. In 1790 one newspaper was published in Kentucky; in 1810, seventeen. In 1790 there were 106 in the entire United States; in 1810, 358.

15. In 1790 Thomas Dobson of Philadelphia began the first American edition of the *Encyclopedia Brittanica*, generally known as *Dobson's Encyclopedia.* He had but 246 subscribers when the first half-volume was ready for delivery. He successfully completed its twenty-one volumes and three supplementary volumes in 1803.

16. Matthew Carey, publisher and economist, came to America in 1784 and issued the first edition of his *Pennsylvania Herald* in January, 1785. Later he borrowed money and set up as a publisher and bookseller. *The Portfolio* of August 10, 1805, carries references to his editions of the Bible.

17. On November 1, 1806, when the Society celebrated its fourth anniversary, it consisted of 120 members. Childs, as president, delivered the oration.

18. Matthew Carey was instrumental in organizing the American Literary Fair, the first being held in June, 1802. It was then decided to hold the fairs twice yearly and alternately in New York and Philadelphia. At the fall gathering in 1802 the idea of auction was introduced. After four or five years of indifferent success the fairs were abandoned. Country printers brought in editions of popular works from worn types and on inferior paper, and thus enjoyed an improper advantage.

19. David Edwin, son of John Edwin an English actor, came to Philadelphia in 1797 and for nearly thirty years was the most prolific workman in America.

20. William Haynes or Haines, an excellent engraver of portraits in the stipple manner, came to Philadelphia in 1802 and returned to England in 1805.

21. William Austin, *Letters from London Written during the Years 1802 and 1803*. Boston, 1804.

22. Austin, *Letters,* pp. 109-10. The phrase "a country where triumph the purest principles of legislation which ever adorned civil society — a country in which human character is already elevated to a superior species of man, compared with the miserable wretches of Europe" does not occur in the source of Janson's quotation.

23. Botany Bay, a bay and landing place on the coast of New South Wales, south of Sydney, Australia. It was one of the earliest European settlements on that continent and formerly a British convict station.

24. See Austin, *Letters,* pp. 88-89.

25. See Austin, *Letters,* pp. 89-90.

26. See Austin, *Letters,* pp. 43-55.

27. Samuel Foote, actor and dramatist, the author of numerous satires in dramatic form.

28. A funeral was held in Philadelphia on December 26, 1799, with a procession, bier and pall, and a service at Christ Church. The accounts make no mention of a burial. Funeral solemnities for Washington were held also in Norfolk. The bier was taken to the church and after the service to the grave, where three volleys were fired. Doubtless this practice was fairly general at that time.

CHAPTER XXXII

THE AMERICAN CAPTAIN LITTLE TAKES A FRENCH CORVETTE — TRIED ON CHARGES BROUGHT AGAINST HIM BY THE PRISONERS, AND SUPERSEDED IN HIS COMMAND — THE FRENCH SHIP REPAIRED AT THE EXPENCE OF AMERICA, AND RESTORED BY CONGRESS — BLOCKADED IN BOSTON BY A BRITISH SHIP — ACTION OFF SANDY HOOK BETWEEN THE AMBUSCADE AND BOSTON — CIRCUMSTANCES ATTENDING THE RETURN OF ADET, THE FRENCH AMBASSADOR — BLOCKADE OF A FRENCH FRIGATE IN NEWPORT BY THE ASIA — JOHN PIERCE KILLED BY A SHOT FROM THE LEANDER — PROCLAMATION OF PRESIDENT JEFFERSON ON THE OCCASION.

IN THE fomer part of this volume I have mentioned the vigorous measures resorted to by President Adams against the depredations daily committing upon the commerce of the United States during his administration, by the French in the West Indies.

The American frigate called the *Boston*, commanded by Captain Little, was one of the cruisers sent by Mr. Adams, to check their piratical depredations.[1] This ship had fallen in with a large French corvette called *Le Berceau*, and took her after a faint resistance. Little brought his prize safely to the harbor of the town from which his ship was named and at this time Mr. Jefferson was seated in the presidential chair. On a similar occasion, when Commodore Truxton captured a French frigate in the presidency of Mr. Adams, she was condemned as a lawful prize, and refitted to cruize against her former owners.

On the arrival of Captain Little with his prize at Boston, the republican prisoners were extremely clamorous against him, and found means to send a remonstrance to President Jefferson. This was a proceeding natural to men who are prevented from following their nefarious career, but that the reigning ruler of the country, subverting in every instance the measures of his predecessors should notice their complaint by degrading Captain Little, was, at the time the circumstance happened, a matter of astonishment. This gallant man, like Colonel Butler, was of the school of Washington.

The *Columbian Centinel*, edited by Major Benjamin Russell, one of the best diurnal prints in the United States,[2] thus mentions this transaction:

> The trial of Captain Little on charges alleged against him by the officers of the French corvette, *Le Berceau*, has excited much sensibility in the breast of every real friend to the American navy. It has been considered *a new thing under the sun*, for a brave and humane officer, without the least previous investigation by the government under which he serves, to be deprived of his *sword* and *ship*, and be compelled to stand a public trial, on the bare complaint of the prisoners he had just captured — whose characters were known to be infamous, and whose conduct to several American vessels has been proved on oath to have been little better than that of pirates. Yet such things we have seen, and on the oath of such men has a gallant naval commander been subject to the ignominy of arrest and trial — whether from a desire to *rescue the American navy from the suspicion of reproach*, or from an undue attachment to *the French republic*, let the manly, good sense of the American public determine.

Captain Little was brought to trial on the charges of the French marauders of *Le Berceau* and on the following accusations:

1. Taking money from the prisoners.
2. Plundering them of articles, their private property.
3. Indecent conduct in searching them, and the corvette in which they were made prisoners.
4. Cruelty towards them.
5. Kidnapping a part of the crew of the prize.

Upon the trial not a charge was proved. It was evident they originated in that vindictive spirit so conspicuous among the nation of the accusers. By the judgment of the court-martial before whom he underwent this derogation, he was, of course, honorably acquitted.

The publication above quoted farther observed, "that it will give pleasure to the public to learn that not one syllable of these charges were founded in truth; on the contrary, they appear to have originated in malice towards an officer who had arrested the piratical career of the complainants; and in the expectation that the government would be more ready to punish than countenance an act so degrading to the French republic as the capture of a national corvette."

It appeared that the secretary of the navy betrayed emotions of disappointment on reading the sentence of the court-martial; and that, failing in fixing the pretended indignities offered to the Frenchmen on the gallant commander, he transferred it in general terms to his crew in order to convince the adverse party of the high consideration he entertained for the sister republic. Captain Little was, notwithstanding, deprived of the command of his ship, being superseded by Captain Daniel M'Niell, and has not since been in the employ of the government. The *Boston,* on the 7th of February, 1806, was condemned as unfit for service.

The French ship was immediately restored, and ordered to be completely repaired, at the cost of 32,000 dollars, and every possible satisfaction was made by the loving government of the United States to the crew, to enable them again to commit fresh depredations on their commerce. A Boston publication of that date says:

Yesterday the Ex-American corvette saluted the morn, noon, and sun-set, with 21 guns each. Whether in honour of the destruction of the Bastille in 1789, or of the establishment of Cayenne bastiles in 1801; or, as might be conjectured from the number of guns, in commemoration of the sixty-three revolutions, constitutions, &c., &c., in France, we have not learnt.

It was quite gallant in *Le Berceau* yesterday to degrade the British colours while lying snug in a neutral port, especially when it is known that an English ship of inferior force has invited her to sea to take a trial at flag-striking.

When the corvette was ready for sailing, a small sloop of war called the *Pheasant,* under the command of Captain Skipsey,* then a master and commander in the British navy, was found ready to dispute her passage into the ocean. The *Pheasant,* I think, is rated at eighteen guns, the corvette at twenty-eight; and yet nothing could prevail upon the Frenchmen to go out of Boston harbour. Here is another instance, to use the language of Mr. John Randolph in the house of representatives, of Great Britain fighting the battles of the United States, in seeking to destroy her own enemy. *Le Berceau* was blockaded in Boston many months by the *Pheasant;* and without this interposition, she would have renewed her ravages upon the American trade. Thus, in spite of the government, did Captain Skipsey save their vessels from falling a prey to the piratical crew of *Le Berceau,* which at length escaped in the usual manner — favored by a gale of wind.

The day of my first arrival in New York was rendered memorable by the severe engagement which took place off Sandy Hook, between the *Boston* and the *Ambuscade.*[3] We heard distinctly the broadsides as we passed down Long Island Sound, but knew not on what account they were fired. This battle being premeditated on the part of the French, various were the conjectures respecting the cause, and I therefore took some pains to gain correct information.

The *Ambuscade,* a large 44 gun frigate, had been some time lying opposite to New York, and it was known that the *Boston* was stationed on the outside of Sandy Hook. Captain Bompard, who commanded the *Ambuscade,* had given no intimation of his intended departure, until, on a sudden, preparations were made to go out, and a report was spread

* This gallant officer was a lieutenant on board the *Berwick* man of war, one of the British squadron under Admiral Parker, which engaged the Dutch fleet on the Dogger bank during the American war.

that Captain Courtenay, the British commander, had sent him a challenge. The circumstance which gave rise to the report was this: A pilot-boat had carried some provisions to the *Boston*, and as the pilot was returning down the side of the ship to his boat, a young midshipman said to him: "Give our compliments to Captain Bompard, and tell him we shall be glad of his company on this side the Hook." This lost nothing by the way in being communicated to the French commander, who was even told that it was a direct challenge from Captain Courtenay. It soon spread over New York, and the French faction began to feel ashamed that their ship should be blockaded, and thus challenged to come out, by an enemy so inferior in force. This was a spur to Bompard, who, having taken on board a number of American seamen that had offered themselves as volunteers, he promised to chastise the haughty foe. He accordingly went out, attended by a great number of vessels and boats crowded with Americans to witness the fight. The *Boston* soon descried the enemy, and was observed to alter her tacks and to prepare for battle, which soon began on the part of the French, while her antagonist waited her nearer approach. The Gallic-Americans assembled on the occasion had already begun to persuade themselves that the little *Boston* was declining an engagement, when she opened a tremendous and incessant fire. I was informed, so rapid were her broadsides, that she gave three to two received from her enemy during the whole engagement. In the heat of battle the brave Captain Courtenay was killed, and the first lieutenant of the *Boston* badly wounded. The latter, having passed through the surgeon's hands, was brought upon deck, and proved an able substitute for his deceased captain during the remainder of the bloody conflict. The mainmast of the *Ambuscade* was shot through, and could barely be supported by the shrouds — a breeze would have carried it by the board. The *Boston* having lost her fore-top-mast, she put about to replace it, and soon after descrying the French fleet from St. Domingo, she made sail towards Halifax, while the *Ambuscade* declined following, happy, no doubt, in getting back. The Democrats set up the cry of victory, and they publicly rejoiced at what I thought a discomfiture. Next morning I mixed among a group going on board the *Ambuscade*, and there, for the only time, saw the horrid issue of battle. The decks were still in parts covered with blood — large clots lay here and there where the victim had expired. The mast, divested of splinters, I could have crept through; and her sides were perforated with balls. I shrunk from this scene of horror, though amongst the enemies of my native country. The wounded were landed, and sent to the hospital. I counted thirteen on pallets, and double that number less severely wounded. Nothing but commiseration resounded through the streets, while the ladies tore their chemises to bind up their wounds. Advertisements were actually issued for linen rags for that purpose, and surgeons and nurses in numbers repaired to the sick ward. The French officers would not acknowledge the amount of their slain. I calculate the proportion to the wounded must have been at least twenty. I afterwards went on board the *Jupiter*, a line of battleship, and one of the St. Domingo squadron. The sons of equality were a dirty ragged crew, and their ship was very filthy. This was before any contagious fever had visited New York — these fellows were alone sufficient to engender disease. I witnessed Bompard's triumphal landing the day after the engagement. He was hailed by the gaping infatuated mob with admiration, and received by a number of the higher order of Democrats with exultation. They feasted him, and gave entertainments in honour of his asserted victory. He was a very small elderly man, but dressed like a first-rate beau, and doubtless fancied himself upon this occasion six feet high! At this moment I verily believe the mob would have torn me piecemeal had I been pointed at as a stranger just arrived from England. I ground this supposition on the fact of a British lieutenant of the navy having been insulted the same day at the Tontine coffee-house; but he escaped farther injury by jumping over the iron railing in front of the house. The flags of the sister republics were entwined in the public room. Some gentleman secretly removed the French ensign, on which rewards were offered for a discovery of the offender, but he remained in secret.

In the preceding part of this volume, I mentioned the dismission of Genet and Duplaine from their diplomatic functions by President Washington. Not long afterwards he thought fit to revoke the powers granted to Mr. Moore, the English vice-consul at Newport in Rhode Island.

Adet, the ambassador from France[4], being recalled, a frigate of his nation lay at Newport ready to receive him; but blockaded by the British man of war *Asia*. He embarked in a Rhode Island packet at New York, in order to proceed to Newport. Of this, with the most minute account of his suite and baggage, Moore received information from a friend, previous to the sailing of the packet; and which he immediately communicated to the captain of the *Asia*, with directions to intercept the Frenchman. Accordingly, as the packet approached, the British ship was in waiting, fired a gun to bring her to, and immediately manned a boat and boarded her. This greatly astonished the Americans on board, who had never, previous thereto, been molested by the cruizers of England. The lieutenant demanded Adet, and upon being answered that he was not on board, he was proceeding to search for him, when he was assured, that being becalmed, the packet had put into Stonington, a port about twenty miles distant, where the ambassador landed, with a great part of his baggage. The officer was furnished with a description, and the number of trunks, which he demanded; but they had, most fortunately for the monsieurs, been landed. Adet passed along the shore while the packet was undergoing this scrutiny. The governor of the state, Arthur Fenner,[5] a quaker, resented the indignity offered to the American flag, and sent an account of the transaction to

President Washington, who immediately revoked the functions of Mr. Moore, and sent a strong remonstrance to the British government. I thus lost a valuable acquaintance with that gentleman's amiable family, who returned with him soon afterwards to England; and I never heard how the affair terminated.

The French frigate was moored in the harbour, while the *Asia* kept her station near the Naraganset shore, about four miles distant. I was alarmed one morning by a great bustle in the street, and enquiring the cause, was informed "that my cursed countrymen were going to take the French frigate, and to massacre the crew." I however ventured out, and saw the *Asia* majestically approaching the frigate under a crowd of sail, while the latter was warping in, nearer to the town. I dreaded the consequences, and had every reason to think that the British ship not only contemplated the seizure of the Frenchmen, but even meant to fire upon the town. This conjecture was founded upon the circumstance of a boat's crew from the *Asia* coming for provisions into the town being grossly insulted by the inhabitants; and the British commander having threatened to bombard the town if the least violence was repeated to any of his men. I naturally concluded that this had again happened, and that he was coming to put his threat into execution. With great anxiety I regarded the manœuvres of the *Asia*, which at half gun-shot wore ship, and returned to her station.*

Adet, weary of being pent up in Newport, determined to risk a flight in a gale of wind; and to this end, early one morning he hastily got on board with his suite, when the frigate slipping her cable, pushed out to sea. The thickness of the atmosphere long sheltered the ambassador from a dis-

* On my return I was followed to my lodgings by a number of boys, singing —

"Englishman no good for me,
Frenchman fight for liberty."

I was told that it would be attended with the utmost danger to chastise the urchins — such are the blessings of liberty and equality!

covery by his enemy. At length the British ship descried the frigate, but she was too far out of the harbor to pursue with any hopes of success. This was, however, attempted, and from the heights of the island the chase was visible as the day cleared, for between two and three hours, when the *Asia* reluctantly gave up the pursuit.

The French captain wrote by his pilot to his agent at Newport an account of his safety, in the true style of *gasconade*. He observed, "that having the ambassador on board, his orders were to decline an engagement, which was a fortunate circumstance for the English ship."

During the latter part of my residence in the United States, the people grew extremely clamorous against Great Britain; and their former rancor was renewed with a spirit doubly vindictive. This temper had been some time agitating, and from the impressment of their seamen, and the detention of their vessels, on their own shores, by British ships of war. Their government, at length, entered into an investigation of the subject, and found various causes of complaint against the conduct of the British commanders stationed on their coast. A list of impressed American citizens was advertised, with directions to their relations and friends to transmit proofs of their citizenship. While these steps were taking in order to ground a remonstrance to Britain, an unlucky ball, fired from the *Leander*, man of war, killed an American citizen at the helm of his vessel, near the entrance of the harbor of New York. This circumstance had nearly inflamed the people to acts of retaliation, and instances actually occurred of unoffending Englishmen being menaced by the exasperated natives. An immediate rupture with Britain was insisted on by the most violent, and the more moderate deprecated the danger of the hostile steps which appeared on the point of being resorted to. They, however, wisely determined to leave the matter to Congress, who passed, after great warmth of debate, an act prohibiting the importation of English manufactures into their ports. This was considered by some as a preliminary step to a declaration of war, which, it is to be hoped, is averted by the recent treaty with that country.

The man whose death excited such an extraordinary sensation, was John Pierce, who had borne through life the character of an industrious citizen. His remains were interred with every demonstration of resentment against those who caused his death, at the public expence; and were attended to the grave by the state officers, corporate bodies, the military, and great numbers of inhabitants, in procession.

The following proclamation of the president, will sufficiently shew the temper of the government on this occasion: —[6]

BY THOMAS JEFFERSON,

President of the United States of America,

A PROCLAMATION

Whereas satisfactory information has been received, that Henry Whitby, commanding a British armed vessel, called the *Leander,* did on the 25th day of the month of April last, within the waters and jurisdiction of the United States, and near to the entrance of the harbor of New York, by a cannon-shot fired from the said vessel *Leander,* commit a murder on the body of John Pierce, a citizen of the United States, then pursuing his lawful vocations within the same waters and jurisdiction of the United States, and near to their shores; and that the said Henry Whitby cannot at this time be brought to justice by the ordinary process of law.

And whereas it does further appear that both before and after the said day, sundry trespasses, wrongs, and unlawful interruptions and vexations on trading vessels coming to the United States, and within their waters and vicinity, were committed by the said armed vessel the *Leander,* her officers and people; by one other armed vessel, called the *Cambrian,* commanded by John Nairne, her officers and people; and by one other armed vessel, called the *Driver,* commanded by Slingsby Simpson, her officers and people; which vessels being all of the same nation, were aiding and assisting each other in the trespasses, interruptions, and vexations aforesaid.

Now therefore, to the end that the said Henry Whitby may be

brought to justice, and due punishment inflicted for the said murder, I do hereby especially enjoin and require all officers having authority, civil or military, and all other persons within the limits or jurisdiction of the United States, wheresoever the said Henry Whitby may be found, now or hereafter, to apprehend and secure the said Henry Whitby, and him safely and diligently to deliver to the civil authority of the place, to be proceeded against according to law.

And I do hereby further require that the said armed vessel, the *Leander,* with her other officers and people, and the said armed vessels the *Cambrian* and *Driver,* their officers and people, immediately and without any delay, depart from the harbors and waters of the United States. — And I do for ever interdict the entrance of all other vessels which shall be commanded by the said Henry Whitby, John Nairne, and Slingsby Simpson, or either of them.

And if the said vessels, or any of them, shall fail to depart as aforesaid, or shall re-enter the harbors or waters aforesaid, I do in that case forbid all intercourse with the said armed vessels, the *Leander,* the *Cambrian,* and the *Driver,* or with any of them, and the officers and crews thereof, and prohibit all supplies and aid from being furnished them, or any of them. And I do declare and make known, that if any person, from or within the jurisdictional limits of the United States, shall afford any aid to either of the said armed vessels, contrary to the prohibition contained in this proclamation, either in repairing such vessel, or in furnishing her, her officers or crew, with supplies of any kind, or in any manner whatever; or if any pilot shall assist in navigating any of the said armed vessels, unless it be for the purpose of carrying them in the first instance, beyond the limits and jurisdiction of the United States; such person or persons shall, on conviction, suffer all the pains and penalties by the law provided for such offences: And I do hereby enjoin and require all persons bearing office, civil or military, within the United States, and all others, citizens or inhabitants thereof, or being within the same, with vigilance and promptitude to exert their respective authorities, and to be aiding and assisting to the carrying this proclamation and every part thereof into full effect.

L. S. " In testimony thereof, I have caused the seal of the United States to be affixed to these presents, and signed the same with my hand.

"Given at the city of Washington, on the third day of May, in the year of our Lord one thousand eight hundred and six, and of the sovereignty and independence of the United States the thirtieth.

(Signed) TH. JEFFERSON.

BY THE PRESIDENT.

(Signed) JAMES MADISON,
Secretary of State."

NOTES — CHAPTER XXXII

1. In his *History of the United States Navy*, I, 208-13 Maclay says nothing about the courtmartial of Captain Little. The *Berceau* was released under the terms of the treaty of February 3, 1801, with France.

2. The *Columbian Centinel* was established in Boston in 1790.

3. Janson arrived in New York on July 31, 1793, the date of the engagement between the *Boston* and the *Ambuscade* in which the British Captain Courtenay was killed. See John Campbell, *Naval History of Great Britain*, VI, 403-04.

4. Ed. Field, *State of Rhode Island and Providence Plantations at the End of the Century: A History*, I, 283-84 says that this controversy arose concerning Fauchet instead of Adet.

5. Arthur Fenner served as Governor of Rhode Island from 1790 to 1805. He was born in 1745 and lived until 1805.

6. This Proclamation may be found in J. D. Richardson, compiler of *Messages and Papers of the Presidents*, I, 390-92.

CHAPTER XXXIII

GYPSUM — LARGE QUANTITIES OF THAT SUBSTANCE IMPORTED FROM CANADA INTO THE UNITED STATES, AND EMPLOYED AS MANURE — PITTSBURG — GENERAL OBSERVATIONS ON THE WESTERN TERRITORIES — MILITARY TAVERN-KEEPERS — QUALITY AND PRODUCE OF THE SOIL IN KENTUCKY — REASON FOR THE LOSS OF TEETH AMONG THE AMERICANS — DIFFICULTY OF BRINGING PRODUCE TO MARKET FROM THE WESTERN COUNTRIES.

IT is surprising to observe the quantities of gypsum, or plaister of Paris, which is carried from the sea-ports of the United States, into the country. The waggons, of late years, make a profitable return load of this article, which is pulverised and used as manure. On certain lands it produces a better crop of wheat and Indian corn than any other kind, and is more durable. When it is known that this valuable substance is not found within the United States, the trade in that article becomes more a matter of surprise. It is procured from the British possessions, and not from the boundary line on the river St. Croix. Vast rocks and quarries of gypsum are found along the coast; and the Americans, unmolested, pilfer it from the inhabitants, who, indeed, seem to account it of little value. When an owner of the soil, which rarely happens, prohibits interlopers from taking it away, he is satisfied with some small tribute. Many scores of vessels are employed in carrying the stone along the coast as far as Savannah, in Georgia. I have often wondered that the British government do not turn the matter to their profit. The Americans would purchase it by weight, as they sell it, to great advantage.

I have seen this valuable manure carried as far as Pittsburg, on the Ohio, between three and four hundred miles. This is the principal commercial place of the new states. The river Ohio is formed by the conflux of the Monongahela and

Allegany, where Pittsburg is situated. The town is well built, principally of brick, has a smoaky appearance, and contains about five hundred houses. The situation is said to be healthy, and agues and intermittent fevers rare. My stay there did not afford time enough to ascertain the truth of this assertion; but the inhabitants of Lexington, and other places in Kentucky, are not only subject to those distressing complaints, but to bilious attacks towards the end of autumn.

Pittsburg is a place of considerable business. It is the staple of the trade to Philadelphia, Baltimore, and Alexandria. Here are two printing-offices, each publishing a newspaper; a glass-house, and an iron-foundry. The exports consist of flour, Indian corn, salted meat and butter, bar iron, and whiskey.* Redstone, an improving town on the river Monongahela, and fifty miles above Pittsburg, also sends a great quantity of produce down the Ohio to New Orleans.

Of late years, ship-building has been carried on here, though upwards of twelve hundred miles from the ocean; and vessels of a size and strength fit for the trade of the most distant parts of the world, have been steered safely down the Ohio and the Mississippi into the gulph of Florida. Vessels of war are now building on the Ohio,[1] intended to have been used as gun-boats against the powers of Barbary, with whom the Americans are generally at war. The cordage for these vessels is manufactured at Redstone and Lexington; and the adjacent district contains abundance of iron. The produce of the country is transported to New Orleans in large barges, which are sometimes forty, and even fifty days on their passage, going with the current.† To return by the same route

* Next to Yankee rum, this is the most execrable of ardent spirits distilled in the United States. Whiskey, made of rye, and at a proper age, is not so very deleterious. The manufacturer will swear to the purchaser that it is genuine whiskey, though made from Indian corn.

† In the spring of the year, the current of the river is so rapid, that there is no occasion for oars or sails. They might, indeed, prove dangerous, being liable, from the great swiftness with which the boat would then go, to turn it out of the current into an eddy, where it might be entangled among sunken branches and roots of trees, rendering the situation extremely dangerous.

would require many months; the barges are therefore sold at New Orleans for some trifling consideration, being frequently cut up for fuel, and the bargemen generally prefer returning by the Atlantic ocean. They procure a passage on very moderate terms to Baltimore or Philadelphia, and return on foot to Pittsburg. This *trip*, in the territory of the United States only, requires two, and sometimes three months. The increase of population in this country, so far removed from the ocean, is astonishing. Previous to the American war, it was an unexplored desart, occasionally penetrated by the savages on their hunting excursions. They opposed the white men on their taking possession of the banks of the Ohio; but they are now driven to a considerable distance; and this country, formed by nature for a distinct empire, comprising the new states of Ohio, Kentucky, and Tennessee, with the territories of Indiana and the Mississippi, contain little short of half a million of inhabitants. The land on the banks of the river is chiefly improved, and it produces on an average, if entirely cleared, fifteen, twenty, and on some spots twenty-five bushels of wheat per acre. It is the custom to notch the trees intended to be felled, the year before, by which the sap no longer running, they perish, and are more easily cut down. The stumps are generally left to the decay of time, and on such land the crop will consequently yield a third less. This plan is adopted, from the great scarcity of working hands. An emigrant eagerly grasps the idea of the cheapness of the land in this part of the world, without ever reflecting on the great difficulty and enormous expence of clearing and tilling it. It is like calculating on the sums of money the timber would produce in England, without allowing the expence of land carriage to his vessel, and for its transportation across the Atlantic, which would render his oak dearer than mahogany. Without a sufficient number of labourers, all his prospects become visionary; and hence we find so many removals from one place to another, and such numbers entirely abandoning the enterprize, and returning impoverished to the sea-coast.

Every article of life in Kentucky is about half the price required on the sea-coast.* Lest any reader should be prepossessed so irretrievably as to be resolved to ascertain the truth of my observations, I beg him first to peruse the following, made by Mr. H. Toulmin, a district judge, and residing at Frankfort.

After describing the difficulty and expense of travelling, which, by the bye, he tells you, "that Englishmen frequently do not learn till they have spent all their money!" or in other and plainer words, that they are ruined by the length, difficulty, and expense, of reaching the place of their destination, Mr. Toulmin descends to the minutiæ of living. He says that wheat is half a dollar per bushel; oats one quarter of a dollar; potatoes the same price; beef 2d. to 3d. per pound; (in order to accommodate the reader, I shall deviate from Mr. Toulmin, and mention the price in British money); fresh pork (generally shot, or otherwise killed in the woods) 2d; bacon 3d. halfpenny to 4d; salt 3s. 9d. per bushel; sugar and tea as dear as in England; but English and other European goods are one-half more at least than in the respective places where they are manufactured.

This gentleman next presents a scheme for purchasing and stocking a farm, and laying in a year's provisions, with the

* At Lexington, in Kentucky, there is a retail store, kept by a Mr. Trotter,[2] who is supposed to do as much business as any trader in the large towns on the sea coast. He sends to market immense quantities of deer skins, the sales of which are said to amount to between thirty and forty thousand dollars annually. This circumstance shews the numerous herds of deer with which the immense forests of that country abound. In winter, the carcases are also frequently brought to the sea-port towns, and sold at the price of fresh beef, and frequently for much less; the Americans not being sufficiently skilled in Epicurism to admire the *haut gout* of a haunch of venison, it is frequently sold at a much lower price as it advances to that state which is so much admired at our city feasts. Mr. Trotter employs many waggons in bringing his goods from Philadelphia, and returning the produce of the country, which he receives in barter for the manufactures of England, and which cost him several thousand dollars yearly.

small sum of 172l. 19s. British; and which, like all other American speculations, is extremely flattering when viewed upon paper. It is as follows:—

	L.	S.	D.
80 Acres of land, with decent cabins, and 30 of which to be cleared (that is, fit for sewing grain)	90	0	0
2 Plough horses	22	0	0
2 Cows and Calves	4	10	0
10 Sheep	4	10	0
1 Plough	1	7	0
Geers and saddles	4	10	0
A one-horse cart	7	10	0
Household furniture	15	0	0
One year's provisions,* viz. 1000 lbs. of pork	4	10	0
300 lbs. of beef	2	10	6
3 bushels of salt	1	7	0
40 ditto of wheat	4	10	0
8 ditto of Indian corn	3	12	0
2000 lbs. of hay	1	10	0
20 bushels of potatoes	1	2	6
Sundries	4	10	0
	£172	19	0

All this sounds pleasing to the ear, and appears satisfactory to the eye, but Mr. Toulmin was no judge, it seems, of the cost of this farmer in arriving with his family at the place of purchase. Indeed, it appears beyond his calculation, for he very judiciously puts it under the sweeping observation—"that Englishmen frequently do not learn it (to travel) until

* In all parts of the United States, families lay in provisions of this kind every winter for the year. In summer time, especially in the back forests, they can have no fresh provisions. The heat of the weather, and the myriads of insects, keep the cattle in the state of *Pharaoh's kine;* and the torment is often so insupportable, that they run off half-mad, and become wild.

they are ruined." At a nearer guess, I can inform him, that it will cost nearly double the contemplated price of this farm before he can place his family upon it; if I may calculate upon the charge of one hundred guineas lately paid by a mercantile friend of mine,* for his passage to New York. It will also be remembered, that the cause of the apparent cheapness of provisions arises from the difficulty of carrying the surplus to market after supplying themselves. Taking this into consideration, together with the advanced price of European goods, tea, and sugar, and above all, the expense of travelling, there will remain no very great balance in favor of the western country over the Atlantic states. This is a subject which writers, who wish to flatter emigrants, will not touch upon; and for the same reason, they will be apt to deny the truth of these observations. It will not be amiss also to take in view that Mr. Toulmin holds a large property on the very spot which he describes; and that, being a man of influence, and a district judge, every emigrant in some degree adds to his fortune and his power.

In travelling these dreary roads, a stranger is amazed at the number of *ci-devant* military officers and infatuated emigrants he meets with. The miserable places of entertainment, which they call taverns, are generally kept by a colonel or a major; and I have known even waggoners who had formerly been field-officers. They are extremely tenacious of their titles, and though many acquired them merely by attending a muster in the militia, and were then displaced, yet, to omit the colonel or the major would imply disrespect, and bring on you some rebuke, if not from the redoubted hero himself, at least some friend or one of the family would immediately supply the defect, or tell you how to accost your host. They rigidly adhere to the vulgar adage, "once a captain always a captain." I have had the honor of being *questioned* by these men of rank, from Colonel Coleman, landlord of the Bunch

* In the first chapter, I have mentioned that I paid for my passage to Boston thirty guineas — such was the price in those times.

of Grapes Inn,[3] State-street, Boston, to Colonel Ripey, who keeps the sign of the General Washington at Shippensburg, in the back part of Pennsylvania.[4] At the house of the latter *commander* ended the line of stages running towards Pittsburg, and the travellers were obliged either to purchase horses, or to walk the remainder of the road — one hundred and seventy miles! There were several horses, it is true, kept for sale; even Colonel Ripey could have accommodated the traveller; but then, aware of his distress, he would have exacted double price. I was sorry to hear that this lucrative part of the colonel's business was destroyed, by a regular stage being lately established the whole way to Pittsburg, for he was good-humored, and dealt out his interrogatories with some decency.

One principal cause of the richness of the land in Kentucky is the thick bed of leaves, and rotting trunks of trees, with which the earth had been covered every year for many generations, and which decayed into a rich and deep vegetable surface that will endure many years' cultivation without being exhausted. This was in some measure the case on the shores of the Atlantic on the discovery of America, but the virtue has been long extracted, and the planter is very sparing of manure, though it may often be made from the weed thrown up by the ocean, which, from its saline particles, is excellent for most of the land, the trouble being the great obstacle to its employment. I have seen thousands of acres *worn out,* as they call it, and lying waste, particularly tobacco-fields, that being a plant which greatly impoverishes wherever it is cultivated.

The goodness of the land is ascertained by the description of the timber with which it is covered. That of the first quality produced black oak, commonly called black jack; white oak, some of which yield acorns nearly the size of hens' eggs; white, black, and blue ash; the white walnut; the cherry tree; the slippery elm; the coffee tree, which bears no fruit of its name; the honey-locust, producing nothing sweet; the sugar maple, from which sugar is made; the beech and plane; the white and yellow poplar; the cucumber-tree, which bears not good fruit; and the tall and weeping willow.

Land of the second quality bears the red oak; black oak, of an inferior quality to the black jack; the sassafrass, the root of which is a great cleanser and purifier of the blood; the sweet and common gum trees, which produce neither a gummy nor resinous substance. On the third quality will be found some inferior kinds of red and black oak, pines, and cedars.

Indian corn thrives in an eminent degree in Kentucky; the best lands producing from thirty to forty bushels per acre, each weighing from fifty to sixty pounds. Some writers on this subject affirm, that in very plentiful years the produce has been known to yield an hundred bushels per acre.* I confess, that I never knew such an instance, nor could I find any planter to corroborate the assertion. This grain, greatly as it is esteemed and used where it is grown, is not suited for consumption either in England or Ireland. In the latter kingdom, during the years of scarcity, 1797 and 1798, when it was brought over in large quantities, it was despised even by the lowest class of the people.

Many reasons have been adduced for the premature loss of teeth among Americans. I am, myself, convinced that the principal cause arises from the constant use of Indian meal, which they make into flat pieces of dough, seven or eight inches in length, three or four in width, and generally half an inch thick, and bake upon a flat board before the fire. This they call Johnny cake, and they eat it with butter quite hot; in fact, it is never used cold but on some emergency. Their salt pork, pickled herrings, and coffee infamously made, drunk almost scalding hot, added to the Johnny cake, the

* The climate here is less subject to summer rains, gusts, and whirlwinds; and these crops are the produce only of what they term *lucky seasons;* yet the crops are in some degree uncertain, while the animals which destroy the seed in the planting season are more numerous than towards the coast.

constant breakfast and supper of the lowest class, must certainly be great enemies to the teeth. At dinner, also, the common bread is this favorite hot cake.

The quantity of Indian corn raised in this western country, has proved another incentive to the emigrants to flock towards the Ohio; but they do not wait to calculate on the small value it bears. A quarter of a dollar per bushel, is about the medium. If the planter sends it to a distant market, New Orleans, a barge load will cost two or three hundred dollars. If sent to the sea-coast, the carriage is still more expensive; and though the price the corn may bring when arrived, should defray expences and leave a profit, yet no one will undertake the long voyage without an advance; and very few emigrants are possessed of superfluous cash for a few years after their arrival.

Tobacco, hemp, and flax, are also cultivated to advantage in the western territory. The price of the former, where grown, is, on an average, two dollars per hundred weight; but when it arrives at the port whence it is shipped, it is advanced to eight dollars. This fact I had an opportunity of ascertaining, having paid that price in Philadelphia, and this is about the ratio of other kinds of produce. Thus, it costs three times the expense of raising, to bring it to market. When in the merchant's hands, the emigrant certainly expects to realize the fruits of his toil. Here he will meet with another impediment, for he must expect no remittance from his commercial agent for at least six months. The merchant ships it as a payment for English goods, on which he has, perhaps, had a year's credit. Every description of business on a large scale in America, is done on very long credit; and if you cannot give that accommodation, you must keep your articles till they perish, or dispose of them at an inferior price.

NOTES — CHAPTER XXXIII

1. The following interesting account of shipbuilding in Pittsburgh is found in George H. Thurston, *Pittsburgh and Allegheny in the Centennial Year*, Pittsburgh, 1876, p. 89: "The building of sea-going vessels was established in

Pittsburgh by a French gentleman, Louis Anastasius Tarascon, who emigrated from France in 1794, established himself in Philadelphia as a merchant. In 1799 he sent two of his clerks, Charles Brugiere and James Berthaud, to examine the course of the Ohio and Mississippi from Pittsburgh to New Orleans, and ascertain the practicability of sending ships, and clearing them ready rigged from Pittsburgh to Europe and the West Indies. The two gentlemen reported favorably. — The first year, 1801, they built the schooner *Amity* of 120 tons, and the *Pittsburgh* of 250 tons, and sent the former loaded with flour to St. Thomas, and the other, also loaded with flour, to Philadelphia from whence they sent them to Bordeaux, France, and brought back a cargo of wine, brandy and other French goods, part of which they sent to Pittsburgh in wagons at a cost of from six to eight cents a pound." Thurston gives a list of four other ships which this company built in 1803 and 1804 and placed in Atlantic service. The same author in *Pittsburgh as It Is*, Pittsburgh, 1857, 68-69, states that the *President Adams* and the *Senator Ross*, galleys launched in Pittsburgh in 1798," were the first sea-going boats which were constructed on the Ohio. — From 1802 to 1805 the business of building sea-going vessels seems to have been flourishing here, as, in a short period there were constructed the ships *Pittsburgh*, *Louisiana*, *General Butler*, *Dean* and *Black Warrior*; schooners *Amity*, *Allegheny* and *Conquest*.

2. General George Trotter died in Lexington, Kentucky, on October 13, 1815, aged 37 years. He served in the Legislature several terms as representative from Fayette County. He was acting Brigadier-General in the battle of the Thames.

3. The Bunch of Grapes Inn was located on the west corner of Kilby Street, formerly Mackerel Lane, and State Street. It was famous as a chosen resort of the patriot leaders in Boston prior to the Revolution.

4. President Washington travelled through Shippensburg during the Whiskey Insurrection in western Pennsylvania. On October 11, 1794, he took dinner at the Branch Inn, operated by William Rippey, and on October 24, he passed the night in Shippensburg. William Rippey enlisted a company of which he was commissioned captain on January 9, 1776. The brigade of which it became a part fought in the campaign in Canada. At Trois Rivieres Captain Rippey and most of his men were captured. Rippey made his escape, and after the war he resumed his management of the Branch Hotel, which he continued until his death in 1819.

CHAPTER XXXIV

THOMAS PAINE

FROM the commencement of this work, it has been my intention to devote a page or two to a character who has caused much disturbance in England, who once acquired great notoriety in France, and who has recently returned to the United States of America to close a mortal career, which has been marked with efforts to cause anarchy in governments, and to subvert even the christian religion. The reader will perceive that I mean the accursed English apostate, Thomas Paine.[1] From one chapter to another I have contemplated the introduction of the hateful subject, until I came to that which gives some American public characters. Here I paused, but, after some deliberation, I considered even the worst set of men would be disgraced by admitting him into a classification. Arnold was a traitor to the country which gave him birth — but Arnold did not add to this crime that of scoffing against the laws of his God. He did not subvert the religion in which he was educated; and though he broke the bonds by which he had bound himself to the service of his country, he did not attempt to warp the minds of his fellow-men, from the homage they owed to an overseeing and indulgent Providence, which, by Paine's own confession, snatched the infidel even from the jaws of death. Here he alludes to some interposition which saved him, though long in prison among the proscribed, from the axe of the guillotine.[2] This interference was the mercy of Providence, who, we must suppose, for a while spared his life, that his obdurate heart might be softened into true repentance, in which all christians found their hope of everlasting salvation. How did this recreant employ the hours of his imprisonment? With death staring him in the face — with momentary expectation of being called to render an account of his misdeeds before a judge omnipoent — he composed a part of his blasphemy called the "Age of Reason,"[3] and when liberated through the agency of the invisible and merciful Divine power, he fell to work to disseminate his impiety through the world. I have therefore determined that he shall stand alone, in order that the reader may either point the finger of scorn, or pass over the despised subject of this chapter.

Mr. Jefferson, the present president of the United States, is, beyond contradiction, in many worldly attainments, of superior abilities — but in Mr. Jefferson we have another proof of the fallibility of man — another strong instance how imperfect is our nature, and that perfection is in God alone. A fatal error committed by the present ruler of a large democracy, was his inviting this apostate to accept an asylum in the bosom of his country, and procuring the means of his escape from France, after he had made himself the detestation even of that nation.[4]

Americans have shrewn their hatred to this fellow, even to such a degree as to attempt his assassination.[5] He was fired at while sitting in his parlour, and again Providence averted the blow. Much as I despise him, I reprobate this worst of crimes which one mortal can commit against another. No, I would not have even Thomas Paine die by the hands of an assassin; but I would, in pity to so great a sinner, let him die a lingering death, that he might still have ample time to make his peace with offended heaven.

Finding at the present moment that I am near the end of my volume, I have taken up the pen on this head. Here have I again hesitated, and resorted afresh to my memorandums and documents. Happily I have found myself spared the necessity of penning my own comments, which might have proved in their progress too violent to be presented to the eye of the reader, by the well-applied sentiments of an American, who signs himself "*A native Virginian*, and which are extracted from a print published at the very seat of government.[6] After many severe strictures on the conduct of President Jefferson, with respect to Paine, this author thus proceeds: —

Citizens of America! I mean ye native born and long-since-adopted citizens: ye who have something at stake; ye who believe in the existence of a God; ye who dread those distressing and those overwhelming scenes of anarchy, rapine, and murder, which have so recently covered with blood a great portion of the ancient world; pause a moment, I beseech you, on this most inglorious and insulting act of the first magistrate of this great and enlightened nation: see the outrages offered to your understandings, and the sovereign contempt in which the good opinions of the religious, the orderly, and most independent characters of our country are held by the man whom we so unfortunately conducted to the most dignified seat in the Union. I mean not to attempt at declamation with a view to inflame your passions, or to beguile your understandings. It will be only necessary to call your attention to a few plain and well established facts, to satisfy you that the invitation to this country of that monster of impiety, Paine, by the president, was an act mean, base, and degrading in itself, and highly dishonorable to the nation; and, as such, be assured it will be viewed by all Europe, and in every quarter of the globe, where christianity or morality shall be revered.

Recollect, that this beastly, drunken infidel was confined in one of the gaols of Paris, under daily expectations of being dragged to the guillotine. Well knowing the temper of the times, and the extreme viciousness and licentiousness of the jacobin, then the ruling faction, he wrote and published that detestable book, the "Age of Reason." This work being congenial with the principles and the new philosophy of that faction, it was patronized and disseminated with great fanatic zeal and industry, for the purpose of destroying the Christian religion, and of corrupting the morals of the people, that they might the more easily be brought within the fangs of arbitrary power and despotism. With what success this was done, let the innocent spirits of the thousands and tens of thousands, of all ages and sexes, with whose blood it is well known that unfortunate country was deluged — answer. Let our own observations too, respecting the rapid advances which atheistical and deistical sentiments have made in this country, within the last ten years, also, answer the question. Know then, that for these *labors*, which the president of the United States calls "useful," the sacrilegious head of the author was then spared. This is a fact too well established to be contradicted. But as the jacobin party sunk in France, that miscreant, Paine, became unnoticed and contemptible. He was only seen and known as a drunken blackguard in the streets, or heard of in the stews and garrets of Paris. And as order and religion gained ground in France, the name of Paine became every day more and more abhorrent to men of character, and consequently to men in power. His insignificance and brutality of demeanour, of course, became more and more despised. Finding himself abhorred by all good men, and shunned for his meanness, bestiality, and perfidy, by infidels like himself, he saw that he had at length got out of his element. Without any prospect of laboring again successfully in his *vocation* of beguiling the uninformed, or of urging to deeds of wickedness and bloodshed the corrupted portion of his fellow-men in that country, he began to give himself up as a last atom. In this situation, a situation truly miserable to infernal spirits, did he receive the consoling and affectionate letter from our philosophic president, '*written in the easy confidence of old acquaintance*,' cordially inviting him to the bosom of his country, with prayers for the '*success of his useful labors!!!*' Gracious Heaven! that ever I should have advocated the views of such a man to the chief magistracy of the Union!

Now that Paine could no longer work evil in Europe; could no longer be supported in reviling the idea of the Son of God, the Saviour of the world, and those who believe in him; could no longer be countenanced in speaking irreverently of your never to be forgotten Washington, the unsullied patriot and father of his country, is he brought hither, to pursue his "*useful labors*" with the prayers of the president of the United States of America for his "success." Pause, reader, and think of this. The *impious* and *atheistical* Paine; the base caluminator and slanderer of your beloved Washington,[7] invited to your bosoms by the chief of your nation, with prayers for the "success of his useful labors!" Can this be true? Yes, fellow-citizens of America, such is the polluted hoary wretch whom your president has brought to your shores. But will the people of this country, no matter what their politics may be (for Heaven forbid that every democrat should be a jacobin), submit to such an outrage on their feelings and understandings? Will they suffer such an infidel to insult them with his blasphemies? or will they listen to the opinions of a man, or *men* or *measures*, who could, like a detestable villain, call our (all but immortal) Washington "a *coward* and a *traitor?*" In one word, will they listen to any thing that may fall from his sacrilegious and prostituted pen? Or will they hold in future estimation the hypocritical, pusillanimous, and degraded character, who has so "*belittled*" himself, as to invite him to our land?

I will now, ye honest, well-meaning citizens of the United States, only call your attention to another fact respecting this mammoth of baseness, this infidel, and despicable ingrate, Tom Paine. — It is upon our own records that he was cashiered and degraded for perfidy of conduct, while holding an office of confidential trust, under the old congress of the United States.[8] It is equally notorious that he had outlived in this country, as it has been proved he had done in England before his migration hither, everything like reputation or respectability of character; and that he was all but kicked out of every honorable or respectable company in Philadelphia, before he returned to Europe. Notwithstanding these things — circumstances well known to our president — and notwithstanding he afterwards became, every day he lived, more and more conspicuously "infamous for his many crimes," still he has found, not only favor and countenance, but protection in the arms of the man, whom the evil genius of America, in an unguarded hour, placed in her presidential chair. To sum up, then, my fellow-citizens, in a few words, the whole of this most shameful and atrocious act, it will stand thus: — that the traitorous officer, the infamous and ungrateful slanderer of our Washington, the reviler and scoffer of our holy religion, and one of the most debauched and immoral beings in existence, has been solicited by Thomas Jefferson, president of the United States of America, to spend the remainder of his days among you, with prayers "for the success of his useful labors."[9]

NOTES — CHAPTER XXXIV

1. Although many of the facts concerning Thomas Paine's life are generally known, no first rate biography of him has yet been written. Born in Thelford, Norfolk, England, on January 29, 1766, Paine died in New Rochelle, New York, on June 8, 1809. His family was Quaker. He was chosen by his associates in the London custom office to embody in a paper a statement of their complaints and objections against the official management. This paper chanced to come before Franklin, who suggested to the author that his abilities would find a

more satisfactory field of activity in America than in England. Armed with letters from Franklin, he came to Philadelphia in 1774.

2. Paine went to France, where in September, 1792, he was elected as a member of the National Convention. At the trial of Louis XVI he proposed that the king be exiled, a suggestion which offended the extreme radicals. In 1793 at Robespierre's instigation, he was ejected from the Convention on the ground that he was a foreigner. For nearly a year he remained in Luxembourg prison in constant expectation of sentence to the guillotine.

3. Written at least in part while Paine was in prison, and published in London and Paris in 1794 and 1795. Although it attacked the Christian religion, it was equally unfavorable to atheism, in spite of the fact that from that time to this he has been branded as an atheist. His religious creed may be summed up in two quotations: "I believe in one God, and no more; and I hope for happiness beyond this life. — I believe that religious duties consist in doing justice, loving mercy, and endeavoring to make our fellow creatures happy."

4. By voting for the exile instead of the execution of Louis XVI.

5. At New Rochelle on Christmas evening in 1804 a man named Derrick, who owed Paine money, fired a gun into his room. Apparently the assailant was drunk, and although he was arrested, the charge was not pressed.

6. Paine returned to America in October, 1802, landing at Baltimore. He was more or less ostracized during his last stay in the United States. Political and theological antipathies were strong. He was the author of the *Age of Reason*, and he immediately became the assailant of the Federalists, personnel and principles.

7. Paine wrote three letters to Washington which he surpressed at Monroe's request. On September 20, 1795, he wrote asking Washington to clear himself of the charge of treachery. This was followed by another dated August 3, 1796, a long and bitter attack on Washington's military career and his policies as President.

8. In April, 1777, Paine was elected clerk to the Committee on Foreign Affairs by the Colonial Congress. Two years later he lost this position because of charges made by the commissioners to France that he had disclosed certain official secrets. That he was not entirely discredited as Janson would lead his readers to believe is indicated by the fact that in 1780 he received the appointment as clerk of the assembly of the Pennsylvania Legislature. In 1781 he associated with Colonel Laurens in obtaining loans from Holland and France, for which service he was rewarded by Congress.

9. See Jefferson's letter to Paine, dated March 18, 1801, in *The Writings of Thomas Jefferson*, edited by Paul Liecester Ford. New York, 1897. VIII, 18-19.

CHAPTER XXXV

EMIGRATION — SMUGGLING — GERMAN REDEMPTIONERS

THE emigration from the British dominions, and more especially from Ireland, to the United States, is almost incredible. I took some pains to gain correct information on this subject, and was astonished at the numbers that of late years have crowded the American ships from different parts of Europe.

In the year 1801, fourteen thousand souls were landed from Ireland by the Philadelphia ships alone; and upon the moderate calculation of the like number arriving at other ports, we find the emigration to be twenty-eight thousand! These people paid, on an average, for their passage, ten guineas each, making 294,000*l.* sterling. Many of them took with them considerable property; and almost the whole had the saving of a year or two in their pockets in specie on their landing on the American shore; but, supposing they drained their country of only ten guineas each more, the loss to Ireland would be 588,000*l.*!!!

Guinea-men with slaves, were never crowded like the American ships from Londonderry to Philadelphia with Irish passengers. A small ship, of only 215 tons, took on board five hundred and thirty passengers, who first paid the captain above 5000l. for their passage. To these must be added the ship's crew, making five hundred and forty-two souls, being nearly double the number ever attempted to be *stowed* in a slave ship of that burthen.

By an act of parliament, vessels are restricted to a certain number of passengers, according to which, the ship above mentioned could legally carry only 43 persons. American ingenuity, added to a little connivance of those who ought to carry the law into effect, produced this destructive increase. The ship of 215 tons, swells into 400, on her arrival in

Derry, and thus it is pretended she can carry eighty passengers. This number, on her departure from the port, are mustered on the deck, before the mayor and procurator of the city, and permission is given for her sailing. She then drops with the tide down the river, on the banks of which she is expected by the surplus of her passengers, who pour on board by hundreds. Some, who could not procure boats, fearful of losing their passage to the "land of milk and honey," have been known to swim after the ship, and sometimes to lose their lives in the attempt. On the passage alluded to, thirty of these unfortunate people perished; and from their crowded situation, and the uncleanliness of the lower order of the Irish, together with their approach to a warm climate, it is a matter of surprise that pestilence did not sweep away the greatest part of them.

Arrived in the river Delaware, the strangers are set on shore upon the banks, as fast as boats can be procured for that purpose; for the laws here too are strict respecting the landing of passengers of this description — for instance, the owner and captain must enter into bonds, that they shall not become a charge to the parish where they are landed, with some other regulations, which have now escaped my memory.

The emigration from Ireland was particularly increased by the political disturbances in that country. To many who acted a conspicuous part in the ranks of rebellion, America has afforded a refuge. Among these Mr. Emmet, who has been mentioned as the counsel of Mr. Ogden, the proprietor of the *Leander*, is now on the road to fortune and reputation. I am indebted to a most respectable friend for a biographical sketch of that gentleman, which, it is true, is rather out of its place here, but not having received it in time to be introduced in a more suitable situation, I trust the indulgence of my readers will dispose them to pardon the digression:

Thomas Addis Emmet, Esq. is the son of Dr. Robert Emmet,[1] an eminent physician, who practised with considerable celebrity in the city of Cork and its vicinity for several years. Having acquired an independent fortune, he removed with his family to Dublin, where he was appointed state-physician, having been previously elected fellow of the royal society.

Doctor Emmet had three sons, Temple, Thomas Addis, and Robert who was considerably younger than his brothers. They were all educated in a most liberal manner — were each early matriculated in the university of Dublin, and made extraordinary progress in every branch of science and of literature. In early life they displayed strong evidence of talents, energy of mind, and attachment to democratic principles, which pervaded the whole family, injured their father materially in his profession, and brought on his sons, Thomas Addis and Robert, the most serious misfortunes. Temple Emmet[2] was bred to the law, and was admitted a barrister in the court of Dublin early in life; and from his great talents must have risen to the zenith of professional emolument and honors, had he not fallen prematurely under the malignant influence of a putrid fever, which blasted his youth, and brought him to the grave. Those who knew him, revere his memory and praise his worth. His forensic abilities were distinguished by accurate and logical argument, scientific knowledge, and brilliant eloquence. He was a powerful advocate, and though young, accounted an excellent legal opinion.

The younger son, Robert,[3] distinguished himself in college when a very young student, as a powerful orator, particularly in the historical society; but his attachment to republican politics, and his bold promulgation of democratic principles, raised him many enemies in the university; and at length being strongly suspected of disaffection to the British government, to avoid a prosecution with which he was threatened, he fled into France, in which country his brother, Thomas Emmet, at that time resided.

Early in 1803, this unfortunate young gentleman returned to his native land, where he joined a band of conspirators who had escaped in the rebellion of 1798, and who had determined upon seizing the castle of Dublin, and making the lord-lieutenant prisoner. On the 23d of July, 1803, this conspiracy broke out into an insurrection about nine at night, and was completely quelled before morning. Lord Kilwarden, the chief justice of Ireland, was murdered in his carriage by a banditti; and Emmet, to adopt his own expression, instead of finding himself a leader of a formidable insurrection, found himself without any influence or command, in the midst of a ruffianly mob. With a few adherents, he escaped into the mountains, but returned in a few days, was taken near Dublin, tried for high treason, convicted and executed, being not more than twenty-four years of age.

This unfortunate youth had early imbibed, under the tutelage of his father, those political doctrines, which caused his ruin. The object of his enthusiastic mind was to separate Ireland from Great Britain, and this he hoped to accomplish without any interference or assistance from France, as appears from his address to the court after his conviction. These are his words: — "God forbid that I should see my country under the hands of a foreign power. If the French should come as a foreign enemy, oh, my countrymen! meet them on the shore with a torch in one hand, a sword in the other — receive them with all the destruction of war; immolate them in their boats before our native soil shall be polluted by a foreign foe! If they proceed in landing, fight them on the strand, burn every blade of grass before them as they advance, raze every house; and if you are driven to the centre of your country, collect your provisions, your property, your wives, and your daughters; form a circle around them — fight while but two men are left; and when but one remains, let that man set fire to the pile, and release himself, and the families of his fallen countrymen, from the tyranny of *France*." As Robert had then recently returned from France, and from communing with his brother, it is but fair to conclude, that on this point they coincided in political sentiments.

From the conduct of this youth, he appears an enthusiast in politics, heated by a sanguine mind even to a degree of insanity, which, though it may not excuse, must palliate his offences. His oratorical abilities were considerable; and his conduct at that awful moment when death stood before him, inexorable and inevitable, proved his courage. He directed the executioner in the preparations necessary to deprive him of life; and did all in his power to impress on the minds of the spectators, that even in the violent manner in which he was about to lose his life, there was neither fear nor terror — "making a virtue of calamity" — and leaving the world without a tremendous nerve.

Mr. Thomas Addis Emmet,[4] at the time of his (Robert's) execution, was in France; nor is it known that he approved of his brother's expedition to Ireland. This gentleman received his education in the university of Dublin, and took out his degree as a doctor of physic in Edinburgh, where he studied for some time with great reputation, not only for his learning, but his pure, honorable, and moral conduct. Soon after his arrival in Dublin, he was joined in the patent of state physician with his father: but this patent was not a gift from government, Doctor Emmet having paid his predecessor a full price for the emolument of the office, so that in this point neither Dr. Emmet nor his son was indebted to the benevolence of the state. On the death of his elder brother, Temple, Mr. Thomas Addis Emmet resolved on quitting the profession of physic, and to substitute that of the law; and accordingly, about the latter end of 1787, he became a student of the Middle Temple, London, and was admitted a barrister in the Irish courts in Michaelmas term, 1790.

In 1790, a confederacy, calling themselves "The United Irishmen of Belfast," was formed in the north of Ireland; on the 9th of November, 1791, the Society of United Irishmen of Dublin commenced their meetings, chosing for their chairman the honorable Simon Butler,[5] second son to Lord Viscount Mountgarret, and for their secretary, the celebrated

James Napper Tandy,[6] who at that time was a citizen of considerable interest and political influence in Dublin, and a member of the Whig Club. This extraordinary demagogue was afterwards convicted of high treason, pardoned, went into France, and died at Bourdeaux, a general in the service of Bonaparte.

Mr. Emmet was an early associate of this society; and their leading resolutions and tests point out his avowed political principles. After a recapitulation of grievances, they say: "In the present great era of reform, when unjust governments are falling in every part of Europe: when religious persecution is compelled to abjure her tyranny over conscience; when the rights of men are ascertained in theory, and that theory is substantiated by practice; when iniquity can no longer defend absurd and oppressive forms against the common sense and common interests of mankind: when all government is acknowledged to originate from the people, and to be so far only obligatory as it protects their rights and promotes their welfare; we think it our duty, as Irishmen, to come forward and state what we feel to be our heavy grievance, and what we know to be its effectual remedy." This declaration then states several resolutions, complaining of the English influence in Ireland, the necessity of an equal representation of all the people in parliament, the rejection of a place bill, of a pension bill, and of a responsibility bill; the sale of peerages in one house; the corruption avowed in the other; the borough traffic between both, symptoms of a mortal disease which corrodes the vitals of the constitution, and leaves to the people in their own government but the shadow of a name.

The society then specially resolves "that the weight of English influence in the government of Ireland is so great, as to require a cordial union among *all* the people of Ireland to maintain that balance of power which is essential to the preservation of liberty, and the extension of their commerce.

"That the sole constitutional mode by which such influence can be opposed, is by a complete and radical reform of the representation of the people in parliament; and that no reform is practicable, which shall not include Irishmen of *every* religious persuasion."

From the above resolutions it is clear that a princiual object of the society was completely to emancipate the Irish Roman Catholics, and to admit them into the house of lords and commons; and, indeed, a great majority of the society were of that religious persuasion; and since its origin, the Catholic claims have been unceasing. Mr. Emmet, and a few others, had, however, two different objects — first, to separate Ireland from England; and, secondly, to establish a republic. This party formed a private society among themselves, and with them originated the system of insurrection which in 1798 broke out into a rebellion, in which several thousands lost their lives, and many of the promoters suffered on the scaffold.

On the 19th of May, 1798, Lord Edward Fitzgerald,[7] who had been an officer in the royal army, and had served with great reputation in America, was taken prisoner, after a conflict in which he displayed uncommon personal courage. Armed with a dagger only, he opposed no less than four persons. Mr. Ryan, an officer in the yeomanry, he slew. Town-major Swan he wounded in several places; but a last one of the party discharged a musket at him, and he received the ball in his shoulder. Of course he was made prisoner, and died in gaol, without being brought to trial.

A silk-weaver of some eminence, and a member of the directory of the rebels, having betrayed his party, the garrison of Dublin was increased by regiments from the country, and a number of persons were made prisoners in the house of Mr. Oliver Bond, an eminent linen-merchant in Dublin. Soon after Messrs. Shears, brothers and barristers, were apprehended. Arthur O'Connor, Mr. Emmet, and Dr. M'Nevin, stood their ground, and were arrested. Henry and John Shears, Mr. Byrne, Mr. M'Cann, and others, were tried and executed. Mr. Bond was capitally convicted, and this produced a very extraordinary negociation between the prisoners in gaol and the government of the country. The executive government were certainly in possession of sufficient evidence to convict all the conspirators in their power, but they were not acquainted with the extent, the plan, or the strength of the conspiracy, to come at which was a material and serious object. Terms were therefore proposed and agreed on, that the life of Mr. Bond should be spared, on condition that Messrs. Emmet, and M'Nevin, a doctor of physic, should make a fair disclosure of all they knew (names of persons excepted) to a committee of the house of lords, and should remain prisoners during the war, then to have permission to retire to any place out of his majesty's dominion. The examination accordingly took place; and from the conduct of the Irish government afterwards, there can be no doubt but the information they received, and which was printed, was not only candid, but ample. On this occasion, Lord Clare, their chancellor, asked Mr. Emmet: "Had you a committee of assassination?" He answered "No: — if we had, you, my lord, would not be here to ask me that question."

Mr. Emmet and coadjutors having performed their compact, were sent prisoners to Fort George, in Scotland; and here a serious dissention took place between him and Arthur O'Connor. After some time, during the temporary peace with France, these prisoners were permitted to go to that country, with the politics of which Mr. Emmet soon became disgusted; and he left the tyranny of Bonaparte to enjoy freedom under the states of America.[8] There he has been permitted to practice as a counsellor-at-law, and his abilities cannot fail of putting him at the head of his profession, particularly as he enjoys the friendship and patronage of Mr. Jefferson. Mr. Emmet is married, and has several children: he is now about forty-five years of age, hale in constitution, moderate in his living, mild in conversation, amiable in manners, and probably will long enjoy the peaceful situation he has chosen.

The Americans carry to Ireland, flax-seed, tobacco, and lumber, but chiefly contraband goods; and return with the living cargo already described. Every voyage is calculated to clear the first cost of the ship, which may be estimated at from three to five thousand pounds — a better voyage, to use a mercantile term, than to China, or the coast of Guinea.

Smuggling is carried on by these American traders to a great extent, and to the shame of the officers of the customs, in the most *bare-faced* manner. On making Tory island, the land-mark for the north of Ireland, boats put off from the shore, the crews of which appear in the very worst shape of human degradation — their outer garments more wretched than London beggars, but the pockets within full of guineas. All the country people next the sea are smugglers, and illegal distillers of whiskey. These fellows open a trade with the captain, the mates, and the crews, all of whom have a plentiful supply of tea in chests, nankeens in bales, tobacco in rolls, bandana, and other silk handkerchiefs, spices, and, in fine, every kind of contraband commodity. While this fraud is practised upon the revenue, government cutters and custom-house boats, whose business it is to prevent smuggling, are lying snug at anchor in Lough Foyle, Lough Swilley, or other convenient harbours.

With such ease and security have they carried on this illicit traffic, that the ship Eliza, of Baltimore, began deliberately to unload her tobacco in Lough Foyle, *in sight* of a revenue cutter at anchor; and what tended to aggravate the matter was, that the crew had the impudence to commence the discharge in the middle of the day, when the inhabitants on either shore witnessed their proceedings. The cutter was consequently *compelled* to do her duty; and the ship was seized and condemned.

To return to the emigrant, whom we must now consider in his earthly elysium; and where, unless he immediately sets off for the woods and mountains, he will find room for his bones before the hot season is past. Look at Philadelphia, New York, Baltimore, Norfolk, Charleston — in short, most towns on the coast, and you will find them in the latter end of the summer scenes of putrefaction. The habit of a stranger, fresh from the salubrious breezes of England and Ireland, instantly imbibes the prevailing disease — and this they call the yellow fever.

The English emigrants are not so numerous, yet the property they carry with them is estimated higher than that drained from Ireland. Hence, English gold is in circulation in all parts of the United States.

From Germany, of late years, there have been considerable importations of redemptioners. These are poor people, who bind themselves to the captain or his assigns, for the price of their passage. Their time of servitude is from three to seven years, which the patient German generally endures without a murmur. These are the most valuable emigrants to America; for they are generally honest and industrious, and often acquire considerable property after the expiration of their servitude. In some parts of Pennsylvania, the country for many miles is inhabited entirely by Germans, who retain their native language, and pursue their ancient customs.[9]

The present situation of the continent can scarcely be supposed to have diminished the importation of redemptioners. Oppressed by all the miseries of war and military tyranny, his habitation burned, his fields laid waste, his relatives perhaps butchered, or sold into worse than negro slavery, can it be surprizing that all the bonds which attached the peasant to his country are dissolved, nay, that he loaths the scene of such complicated horrors; and having lost all that he possessed in the world, is ready to compromise his liberty for a stated period, in order to obtain the present blessings of security and repose, with the prospect of future competence and ease! But that men, who enjoy all the blessings and privileges of British citizens, to whom the calamities of war are known only by name, should renounce those advantages to condemn themselves to a life of mortification and toil, in an unfriendly clime, must be attributed to the delusions which the human mind is fond of cherishing with respect to distant objects, which often neither the evidence of facts nor argument is able to remove, and which experience, like the morning sun chasing the nocturnal vapors that shroud the horizon, is alone capable of dissipating.

NOTES — CHAPTER XXXV

1. Physician to the viceroy in Ireland.

2. Christopher Temple Emmet, oldest son of Dr. Robert Emmet, was admitted to the bar in Dublin in 1781 and advanced to the rank of king's council in 1787. He died the following year while on the circuit in the south of Ireland.

3. Robert Emmet belonged to the United Irishmen, and in politics was a violent nationalist. He was executed on September 20, 1803, at the age of twenty-five years.

4. Also a member of the United Irishmen. Janson's account of the rebellion is substantially correct.

5. The third son of Edmund, tenth Viscount of Mountgarret, and the first president of the United Irishmen. He was called to the Irish bar in 1778. In 1792 he published a digest of the property laws. After being imprisoned for six months in 1793 because of a paper issued by the Society of United Irishmen, he went to Scotland, where he continued to direct the proceedings of the Society until compelled to flee from that country.

6. Tandy supposedly began his career as an ironmonger, but soon interested himself in politics. His mind turned especially towards the expansion of the rights of the people. He tried, also, to cultivate a better understanding between the Catholics and Protestants. He is best known as the hero of "The Wearing of the Green."

7. Fitzgerald served with the 96th Infantry as lieutenant in Ireland. He exchanged to the 19th in order to get into foreign service, and in 1781 went to Charleston. He was wounded at Eutaw Springs, went to Ireland, then returned to New Brunswick, and finally went down the Mississippi to New Orleans. In 1796 he joined the United Irishmen. He died on June 4, 1798, from a wound received in the encounter which Janson describes.

8. Emmet came to the United States in 1804 from France. He joined the New York bar, where he soon took a leading position. He continued prosperous until his death, which occurred while he was pleading in a New York court on November 14, 1827.

9. A. B. Faust, *The German Element in the United States*, gives probably the most complete study of the life and customs of the early German settlers.

APPENDIX

APPENDIX

THE documents which the author has thought proper to bring together in the form of an Appendix, not only contain much interesting and authentic matter relative to the American republic, but will likewise serve to illustrate many of the subjects of which he has treated in the preceding sheets.

ABSTRACT OF A REPORT ON AMERICAN ROADS

THE committee of the senate of the United States, to whom was referred the examination of the act entitled "An act to enable the people of the eastern division of the territory northwest of the river Ohio to form a constitution and state-government, and for the admission of such state into the union, on an equal footing with the original states, and for other purposes," and to report the manner the money appropriated by said act ought to be applied, report as follows:

That, upon the examination of the act, they find the one-twentieth part, or five per cent. of the nett proceeds of the lands lying within the state of Ohio, and sold by congress after the 30th June, 1802, is appropriated for laying out and making public roads, leading from the navigable waters emptying into the Atlantic to the river Ohio, to said state and through the same; such roads to be laid out under the authority of congress, with the consent of the several states through which the roads shall pass.

By a subsequent law, passed on the 3d of March, 1803, congress appropriated three per cent. of the said five per cent. to laying out and making roads within the state of Ohio, leaving two per cent. of the appropriation contained in the first-mentioned law unexpended; which now remains for "the laying out and making roads from the navigable waters emptying into the Atlantic, to the river Ohio, to said state."

The nett proceeds of sales of lands in the state of Ohio, from July 1st, 1802, to June 30th, 1803, inclusive, was

	$124,400 92
From 1st July, 1803, to June 30th, 1804	176,203 35
From 1st July, 1804, to June 30th, 1805	266,000
From 1st July, 1805, to 30th September, 1805 . .	66,000
Amounting in the whole to	$ 632,604 27

Two per cent. on which sum amounts to 12,652 dollars.

Twelve thousand six hundred and fifty-two dollars was, therefore, on the 1st of October last, subject to uses directed by law, as mentioned in this report. The fund is constantly accumulating, and will probably, by the time preparations can be made for its expenditure, amount to eighteen or twenty thousand dollars.

The committee have examined, as far as their limited time, and the scanty sources of facts within their reach, would permit, the various routes which have been contemplated for laying out roads, pursuant to the provisions of the act first mentioned.

The distance from Philadelphia to Pittsburgh is 314 miles, by the usual route, and on a straight line about 270.

From Philadelphia to the nearest point on the river Ohio, contiguous to the state of Ohio, which is probably between Steubenville and the mouth of Grave Creek, the distance by the usual route is 360 miles, and on a straight line about 308.

From Baltimore to the river Ohio, between the same points, and by the usual route, is 275 miles, and on a straight line 224.

From this city (Washington) to the same points on the river Ohio, the distance is nearly the same as from Baltimore, probably the difference is not a plurality of miles.

From Richmond, in Virginia, to the nearest point on the Ohio, the distance by the usual route is 377 miles, but new roads are opening which will shorten the distance 50 or 60 miles; 247 miles of the proposed road from Richmond north-westerly will be as good as the roads usually are in that country, but the remaining 70 or 80 miles are bad for the present, and probably will remain so for a long time, as there seems to be no present inducement for the state of Virginia to incur the expence of making that part of the road passable. From Baltimore to the Monongahela, where the route from Baltimore to the Ohio will intersect it, the distance, as usually travelled, is 218 miles, and on a straight line about 184. From this point, which is at or near Brownsville, boats can pass down with great facility to the state of Ohio, during several months in the year.

The above distances are not all stated from actual mensuration, but they are sufficiently correct for the present purpose.

The committee have not examined any routes northward of that leading from Philadelphia to the Ohio, nor southward of that leading from Richmond, because they suppose the roads to be laid out must strike the Ohio, in order to fulfil the law.

The mercantile intercourse of the citizens of Ohio, with those of the Atlantic states, is chiefly with Philadelphia and Baltimore; not very extensive with the towns on the Potomack within the district of Columbia, and still less with Richmond in Virginia. At present, the greatest portion of their trade is with Philadelphia; but their trade is rather increasing with Baltimore, owing to the difference of distance in favour of Baltimore, and to the advantage of boating down the Monongahela, from the point where the road strikes it, about 70 miles by water, and 50 by land, above Pittsburgh.

The sum appropriated for making roads is so small, that the committee have thought it most expedient to direct an expenditure to one route only; they have therefore endeavored to fix on that which, for the present, will be most convenient to the citizens of Ohio, leaving to the future benevolence and policy of congress an extension of them on this or any other route, and an increase of the requisite fund; as experience may point out their expediency or necessity. A wise government can never lose sight of an object so important as that of connecting a numerous and rapidly-increasing population, spread over a fertile and extensive country, with the Atlantic states, now separated from them by mountains, which, by industry and expense, moderate compared with the advantages, can be rendered passable.

The route from Richmond must necessarily approach the state of Ohio in a part thinly inhabited; and which, from the nature of the soil, and other circumstances, must remain so, at least for a long time; and, from the hilly and rough condition of the country, no roads can be conveniently made leading to the principal population of the state of Ohio. These considerations have induced us to postpone, for the present, any further consideration of that route.

The spirit and perseverance of the people of Pennsylvania are such, in road making, that, no doubt, they will, in a little time, complete a road from Philadelphia to Pittsburgh, as good as the nature of the ground will permit. They are so particularly interested to facilitate the intercourse between their trading capital Philadelphia, not only to Pittsburgh, but also to the extensive country within their own state, on the western waters, that they will of course surmount the difficulties presented by the Alleghany, Chestnut ridge, and Laurel hill, the three great and almost the sole impediments which now exist on that route.

The people of Maryland, with no less spirit and perseverance, are engaged in making roads from Baltimore, and the western boundary of the district of Columbia, through Fredericktown to Williamsport.

Were the government of the United States to direct the expenditure of the fund in contemplation upon either of these routes, for the present, in Pennsylvania or Maryland, it would probably so far interfere with the respective states as to produce mischief instead of benefit; especially as the sum to be laid out by the United States is too inconsiderable alone to effect objects of such magnitude. But as Maryland has no particular interest to extend its road across the mountains, and if it had it would be impracticable, because the state does not extend so far, the committee have thought it expedient to recommend the making of a road from Cumberland, on the north bank of the Potomack, and within the state of Maryland, to the river Ohio, at the most convenient place between a point on the eastern bank of said river, opposite to Steubenville and the mouth of Grave creek, which empties into the Ohio, a little below Whelen, in Virginia. This route will meet and accommodate the roads leading from Baltimore and the district of Columbia; it will cross the Monongahela at or near Brownsville, sometimes called Redstone, where the advantage of boating can be taken, and from the point where it will probably intersect the Ohio, there are now roads, or they can easily be made over feasible and proper ground, through the principal population of the state of Ohio.

Cumberland is situated at the eastern foot of the Allegany mountain, about eighty miles from Williamsport by the usual route, which is circuitous, owing to a large bend in the Potomack, on the bank of which the road now runs; the distance on a straight line is not more than 50 or 55 miles, and over tolerable ground for a road, which will probably be opened by the state of Maryland, should the proposed route be established over the mountains.

From Cumberland to the western extremity of Laurel hill, by the route now travelled, the distance is 66 miles, and on a straight line about 55. On this part of the route, the first and very considerable expenditures are specially necessary. From Laurel hill to the Ohio river, by the usual route, is about 70 miles, and on a straight line 54 or 55; the road is tolerable, though capable of improvement.

To carry into effect the principles arising from the foregoing facts, the committee present a bill for the consideration of the senate. To take the proper measures for carrying into effect the section of the law respecting a road or roads to the state of Ohio, is a duty imposed upon congress by the law itself.

To enlarge on the high importance of cementing the union of our citizens on the western waters with those of the Atlantic states, would be unnecessary. Politicians have generally agreed that rivers unite the interests and promote the friendship of those who inhabit their banks; while mountains, on the contrary, tend to the disunion and estrangement of those who are separated by them. In the preceding case, to make the crooked ways straight and the rough ways smooth, will, in effect, remove the intervening mountains, and, by facilitating the intercourse of our western brethren with those of the Atlantic, essentially unite them *in interest,* which is the most effectual means of uniting the human race.

ABSTRACT OF THE REPORT OF THE SECRETARY OF THE TREASURY.

Revenue and Receipts

	Dollars.
Nett revenue arising from duties on merchandize and tonnage, during the year 1801	12,020,279
Nett revenue arising from the same source, during 1802	10,154,564
That which accrued during 1803	11,306,430
And that which accrued during 1804, deducting the additional duties constituting the Mediterranean fund	12,672,323

The nett revenue accrued during the three first quarters of 1805, does not fall short of that of the corresponding quarters of 1804; and that branch of the revenue may, exclusively of the Mediterranean fund, be safely estimated at twelve millions of dollars, which is nearly the average of 1803 and 1804.

The defalcation which took place in 1802, and the increase in the following years, sufficiently show that no inconsiderable portion of that branch of the revenue is due to the neutrality of the United States during the continuance of war in Europe. Yet if the revenue of 1802, the only year of European peace since 1792, be the basis on which to form an estimate, this, with an addition of ten per cent., the increase of population for three years, and of near three hundred thousand dollars computed revenue of New Orleans, will give near eleven millions and a half.

The revenue arising from the sale of public lands has been greater during the year ending 30th of September, 1805, than that of any preceding year. During that period, besides one hundred and forty-five thousand acres sold to persons claiming a right of pre-emption, four hundred and seventy-four thousand acres have been disposed of at the ordinary sales, making altogether, with the preceding sales, from the time when the land-offices were opened in 1800 and 1801, near two millions of acres. The actual payments by purchasers, which, during the year ending the 30th of September, 1804, had amounted to four hundred and thirty-two thousand dollars, and had not, in any one previous year, exceeded two hundred and fifty thousand dollars, have, during the year ending 30th September, 1805, amounted to five hundred and seventy-five thousand dollars, of which five hundred and thirty-five thousand dollars were paid in specie, and the residue in stock of the public debt. The specie receipts from that source may, for the ensuing year, be safely estimated at five hundred thousand dollars.

The permanent revenue of the United States may, therefore, without the duties on postage, and other small incidental branches, be computed, for 1806, at......	12,500,000
The payments during the same year, on account of the temporary duties, constituting the Mediterranean fund, to the 31st March next, are estimated at nine hundred thousand dollars, and about one hundred thousand may be expected from the arrears of internal duties and direct tax, and from other incidental branches, making, for temporary and incidental receipts......	1,000,000
Balance in the treasury, which, on the 30th September last, amounted to four million, five hundred and seventy-five thousand, six hundred and fifty-four dollars, will (as the receipts and expenditures of the present quarter may be considered as nearly equal) be diminished, at the end of this year, only by the payments on account of the American claims, assumed by the convention with France, and as the whole amount of those claims, unpaid on the 30th September last, will, in this estimate, be stated among the expenditures of 1806, the whole of the above-mentioned balance may be added to the receipts of that year, viz.	4,575,000
Making in the whole..........................	18,075,000

Expenditures.

The expences of 1806, defrayed out of those resources, are either permanent or temporary, viz., the permanent expences are estimated at eleven millions, four hundred and fifty thousand dollars, and consist of

1. The annual appropriation for payment of the principal and interest of the public debt, of which more than one half will go to the discharge of the principal, and the residue to the payment of interest	8,000,000
2. For the civil department, and all domestic expences of a civil nature, including invalid pensions, light-house and mint establishments, surveys of public lands, the third instalment of the loan due to Maryland, and one hundred and fifty thousand dollars to meet claims allowed by congress	1,150,000
3. For expences incident to the intercourse with foreign nations, including the permanent appropriations for Algiers	200,000
4. For the military and Indian departments, including the permanent appropriations for certain Indian tribes	1,030,000
5. For the naval establishment, exclusive of the deficiencies for the service of 1804 and 1805, estimated at six hundred thousand dollars	1,070,000
	11,450,000

The extraordinary demands for 1806, are

The navy deficiencies of 1804 and 1805	600,000	
Balance of American claims assumed by the French convention, unpaid the 30th September last	3,400,000	
		4,000,000
Making altogether		15,450,000

It hence appears, that the permanent revenues of the United States will, during the ensuing year, exceed the permanent expenditures by more than one million of dollars, and that the money in hand, with the temporary resources of the year, will, after leaving the sum always necessary to keep in the treasury, discharge the navy deficiencies, and the whole amount of the claims assumed by the convention with France, the large receipts of last year rendering it unnecessary to recur to the loan authorised by law.

Mediterranean Fund.

The additional duty of two and a half per cent. on goods paying duties ad valorem, which constitutes the Mediterranean fund, amounted, during the six last months of 1804, to five hundred and sixty-three thousand and thirty-eight dollars. The amount of the duty accrued, during the year ending on the 30th June, 1805, was nine hundred and ninety thousand dollars. This product will, it is true, be diminished by subsequent exportations: but from a view of the value of goods imported in 1803 and 1804, charged with that duty, the final may be estimated at nearly nine hundred thousand dollars a year. The fund will, therefore, ultimately produce, during one year and nine months, commencing the 1st July, 1804, and ending the 31st March, 1805 1,575,000

The expences heretofore charged on that fund have been

Paid in 1804, to the said department, under the act constituting the fund 525,000

Paid in 1805, to the said department under the second section of the act of 25th January, 1805 590,000

Making a total of 1,115,000

and leaving a surplus of four hundred and sixty thousand dollars, but which will be more than absorbed by the navy deficiencies above-mentioned. The monies actually received or to be received into the treasury on account of that fund, prior to the 1st of January, 1806, are about six hundred thousand dollars. The residue will be received between that day and the 31st of March, 1807; and credit has been taken for a sum of nine hundred thousand dollars, on that account, in the preceding estimate of the receipts of 1805.

Public Debt.

The payments on account of the principal, during the year ending on the 30th September, 1805 . . . . . 4,377,898.63

The two last instalments due to Great Britain, discharged during the same period 1,776,000.00

Making 6,153,898.63

As the exportation of the specie necessary to discharge the last-mentioned instalment would have been sensibly felt, it was found eligible to pay it in London, in conformity to the act of the 3d of March, 1805, and this was effected, at par, by the Bank of the United States.

		DOLL. CTS.
Payments on account of the public debt, from the 1st of April, 1801, to the 30th of September, 1805		17,954,790.49
Paid to Great Britain, in satisfaction of what the United States might have been liable to pay, by the sixth article of the treaty of 1794		2,664,000.00
Balance in the treasury on the 1st of April, 1801	1,794,052.59	
On the 30th of September, 1805	4,575,654.37	
Making an increase of	2,781,601.78	
Which, deducting proceeds of sales of bank shares	1,287,600.00	
Leaves for the increase from the ordinary revenue		1,494,001.78
Making a difference in favor of the United States during four years and a half of		22,112,792.27

During the four years, commencing on the 1st of April, 1801, and ending on the 31st of March, 1805, there has been paid into the treasury,

By duties on tonnage and foreign merchandise	45,174,837.22
By all other sources, including 1,596,171 dollars, and 43 cents, from the sales of bank shares and public vessels	5,492,639.82
	50,667,467.04

1. Less than one-third of this whole has defrayed all the current expences of the United States, viz.:

		DOLL. CTS.
For the civil list, and all domestic civil expences	3,786,114.79	
For the military establishment and Indian department	4,405,192.26	
For the naval establishment	4,842,635.15	
For the expences attending the intercourse with foreign nations	1,071,437.84	
Amounting to		14,105,380.04

2. Near one-third was necessary to pay the interest on the public debt, viz.		16,278,700.95
Part of that sum (3,160,000 dollars) was paid on account of the interest on the deferred stock, a charge which commenced only in 1801, and was therefore in addition to the annual sum wanted before that year for the payment of interest on the public debt.		
3. More than one-third, and which may be considered as the surplus revenue of the United States, during that period, has been applied towards the extinguishment of the debt, viz.		
On account of the principal	16,317,663.92	
In payment of debts contracted before the 1st of April, 1801, under the British treaty and the French convention	2,963,782.64	
		19,281,446.56
		49,665,527.55

While one-third of the national revenue is absorbed by the payment of interest, a presevering application of the resources afforded by seasons of peace and prosperity to the discharge of the principal, in the manner directed by the legislature, is the only mode by which the United States can ultimately obtain the full command of their revenue, and the free disposal of all their resources. Every year produces a diminution of interest, and a positive increase of revenue. Four years more will be sufficient to discharge, in addition to the annual reimbursements on the six per cent. and deferred stocks, the remainder of the Dutch debt, and the whole of the eight per cent., navy six per cent., five and a half per cent., and four and a half per cent. stocks. As the portion of the public debt which shall then remain unpaid will consist of the six per cent. deferred, and Louisiana stocks, neither of which can be reimbursed, except at the periods and in the proportions fixed by contract, and of the three per cent. stock, which its low rate of interest will render ineligible to discharge at its nominal value, the rapidity of the reduction of the debt, beyond the annual reimbursements permitted by the contracts, will, after 1809, depend on the price at which purchases may be effected.

DUTIES OF THE SEVERAL PORTS OF THE UNION.

THE following statement of payments made into the treasury of the United States, by the several collectors of customs, during four years, commencing April 1, 1801, and ending March 31st, 1805, exhibits the amount of revenue of the respective ports in the Union:

Ports	*Payments*	*Ports*	*Payments*
New York	$12,862,020.87	Camden	$32,900.00
Philadelphia	7,777,965.14	Fort Adams	26,900.00
Boston	6,408,400.26	York (Mass.)	26,698.72
Baltimore	3,861,963.08	New Orleans	23,791.83
Charleston	3,031,639.54	Edgartown	21,879.21
Norfolk	1,761,673.77	Detroit	18,132.00
Salem (Mass.)	1,034,498.07	Georgetown (Col.)	15,950.00
Savannah	914,039.73	Barnstaple	15,042.58
Providence	781,556.12	Hudson	14,200.43
Portland	545,265.66	Snowhill	12,156.48
Newhaven	510,637.15	Brunswick	11,318.54
Petersburg	510,506.17	Beaufort (N. C.)	10,000.00
Portsmouth	484,513.41	Folly Landing	8,900.00
Alexandria	467,761.23	Cherrystone	7,134.63
Newburyport	400,614.30	East River	6,624.00
Newport	390,916.70	Great Egg Harbor	5,700.00
Middletown	382,757.31	Perth Amboy	5,150.00
Wilmington (N. C.)	319,110.07	Beaufort (S. C.)	4,500.00
Richmond	290,032.43	Vermont	4,022.83
New London	282,049.88	Oxford	3,840.56
Wilmington (Del.)	230,327.87	St. Mary's	3,551.27
Kennebunk	168,984.64	Massac	3,400.00
Newbern	146,429.95	Vienna	2,500.00
Edenton	129,505.57	Sag-Harbor	2,456.76
Bristol (R. I.)	106,600.00	Burlington	2,152.00
Gloucester	104,049.61	Yorktown	1,500.00
Bath	96,927.19	Palmyra	1,370.00
Rappahannock	93,249.97	Champlaine	1,200.00
Marblehead	92,439.48	Allburgh	1,145.00
Wiscasset	89,422.45	Bridgetown	1,000.00
Fairfield	70,900.46	Havre de Grace	950.00
New Bedford	71,227.52	Frenchman's Bay	614.43
Washington* (N.C.)	67,234.64	Ipswich	600.00
Biddeford	61,941.62	Machias	500.00
Nantucket	58,395.41	Chester (Md.)	350.00
Plymouth	57,256.99	Dumfries	340.00
Waldoborough	52,932.96	Passamaquoddy	212.42
Penobscot	51,366.63	Louisville	20.00
Dighton	35,200.61		
Georgetown (S.C.)	33,786.59	Total	$45,174,837.22
Michilimackinack	33,005.05		

SALARIES OF PUBLIC OFFICERS.

THE President — Twenty-five Thousand Dollars.
The Vice-President — Ten Thousand Dollars.
The Secretary of State — Five Thousand Dollars.
The Secretary of the Treasury — Five Thousand Dollars.
The Secretary of War — Four Thousand Five Hundred Dollars.
The Secretary of the Navy — Four Thousand Five Hundred Dollars.
The Attorney-General — Three Thousand Dollars.
The Comptroller of the Treasury — Three Thousand Five Hundred Dollars.
The Treasurer — Three Thousand Dollars.
The Auditor of the Treasury — Three Thousand Dollars.
The Register of the Treasury — Two Thousand Four Hundred Dollars.
The Accountant of the War Department — Two Thousand Dollars.
The Accountant of the Navy Department — Two Thousand Dollars.
The Post-Master General — Three Thousand Dollars.
The Assistant Post-Master General — One Thousand Seven Hundred Dollars.

Payable quarterly — to continue for three years from January 1, 1804.

PUBLIC EXPENSES OF THE UNITED STATES, FOR 1805.

	DOLL. . CTS.
CIVIL LIST, including the civil expenses of the territory of New Orleans	611,911.50
Miscellaneous expenses	310,982.31
Intercourse with foreign nations	269,550.00
Military establishment	942,992.48
Naval establishment, including 71,340 dollars, 76 cents, as an appropriation for the crew of the frigate Philadelphia	1,240,445.29

ESTIMATE

Legislature, including stationary, printing, fuel, &c.	228,565.00
Executive, president and vice-president	30,000.00
Department of State	27,304.00

Treasury Department	73,277.27
War department	29,450.00
Naval department	21,170.00
General post-office	11,360.00
Compensations to loan-officers, &c.	26,250.00
Surveyor general department	2,000.00
south of Tennessee	3,200.00
Officers of the mint	10,600.00

GOVERNMENTS IN TERRITORIES OF THE UNITED STATES.

Territory of New Orleans	21,240.00
Mississippi territory	5,500.00
Indiana territory	5,500.00
Valuation of lands, &c.	13,595.23
Miscellaneous	2,000.00

JUDICIARY.

Chief justice and five associates	21,500.00
Nineteen district judges	26,200.00
District of Columbia	5,200.00
Attorney-general	3,000.00
District attornies	3,400.00
Marshals	1,600.00
Expenses of courts, &c.	4,600.00
Light-house establishment	126,776.52

DURING the passage of the Non-importation Act, the secretary of the treasury was called upon by the senate for an account of the imports from Great Britain. Mr. Gallatin, the secretary, in consequence thereof, made the following reports of the value, agreeably to prime cost, of goods paying duties ad valorem, imported during the years 1802, 1803, and 1804, from the dominions of Great Britain in Europe, and in the East Indies; and also, from all other parts of Europe, and from China; and the quantity of salt, rum, and nails, imported during the same years from Great Britain and her dependencies.

A STATEMENT,

Exhibiting the value (agreeably to the prime cost) in sterling money, of Goods, paying duties ad valorem, imported from the dominions of Great Britain in Europe, and from her dominions in the East Indies; and also, from all other parts of Europe, and from China.

For the years	From the dominions of Gt. Britain in Europe.			From all other parts of Europe.			From the British dominions in the East Indies.			From China.		
Ending on the 30th Sept.	At 12½ per cent.	At 15 per cent.	At 20 p.cent.	At 12½ per cent.	At 15 p. cent.	At 20 p.cent.	At 12½ p. cent.	At 15 p. ct.	At 20 p. ct.	At 12½ p. cent.	At 15 p.cent.	At 20 p.ct.
1802, £. sterl.	3,907,582	1,315,946	49,650	1,306,183	343,864	65,976	594,506	1,453		456,135	37,328	4
1803,	4,091,692	1,254,852	39,273	678,513	259,922	40,980	467,718	5,162	2	398,169	58,691	358
1804,	4,088,450	1,211,060	49,923	1,106,564	318,575	34,676	733,497	9,705		408,218	34,036	65

A STATEMENT,

Exhibiting the quantity of Salt, Rum, and Nails imported from the dominions of Great Britain in Europe, from the British West Indies, and from other British dependencies.

For the years	From the dominions of Great Britain in Europe.			From the British West Indies.			From other British dependencies.		
	SALT.	RUM.	NAILS.	SALT.	RUM.	NAILS.	SALT.	RUM.	NAILS.
Ending on the 30th September,	Bushels.	Gallons.	Pounds.	Bushels.	Gallons.	Pounds.	Bushels.	Gallons.	Pounds.
1802,	1,262,039	5,816	3,051,782	801,802	4,213,087	65,811	4,608	11,872	
1803,	1,431,274	45,459	3,841,185	758,421	3,628,264	4,426	12,688	7,883	7,469
1804,	1,260,122	17,778	3,924,803	803,668	4,368,316	10,692	30,050	14,940	6,598

MESSAGE OF THE PRESIDENT, COMMUNICATED DECEMBER 2, 1806.

To the Senate and House of Representation of the United States of America in Congress assembled.

It would have given me, fellow citizens, great satisfaction to announce, in the moment of your meeting, that the difficulties in our foreign relations, existing at the time of your last separation, had been amicably and justly terminated.

I have lost no time in taking those measures which were most likely to bring them to such a termination, by special missions, charged with such powers and instructions as, in the event of failure, could leave no imputation on either *our moderation or forbearance*. The delays which have since taken place in our negociation with the British government, appear to have proceeded from causes which do not forbid the expectation that, during the course of the session, I may be enabled to lay before you their final issue.

What will be that of the negociation for settling our differences with Spain, nothing which had taken place, at the date of the last dispatches, enables us to pronounce. On the western side of the Mississippi she advanced in considerable force, and took post at the settlement Bayou Pierre, on the Red River. This village was originally settled by France, was held by her as long as she held Louisiana, and was delivered to Spain only as a part of Louisiana. Being small, insulated, and distant, it was not observed at the moment of redelivery to France and the United States, that she continued a *guard of half a dozen men*, which had been stationed there. A proposition, however, having been lately made by our commander-in-chief, to assume the Sabine river as a temporary line of separation between the troops of the two nations, until the issue of our negociations shall be known, this has been referred by the Spanish commandant to his superior, and in the meantime he has withdrawn his force to the *western side of the Sabine river*. The correspondence on this subject, now communicated, will exhibit more particularly the present state of things in that quarter.

The nature of the country requires indispensably that an unusual proportion of the force employed there should be cavalry, or mounted infantry. In order therefore that the commanding officer might be enabled to act with effect, I had authorised him to call on the governors of Orleans and Mississippi, for a *corps of five hundred volunteer cavalry*. The temporary arrangement he has proposed, may, perhaps, render this unnecessary. But I inform you with great pleasure of the promptitude with which the inhabitants of those territories have tendered their services in defence of their country. It has done honor to themselves, entitled them to the confidence of their fellow-citizens in every part of the Union, and must strengthen the general determination to protect them efficaciously under all circumstances which may occur.

Having received information that in another part of the United

States a great number of private individuals were combining together, arming and organizing themselves, contrary to law, to carry on a military expedition against the territories of Spain, I thought it necessary, by proclamation, as well as by special orders, to take measures for preventing and suppressing this enterprise, for seizing the vessels, arms, and other means provided for it, and for arresting and bringing to justice its authors and abettors. It was due to that good faith which ought ever to be the rule of action in public as well as in private transactions; it was due to good order and regular government, that, while the public force was acting strictly on the defensive, and merely to protect our citizens from aggression, the criminal attempts of private individuals to decide, for their own country, the question of peace or war, by commencing active and unauthorized hostilities, should be promptly and efficaciously suppressed.

Whether it will be necessary to enlarge our *regular force* will depend on the result of our negociations with Spain. But as it is uncertain when that result will be known, the provisional measures requisite for that, and to meet any pressure intervening in that quarter, will be a subject for your early consideration.

The possession of both banks of the Mississippi reducing to a single point the defence of that river, its waters, and the country adjacent, it becomes highly necessary to provide for that point, a more adequate security. Some position above its mouth, commanding the passage of the river, should be rendered sufficiently strong to cover the armed vessels which may be stationed there for defence; and, in conjunction with them, to present an insuperable obstacle to any force attempting to pass. The approaches to the city of New Orleans, from the eastern quarter, also will require to be examined, and more effectually guarded. For the internal support of the country, the encouragement of a strong settlement on the western side of the Mississippi, within reach of New Orleans, will be worthy the consideration of the legislature.

The gun-boats, authorized by an act of the last session, are so far advanced that they will be ready for service in the ensuing spring. Circumstances permitted us to allow the time necessary for their more solid construction. As a much larger number will be wanting to place our seaport towns and waters in that state of defence to which we are competent, and they entitled, a similar appropriation for a further provision of them is recommended for the ensuing year.

A further appropriation will also be necessary for repairing fortifications already established, and for the erection of such other works as may have real effect in obstructing the approach of an enemy to our seaport towns, or their remaining before them.

In a country whose constitution is derived from the will of the people, directly expressed by their free suffrages, where the principal executive functionaries, and those of the legislature, are renewed by them at short periods — where, under the character of jurors, they exercise in person the greatest portion of the judiciary powers — where the laws are consequently so formed and administered as to bear with equal weight and favour on all, restraining no man in the pursuits of honest industry, and securing to every one the property which that acquires — it would not be supposed that any safeguards could be needed against insurrection or enterprize on the public peace or authority. The laws however, aware, that these should not be trusted to moral restraint only, have wisely provided punishments for these crimes when committed. But would it not be salutary to give also the means of preventing their commission. Where an enterprize is meditated by private individuals, against a foreign nation, in amity with the United States, powers of prevention, to a certain extent, are given by the laws. Would they not be as reasonable and useful where the enterprise preparing is against the United States? While adverting to this branch of the law, it is proper to observe, that in enterprizes meditated against foreign nations, the ordinary process of binding to the observance of the peace and good behaviour, could it be extended to acts to be done out of the jurisdiction of the United States, would be effectual in some cases where the offender is able to keep out of sight every indication of his purpose which could draw on him the exercise of the powers now given by law.

The states on the coast of Barbary seemed generally disposed at present to respect our peace and friendship. With Tunis alone some uncertainty remains. Persuaded that it is our interest to maintain our peace with them on equal terms, or not at all, I propose to send in due time a reinforcement into the Mediterranean; unless previous information shall shew it to be unnecessary.

We continue to receive proofs of the growing attachment of our Indian neighbours, and of their disposition to place all their interests under the patronage of the United States. These dispositions are inspired by their confidence in our justice, and in the sincere concern we feel for their welfare. And as long as we discharge these high and honourable functions with the integrity and good faith which alone can entitle us to *their* continuance, we may expect to reap the just reward in their peace and friendship.

The expedition of Messrs. Lewis and Clarke, for exploring the river Missouri, and the best communication from that to the Pacific Ocean, has had all the success which could have been expected. They have traced the Missouri nearly to its source, descended the Columbia to the Pacific Ocean, ascertained with accuracy the geography of that interesting communication across our continent, learnt the character of the country, of its commerce, and inhabitants; and it is but justice to say, that Messrs. Lewis and Clarke, and their brave companions, have, by this arduous service, deserved well of their country.

The attempt to explore the Red river, under the direction of Mr. Freeman, though conducted with a zeal and prudence meriting entire approbation, has not been equally successful. After proceeding up to about six hundred miles, nearly as far as the French settlements had extended, while the country was in their possession, our geographers were obliged to return without completing their work.

Very useful additions have also been made to our knowledge of the Mississippi, by Lieutenant Pike, who has ascended it to its source, and whose journal and map, giving the details of his journey, will shortly be ready for communication to both houses of congress. Those of Messrs. Lewis, Clarke, and Freeman, will require further time to be digested and prepared. These important surveys, in addition to those before possessed, furnish materials for commencing an accurate map of the Mississippi and its western waters. Some principal rivers, however, remain still to be explored, towards which the authorization of congress by moderate appropriations, will be requisite.

I congratulate you, fellow citizens, on the approach of the period at which you may interpose your authority, constitutionally, to withdraw the citizens of the United States from all further participation in those violations of human rights which have been so long continued on the unoffending inhabitants of Africa, and which the morality, the reputation, and the best interests of our country, have long been eager to proscribe. Although no law you may pass can take a prohibitory effect till the first day of the year one thousand eight hundred and eight, yet the intervening period is not too long to prevent, by timely notice, expeditions which cannot be completed before that day.

The receipts of the treasury, during the year ending on the 30th day of September last, have amounted to near fifteen millions of dollars, which have enabled us, after meeting the current demands, to pay two millions seven hundred thousand dollars of the American claims, in part of the price of Louisiana; to pay of the funded debt upwards of three millions of principal, and nearly four of interest; and in addition, to reimburse in the course of the present month nearly two millions of five and a half per cent. stock. These payments and reimbursements of the funded debt, with those which had been made in the four years and a half preceding, will, at the close of the present year, have extinguished upwards of twenty-three millions of principal.

The duties composing the Mediterranean fund will cease, by law, at the end of the present session. Considering, however, that they are levied chiefly on luxuries, and that we have an impost on salt, a necessary of life, the free use of which otherwise is so important, I recommend to your consideration the suppression of the duties on salt, and the continuation of the Mediterranean fund instead thereof, for a short time, after which that also will become unnecessary for any purpose of contemplation.

When these branches of revenue shall in this way be relinquished, there will still ere long be an accumulation of money in the treasury beyond the instalments of public debt which we are permitted to contract to pay. They cannot, then, without a modification, assented to by the public creditors, be applied to the extinguishment of this debt, and the complete liberation of our revenues, the most desirable of all objects. Nor, if our peace continued, will they be wanting for any other existing purpose. The question, therefore, now comes forward, to what other object shall these surplusses be appropriated, and the whole surplus of the impost, after the discharge of the public debt, and during those intervals when the purposes of war shall not call for them? Shall we suppress impost, and give that advantage to foreign over domestic manufactures? Of a few articles of more general and necessary use, the suppression, in due season, will doubtless be right; but the great mass of articles on which impost is paid, are foreign luxuries, purchased by those only who are rich enough to afford themselves the use of them. Their patriotism would certainly prefer its continuance, and application to the great purposes of the public education, roads, rivers, canals and such other objects of public improvement as may be thought proper to add to the constitutional enumeration of federal powers. By these operations, new channels of communication will be opened between the states; the lines of separation will disappear; their interests will be identified; and their union cemented by new and indissoluble ties. Education is here placed among the articles of public care, not that it would be proposed to take its ordinary branches out of the hands of private enterprise, which manages so much better all the concerns to which it is equal; but a public institution alone can supply those sciences which, though rarely called for, are yet necessary to complete the circle; all parts of which contribute to the improvement of the country, and some of them to its preservation. The subject is now proposed for the consideration of congress, because, if improved, by the time the state legislature shall have deliberated on this extension of the federal trusts, and the laws shall be passed, and other arrangements made for their execution, the necessary funds will be on hand without employment. I suppose an amendment of the constitution, by the consent of the states, necessary; because the objects now recommended are not among those enumerated in the constitution, and to which it permits the public monies to be applied.

The present consideration of a *National Establishment for Education, particularly*, is rendered proper by this circumstance also, that, if congress, approving the proposition, shall yet think it more eligible to found it on donations of lands, they have it now in their power to endow it with those which will be the earliest to produce the necessary income. This foundation would have the advantage of being independent on war, which may suspend other improvements by requiring for its own purposes the resources destined for them.

This, fellow-citizens, is the state of the public interests at the present moment, and according to the information now possessed. But such is the situation of the nations of Europe, and such, too, the predicament in which we stand with some of them, that we cannot rely with certainty on the present aspect of affairs, that may change from moment to moment, during the course of your session, or after you shall have separated. Our duty is, therefore, to act upon the things as they are, and to make a reasonable provision for whatever they may be. Were armies to be raised whenever a speck of war is visible in our horizon, we should never have been without them. Our resources would have been exhausted on dangers which have never happened, instead of being reserved for what is really to take place. A steady, perhaps a quickened pace, in defence of our sea-port towns and waters, an early settlement of the exposed and vulnerable part of our country, a militia, so organized, that its effective portions can be called to any point in the nation, or volunteers instead of them, to serve a sufficient time, are means which may always be ready, yet never preying on resources until actually called into use. They will maintain the public interests, while a more permanent force shall be in a course of preparation. But much will depend on the promptitude with which these means can be brought into activity. If war be forced upon us, in spite of our long and our vain appeals to the justice of nations, rapid and vigorous movements, in its outset, will go far towards securing us in its course and issue, and towards throwing its burthens on those who render necessary the resort from reason to force.

The result of our negociations, or such incidents in their course as may enable us to infer their probable issue; such further movements also on our western frontier as may shew whether war is to be pressed there, while negociation is protracted elsewhere, shall be communicated to you from time to time, as they become known to me; with whatever other information I possess or may receive, which may aid your deliberations on the great national interests committed to your charge.

TH. JEFFERSON.

INDEX